CW00450195

A DATE WITH LANGUAGE

A Date
with Language

DAVID CRYSTAL

BODLEIAN
LIBRARY
PUBLISHING

First published in 2023 by the Bodleian Library
Broad Street, Oxford OX1 3BG
www.bodleianshop.co.uk

ISBN 978 1 85124 611 3

Publisher: Samuel Fanous
Managing Editor: Susie Foster
Editor: Janet Phillips
Picture Editor: Leanda Shrimpton
Cover design by Dot Little at the Bodleian Library
Designed and typeset by Lucy Morton of illuminati in 11½ on 15 Fournier
Printed and bound in Great Britain by by TJ Books Limited
on 70 gsm TJ Mechanical Creamy paper

British Library Catalogue in Publishing Data
A CIP record of this publication is available from the British Library

Contents

PREFACE
vi

A DATE WITH LANGUAGE
I

APPENDIX
368

REFERENCES
369

INDEX
387

Preface

Anniversary events have long had a widespread appeal, judging by the
number of 'On This Day' books that have been published since the
eighteenth century. On my shelves I have a huge two-volume *Book of
Days* from the Scottish firm of Chambers, 1881. There's a similarly large
Dictionary of Dates, from Macmillan, 1934. And then, by contrast, my
own tiny *Pocket On This Day*, produced for Penguin in 2006. There
are 'On This Day' websites beyond number, often with a slant, such as
'On This Day in History... in Music... in Football'. Or 'Famous People
Born On This Day?' '...Died On This Day'. But I've never found an
anniversary collection that focused just on Language. Hence the present
book, inspired by a suggestion from Bodleian's Head of Publishing,
Samuel Fanous.

   I had originally thought there would be enough officially designated
days – such as Mother Tongue Day and the European Day of Languages
– to fill the year. I was wrong. Only half of the days in this book
are 'named days' or days on which a significant linguistic event took
place. This however had a plus side, as it allowed me the opportunity
to look for personalities who have had interesting things to say about
language – not just by using it in interesting ways (which all authors
do), but by stepping back and commenting on it (which not so many
do). My search was global, so in these pages you'll find writers from all
over the English-speaking world, including those for whom English is
a second or foreign language, and who comment on the special issues
that bilingualism encounters. The book is written for an English-reading
audience, but several days focus on other languages.

I also wanted the selection of days, events and personalities to display the extraordinary breadth of the subject of language. So within these pages you'll find represented the different elements in language structure – pronunciation, orthography, grammar, vocabulary, discourse – and how they are studied in dictionaries, thesauri, style manuals and etiquette books; uses of language in such domains as science, religion, politics, broadcasting, publishing, the Internet and the arts; and the various applications of language study, such as in language teaching, speech therapy, deaf education and forensic science. Communication technologies are represented, from the humble pencil to digital software. Everyday usage is also an important theme, and especially the ludic dimension, which turns up in an unexpectedly large number of ways – some really quite bizarre, but nonetheless interesting. Individual languages mustn't be forgotten, both the 'big' ones (such as the UN's official languages) and those spoken by small groups, along with their associated cultural identities. And then there's the historical dimension – those times and people who helped to shape the current language, from Anglo-Saxon times to the present day. Many brilliant writers of earlier centuries have fascinating things to say about language, but they are rarely or never mentioned in textbooks on the history of English. And several countries have writers who have made insightful linguistic observations, but they're little known because they fall outside the traditional mainstream of English language and literature, with its focus on (predominantly white, male) British and American authors.

If there's a major theme throughout this collection, it's linguistic diversity: people who use different languages, dialects and styles; who use language creatively in individual ways; who reflect on how language expresses their identity or culture, especially when this relates to gender, race or ethnicity. For some, writing is a way of earning a living; for others, it's just a part of everyday life. The book is as much about the social context in which language is used as about language itself. I came across this quotation while researching the book. It's from Samuel Richardson's epistolary novel *The History of Sir Charles Grandison* (1754). In volume 1, letter 12, Miss Byrom observes: 'I have been taught to think, that a learned man and a linguist may very well be two persons…

In other words, that science, or knowledge, and not language merely, is learning.' Yes, language has always to be seen in its wider cultural setting, and many of my comments in these pages reflect Miss Byrom's distinction.

As far as possible, within my 350-word limit per day, I've let people tell their own story, using extracts from their books, speeches and interviews. What I hope is that my selection of their work will be sufficiently intriguing to make you want to read more, if the writers are new to you (and I've included some further reading within the references at the end of the book). That's certainly what happened to me. There are several authors and works in these pages I'd not read before, and exploring their works to find out what they had to say about language (if anything) was a charter to read. My book would have been ready six months ago otherwise, but I don't begrudge the time it took for an instant. I haven't had so much fun since Hilary and I compiled our language quotations book, *Words on Words*, twenty years ago.

Over the years I've often had requests asking for 'On This Day' facts. Sometimes they're from language teachers wanting to add a bit of variation to their daily curriculum. Sometimes they're from people who've been asked to give a talk or a speech on some language-related topic, who want to find something of current relevance to say in their introductory remarks. They often use the word 'celebrate' when talking about language, and that's what I hope my entries do: act as a celebration of the remarkable creativity of all – artists and scientists, professionals and amateurs alike – who have illuminated our understanding of language.

DAVID CRYSTAL

A DATE WITH LANGUAGE

Maria Edgeworth was born in 1768

Born in Oxfordshire, Edgeworth accompanied her father to his Irish estate, which she eventually helped to manage, and stayed in Ireland until her death in 1849. She was the first to write a novel in a regional variety of English: *Castle Rackrent; An Hibernian Tale Taken from the Facts and from the Manners of the Irish Squires before the Year 1782*. It's narrated by Thady Quirk, an illiterate old family steward, who tells the story in his 'vernacular idiom'. The book, published in 1800, is full of the rhythms and idiom of Irish speech. Here's a typical example, as the novel nears its close:

> 'Oh! King of Glory!' says I, 'hear the pride and ungratitude of her, and he giving his last guineas but a minute ago to her childer, and she with the fine shawl on her he made her a present of but yesterday!'

It was a daring choice in an age when regional speech wasn't considered to be a proper literary medium, other than for comic purposes, and which pilloried any departure from what was considered to be 'correct' grammar and 'polite' vocabulary.

Edgeworth is well aware of a possible problem in using local dialect. In her preface she adds an apologia for the benefit of 'the ignorant English reader', and at the end provides a glossary of some of the local expressions. She comments: 'Thady's idiom is incapable of translation, and besides, the authenticity of his story would have been more exposed to doubt if it were not told in his own characteristic manner.' There's actually very little that would make an English reader struggle, but more than enough to give the story a linguistic character that captures Irish identity. She heralds the flowering of dialect writing that became a feature of the nineteenth-century novel in the works of Emily Brontë, Walter Scott, George Eliot and others.

Stylistic diversity is the main driving force behind my selection of people and topics in this book, and I can think of no better way of introducing that theme than through the writing of Maria Edgeworth.

Peter Sutcliffe, dubbed the 'Yorkshire Ripper', was arrested in 1981

Dialect had a small but significant role to play in the investigation into the series of murders of women that took place mainly in Yorkshire between 1975 and 1980. It came about because in 1979, when little progress had been made, the police received a tape recording from someone the media called 'Wearside Jack', because of the way the speaker introduced himself: 'I'm Jack. I see you are still having no luck catching me.' It went on for 3 minutes and 16 seconds.

The detective in charge of the case was convinced the tape was genuine, and valuable time and resources were devoted to following it up. Two phoneticians from the University of Leeds, experts in regional accents, worked out that the voice was indeed from the area of the River Wear, in the north of England – specifically from Sunderland – and they suggested a good starting point for inquiries would be the districts of Castletown or Southwick, near the river. They were convinced it was a hoax, as such a voice would have stood out a mile in Yorkshire, where the murders took place. The man had to be living on Wearside, where the voice would not have been so identifiable. When Sutcliffe was caught, his voice was nothing like the one on the tape. He was from Bradford.

The hoaxer was eventually found through DNA evidence in 2005, and pleaded guilty at a trial a few months later. He'd been living just south of the river, less than a mile from Castletown, and had gone to school there.

This is one of most successful instances of the role played by the branch of linguistics that has come to be called forensic phonetics. The subject includes a wide range of investigations, all focused on the way pronunciation does far more than make our speech understandable. It can identify individuals, communities, settings, emotions and other features of interaction that are useful sources of evidence in criminal investigations.

Tolkien Day

J.R.R. (John Ronald Reuel) Tolkien was born on this day in 1892. A philologist by training, he specialized in Old English, and became professor of English language and literature at Oxford. Universally known for *The Hobbit* and *The Lord of the Rings* trilogy, he has a special following among linguists for his invented languages – a process he called *glossopoeia* ('language making').

He began constructing languages while a teenager, and it developed into something far more than a hobby. His philological background motivated him to think in terms of families of languages, in which a 'parent' language gives rise to 'daughter' languages, distinct but interrelated. The exercise wasn't solely a task of mechanical reconstruction of sounds, words and grammar. For Tolkien, a constructed language had to have a historical and cultural identity, just as real languages have. So his best-known creation, Elvish, isn't simply 'the language spoken by the elves', but the expression of elvish history, legends and culture, and a source from which other languages evolved, such as Entish, the language spoken by the tree-like beings, the Ents. Middle-earth is a highly multilingual world.

Here's an example. In *The Fellowship of the Ring* (1954, chapter 8), Lady Galadriel sings a farewell song to Frodo 'in the ancient tongue of the Elves beyond the Sea ... the language was that of Elven-song and spoke of things little known on Middle-earth'. These are the opening two lines:

Ai! laurië lantar lassi súrinen,	*Ah! like gold fall the leaves in the wind*
Yéni únótimë ve rámar aldaron!	*long years numberless as the wings of trees!*

There are hints of real languages in the words, and a powerful phon-aesthetic in the recurring use of the continuant consonants *l*, *r*, *m* and *n*.

The Tolkien Society was founded in 1969, four years before his death. Apart from celebrating Tolkien Day, it also instituted in 2003 a Tolkien Reading Day, on 25 March. Why then? It's the date of the downfall of Sauron, the Lord of the Rings.

United Nations World Braille Day

⠠⠃⠗⠁⠊⠇⠇⠑

Reading about Louis Braille, born on this day in 1809, and blinded through an accident at age 3, I'm struck by two facts. The first is that he had devised his system of tactile reading by the age of 15, while attending the Institute for Blind Youth in Paris; the second is that this system, though greatly superior to earlier methods, was rejected by the Institute, when he began to teach there, because of a reluctance to depart from traditional methods. It wasn't adopted until 1852, two years after his death. The demand came from the students, who welcomed its greater simplicity and functionality, and it was soon being used internationally.

The traditional method was to make books with letters embossed into heavy paper – a system that was cumbersome, difficult to read, costly to produce, and unusable for personal writing. A crucial development came in 1815, when Charles Barbier, an inventor of simplified writing systems, responded to Napoleon's demand for 'night writing', so that soldiers on the battlefield could communicate silently without light. His method used a punch to press patterns of up to 12 dots into paper, so that letters could be read with the fingers, using an apparatus to ensure that lines were even and dots correctly aligned. The military never took up the idea, but the Institute eventually began to use it, and one of the students who learned it was Louis Braille.

The teenager soon realized the main difficulty with Barbier's system – that a single finger couldn't easily sense a 12-dot configuration. He reduced the number of dots to six, arranged in two columns, and extended the patterns to include numerals, punctuation and other symbols. Today there are several derivatives and styles and many computational applications, though screen reading software on portable devices seems to have somewhat reduced its use.

Leung Ping-kwan (Yesi) died in 2013

This writer is a perfect illustration of the intimate way language and culture interact. Born in Guangdong on the Chinese mainland in 1949, he grew up in nearby Hong Kong. He wrote mainly in Chinese under the pen name Yesi, but translated a great deal into English, his main theme being the complex multicultural and changing character of his home city and island. An obituary headline in the *South China Morning Post* (15 January 2013) described him as 'the poet who put Hong Kong into words'.

Eating and drinking show how a language expresses cultural identity. Here are lines from 'Yellow Rice', in a series titled 'Tasting Asia' (2005):

> India brought over spices and curry
> Arabian Shish Kebab became satay
> The Dutch seized the nutmeg and cumin
> The Chinese came with black beans and vegetable seeds
> The soy sauce landed here from afar became sweet
> Numerous islands line the coastline on the dining table
> Nobody can colonize spices
> Turmeric dyes my fingers yellow
> Padan leaves always have a strong fragrance
> The fiery chili pepper refuses to bow to anyone
> Hot as volcanic lava
> Rugged as ocean rock. Only
> Rice is our common language…

In an interview, he wryly reflects on the name of another poem, 'Comprador Soup':

> a Western cream soup elevated by adding shark's fin… [the name] came from the nouveau riche of the time, the popular middlemen that played important roles in the trade business between the Chinese and the foreigners in the early twentieth century. … I recently tasted this soup in a nostalgic-style restaurant in Vancouver. It has become a sort of mushroom cream soup, with the name re-translated into English as 'Cambridge Soup'. So it has been elevated to another status with a new identity and a forgotten memory.

Forgotten no more, thanks to Yesi.

The Royal College of Speech and Language Therapists was founded in 1945

There are references to 'speechlessness' in ancient Egypt, 'stammering' in ancient Rome, and 'deafness' in Anglo-Saxon England. I imagine disorders of communication were present when the human race first began to speak and sign. But it's only relatively recently that their scientific study has taken place, accompanied by a cadre of professionals trained to assess, diagnose and treat them.

If you were living in Britain in 1900, and had a speech defect, little help was available. You might approach a teacher of elocution or oratory; but they fostered the art and practice of good speaking in people who had their faculties intact – promoting eloquence, training actors, and correcting accents thought to be inferior. Alternatively, you might find a doctor who had specialized in medical conditions affecting communication, such as the loss of speech (aphasia) following a stroke; but there was little to offer by way of treatment, especially for those with no obvious physical disability (such as a child with delayed speech development).

The situation changed in the twentieth century. In Britain, the first departments of speech therapy were set up in the 1920s, and in 1945 the artistic and medical strands merged to form the College of Speech Therapists, which established a three-year diploma training course. During the 1980s there was lengthy debate about the name of the profession, as in other parts of the world speech therapists were being called 'speech pathologists', 'orthophonists' and other such names. In the end, to avoid the misleading impression that 'speech' meant only pronunciation, 'language' was added in 1991, and four years later the profession was given royal patronage, leading to its present title: the Royal College of Speech and Language Therapists. Linguistics, psychology and education are now major elements of the training, alongside medicine, and the profession has proved to be an attractive option for students who want to add a practical and rewarding dimension to their interest in language.

Scottish *makar* Allan Ramsay died in 1758

A *makar* (or 'maker') is the name describing the poets who wrote in Scotland during the fifteenth and sixteenth centuries; and when there was a revival of Scottish poetry in the eighteenth century the old name was used again. Indeed, it's had a further lease of life in modern times, with several cities now recognizing their own Poet Laureates as *makars*, and a national Scots Makar was recognized by the Scottish parliament in 2004.

Allan Ramsay was born in Lanarkshire in 1686, and is remembered as an editor of poetry as well as a poet in his own right, sometimes writing under the pen names of Isaac Bickerstaff and Gawin Douglas. His editorial achievement was to revive public interest in the earlier vernacular literature of Scotland. In 1724 he compiled *The Ever Green, being a Collection of Scots Poems, Wrote by the Ingenious before 1600*. In his Preface he expresses his antipathy to the fashionable favouring of English expressions from south of the border:

> When these good old Bards wrote, we had not yet made Use of imported Trimming upon our Cloaths, nor of foreign Embroidery in our Writings. Their Poetry is the Product of their own Country, not pilfered and spoiled in the Transportation from abroad...

In his own writing he was the first in the eighteenth century to explore the literary potential of Scots, and would prove to be a major influence on Robert Burns (SEE 25 JANUARY). A sense of his style can be seen in his widely acclaimed pastoral comedy *The Gentle Shepherd* (1725). Here are its opening lines:

Beneath the south-side of a craigy bield,	*rocky shelter*
Where crystal springs the halesome waters yield,	*wholesome*
Twa youthfu' shepherds on the gowans lay,	*two, daisies*
Tenting their flocks ae bonny morn of May.	*attending, one beautiful*

He was a major cultural figure of his time, founding the first established theatre in Scotland, and the first subscription library in the British Isles. Amazing achievements!

Evelyn Wood was born in 1909

How fast are you reading this page? I've just timed myself reading it, and it took me a little over a minute. Most people read at 250–300 words a minute. But could you read it in half the time, and still take it all in? Approaches to speed reading claim that you can.

Evelyn Wood is one of the great names when the subject of speed reading comes up. She was an American teacher who created one of the most popular systems, called 'dynamic reading'. She'd observed people reading very quickly yet with apparent comprehension – over a thousand words a minute – and wondered if it was possible to teach others their strategy. Thanks to intense marketing campaigns, her approach became widely known, and was taken up by some high-profile names, such as Presidents Kennedy and Carter. At her death in 1995, there were several systems being promoted, and many can now be found online.

Speed-reading systems operate by getting you to focus on the important words and skimming over the less important ones. You read downwards, rather than from left to right, reducing back-and-forth eye movements on each line, and assimilating thoughts rather than single words.

Claims about super-fast speeds have been controversial, and there have been several serious criticisms. Linguists worry about what counts as a word, what kind of text is being read, and how comprehension can be accurately tested. A text full of long words and complex constructions presents a different challenge compared to one where words and sentences are short. The risk of misunderstanding varies, depending on text type: a fast read of a domestic email is unlikely to cause problems, but skimming through a health instruction manual could lead to serious issues. The reason for reading is also a factor. If I were to tell you that, after reading this, you will be examined on its content, you would read it much more slowly!

The best way of improving reading ability, to my mind, is just to read more often and more widely, at whatever speed you find comfortable.

Word Nerd Day

This day wouldn't exist without the fortuitous rhyme. It wouldn't work if a day celebrating words was called Vocabulary Nerd Day, or the like. Rhyme carries a powerful communicative punch, when used outside of poetry. It takes us back to our earliest years, when we were enthralled by nursery rhymes.

Nerd has ameliorated over time. Its first recorded use in the *Oxford English Dictionary* was in *Newsweek* in 1951, and all the early citations are derogatory, referring to a socially inept or boringly conventional person. But today it has acquired positive or jocular connotations. Anyone who pursues an interest in a dedicated or obsessive way would be classed as a nerd, especially if the interest is in a niche or unfashionable domain. And they would happily call themselves one.

The etymology of *nerd* is uncertain. The most popular theory is that it came from one of Dr Seuss's books for young readers: *If I Ran the Zoo*. The new zookeeper is a child named Gerald McGrew (rhymes with *zoo*), and he discovers a wealth of imaginary animals, including, towards the end of the story, *preeps*, *nerkles* and – *nerds*. The book was published in 1950, so it does tie in with the first recorded use the next year. But if that's where it came from, it's a puzzle why it became popular when the other nonsense names didn't. Maybe the accompanying illustration promoted it.

Word Nerd Day has caught on, so I wouldn't be surprised to encounter Word Geek Week in due course. *Geek* is much older – 1876 American slang – with an etymology that may relate it to earlier English *geck*, meaning 'simpleton'. Here too there has been amelioration. Originally referring to a foolish or worthless person, by the 1980s it was being used for anyone very devoted to a subject, or knowledgeable about it, especially in the digital world. The two terms are very close. As a 1993 *OED* citation puts it: 'Geek is the proud, insider term for nerd.'

Who created this day? Why 9 January? No idea.

The League of Nations
held its first meeting in 1920

The League of Nations was a wonderfully optimistic attempt, following the devastation of the First World War, to provide a forum for resolving international disputes. It was created following the Paris Peace Conference in 1919, and held its inaugural meeting in London. Its first General Assembly took place in Geneva later in 1920, with forty-one nations attending. Although it had some successes, the advent of the Second World War demonstrated that its mission had failed, and it was replaced by the United Nations in 1946.

How would so many nations manage to talk to each other? By designating certain languages as 'official'. French and English were initially chosen – the former because of its traditional status as an international language; the latter as the language with an increasing global presence, following the growth of the British Empire in the nineteenth century. Spanish was added in 1920.

An additional question was whether a constructed language should be given official status, to provide a 'neutral' tool of communication, thereby avoiding the competitive tension that existed between speakers of English and speakers of French. The prime candidate was Esperanto, gaining ground following its creation in 1887 (SEE 26 JULY). A proposal was formally made, and ten of the eleven delegates voted in favour. The dissenting voice was that of the French delegate, who saw Esperanto as a serious threat to the status of French as the language of global diplomacy. An article in *Time* magazine in 1923 summed up the situation:

> The Commission decided to eschew synthetic languages, and to invite the League to favor the selection of a living language as one of the most powerful means for bringing the nations of the world together. English and French must fight it out.

Although two years later the League did recommend that member states included Esperanto in their educational systems, the rise of English as a global language subsequently proved to be unstoppable.

International Thank-you Day

This is another of those days whose origin is unknown – perhaps a company specializing in greetings cards, flowers or some other kind of giving. Whoever it was, the intention was plain: to make a point of expressing your gratitude to those who do things for you – friends, employees, colleagues, family... G.K. Chesterton summed it up well (in chapter 6 of *A Short History of England*): 'I would maintain that thanks are the highest form of thought, and that gratitude is happiness doubled by wonder.'

Psychologists have studied this a lot. In a nicely titled 2010 paper, 'A Little Thanks Goes a Long Way', Adam Grant and Francesca Gino showed in a series of experiments how gratitude expressions increased pro-social behaviour by enabling people to feel valued. Gratitude helps us cope with stress, strengthens our personal relationships, and improves our mental and physical well-being. It makes us feel pleased and want to reciprocate, or to do things for others.

For me, the interest lies also in the words people use to express their gratitude. They go well beyond the simple 'thank you'. There are more informal forms, such as *thanks* and *ta*. Intensified forms, such as *thank you so/very much* and *thanks a million*. Jocular forms, such as *ta muchly*. And, especially among young people, the *thank* element may not appear at all.

I read through a collection of emails and online posts, and saw a remarkable number of ways in which people are thanked for a message, suggestion, favour or any kind of assistance: *cheers, wicked, cool, great, nice, awesome, way to go...* These days the gratitude is often shown by an emoticon with a big smile or a thumbs up, or an emoji such as two hands placed firmly together with the fingers pointing upwards. And then, in a further stage, there's the acknowledgement – 'thank you for thanking', as it were: *a pleasure, you're welcome, don't mention it*, and the ubiquitous (especially in restaurants) *No problem* and *No worries*. Presumably all celebrated today.

HAL 9000 became operational in 1992

Spoiler alert! In Stanley Kubrick's epic science-fiction film *2001: A Space Odyssey* (1968), the spacecraft onboard computer, HAL 9000, misbehaves, so the astronaut has to shut it down. As HAL 'dies', we hear him regressing to his 'birth', speaking with increasing slowness and lower pitch:

> Good afternoon ... gentlemen. I am a HAL 9000 computer. I became operational at the H.A.L. plant in Urbana, Illinois on the 12th of January 1992. My instructor was Mr. Langley and he taught me to sing a song. If you'd like to hear it I can sing it for you...

And he then sings a fragment of the old song 'Daisy Bell' ('Daisy, Daisy, give me your answer do...') before giving up the ghost.

For those in the know, this was a reference to the song programmed into the first attempt by a computer to generate continuous speech artificially using a system of speech synthesis. That computer's name was PAT, standing for 'Parametric Artificial Talker', the parameters referring to six of the most important acoustic variables that control the character of speech: fundamental frequency (governing voice pitch), loudness, hiss (as in *s* sounds), and the frequency of the vowel resonances made by the different positions of the tongue, jaw and lips.

PAT was built at the University of Edinburgh, and the acoustic analysis was informed by analyses of speech made by the Phonetics Department there. Tracings of human speech patterns were made from recordings displayed on paper spectrograms and used to make tracks drawn in conductive ink on plastic sheets or glass slides. These were then fed into a device that turned the tracks into signals of varying voltage, and these triggered PAT's sound-producing mechanisms.

I remember hearing her singing 'Daisy' on an early visit to the Edinburgh department, and the memory stayed with me. I'd never heard anything like it before. So when I first heard HAL sing it, I came over all emotional!

Poetry Break Day

The name doesn't mean 'take a break from writing poetry'. It is 'take a break from whatever else you do and write some poetry'. The poem(s) can be about anything and in any style. Most people in English think immediately of rhyming, as is suggested by nursery rhymes, limericks and all kinds of rap. But poems don't have to rhyme. All you need to do is express your thought in lines which have an effective auditory rhythm or visual appeal.

A poem about an everyday object or event raises the subject matter to new heights. The lines make you think about the meaning in a new way, as words are given fresh emphasis. Like this:

A poem
About an everyday object
Raises the subject matter
To new
Heights.

You could arrange the words in many other ways, of course. And add lines, as your imagination takes hold. How would you insert a new line 3, beginning 'Such as …'? I can imagine some quite surreal responses.

Whatever the subject – a description of the world around us, an expression of emotion, a reflection on an event, a funny situation, a personal insight into what life is all about – poems are a way of making it special and memorable (SEE 21 MARCH). So, the suggestion goes, whatever mundane activity you encounter today, turn it into a poem. There are poems in everyone – which is what those who created this day, whoever they were, are suggesting.

World Logic Day

This day was proclaimed by UNESCO in association with the International Council for Philosophy and Human Sciences in 2019. The aim was to draw attention to the importance of logic in the development of knowledge. As director-general Audrey Azoulay said at the time:

> Logic is ever-present: when you use AI software, when you turn on your computer, when you develop an argument. Logic is a contemporary universal. Yet despite being surrounded by logic, we remain quite unaware of its ubiquity.

Why did they choose this date? Because of a birthday and a deathday of two of the most important logicians of the twentieth century: Alfred Tarski, born in 1901; Kurt Gödel, died in 1978. They might also have thought of Charles Dodgson (Lewis Carroll), respected for his work in mathematical logic, who died on this day in 1898 (SEE 2 AUGUST).

It's easy to see the link between logic and language. If we view logic as the investigation of the principles of human reasoning, language is the means through which our reasoning is given expression. The problem is that natural languages are not logical: they contain irregularities and alternatives influenced by history and social convention. Which is more logical, an adjective before a noun (as in English) or after a noun (as in French): *white wine* or *vin blanc*? Is it more logical to mention the colour first or the object first? And, whichever logic you choose, there are exceptions, such as *the people responsible* and *le petit chien* ('the little dog'). This is why linguists talk about languages as being 'arbitrary'.

It's the arbitrariness that has motivated the search for a language based on totally regular principles, and many systems have been proposed, such as John Wilkins's *Essay Towards a Real Character, and a Philosophical Language* (1668), and artificial languages such as Esperanto (SEE 26 JULY) and Interlingua, but none has achieved the usage that their enthusiastic inventors hoped to see.

Incidentally, dates aren't logical either. 14 January was New Year's Day in Julius Caesar's calendar.

The Book of Common Prayer
was presented to Parliament in 1549

This was in the House of Lords. A few days later it was accepted by the Commons, and it became law on the 21st. All churches had to use it from Whit Sunday (9 June) that year.

The Book was drafted by Archbishop Thomas Cranmer, along with a committee of clergy, and it's one of a trio of candidates for the title of 'greatest influence on the English language' – the others being the King James Bible and Shakespeare. The 1549 edition was in use for only three years, when it was given a major revision, but much of its liturgy and language remains in the prayer books used today.

The influence has been mainly in vocabulary and idiom. The marriage service provides one of the clearest illustrations, as several of its expressions have come to be used in secular contexts. Such as:

> wilt thou have this woman to thy wedded wife
> to have and to hold
> for better for worse
> for richer for poorer
> in sickness and in health
> to love and to cherish
> forsaking all other
> so long as ye both shall live
> with this ring I thee wed
> with all my worldly goods I thee endow

and many more.

Film and television in the twentieth century have repeatedly milked these expressions, almost always in a comedy setting. *To Have and to Hold* has been the title of several films, as has *For Richer for Poorer*. Writers vacillate between *for* and *or*. *For Better or Worse* named an American television sitcom that ran between 2011 and 2017. One of the most successful series was the BBC's *Till Death Us Do Part* in the late 1960s and early 1970s, followed by a sequel in the 1980s. And the title of the sequel? *In Sickness and in Health*.

Book Publishers Day

Publishers celebrate books on World Book Day (23 APRIL). But who celebrates publishers? This day reminds us just how important publishers are, and what a complex business it is. It's a curiously neglected topic. I don't recall ever being taught in school about how books come to be, and how the book trade is organized globally. It's a fascinating world, and it would be good to teach children about it.

What would they learn?

— the process of book production – from agents, submissions and contracts to deadlines, print runs and marketing
— types of books – fiction and nonfiction, educational, academic, trade, children's, young adult ...
— the different media – print, electronic, audio, self-publishing
— the publishing team – editors, designers, illustrators, typesetters, copy-editors, indexers ...
— the structure of big companies, with their divisions and imprints, and the world of independents ('indies')
— the printers – hardbacks, paperbacks, paper sizes, proofs ...
— what goes on the publication data page in a book
— how much does it all cost, and how is the money divided.

Then they'd learn about broader issues, such as:

— the International Publishers Association, protecting copyright, defending freedom to publish, promoting literacy
— book events – reviews, prizes, fairs, festivals, cities, book days ...
— the legal deposit system – how books are sent to a repository, such as (for the UK) the British Library, to preserve intellectual and cultural heritage
— the monitoring system, notably Nielsen BookScan, which collects data directly from booksellers and retailers
— the cataloguing system, especially the International Standard Book Number (ISBN) identifying each publication, consisting of five elements: a prefix, country, publisher and edition, ending with a validating check digit.

It's a huge industry, with over 15,000 publishers worldwide. How much of all this is widely known? I suspect very little. Should it be part of a school curriculum? Today prompts us to think about such things.

Benjamin Franklin was born in 1706

The visionary polymath Benjamin Franklin, one of the Founding Fathers of the United States, has a huge reputation as a writer, publisher, scientist, inventor and statesman, but for a linguist his appeal lies also in his interest in the reform of English spelling. Like many others since the sixteenth century, he wanted to give the alphabet – as he put it in the introduction to *A Scheme for a new Alphabet and a Reformed Mode of Spelling, with Remarks and Examples* (1768) – 'a more natural Order'. It was a vision whose time seemed to be right – a new language for the new nation that would emerge out of the War of Independence a few years later.

Towards this end, he removed six letters from the alphabet (*C, J, Q, W, X, Y*), – *we* is written *ui* – and added six of his own devising, such as new symbols for 'sh' and 'ng', and separate letters for the two 'th' sounds (as in *thin* and *this*). Long vowels were shown by double letters, such as *diir* for *dear*. The system reflects an eighteenth-century American pronunciation – *have* is *hev*, *lost* is *last*, *new* is *nu*. On the other hand, several irregular features are retained, such as *our* and *uuld* (*would*).

His scientific background coloured the approach, which showed an awareness of the phonetics of speech that was rare at that time. But he quickly encountered the problems that have to be faced by anyone wanting to improve English spelling, such as the reluctance of society to leave traditional orthography, the impossibility of finding a single simplified system that would reflect the many English accents, and the real difficulty – which all reformers encounter – of persuading people that their individual method of simplification is superior to the many competitors that have been proposed. Franklin soon lost interest in his system, though by the time of his death in 1790 some of his ideas were being taken up by Noah Webster (SEE 16 OCTOBER).

Thesaurus Day

Peter Mark Roget was born on this day in 1779. Nobody ever uses his first names. To the lexicological world he is simply Roget, known for his Thesaurus, published in 1852. For many people, *Roget* has come to mean 'thesaurus', and they say 'pass me a Roget', even though it might not be by Roget at all. Few have achieved the accolade of becoming a generic noun.

His book has sometimes been described as a dictionary, but that is hugely misleading. We use a dictionary because we encounter a word and want to look up its meaning. We use a thesaurus for the opposite reason: we have a meaning in mind and want to look up a word that expresses it. Or a phrase. And that is how Roget described his book: *A Thesaurus of English Words and Phrases Classified and Arranged so as to Facilitate the Expression of Ideas and Assist in Literary Composition.*

He began working on what he called a 'system of verbal classification' in 1805, but it took him over forty years to complete. He had trained as a doctor, and held a series of posts at medical institutions in Manchester and London, which left him little opportunity for the rigorous and time-consuming task of thesaurus creation. This changed after he retired from medical life in 1840.

A thesaurus has uses far greater than the literary. It helps anyone who wants to find the 'best word' for a meaning. In a print edition, you look a word up in its alphabetical index, and this sends you to the place where words of similar meaning (synonyms) are located – and in some thesauri, words of opposite meaning (antonyms) too. In an electronic edition, simply typing a word into the search box shows the listings.

Roget's son and grandson both inherited his passion, editing enlarged revisions after his death in 1869. None of the family could ever have imagined the scale of the genre's afterlife. The original had some 15,000 entries; the largest thesauri today have over half a million (SEE 22 OCTOBER).

Victoria Fromkin died in 2000

One of the biggest challenges in linguistic research is to understand how the brain works when it is processing language. Vicki (as she was known to everyone) Fromkin made a major contribution to that. She was born in New Jersey in 1923, and spent her academic life at UCLA (Los Angeles). An indication of her standing in the profession is that the Linguistic Society of America, where she had periods as its secretary, vice-president and president, now has a Lifetime Service Award in her name.

Her main research field was an area of linguistic behaviour that affects everyone: slips of the tongue, as well as other breakdowns that temporarily interfere with our flow of speech, such as when we say that something is 'on the tip of our tongue'. She made a huge collection of what she called 'speech errors', showing how diverse they are, and yet not random: in tongue-slipping, sounds replace sounds, words replace words, affixes replace affixes, and so on.

Here are some examples from her collection. Deletion: *pants* for *plants*. Addition: *moptimal number*. Anticipation: *a leading list* (for *reading*). Perseveration: *beginning of the burn* (for *turn*). And then there are the famous reversals, such as *Yew Nork*, or those involving whole words, such as *fool the pill* for *fill the pool* – Spoonerisms (SEE 22 JULY). Two words can form a blend: *splinters* and *blisters* become *splisters*. Lewis Carroll called these 'portmanteau' words.

And tip of the tongue? The words that come to mind predict features of the one that is lost. Try writing them down, and look for recurring sounds. The stress pattern will usually be the same. So, once I was searching for the name of a city I worked out was *Verona*. I had guessed *Havana* and *Granada*. Same stress; all ending in *a*; *v*, *r* and *n* are present; *d* seems a distraction until one realizes that it's articulated in exactly the same place as *n*. The evidence was there. All I had to do was put the pieces together in the right way.

Myles Coverdale died in 1568

In 1534 the Convocation of Canterbury asked Henry VIII to authorize
a translation of the whole Bible into English – an English that people of
the sixteenth century could understand. (The earlier translation by John
Wycliffe in the late fourteenth century was into Middle English, which
would become increasingly unfamiliar to people during the 1400s.)
The task fell to Myles Coverdale, born in 1488, who had worked with
William Tyndale on his partial translation. His edition, published in 1535,
was the first complete Bible to be printed for use in England, and was
dedicated to the king.

All early Bible translations have left their mark on the language,
introducing new words and idioms, and passages that have proved
memorable because of their poetic quality. Most of Coverdale's text was
superseded by later versions, though his translation of the Psalms was
used in the Book of Common Prayer (SEE 15 JANUARY), and is thus still
to be heard. But his role in the development of English vocabulary is
notable.

There are 189 words that have their first recorded use in Coverdale's
1535 edition, according to the files of the *Oxford English Dictionary*, as
revised up to 2022. Some are specifically biblical terms, and some have
become obsolete (such as *Babylonical*, later replaced by *Babylonian*);
but most have achieved a permanent place in the language. There are
items immediately recognizable to anyone familiar with Bible stories,
such as *behold, fig leaves* and *swaddling-clothes*; but the majority have no
specifically biblical association, such as *brawling, doorkeeper, evening star,
killer, morning star* and *zeal*, and items like *bellyful* and *off and on* have a
strong colloquial presence.

As always with earlier stages of the language, we might regret the
passing of some words and phrases in standard English, and wish they
had stayed. I have a particular affection for *yonside* ('farther side'),
overmorrow ('the day after tomorrow') and *out-quencher* ('candle snuffer'),
and wouldn't be at all surprised to encounter them in regional dialect use
still.

George Orwell died in 1950

Orwell's 'Politics and the English Language' is to my mind one of the most important articles on language from the twentieth century. Published in 1946, when he was 43, it is a short essay, but it had an immediate impact because it drew attention to an issue that had simply not been addressed. Today, we've learned to be sceptical of political language that obscures or deliberately hides realities; but at the time nobody had read anything quite like this:

> In our time, political speech and writing are largely the defence of the indefensible. Things like the continuance of British rule in India, the Russian purges and deportations, the dropping of atom bombs on Japan, can indeed be defended, but only by arguments which are too brutal for most people to face, and which do not square with the aims of political parties. Thus political language has to consist largely of euphemism, question-begging and sheer cloudy vagueness.

Orwell frequently alludes to the way words hide realities, or are not up to the task of describing realities, even in the most mundane of circumstances. He comments, after visiting poor housing in *The Road to Wigan Pier*:

> Words are such feeble things. What is the use of a brief phrase like 'roof leaks' or 'four beds for eight people'? It is the kind of thing your eye slides over, registering nothing. And yet what a wealth of misery it can uncover!

His legacy is that people are now prepared to criticize public figures who use euphemistic jargon, who fail to 'tell it as it is'. We notice when the telling is obscured by cliché. We can be fairly certain that any politician who says 'let me be perfectly clear about this' is about to give us some Orwellian politicalspeak. And there are now words in the language to help us describe what is going on. *Gobbledegook* was first recorded in 1944. *Double-talk* is from the same decade. And Orwell was the first to use *-speak* as a derogatory suffix — *Oldspeak* and *Newspeak*, in the novel *Nineteen Eighty-four*.

The BBC broadcasts its first
live football commentary in 1927

It was a First Division game, between Arsenal and Sheffield United, played at the Highbury stadium in London. The commentator was Henry Blythe Thornhill Wakelam, known conveniently as 'Teddy'. His commentary box was a primitive affair – said at the time to be more like a garden shed than a studio – located in one of the stands opposite the halfway line.

Why did commentary arrive so late? The BBC had already been broadcasting for five years. The reason was that the sporting authorities and the press were antagonistic, thinking that live radio would stop people attending games and buying newspapers. But at the beginning of 1927 the BBC became a public corporation, and its charter gave it the right to broadcast live coverage of sporting events.

How was it to be done? The producer published in the BBC's magazine, *Radio Times*, a plan of the pitch divided into eight numbered squares. Squares 1 and 2 were on the commentator's right, in front of the goal, 3 and 4 reached the halfway line, 5 and 6 were the other side of the halfway line, and 7 and 8 were in front of the goal on the left.

Two commentators were used. Wakelam described the action on the pitch while a colleague called out which square the ball was in: 'now up field (7)... a pretty pass (5, 8)...', and so on. It's not the commentary style we know today, as knowledge of the layout of the pitch can be taken for granted, but there's a great deal linguistically in common, as seen in those punchy, elliptical sentences. It was a widely acclaimed innovation, and Wakelam went on to cover cricket and Wimbledon later in the year.

Two other points of interest: one for football enthusiasts, the other for linguists. The match ended in a 1–1 draw. And a notice pinned to the wall of the commentary box read 'Don't swear'.

National Handwriting Day

The day began in the United States, but the concept is so relevant to modern times that *National* should really be replaced by *International*. As people increasingly rely on computers, smartphones and tablets to communicate, there's a real risk that the art of handwriting could be lost – and it *is* an art, as the form of calligraphy shows.

The day had an originally commercial aim. It was established by a North American organization, the Writing Instruments Manufacturers Association, in 1977, to bring together the concerns of all industries involved in handwriting – makers of pens, pencils, markers, inks, erasers, writing paper, and related devices. They chose this day to promote its use: the birthday of the first person to sign the Declaration of Independence, John Hancock.

The benefits of handwriting go well beyond its artistic character, though the pleasure we gain from a piece of nice handwriting should never be underestimated. Here are some:

— the tactile experience of holding an implement and feeling the writing surface
— the calming effect that can accompany a piece of extended handwriting, arising out of the simple fact that it slows us down
— for children learning to read and write, the development of motor skills
— the recognition experience, for handwriting reveals our identity – as seen in forgery detection or character analysis: graphology
— the functional value, seen in such settings as post-it notes, envelopes, graffiti, signing for a parcel and legal signatures

And it is salutary to reflect on

— the fall-back experience, when there is no electronic device to hand, or its battery or power supply is dead.

It's a day that prompts us to use handwriting in a fresh way, perhaps by sending someone an appreciative note, writing a letter or card, or engaging in a piece of creative writing. Or we might simply admire someone else's handwriting, such as the manuscript of a famous author, or a famous illuminated manuscript – these days easy to find online.

International Day of Education

This is a recent day, first celebrated in 2019. The UNESCO website tells us why:

> Education is a human right, a public good and a public responsibility.

The right to education is enshrined in article 26 of the Universal Declaration of Human Rights. School, it goes on to say, is more than just a place of learning: it is also a place that provides protection, well-being, food and freedom. And the UN provides disturbing statistics for 2021: 258 million children do not attend school; 617 million children cannot read.

Language education is only one element in the mix of content that provides a good education; but it's an important topic that, surprisingly, is often missing from the curriculum. At primary level, the teaching of literacy (reading and writing) is a given; but the other two skills of communication – listening and speaking (often referred to as oracy) – are commonly left to chance. The learning of at least one other language is also a given in many countries. And countries are enormously varied, and often uncertain, over how much emphasis to devote to teaching *about* language – studying the way language is structured and how it is used.

There have been several initiatives to increase the awareness of language at older levels. The most enthusing one I know is the Linguistics Olympiad – one of many International Science Olympiads for secondary-school students, held annually since 2003. Each year, teams of young linguists compete to solve puzzles about the way the structure of a language works. I've seen some events, and can testify to the brilliant linguistic insights that these young people demonstrate.

But learning about the history, structure and use of language – KAL (knowledge about language), as it's sometimes called – is still not something students routinely experience in most schools. It's a pity, as they enjoy finding out about the people, places and events that have contributed to linguistic knowledge. Perhaps an 'On This Day' will help?

Burns Night/Nicht

The event is unique, celebrating the birth on this day in 1759 of Robert Burns – or Rabbie Burns, to use the localized spelling in which he's affectionately known in Scotland. No other writer has achieved the distinction of being celebrated not only in the daytime, but also in the evening, when a Burns Supper has been traditionally held since 1801, five years after his death at the young age of 36. His remarkable poetic achievement is recognized in his standing as the national poet of Scotland, but included in that is his prolific creativity as a songwriter – best known for the New Year paean 'Auld Lang Syne', sung all over the world.

People responded to his writing because they were able to identify with its homely and humorous character – a famous example is his poem 'To a Mouse' – and appreciated his choice of a local variety of English with its roots in the Middle Ages, now known proudly as Scots. After him, Scottish writing was no longer dominated by the literary norms of England, and a regional Scottish literature soon evolved, with authors adapting the language to create their own linguistic identities.

As an illustration, here are the opening lines of the poetic 'Address to a Haggis', spoken ceremonially at every Burns Supper, after this savoury meat dish is brought into the dining room, traditionally accompanied by a bagpiper:

Fair fa' your honest, sonsie face,	*fall, jolly*
Great chieftain o' the puddin-race!	*of*
Aboon them a' ye tak your place,	*above, all, take*
Painch, tripe, or thairm:	*paunch, intestine*
Weel are ye wordy o' a grace	*well, worthy*
As lang's my arm.	*long*

We don't find uniformity when we look across the range of writing in Scots. Some of the words in this extract you'll see spelled in slightly different ways, such as *weill* for *well*, and *airm* for *arm*. Scots has diversity, just as all varieties of English do.

Toad Hollow Day of Encouragement

I had no idea this day existed until I started to research this book – but I wish I had, for the world needs more days like this one, and I would have liked to have spread news of it. The story begins in the 1980s, in Kalamazoo, a city in south-west Michigan, USA. Ralph C. Morrison, a teacher at a community college there, and a storyteller, had an elderly student who as a child had attended Toad Hollow Country School, situated in the south of the city in a schoolhouse built in 1834. He came across its name when he read a newspaper article about his student, and was so struck by it that he began to use it in his stories. It became a town, and when asked where it was he would say 'in your heart'.

The town became a physical reality when the local government let him use a local park to tell his stories, and in the early 1990s a team of volunteers ('voluntoads') built a small nineteenth-century township, which they christened Toad Hollow, and used it as a centre for creative arts, crafts and historical re-enactments. The enterprise didn't last long, as the government had other plans for the park, but the voluntoads continued the spirit of the initiative into the 2000s, and one of the outcomes was this day. As a website describing the history puts it: 'The day is for supporting, encouraging, and making heartfelt connections with others ... a day for volunteering, to show others the things you love, and to encourage them to share as well.'

Why the 26th? Probably because this was the date Michigan achieved statehood in 1837, but there may have been other, unrecorded reasons. There are more places called Toad Hollow in the USA, with different functions, and I've come across a Toad Hollow Archers Club in Cornwall. But the name deserves to be more widely known in its Kalamazoo incarnation – and perhaps copied? I make up for my own neglect now.

The inaugural naming of tennessine took place in 2017

It isn't often that new chemical elements are discovered, and added to the periodic table, but in 2016 four new superheavy elements were given official recognition: nihonium (element 113), moscovium (115), tennessine (117) and oganesson (118). All were synthetic elements produced through lab experiments. Why those names?

It's the procedure authorized by the International Union of Pure and Applied Chemistry (IUPAC): elements can be named after a mythological concept, a mineral, a place, a property or a scientist. So in the above we see Nihon (Japan), Moscow, Tennessee, and Nobel prize-winner Yuri Oganessian. To maintain historical and chemical consistency, the word endings are *-ium* for elements belonging to groups 1 to 16, *-ine* for those in group 17, and *-on* for those in group 18.

Each country celebrated its achievement in its own way, and this was the day chosen to inaugurate tennessine. Why Tennessee? Because this is where the famous Oak Ridge National Laboratory, established in 1943, is situated, in the east of the state near Knoxville. Researchers there, along with collaborators at Vanderbilt University and the University of Tennessee, made the discovery in 2010, but it took over five years to verify it, and another year to gain approval for the new name.

Neologisms are usually the result of an immediate and unconstrained process of creation: I can invent a new word today without it having to go through a formal process of acceptance. Some countries do establish committees in an attempt to control their character, and these can play a useful role (in respecting the lexical traditions of an endangered language, for instance), but in the end it's the weight of public opinion that decides whether a new word lives or dies in everyday usage. Not so in the case of scientific nomenclature. Organizations such as IUPAC play a critical role in ensuring terminological consistency and precision.

Data Protection Day/Data Privacy Day

The Council of Europe showed great prescience when it signed its Convention for the Protection of Individuals with Regard to Automatic Processing of Personal Data – known succinctly as 'Convention 108'. This was as early as 1981, long before concern about online privacy became the public issue it is today.

The need for greater awareness of the issues grew rapidly in the early 2000s, following the development of search engines in the 1990s and the arrival of social media a decade later, such as Facebook (2004), YouTube (2005) and Twitter (2006). The Council of Europe therefore launched a Data Protection Day, recognized for the first time on this day in 2007 – the date on which Convention 108 was signed. A year later, the United States and Canada instituted a Data Privacy Day, to be celebrated on the same date.

The idea is to get governments, data protection agencies and other bodies to take steps to raise awareness of the problems in safeguarding personal data. Events have included conferences, school projects and campaigns targeting the general public. Surveys have shown that a remarkable number of individuals are unfamiliar with the risks associated with how their personal information can be used and exploited online. An apparently innocent purchase of goods or services, a casual browsing of the Internet or the downloading of an interesting app can have unexpected consequences. What can you do if you think your privacy has been disrespected? What are your rights? This is the day when a special effort is made to empower businesses and individuals to respect privacy and foster trust.

The two-way nature of this effort needs underlining: businesses *and* individuals. Companies have the responsibility of developing a culture of privacy, keeping data safe and routinely assessing their practices, especially if other agencies are carrying out work on their behalf. But a lot can be done by people learning as much as possible about how to manage their privacy and security settings, and not giving websites and apps more data than the bare minimum.

Susan Coolidge was born in 1835

This was the pen name of Sarah Chauncey Woolsey, born in Ohio. She was a prolific writer – over thirty children's books, numerous short stories and poems, and edited works such as an edition of Jane Austen's letters. She is best known for her classic children's novel *What Katy Did* (1872) and its sequels. Although her popularity has varied since her death in 1905, the Katy series is still in print, and was actually ranked among the ten most popular reading choices for 12-year-old girls, in a British study of reading preferences in the 1990s.

For a book on language, to celebrate her work I've chosen the first four stanzas of a poem she published in *A Few More Verses* (1889), titled simply 'Words'. The phrasing is of its period, but the personification is ingenious.

A little, tender word,
  Wrapped in a little rhyme,
Sent out upon the passing air,
As seeds are scattered everywhere
  In the sweet summer-time.

A little, idle word,
  Breathed in an idle hour;
Between two laughs that word was said,
Forgotten as soon as uttered,
  And yet the word had power.

Away they sped, the words:
  One, like a wingèd seed,
Lit on a soul which gave it room,
And straight began to bud and bloom
  In lovely word and deed.

The other careless word,
  Borne on an evil air,
Found a rich soil, and ripened fast
Its rank and poisonous growths, and cast
  Fresh seeds to work elsewhere.

Angela Thirkell was born in 1890

Sometimes a snatch of dialogue triggers an association with a linguistic domain, and provides a fresh angle on it. This happened to me when I came across this extract from Angela Thirkell's 1935 novel *O These Men, These Men*. She was a prolific and popular mid-century novelist, born in London, writing over thirty novels between the 1930s and 1960s, mainly set in fictional Barsetshire – continuing the world created by Trollope in the nineteenth century. She died in 1961. An Angela Thirkell Society celebrates her work.

This isn't a Barsetshire novel, but its intriguing title would motivate any Shakespearean to read it, as the words are spoken by Desdemona to Emilia in *Othello*. In chapter 3, Caroline Danvers is talking to her cousin Hugh, who has asked her if she still cares for her alcoholic former husband, James.

> Caroline shrank from him as if he were James himself and shook her head.
> 'No, no,' she said. 'I hardly even remember him.'
> 'But you don't like talking of him?'
> Caroline put her hand on his arm.
> 'No, I hate it. But I feel I ought to do a kind of five finger exercises by saying his name till I can say it without making a fool of myself. Not because of hating him, because you don't hate a person that you never think of. ... But a person's name can suddenly hurt one so much. Do you know what I mean?'
> 'I do. There are some names that one can't even say in a normal voice because they lay open some nerve. I was frightfully in love with a woman once. Her name was Susan and she came from Norwich and she lived with her husband in Ovington Square. I fell out of love with her, and I haven't seen her or heard of her for years, but if I read or hear the words Susan, or Norwich, or Ovington, I go all queer.'

These are personal associations for Hugh, but I wonder how far names generate more widely held associations and language-specific collocations. Stratford, and the Bard of Avon, for a start.

National Backward Day
or
Yad Drawkcab Lanoitan

This day might get the prize for the strangest celebration in this book, but it's proved to be a popular fun occasion in the United States. It's said to be the brainchild of two women – Megan Emily Scott and Sarah Nicole Miller – who in 1961 were milking cows on a farm while thinking of what they'd rather be doing: making crafts. The idea caught on in their home town, and then spread. The first official DBN was celebrated the following year. They chose this date because, in the American system of dating, 31 January is 1/31 – which backwards is also 1/31.

As one of the explanatory websites puts it: 'The day provides an opportunity to reverse our ways, our direction, or simply our shirt.' Examples include adding coffee to your milk and having breakfast for dinner. Linguistic recommendations include learning to write your name and address backwards, saying 'Goodbye' instead of 'Hello', and reading a book starting with the last page.

Actually, there are lots of examples of backward(s) usage (*ananyms* – from Greek *ana-* 'back') in the history of language study. 'Back slang', in which words are spoken or spelled backwards, has been recorded for well over a century in English. *Rouf* and *neves* is known in market and criminal argot. *Yob* is standard colloquial. Speaking backwards has long been a popular children's game, once they've learned to read.

There's a serious side to all this. Psychologists have pointed to the value of sometimes doing things in the order we don't usually follow, changing work routine, trying a different approach to solving a problem, and so on. Car drivers regularly encounter 'mirror writing', as when they see AMBULANCE correctly in a car rear-view mirror. And the history of ignoring or reversing social rules and roles is ancient, as evidenced by the December festival of Saturnalia in classical Rome, when – amongst many events – masters served their slaves.

The patron of today would have to be Leonardo da Vinci, whose personal notes were in mirror writing.

Langston Hughes was born in 1902

Born in Missouri, Hughes became a leader of the movement of African-American writers and musicians that evolved in 1920s' New York City, known as the Harlem Renaissance, but anyone interested in language needs to remember him also as the father of a new stylistic genre: jazz poetry. The term applies to the content of the poetry as well as its formal structure: it's both about jazz and, in its rhythms, influenced by jazz.

In its early days the focus was on the people, places, instruments and styles that made up the jazz world. Later it incorporated the syncopation, repeated phrasing and improvisation that characterize the musical genre. A good illustration is the second stanza of 'The Weary Blues':

Thump, thump, thump, went his foot on the floor.
He played a few chords then he sang some more –
   'I got the Weary Blues
   And I can't be satisfied.
   Got the Weary Blues
   And can't be satisfied –
   I ain't happy no mo'
   And I wish that I had died.'
And far into the night he crooned that tune.
The stars went out and so did the moon.
The singer stopped playing and went to bed
While the Weary Blues echoed through his head.
He slept like a rock or a man that's dead.

He died in 1967, but his legacy lives on in the creativity of many modern poets, singers and instrumentalists, as well as in the quick-fire rhyming rhythms of rap. One of my favourites is Shake Keane, poet and flugelhorn player from St Vincent, described in a 2021 biography by Philip Nanton as someone who was 'at the crossroads between jazz and poetry'. Along with Michael Garrick, he was influential in introducing jazz poetry to Britain in the 1960s. Why favourite? Because I got to know him when I started to read English as an undergraduate in 1959. He was a mature student in the same class.

Hannah More was born in 1745

She came to be one of the most important literary figures in the later decades of the eighteenth century, a successful poet and playwright, and a member of the literary and intellectual women's coterie known as the Bluestockings (from their informal and unconventional wear). Thanks to her literary success, she was able to engage in philanthropy, establishing several schools in the Bristol area, where she was born, and supporting the foundation of a liberal arts college in Gambier, Ohio: Kenyon College. In her middle and later years (she died in 1833) she was a leading campaigner for social reform, especially in the fields of women's education and the abolition of slavery.

She was an admirer of Dr Johnson, praising his work in her writing. In Boswell's *Life of Johnson* he is said to have been totally unimpressed by her flattery; but later, according to the Scottish philosopher James Beattie, he is reported to have acknowledged her as 'the most powerful versificatrix in the English language'. This unusual word for a female versifier seems to be a Johnsonian creation: the historical *Oxford English Dictionary* has no further instances of its use apart from this one. But it clearly indicates the esteem in which she was held. And, indeed, there are no parallels during this period to her major poems in rhyming couplets, such as 'The Bleeding Rock', 'Florio' and 'Bas Bleu' (Blue Stocking).

As an indication of her style, below are a few lines (59–66) from her long poem 'Slavery' written in 1788 – an impassioned attack on the practice – which anticipates many of the themes of a postcolonial era:

> Perish th' illiberal thought which wou'd debase
> The native genius of the sable race!
> Perish the proud philosophy, which sought
> To rob them of the pow'rs of equal thought!
> Does then th'immortal principle within
> Change with the casual colour of a skin?
> Does matter govern spirit? or is mind
> Degraded by the form to which 'tis join'd?

And she answers her own questions with an emphatic 'No'.

Feast day of St Blaise, patron saint of throat diseases

Linguists who have a Christian belief would do well to remember St Blaise; and those who don't might nonetheless appreciate the attention that the story of his life gives to diseases and injuries of the throat, for many of them interfere with speech production. The throat contains the larynx, situated behind the prominence known as the Adam's apple. Air from the lungs makes the vocal folds in the larynx vibrate, resulting in the voicing of many speech sounds as well as controlling pitch and loudness, and several other voice qualities.

Our voice and speech are affected when anything goes wrong with the anatomy, physiology or neurology of the larynx. A range of disorders can lead to a breathy or husky voice quality (technically called *dysphonia*), or total loss of voice, and in an extreme case serious disease can lead to the surgical removal of the larynx, and the need to replace the lost vibrations with a device that generates them artificially. Phonetic disorders of speech form a major part of the work of the speech and language therapist (SEE 6 JANUARY).

What did Blaise do to warrant this patronage? He was a third-century physician who became Bishop of Sebastea in historical Armenia – present-day Sivas in Turkey. The local governor had been given orders from the Roman emperor Licinius to kill any Christians. As Blaise was being led away to prison, the story goes, a mother set before him her son, choking to death on a fish bone; he prayed for him, and the child was cured. Blaise was beheaded soon after. The story is first recorded in the writings of a fifth-century Greek physician, Aëtius Amida.

In many places around the world, today's feast (recognized in the Western Church) is celebrated by a priest holding a pair of crossed candles over the head or near the throat of those wishing to participate, and a blessing is given with an invocation to protect the recipient from throat disease. In the Eastern Church, the feast day is 11 February.

Frederick Furnivall was born in 1825

One of the books on my shelves I most often refer to is *The Oldest English Texts*, edited by Henry Sweet in 1885, and published on behalf of the Early English Text Society (EETS). It includes all extant Old English texts up to about 900 that are preserved in contemporary manuscripts, with the exception of the Anglo-Saxon Chronicle and the works of Alfred. Anyone interested in the origins of English will find it invaluable, along with the many other publications of the EETS on Old and Middle English. And we have Furnivall to thank for that, because he founded it in 1864.

Born in Surrey, he became a barrister, though his linguistic interests soon replaced his legal work. A lifetime socialist, he went so far as to say, later in life: 'I never cared a bit for philology: my chief aim has been throughout to illustrate the social condition of the English people in the past.' This was unduly self-dismissive. He was a crucial figure in the development of historical English-language study. He joined the Philological Society in 1847 and served as its secretary from 1853 until just before his death in 1910. He was a member of the three-man committee formed in 1857 to find a way of collecting all the 'unregistered words' in English; and the *New English Dictionary* – later called the *Oxford English Dictionary* – was the result (SEE 15 FEBRUARY). He had a leading role during its early development, and after James Murray took over as editor he continued to provide thousands of examples of word usage for its files.

As if this wasn't enough, he founded several other literary societies, and edited a major 'six-text' edition of *The Canterbury Tales*. But I remember him mainly for his lexicological aims, which he described in 1862, in a typical rhetorical flourish, as a National Portrait Gallery of words, adding: 'No winged messenger who bears to us the thoughts and aspirations, the weakness and the littleness, of our forefathers; who is to carry ours to our descendants: is to be absent.' And he quotes Tennyson in a rousing conclusion: 'Fling our doors wide! all, all, not one, but all, must enter.'

Reader's Digest magazine was first published in 1922

The magazine arrived in our house every month when I was little, and I remember avidly reading the vocabulary quiz, 'It pays to increase your word power', and thinking this was a very good idea. It had only been going for a few years: the first column appeared in January 1945. The writer was dictionary editor and lexical enthusiast Wilfred J. Funk, and after his death in 1965 his son Peter took over, with 'increase' replaced by 'enrich'. There have since been several lexical compilations, books, competitions and games.

I got to know the magazine well when I wrote the chapter on 'Language and Communication' for the *Reader's Digest Library of Modern Knowledge* (1978). Looking back at it now, I'm surprised to see only a short entry on vocabulary size, saying little more than the rather obvious point that some people have more words at their disposal than others. Today, this observation can be given much more substance.

People have two kinds of vocabulary: active (the words they use) and passive (the words they know but don't use). Obtaining an estimate about passive vocabulary isn't difficult, though it takes a bit of time. All you have to do is go through a medium-sized dictionary (1,000–1,500 pages, or around 150,000 entries) and tick the words you know! Or, easier, take a few samples and work out an average per page. People who've done this are always surprised at the outcome. With few exceptions, they know over 50,000 words. But when we note how word families soon build up – *happy, happily, happiness, happy-go-luck*y... – perhaps this isn't so surprising. Well-read people can easily reach 100,000 – though that's still nowhere near 'all the words in the dictionary'.

Active vocabulary is much harder to estimate. It would mean recording all the words we say over a period of time; and, as the words we use change according to the seasons and festivals, that period needs to be a year. Samples suggest that our active vocabulary is likely to be about a third of our passive. Still a lot, though.

Waitangi Day

The day remembers the Treaty of Waitangi, the founding document of the country of New Zealand. Waitangi is on the coast of the Bay of Islands, in the far north of North Island, and it is there that an agreement was signed on this day in 1840 between the British Crown and over 500 Māori chiefs (*rangatira*). It's now a public holiday in New Zealand.

It took a long time for the Māori language to achieve the kind of public celebration that it receives today. As with many minority languages around the world, its use was often opposed and its character reviled. A century of neglect and seriously diminishing use began to be reversed in the 1970s. Every year since 1975 there has been a Māori Language Week during September, in which the language is displayed in all its variety, and people are encouraged to use more Māori phrases in everyday life. It became an official language of New Zealand in 1987, and there are now schools, radio stations and a television channel functioning through the medium of Māori.

With over a century of contact between English and Māori, it's not surprising to find that both languages have changed their lexical character. Many English words have entered Māori, adapted to suit its sound system and spelled accordingly, such as *etita* (editor), *kirikiti* (cricket) and *tiakarete* (chocolate). And these days we find an increasing number of Māori words entering New Zealand English. The *Oxford English Dictionary* has over 300 examples, such as the greetings *aloha* and *kia ora*, the *tui* and *kiwi* birds, the *kauri* tree, the *haka* ceremonial dance, and the name for a New Zealander of European descent, *pakeha*. And not forgetting the word for the Māori language itself, *te reo*. There are fusions too, such as *cyber-hui*, from *hui* (a social gathering). Some, such as *kiwi* (in both its national and its ornithological sense), as well as *kiwifruit*, have travelled far outside the country, becoming a part of international standard English. The most comprehensive account is in the *Dictionary of New Zealand English*, first published in 1997.

Charles Dickens was born in 1812

One day to celebrate the writing of Dickens would never be enough, given the prolific and wide-ranging output of his 58-year life. And how could anyone make a principled choice, given that so many of his works compete to be favourites? Even from a stylistic point of view, there are so many intriguing facets to explore, such as his vivid character descriptions, his use of local dialect and speech idiosyncrasies, and his humorous comments on the way a dialogue is developing.

But I have to write something; so here's an example, from *Sketches by Boz*, which I choose because it was first published on this day in 1836. Its full title was *Sketches by 'Boz,' Illustrative of Every-day Life and Every-day People*, and comprised a collection of fifty-six short pieces he'd published in newspapers and periodicals over the previous three years. In 'Seven Dials', we read a description of a quarrel building up into a fight in the heart of that district in London:

> On one side, a little crowd has collected round a couple of ladies, who having imbibed the contents of various 'three-outs' of gin and bitters in the course of the morning, have at length differed on some point of domestic arrangement, and are on the eve of settling the quarrel satisfactorily, by an appeal to blows, greatly to the interest of other ladies who live in the same house, and tenements adjoining, and who are all partisans on one side or other.

An insult by one side uses the word 'hussies'.

> 'What do you mean by hussies?' interrupts a champion of the other party, who has evinced a strong inclination throughout to get up a branch fight on her own account ('Hooroar,' ejaculates a pot-boy in parenthesis, 'put the kye-bosk on her, Mary!') ...

Kye-bosk catches the eye of anyone interested in etymology, for it's a first recorded use of the word, later spelled *kibosh*. In fact Dickens has 252 entries attributed to him in the *Oxford English Dictionary*, such as *scrunched*, *rampage* and *dustbin*. *Three-out* is another: a measure of liquor poured into three glasses.

Robert Lowth's grammar
was published in 1762

In fact it was published anonymously, with only the publisher's name on the title page. But its author was widely known, and he became even more of an iconic figure as a grammarian when he became Bishop of Oxford (1766) and Bishop of London (1777). Born in Hampshire in 1710, Lowth grew up in a social milieu where people increasingly wanted guidance about 'polite' linguistic usage. Dr Johnson had provided this for vocabulary, and Lowth wanted to do the same for grammar, as the section on grammar in Johnson's *Dictionary*, published in 1755, was generally thought to be a weakness. By the time he died in 1787, his *Short Introduction to English Grammar* had gone through many editions and reprintings, and was often pirated and plagiarized.

He wrote it, he says, 'for the use of my little Boy' – an 8-year-old in 1762 – but the level of his exposition, and his use of illustrations, gave it an entirely adult appeal. Adaptations for schools came later. The popularity lay chiefly in the way Lowth identified what he considered to be grammatical 'errors' in the writings of the 'best authors' of the past. He was the first to describe these, especially in syntax – such as placing a preposition at the end of a sentence. The implication, of course, is that these usages should be avoided, and later grammarians would develop this approach to grammar, known now as prescriptivism, that has lasted to the present day.

His book is one that, unusually, has received its own biography, by the Dutch linguist Ingrid Tieken-Boon van Ostade in 2011. She called her study *The Bishop's Grammar*, and sums it up on page 85 by saying it was 'the most authoritative English grammar published during the eighteenth century'. She's right. Some 200 English grammars came out in the later decades of the 1700s, but none achieved the prestige and popularity as Lowth's, and it exercised a huge influence on the grammars that would become even more successful in the nineteenth century.

International Greek Language Day

Obviously there's much to celebrate in the history of Greek literature and culture, and it's only right that the language through which this literature and culture has been expressed should have its own day too. This date was chosen because it's the commemoration day of Dionysios Solomos, the country's national poet, whose works include the Greek national anthem. It has been recognized since 2017.

The history of the language, still spoken today with writings dating back over 3,500 years, has no parallel in Western culture. Only Chinese matches it. And only Latin matches its influence on the lexical character of English and many other European languages. There are over 18,000 derivations from Greek in the *Oxford English Dictionary*, such as *virus*, *theatre*, *ethics*, *temperature*, *philosophy*, *silicon*, *chloroform*, *triassic*, *laryngitis*; and when the entirety of the highly specialized vocabulary of such subjects as chemistry, geology and medicine is included, this total is greatly increased.

Some subjects have grown their terminology largely as a result of Greek. Where would linguistics be, I wonder, without *acoustics*, *antonym*, *calligraphy*, *dialect*, *etymology*, *grammar*, *homonym*, *lexicon*, *metaphor*, *morphology*, *philology*, *phonetics*, *phonology*, *rhetoric*, *rhythm*, *semantics*, *synonym*, *syntax*, *thesaurus*...? But the power of the language in present-day English is best illustrated from the number of combining forms that use a Greek prefix or suffix: *anti-*, *hyper-*, *micro-*, *mono-*, *neo-*...; *-graph*, *-ism*, *-meter*, *-phobe*, *-phone*...

Hundreds of words already exist using these elements. Take *cyber-*: *cyberfriend*, *cybercafé*, *cyberbully*, *cybercrime*, *cyberterrorism*... Or *-(o)logy*, as in *theology*, *psychology*, *astrology*, *mineralogy*, and dozens more, with the suffix becoming a separate word, meaning a specialized field of knowledge, as in the title of Maureen Lipman's book *You Got an Ology?* (1989). And there are hundreds more waiting to be coined. Once we know the meaning of the basic element, the word-coining sky's the limit. The study of London? *Londonology*. Online? *Cyberlondonology*. Don't like that idea? *Anticyberlondonology*.

Fleur Adcock was born in 1934

Fleur Adcock was born in New Zealand, but spent part of her childhood in England, returning to live in London in 1963. From her many collections of poetry, I choose a tiny fragment below, introducing it by this extract from an interview in 2018 for the literary website Jogos Florais, because of the way she draws attention to the central notion of rhythm, and how she deals with it. The interviewer has asked her if there are any words or stylistic figures she particularly likes.

> Yes, I like to get the rhythm right. Not the metre, but the rhythm. There is such a profound difference between rhythm and metre. You can't describe it or talk about it, you can only give examples now and then. If it sounds a bit off, then that's part of the joy of it. … Things stick in my mind, strange rhythms. I listen to the rhythm in my mind all the time when I'm walking.

Because metre is so central to the English tradition, it tends to attract all the attention in teaching about poetry, with free verse left to fend for itself. Remarks like this are a valuable corrective.

'Dragon Talk' (2010) is a humorous yet affectionate and at times moving poem about the ups and downs of dictating to the well-known speech recognition software. These two stanzas nicely illustrate the way poetic lines can be crafted to express rhythmical sense units of meaning, with the line breaks controlling the pace at which we're led through the narrative. Line endings tease us with a semantic puzzle: what will happen next? The humour lies in the unexpected resolution.

> All the come-ons
> you transcribed as commas —
> how can we conduct a flirtation
> in punctuation? —
>
> Particularly when,
> money-mad creature,
> you spell doom to romance
> by writing 'flotation'.

The feast day of St Cædmon

Cædmon, who lived in the seventh century CE, is the first English poet of known name. (The letter æ, 'ash', is pronounced like the *a* in *cat*.) His story is told by Bede in his *Ecclesiastical History of the English People* (book 4, chapter 24), written in the following century.

Cædmon was a stable boy at Whitby Abbey in Yorkshire. He leaves a community banquet ashamed that he can't participate: 'being sometimes at entertainments, when it was agreed for the sake of mirth that all present should sing in their turn, when he saw the instrument come towards him, he rose up from table and returned home.' He falls asleep, and someone appears to him in a dream. This exchange follows, the first recorded fragment of English conversation, here in Modern English:

> Cædmon, sing me something.
> 'I can sing nothing; and therefore I went out from the banquet
>   and came here, because I didn't know how to sing anything.'
> However, you can sing for me.
> 'What shall I sing?'
> Sing me creation.

He then creates a piece today called 'Cædmon's Hymn'. Any translation does no justice to the rhythm, alliteration and balanced lines that form the structure of the Old English original.

> Now we must praise the guardian of the heavenly kingdom
> the might of the Creator and his mind's purpose,
> the work of the Father of Glory, as he for each of his wonders,
> the eternal Lord, established a beginning.
> He shaped first for the sons of the earth
> heaven as a roof, the holy shaper;
> then the middle-world, mankind's guardian,
> the eternal Lord, afterwards made,
> solid ground for men, the Lord almighty.

'Sing me creation' – *Sing me frumsceaft* in Old English – might sound stilted, but it's a construction that has lasted down the centuries. Type 'Sing me a story' into a search engine and you'll see.

43

Darwin Day

Charles Darwin was born in Shropshire on this day in 1809, and it's celebrated around the globe to remember his contribution to evolutionary biology, as well as to promote all scientific endeavour. But what is he doing in a book on language? Because the most famous phrase we associate with him has a direct application to speech.

This is, of course, 'the survival of the fittest' – a succinct way of describing the mechanism of natural selection. In fact the phrase didn't originate with him – it belongs to his contemporary Herbert Spencer – but he was sufficiently impressed with it that he included it in the fifth edition of *On the Origin of Species* (1869).

The most obvious linguistic application is in relation to accents. Accents exist to express identity – who we are, which community we belong to, which community we *don't* belong to. They perform this function better than other methods, such as badges or clothing, because they can be perceived around corners and in the dark, and develop naturally and unconsciously, without financial cost.

Perceiving identities in the dark would have been critical in the early development of the human race, when speech was first emerging. Imagine you're in a cave, and you hear noises outside. Are they friends or enemies? You call out, and a voice replies. If the voice has the same accent as yours, it's probably safe to go outside, as the speaker is likely to be a member of your tribe. If the voice has a different accent, you can still go outside, but you'd better take your club with you! The better you are at identifying different accents, then, the more likely you are to survive.

I find this scenario plausible because it still happens today. A street-wise young man once told me he knew not to round a corner into a street, or go into a club or pub, if he heard a particular accent being used there. In a society where different groups don't get on, listening to accents can still be a matter of survival. The survival of the linguistically fittest.

World Radio Day

UNESCO established this day in 2012, remembering the date
when United Nations Radio started broadcasting in 1946. Its aim is
summarized in a mission statement on the UNESCO website:

> Radio is a powerful medium for celebrating humanity in all its diversity
> and constitutes a platform for democratic discourse. At the global level,
> radio remains the most widely consumed medium. This unique ability
> to reach out the widest audience means radio can shape a society's
> experience of diversity, and stand as an arena for all voices to speak out,
> be represented and heard.

Each year the day has a theme. In 2014 it was gender equality and
women's empowerment in radio, in 2015 youth and radio, and in 2016
radio in times of emergency and disaster. More recent years have
celebrated radio in relation to audiences, diversity, dialogue, innovation,
and other watchwords of the times. It was 'Radio and Trust' in 2022,
'Radio and Peace' in 2023.

From a linguistic point of view, the day provides a moment to
reflect on the way the medium has broadened the expressive richness of
language, as it lives up to its promise 'to inform, educate and entertain'
(as Lord Reith put it in an early comment about the role of the BBC).
Its many formats provide a range of new varieties and styles – news-
reading, weather-forecasting, documentaries, radio plays, sports
commentary (SEE 22 JANUARY), phone-ins, talkbacks, quiz programmes,
interviews, traffic reports, DJ speech, magazines, discussions and (on
commercial radio) advertisements.

By putting all the information into the voice, the medium foregrounds
aspects of language that are often taken for granted, such as accent,
voice quality and speech mannerisms. And that awareness is reflected
in the many letters, cards, emails and other reactions that listeners send
in to radio stations, commenting – usually intemperately – on anything
perceived to be infelicitous.

P.G. Wodehouse died in 1975

Pelham Grenville Wodehouse was born in Surrey in 1881. He wrote articles, plays and lyrics for musicals, before becoming known for his comic fiction. His most famous creations are the disaster-prone Bertie Wooster and his rescuing valet Jeeves.

His writing is full of language play, such as coining new words ('gruntled' from 'disgruntled'; 'I out-Fred the nimblest Astaire'), transferring adjectives ('I balanced a thoughtful lump of sugar on the teaspoon'), and playing with idioms ('if he had a mind, there was something on it'). Less known are his humorous takes on language, as in 'On the Writing of Lyrics' (1917):

> Whoever invented the English language must have been a prose-writer, not a versifier, for he has made meagre provision for the poets. Indeed, the word 'you' is almost the only decent chance he has given them. You can do something with a word like 'you'. It rhymes with 'sue', 'eyes of blue', 'woo', and all sorts of succulent things, easily fitted into the fabric of a lyric.
>
> But take the word 'love'.
>
> When the board of directors, or whoever it was, was arranging the language, you would have thought that, if they had a spark of pity in their systems, they would have tacked on to that emotion of thoughts of which the young man's fancy lightly turns in spring, some word ending in an open vowel. They must have known that lyricists would want to use whatever word they selected as a label for the above-mentioned emotion far more frequently than any other word in the language. It wasn't much to ask of them to choose a word capable of numerous rhymes. But no, they went and made it 'love', causing vast misery to millions.
>
> No lyricist wants to keep linking 'love' with 'skies above' and 'turtle dove,' but what can he do? You can't do a thing with 'shove'; and 'glove' is one of those aloof words which are not good mixers. And – mark the brutality of the thing – there is no word you can substitute for 'love'. It is just as if they did it on purpose.

Announcement of the completion of the *Oxford English Dictionary* in 1928

This was the day when the in-house journal of Oxford University Press, *The Periodical*, made the announcement in a special issue, with the long-awaited words emblazoned on the front cover: 'The Oxford English Dictionary Completed'. The official publication day was 19 April. In *The Times* on that day a celebratory article appeared, with the opening words: 'This year, whatever else it may be, is the Year of the Dictionary.'

It had been the longest of hauls. It was 1857 when the Philological Society of London established a committee to collect unregistered words in English. The following year it was proposed to start preparing a new dictionary. In 1879 Oxford University Press agreed to publish the project, and James Murray was appointed the founding editor (SEE ALSO 22 JUNE). It took five years to produce the first section of letter A, and another forty-four years before the final pages were completed. Its twelve volumes contained 414,825 words.

But the story didn't stop there. A one-volume Supplement was issued in 1933, and a further three Supplements came after, the last published in 1986. The next year a version was produced as a double CD-ROM. In 1989 the second edition of the *OED* appeared – twenty volumes now, and over half a million words. In 2000 the online edition arrived. Work continues on the preparation of a third edition.

The whole story is told in great detail in Peter Gilliver's monumental account, *The Making of the Oxford English Dictionary* (2016). It illustrates the enormous personal, administrative and financial difficulties that had to be faced, as well as the myriad linguistic issues – such as how to handle scientific terms and the inclusion of regional dialect words – which meant that the first estimates of the time it would take to finish the *Dictionary* proved wholly unrealistic. In a talk to the Philological Society in 1882 Murray gave an estimate that 'The dictionary might be out by 1900 A.D., but probably not much before.' He was over a quarter of a century out.

The founding in 1857 of
what would become Gallaudet University

Gallaudet, in north-east Washington DC, is the only university in the world where students live and learn using American Sign Language and English. Its origins lie on this day in 1857, when President Franklin Pierce signed a federal law creating the Columbia Institution for Instruction of the Deaf and the Dumb [as deaf people were misleadingly described in those days] and the Blind. It became a university when it was authorized to issue degrees, in 1864. Its name change took place in 1894: Gallaudet College became Gallaudet University in 1986.

The name honours Thomas Hopkins Gallaudet (1787–1851), who opened the country's first school for the deaf in 1816. A neighbour where he lived in Hartford, Connecticut, had a 9-year-old deaf daughter, whose father, concerned about getting her a good education, persuaded Gallaudet to travel to Europe to study methods for teaching deaf students. At the Institute for the Deaf in Paris he learned about ways of using manual communication, and returned to the USA with one of its teachers, Laurent Clerc (SEE ALSO 23 DECEMBER). Together they raised funds to found a school, and Gallaudet served as its principal until 1830. It began with just twelve students.

Today, the University serves nearly 1,500 students (as of 2022) from all over the USA as well as from abroad. They can choose from over forty courses leading to BA or BSc degrees. Its website (gallaudet.edu) summarizes its development into a leading institution for deaf education and research: 'viewed by deaf and hearing people alike as a primary resource for all things related to deaf people, including educational and career opportunities; open communication and visual learning; deaf history and culture; American Sign Language; and the impact of technology on the deaf community'. Its philosophy is proudly affirmed:

> Here being deaf is not something to overcome, but the place to embrace oneself, and to build connections within and beyond the signing and deaf community.

'Banjo' Paterson was born in 1864

It doesn't take long for a new variety of English to be born in a country, but it takes a lot longer for it to be recognized and accepted, both nationally and internationally. It needs to be institutionalized – that is, included as part of the institutions of a country, by being used on radio and television, in the press, in the law courts, and above all in local literature. Australian English has been steadily growing in regional character since the arrival of the First Fleet in 1788. A century later one of the leading writers who exploited the newly developing lexicon was Andrew Barton Paterson, who wrote poems, ballads and stories under the pseudonym 'The Banjo', the name of his favourite horse. He died in 1941.

Born in New South Wales, his main theme was life in the outback country, presenting a romanticized picture of the bushman as heroic, tough and independent. His most famous piece, often called the unofficial Australian national anthem, is 'Waltzing Matilda', about an itinerant farmhand who steals a sheep and kills himself to avoid arrest. To 'waltz Matilda' is to travel with your belongings wrapped up in a cloth or blanket on your back (a *swag*). Here are the opening verses and chorus as found in the original 1895 manuscript (there are several later variant texts, as well as modifications when it's sung):

Oh there once was a swagman camped in the billabong,	*oxbow lake*
Under the shade of a Coolibah tree,	*eucalyptus*
And he sang as he looked at the old billy boiling,	*can*
Who'll come a waltzing Matilda with me?	

    Who'll come a waltzing Matilda, my darling,
    Who'll come a waltzing Matilda with me?
    Waltzing Matilda and leading a water-bag,
    Who'll come a waltzing Matilda with me?

Down came a jumbuck to drink at the water hole	*sheep*
Up jumped the swagman and grabbed him in glee,	
And he sang as he put him away in the tucker bag,	*food*
You'll come a waltzing Matilda, with me.	

49

Stanley Ellis was born in 1926

Born in Yorkshire, he became principal researcher on the four-volume *Survey of English Dialects*, based at the University of Leeds and published between 1962 and 1971 (SEE 23 OCTOBER). Well known during the 1980s as a broadcaster, Ellis, in his programmes on BBC Radio 4, especially *Talk of the Town*, *Talk of the Country*, brought dialectology to life through illuminating discussions with local people about their culture, folklore and speech. He also presented late-night phone-ins on local radio, answering questions on accents, dialects, place names and surnames.

He spent over a decade in the 1950s doing fieldwork for the *Survey*, travelling all over the country interviewing mainly elderly agricultural people, tape-recording their accents, grammar and vocabulary, and making copious notes about their cultural knowledge and practices, many of which were disappearing. He began his travels using a motorbike and sidecar, but the *Survey* was later able to upgrade him to a Land Rover to tow his caravan, in which he lived with his wife as he visited locations, parking in a farmer's field. In his lectures he would entertain his listeners with stories of the risks involved in a life as a travelling dialectologist, such as being chased by angry sheepdogs.

Ellis was the first person to provide expert evidence for speaker identification in an English court, and appeared frequently in the witness box as an expert in forensic phonetics. It was thanks to his dialect work that he was able to help identify the geographical origin of the hoax Yorkshire Ripper in the 1980s (SEE 2 JANUARY). He died in 2009.

He would have appreciated the fact that his birthday coincides with a language day in another part of the world – Island Languages Day, first celebrated in 2007 in the Amami Islands, part of the long arc of Ryukyuan Islands south of Japan. Although often referred to as dialects, the languages of these islands aren't mutually intelligible with Japanese, so, although historically related, they now have to be considered as distinct languages. But many are seriously endangered. The disappearing dialects that Stanley Ellis studied in England are now part of a global linguistic phenomenon.

Elizabeth Carter died in 1806

Born in Kent in 1717, Carter was one of the leading women writers and correspondents of the eighteenth century, a member of the intellectual circle that included Dr Johnson, and by all accounts the most scholarly of his female contemporaries. She wrote poetry under the pen name Eliza, learned several languages, and made her name by making the first translation into English of the Greek philosopher Epictetus. Johnson is recorded as saying, of some well-known scholar, that 'he understood Greek better than any one whom he had ever known, except Elizabeth Carter'. And again: 'I have composed a Greek epigram to Eliza, and think she ought to be celebrated in as many different languages as Lewis le Grand' (Louis XIV).

Boswell tells an anecdote that reflects her determination:

> I talked of the difficulty of rising in the morning. Dr. Johnson told me, 'that the learned Mrs. Carter, at that period when she was eager in study, did not awake as early as she wished, and she therefore had a contrivance, that, at a certain hour, her chamber-light should burn a string to which a heavy weight was suspended, which then fell with a strong sudden noise: this roused her from sleep, and then she had no difficulty in getting up.'

Another of Johnson's comments about her has often been quoted, illustrating the difficulty facing a woman at that time trying to balance domestic and intellectual skills in a man's world. It comes from a nineteenth-century writer, George Birkbeck Hill, who quotes it in his *Johnsonian Miscellanies*:

> Upon hearing a lady of his acquaintance commended for her learning, he said: – 'A man is in general better pleased when he has a good dinner upon his table, than when his wife talks Greek. My old friend, Mrs. Carter, said he, could make a pudding, as well as translate Epictetus from the Greek, and work a handkerchief as well as compose a poem.' He thought she was too reserved in conversation upon subjects she was so eminently able to converse upon, which was occasioned by her modesty and fear of giving offence.

IATEFL was founded in 1967

It was originally ATEFL – the Association of Teachers of English as a Foreign Language. The 'I' for International was added in 1970, and it's now pronounced *eye*-a-*teff*-ul. It's difficult to appreciate today, with English Language Teaching (ELT) to speakers of other languages having become a major world industry, that there was a time when teachers in this field had little opportunity for formal training or professional development, and negligible public recognition. The first academic courses were being introduced in the 1960s, and organizations were beginning to be formed around the language-teaching world (SEE 17 MARCH), but in the UK there was no forum for ELT professionals to make contact with one another and to share ideas.

The initiative came from a well-known teacher, writer and teacher trainer, W.R. Lee (1911–1996), universally known as Bill Lee, who got the inspiration just before Christmas in 1966. He wrote to as many contacts as he could think of, asking them whether a teacher organization was a good idea. He got over sixty positive responses, and an initial group of what came to be called 'sponsors' met on this day in 1967 at the London offices of Oxford University Press. All the paraphernalia of a new organization soon followed – committee, constitution, newsletters, conferences...

I got to know IATEFL intimately in the 1990s, when I became its honorary president in 1993 and then patron in 1994. An official *History of IATEFL* was published for its 50th anniversary in 2017. By then it had become one of the largest professional associations of English language teachers in the world, with 4,000+ members in over 120 countries. Regional conferences are held in several countries, and the annual conference in the UK can attract 2,000 or more participants. I wrote in my Foreword to the *History* how the editors had managed to capture the 'feel' of the organization. They talk about the IATEFL 'family' – a word one never uses lightly, and usually inapplicable to annual conferences. But it's certainly appropriate to this one.

International Mother Language Day

Surely this has to be the greatest day in the linguistic calendar? It's often called Mother Tongue Day, and its aim is to celebrate the importance of cultural and linguistic diversity for sustainable societies, and to foster a climate of mutual tolerance and respect for all languages – and not forgetting dialects. It's been observed by UNESCO since 2000, and felt to be increasingly necessary as more and more languages become extinct. It's estimated that a language dies on average every three months or so, and that by the end of the present century the number of viable languages in the world will be half the present total of around 6,000.

Why this day? It's the anniversary of a period when people in Bangladesh fought for recognition of Bangla – or Bengali, as it's more widely known. At the time, the country was East Pakistan, part of the country that had been established in 1947. The following year, the Pakistani government declared Urdu to be the sole national language. As a result, a movement grew for Bangla also to be recognized. Several public rallies were organized, and at one of these, on this day in 1952, police fired on students from the University of Dhaka, killing five and injuring many. Some years later, Bengali became the official state language, with the day commemorated within the country as Language Movement Day or Language Martyrs' Day, and given international recognition.

Each year, UNESCO chooses a theme for the day. In 2021 it was 'Fostering multilingualism for inclusion in education and society' and in 2022 'Using technology for multilingual learning'. The UN also established an International Decade of Indigenous Languages, beginning in 2022, emphasizing indigenous peoples' rights to freedom of expression, to an education in their mother tongue, and to participation in public life in such areas as justice systems, the media, and programmes of labour and health.

In 1712 Jonathan Swift published a proposal to regulate English

There was a widely voiced concern during the seventeenth century that English was deteriorating, and in urgent need of help. The Royal Society set up a committee in 1664 'for improving the English language', and they explored the idea of an Academy. It came to nothing, as did similar suggestions over the following fifty years. Jonathan Swift's is probably the best known. Its title in full is: 'A Proposal for Correcting, Improving and Ascertaining [fixing] the English Tongue'.

It takes the form of a long letter to the first minister, Robert Harley, who he hopes will provide the necessary protection. It opens:

> My LORD, I do here, in the Name of all the Learned and Polite Persons of the Nation, complain to Your LORDSHIP, as *First Minister*, that our Language is extremely imperfect; that its daily Improvements are by no means in proportion to its daily Corruptions; that the Pretenders to polish and refine it, have chiefly multiplied Abuses and Absurdities; and, that in many Instances, it offends against every Part of Grammar.

The corruptions have been introduced, Swift thinks, by playwrights, poets, reformers and young academics, who have introduced 'Manglings and Abbreviations' – such forms as *disturb'd* for *disturbed*. His solution:

> a free judicious Choice should be made of such Persons, as are generally allowed to be best qualified for such a Work, without any regard to Quality, Party, or Profession. These, to a certain Number at least, should assemble at some appointed Time and Place, and fix on Rules...

Swift's proposal fared no better than those of his predecessors. The Tory ministry fell in 1714, and Harley with it. The problem, of course, is deciding who the 'best qualified' people would be. Every generation since has had individuals who think themselves the right people to regulate the language, and some have indeed influenced usage, such as Samuel Johnson for vocabulary, Robert Lowth for grammar and John Walker for pronunciation. But Swift's pipe dream of finding a method 'for ascertaining and fixing our language for ever' was never a possibility.

The traditional date for the printing of the Gutenberg Bible in 1455

It's not known exactly when the first complete printing of the Bible – the Latin text of St Jerome, both Old and New Testaments – came off the new press built by Johannes Gutenberg (*c.* 1400–1468). Various dates have been suggested, but this is the one most widely accepted. Certainly it has to be before 12 March 1455, as that's the date of a letter written by Aenias Silvius Piccolomini (later Pope Pius II) to the Spanish cardinal Juan de Carvajal, in which he mentions that he'd seen in Frankfurt several sheets of a printed Bible with such neat lettering that Carvajal would be able to read it without his glasses! This was Europe's first mass-produced book – probably fewer than 200 copies made, but a dramatic change in book production. Previously books could only have been handwritten, with all the expense, time and error-prone copying that characterized the older scribal process.

This wasn't the first printing press in the world. Printing had been known in China and other parts of the Far East for many centuries. But it was certainly the first such press in Europe, and Gutenberg's system of movable metal type, allowing the rearrangement and reuse of individual letters and other characters, was able to cope with big books and large print runs. It involved innovations in the way the metal type was formed and in the ink needed for clear printing. The press was an adaptation of the traditional screw-type wine press, which enabled the application of even pressure to the arrays of inked metal type. The result was greater clarity and legibility, with even spacing between letters and words – hence Piccolomini's cheeky remark.

The invention quickly caught on. By 1500 over a thousand Gutenberg presses were operating throughout Europe. The opportunity to read books and other printed material became increasingly widespread. Information could be shared more quickly and – of special importance to the scientific world – more accurately. A new age of literacy had dawned.

The name day for Matthias and Modeste

I might have chosen any day in the year to illustrate the tradition of 'name days'. They're known in several countries with a strong Catholic, Protestant or Eastern Orthodox presence, sometimes with a history that dates back to the Middle Ages. The practice arose from the list of saints' feast days recognized by the churches. Anyone named after a saint would have that day as a name day. Eventually, other first names were added, so that sometimes a day has several candidates.

Today is the feast day of the first-century Saint Matthias, and is thus a name day – in a variety of spellings and variants – in Austria, the Czech and Slovak Republics (Matej), Estonia (Madi, Madis, Mäido), Finland (Matias, Matti), Lithuania (Motiejus), Poland (Maciej), Germany and Sweden, and perhaps in other countries too. It's also the feast day of the fifth-century Saint Modestus of Trier, so it would relate to anyone called Modest (again, in various spellings), as in Croatia and France. And other saints who share this day are recognized in several countries, such as Edilberto in Italy and Taras (Tarasius) in Ukraine.

A colleague in the Czech Republic tells me that on a name day it's common to give a present, such as chocolate, flowers or a bottle of wine, and many people take it very seriously – though, he says, not everyone remembers (and cites himself!). In Latvia, you might see the name days printed on calendars and diaries, or shown next to the issue date of a newspaper. Morning radio and television programmes might announce it. Mobile phones would receive a text-message greeting or reminder. At home, there could be a special name-day cake, and friends or relatives might pay the recipient an unexpected visit. I can find no trace of such a tradition in Britain, though informally the most widely known feast days could trigger an activity. I imagine anyone called Valentine might receive some sort of shout-out on 14 February.

Eliza Haywood died in 1756

'Mrs Haywood', as she was usually called, was one of the most prolific writers of her time. Little is known about her early life – not even her exact birth date (*c.* 1693) – other than the milestones of a career as an actress and playwright, but she matured into a writer characterized by a remarkable diversity of genres, including poetry, essays, manuals of social conduct, and above all novels. She also wrote and published a periodical which she called *The Female Spectator* – a response to the contemporary *Spectator* of Joseph Addison and Richard Steele – which ran for twenty-four issues in 1745–46. It was the first such work written by a woman, and aimed at women, and is appreciated for its originality today.

Its breadth of subject matter was very wide, written with imagination and stylistic elegance, and included several insightful comments on language. Here are two extracts on the subject of 'conversation' – the first from issue 3 (p. 154), the second from issue 4 (p. 163):

> Can any thing, if we consider rightly, be more rude than to disturb the chearfulness of whatever conversation we come into, with a melancholy detail of our private misfortunes! – They are our own, and ours alone, and a man ought no more to wish to infect others with his griefs, than with his diseases.

> Conversation, in effect, but furnishes matter for contemplation; – it exhilarates the mind, and fits it for reflection afterwards. Every new thing we hear in company raises in us new ideas in the closet or on the pillow; and as there are few people but one may gather something from, either to divert or improve, a good understanding will, like the industrious bee, suck out the various sweets, and digest them in retirement. But those who are perpetually hurrying from one company to another, and never suffer themselves to be alone but when weary Nature summons them to repose, will be little amended, tho' the maxims of a *Seneca* were to be delivered to them in all the enchanting eloquence of a *Tully*.

Tell a Fairy Tale Day

It's celebrated every year in the United States on this day. Who started it? Nobody seems to know, though I suspect a children's publisher or greetings-card company. But the intention is laudable and could well resonate with other countries that have a fairy-tale tradition – which means all countries. Storytelling to children is probably as old as humanity, though the actual names *fairy tale/story* are recorded in English only from the seventeenth century.

Most of the stories we know today were collected in the nineteenth century by the German brothers Wilhelm and Jacob Grimm, and those created by the Danish writer Hans Christian Andersen, but some have ancient origins, such as the fables of Aesop from Ancient Greece. Despite their sometimes dark and horrifying situations, their continuing appeal is evident, and given new imaginative renditions in the cinema, notably by Walt Disney.

From a linguistic point of view, the importance of fairy tales in children's language acquisition has been well recognized. Over and above the appeal of the characters and plots, repeated storytelling instils vocabulary, idiom, grammatical structures and expressive pronunciations that go well beyond the everyday speech children hear and use. Formulaic structures – such as fixed opening and closing sequences ('Once upon a time… lived happily ever after') or a repeated action ('he huffed and he puffed…') develop an awareness of broader patterns of discourse.

The aim of the day is to encourage anyone – adults and children – to read fairy stories and tell them to each other. And to have a go at writing one, or adapting one to meet modern settings – something children themselves love to do, once a favourite story has been thoroughly internalized. Some writers have published alternative versions. My favourite is *The True Story of the Three Little Pigs* (1989) by Jon Scieszka, told from the point of view of the wolf. This is how it begins:

> I'm the wolf. Alexander T. Wolf. You can call me Al. I don't know how this whole Big Bad Wolf thing got started, but it's all wrong…

Joseph Wright died in 1930

His masterwork was the six-volume *English Dialect Dictionary*, published
between 1898 and 1905, which laid the foundation for the study of
dialects in the British Isles. It took him twenty-three years to collect all
the material, and the scale of the project – in a pre-computer age – has
to be appreciated. The dictionary contains around 117,500 word-senses,
with examples taken from over 3,000 dialect glossaries, works containing
dialect words, and the contributions of hundreds of voluntary readers,
all of whom had to be contacted by letter. The information, as it came in,
was handwritten onto slips – 1.5 million for the first volume alone.

Wright's story is extraordinary. He was born in Thackley, a village
in West Yorkshire, in 1855. When he was 6 he got a job driving a
donkey cart, and a year later a part-time job as a doffer in the cotton
mill at Saltaire, working from 6.00 until 12.30 each morning; during the
afternoons he attended a local school. His dictionary tells us that a doffer
was 'a boy or girl employed in a factory to remove the full bobbins from
the throstle-frame and replace them by empty ones'.

In his teenage years he worked at a woollen mill, and during his
dinner hour taught himself to read and write, using the Bible and
Bunyan's *The Pilgrim's Progress*. Two or three evenings each week he
went to a local night school, where he learned French and German.
By the time he was 20 he had taught himself Latin and shorthand. He
saved enough to pay for a term at Heidelberg University, then began
work as a schoolteacher in Yorkshire. Returning to Heidelberg in 1882,
he began his studies as a philologist, eventually gaining a doctorate. He
joined Oxford University in 1888, and went on to become professor of
comparative philology there.

In later life he had to get used to eye-catching newspaper headlines
– such as 'From Donkey-boy to Professor' – whenever he carried out a
public engagement. Certainly, there's no other linguistic story quite as
dramatic as his.

Global Scouse Day

They weren't thinking of language when this day was invented. It was a culinary thought. *Scouse* is the abbreviated form of *lobscouse*, a meat stew originally associated with sailors, and recorded in English from the eighteenth century. Its etymology is unknown, but an association with the port of Liverpool is long established. The word later came to relate to the city itself, with its inhabitants referred to as *Scousers*, and their local accent and dialect as *Scouse*. These usages date only from the 1940s.

The day was begun by Liverpudlian travel adventurer Graham Hughes, who arranged a 'scouse supper' on this day, his birthday, and the tradition was continued during his round-the-world-without-flying visit to all countries between 2008 and 2013 – a feat recognized by Guinness World Records. Eateries in Liverpool and many elsewhere now put scouse on their menu for the day; and other events in music and the arts take place.

For a linguist, though, it's not the stew that counts. It's the speech. The accent is a unique blend of features from surrounding south Lancashire and the speech of immigrant groups, especially from Ireland in the nineteenth century, but also from Wales and Scotland. Informal glossaries of the dialect began to be made in the 1960s, notably those initiated by Irish-born Frank Shaw, the first person recorded as using *Scouse* to refer to the language, who collaborated with Fritz Spiegel and Stan Kelley to write a series of booklets, beginning with *Lern Yerself Scouse*. The dialect came to maturity in 2017, when Liverpool University Press published Tony Crowley's *The Liverpool English Dictionary*. Here's a short selection:

> *ackers* (cash), *barney* (argument), *chuffed* (happy), *doddle* (easy task), *entry* (alleyway), *flicks* (cinema films), *giss* (give me), *hard knock* (tough person), *in tucks* (laughing), *jigger* (back alley), *kecks* (trousers), *lecky* (electric), *made up* (very pleased), *not on* (unacceptable), *ollies* (marbles), *parkie* (park-keeper), *quod* (prison), *ran-tan* (loud knocking), *sag* (play truant), *ta-ra well* (goodbye), *us* (me), *vinegar trip* (wasted journey), *wack* (Liverpudlian), *yocker* (spit).

Janet Kagan died in 2008

Every culture I've ever studied has a myth about the origins of language, sometimes recorded in its earliest literature. Divine origins are usually invoked. In the Bible, Adam is given the power of naming creatures. In a Chinese myth, writing is brought by a heaven-sent sea turtle with marks on its back. Brahma is reputed to have given the knowledge of writing to the Hindu people. But every now and then a modern writer introduces a new story. The American author Janet Kagan is one, born in New Jersey in 1946, and known for her science-fiction and fantasy tales. One of them is a captivating folk tale about the origins of language: 'How First Woman Stole Language from Tuli-Tuli the Beast' (2005). I can give only a hint of its vivid narrative and wistful tone in the short extracts below.

> The story begins with a dream of a beast called tuli-tuli, who lived among the sea crags, and who 'had a most powerful magic called language. She knew everything by its name and when she named the thing, it belonged to her'. The beast would call First Woman's people down to the sea and then eat them. Eventually, First Woman has had enough. Day after day she follows the beast's movements, with the help of the sea and the moon, and finds a way to defeat it. There is a fight, and tuli-tuli is mortally wounded. Then, just as she dies...
>
> At that moment tuli-tuli's claws struck First Woman's face and left two scars there forever. They are tuli-tuli the beast's punishment – for they gave First Woman the power to tell a lie – thereafter language needed never to be true.
>
> That is how First Woman stole language from tuli-tuli the beast. And that is why language is no longer the same from year to year.
>
> And who's to say if tuli-tuli the beast's heart was in her punishment – for it is only the ability to lie that makes possible the telling of a tale or the dreaming of a dream.

The International Air Transport Association agrees the radiotelephony spelling alphabet in 1956

It seems like a simple idea, to find a set of words to pronounce the letters of the alphabet and the numbers 1 to 9 in an unambiguous way; but it took many years of trial and error before a system was accepted by the International Civil Aviation Organization. The result is the *International Radiotelephony Spelling Alphabet* – also called the *NATO phonetic alphabet*.

Those who devised the system had to bear several criteria in mind. They knew it was easy to confuse some traditional alphabet names, such as *n* and *m*, *s* and *f* or *d* and *b*, especially when there's noise interference. Accent variation can be an additional problem.

It wasn't just a matter of finding words that begin with the appropriate first letter. The words had to be current, easily pronounced, readily recognized when written down, and not have any unfortunate semantic associations. The proposed words were initially tested with reference to English, French and Spanish, and then received reactions from people with various language backgrounds in over thirty countries. Several changes had to be made. At one point, *zebra* was proposed, but this ignored the fact that the *zeb* is pronounced differently between British and American English – *zeb* as in *bed* vs *zeeb* as in *seed*.

This is the list approved in 1956:

Alfa, Bravo, Charlie, Delta, Echo, Foxtrot, Golf, Hotel, India, Juliett, Kilo, Lima, Mike, November, Oscar, Papa, Quebec, Romeo, Sierra, Tango, Uniform, Victor, Whiskey, X-ray, Yankee, Zulu.

Numbers are in English, but the pronunciation of *three, four, five, nine, hundreds* and *thousand(s)* is altered to *tree, fower, fife, niner, hundred* for *hundreds*, and *tousand* for both *thousand* and *thousands*.

The word list came to be used in other radio domains, and sometimes have an extended life. A 2016 movie was called *Whiskey Tango Foxtrot*. And many will know of Checkpoint Charlie in Berlin.

Susanna Rowson died in 1824

'Mrs Rowson', as she's named on her books, was born in England in 1762, and as a child went with her father to live near Boston, where she experienced the dramatic events in that area during the American War of Independence. She grew up to become a significant literary figure, known for her novels, poems, essays and textbooks, and at one point edited (and contributed to) a new Boston periodical. Her novel *Charlotte: A Tale of Truth* (1791), titled *Charlotte Temple* in the United States, became a bestseller – a remarkable 25,000 copies in just a few years, according to her memoirist Elias Nason, who thought it comparable to several nineteenth-century novels. *A Memoir of Mrs. Susanna Rowson*, published in 1870 and available online, contains many transcriptions from her novels, poems and letters.

Her varied career included a period with her family as an actress, both in England and in the USA. When she retired from the stage she established in Boston in 1797 the first 'female academy': 'Mrs Rowson's Academy for Young Ladies'. She wrote prolifically for her students, including an innovative geography textbook, and a 156-page dictionary of spelling, published in 1807, the full title of which reads: *A spelling dictionary: divided into short lessons, for the easier committing to memory by children and young persons, and calculated to assist youth in comprehending what they read: selected from Johnson's Dictionary.* That last phrase is important, for it distanced her from the bestselling spelling dictionary published by Noah Webster some years before.

She compiled her dictionary, she says, because as a teacher she felt that existing books didn't meet the needs of her students. She points out that most children don't understand two-thirds of the words in their readers; and even the smallest edition of Dr Johnson's *Dictionary* she thinks is unsuitable. Another difference from Webster is an end-placed encyclopedic section: 'A Concise Account of the Heathen Deities, and Other Fabulous Persons, with the Heroes and Heroines of Antiquity'. Children, she asserts, have to learn to spell proper names correctly, as well as common words. Her point is just as relevant today.

Talk in Third Person Day

Well, according to the enthusiasts, what else would David want to do, on the third day of the third month, but talk and write in the third person? Under no circumstances should he refer to himself using such pronouns as *I* or *me*, but only *he*. Others would choose a pronoun to suit their gender preference – *he*, *she* or *they* – as many do these days when identifying themselves. It's unclear whether *you* also falls under the ban. Presumably it would, if one's intention is to use only the third person.

The day was initiated in 2006 by someone called Russell. David was able to find a website about it, but it has entries only up to 2008, so perhaps enthusiasm waned thereafter. The day remains recognized, though, in websites that collect holidays. Judging by Russell's examples, there was an element of language play lying behind the initiative – rewriting famous quotations in the third person. So one finds, from *Star Wars*, 'May the force be with Luke'. With longer passages, it's more difficult to maintain the convention, and one suddenly finds oneself in deeply ambiguous water. 'I wouldn't do that, if I were you' becomes, what – 'He or she wouldn't do that if they were them'?

Third-person expression has a long linguistic history, especially in such varieties as sports commentary and legal prose. It's a common choice of novelists – as in the opening lines of Jane Austen's *Pride and Prejudice*:

> It is a truth universally acknowledged, that a single man in possession of a good fortune, must be in want of a wife.
>
> However little known the feelings or views of such a man may be on his first entering a neighbourhood, this truth is so well fixed in the minds of the surrounding families, that he is considered as the rightful property of some one or other of their daughters.
>
> 'My dear Mr. Bennet,' said his lady to him one day, 'have you heard that Netherfield Park is let at last?'
>
> Mr. Bennet replied that he had not.

National Grammar Day

This is a national day in the United States, but one that's been noted more widely. It was promoted in 2008 by Martha Brockenbrough, founder of the Society for the Promotion of Good Grammar. As she's reported to have said: 'March forth on March 4 to speak well, write well, and help others do the same!' The aim was to help her students with their grammar in a lively and positive way. Unfortunately that positiveness isn't reflected in the websites I looked at, where we see expressions like 'grammar police' and 'worst grammar mistakes', as if this was the only issue. It seems that the day is in danger of becoming no more than another example of the 'complaint tradition', in which pedants focus on a tiny number of grammatical points, and pay no attention to the broader issues of what actually controls comprehension and clarity of expression.

That would be a shame, as there's far more to grammar than questions of divided usage among people of different social or regional backgrounds. Grammar is the underlying organizational principle of a language, without which there can be no linguistic communication at all. Words by themselves don't make sense, because most are ambiguous. What does *charge* mean? Is it to do with electricity, money, the military, sudden movement...? We resolve the ambiguity by putting it into a sentence. *The children charged in. The garage charged too much.* It's the association of *charge* with other words, related by a grammatical construction, that allows us to understand what's being said.

That's what sentences are for. Their job is, literally, to 'make sense'. And grammar is the study of sentences – their internal structure and how they combine to make dialogues, discourses, paragraphs, and all the other manifestations of speech and writing. It's a subject that deserves to be celebrated, and I've tried to capture the more positive view in a larger work: *Making Sense: The Glamorous Story of English Grammar.* It *is* glamorous, when approached in the right state of mind. And it's worth remembering that *grammar* and *glamour* are etymologically the same.

Leslie Marmon Silko was born in 1948

This American author grew up on the Laguna Pueblo Reservation in New Mexico, and became a leading figure in Native American literature, known for her poetry, novels and essays. One essay provides a perspective on language that's illuminating to anyone unfamiliar with her culture. It's available online, and titled 'Language and Literature from a Pueblo Indian Perspective'. Her words need little extra commentary from me:

> Where I come from, the words most highly valued are those spoken from the heart, unpremeditated and unrehearsed. Among the Pueblo people, a written speech or statement is highly suspect because the true feelings of the speaker remain hidden as she reads words that are detached from the occasion and the audience. I have intentionally not written a formal paper because I want you to *hear* and to experience English in a structure that follows patterns from the oral tradition. For those of you accustomed to being taken from point A to point B to point C, this presentation may be somewhat difficult to follow. Pueblo expression resembles something like a spider's web – with many little threads radiating from the center, crisscrossing each other. As with the web, the structure emerges as it is made and you must simply listen and trust, as the Pueblo people do, that meaning will be made.

A distinctive element in her approach to narrative is the way individual words are said to have their own stories.

> Often the speakers or tellers will go into these word-stories, creating an elaborate structure of stories-within-stories. This structure, which becomes very apparent in the actual telling of a story, informs contemporary Pueblo writing and storytelling as well as the traditional narratives. This perspective on narrative – of story within story, the idea that one story is only the beginning of many stories, and the sense that stories never truly end, represents an important contribution of Native American cultures to the English language.

For her, 'language is story'.

Artemus Ward died in 1867

During the nineteenth century there emerged a genre of comic nonstandard usage, and the American journalist Charles Farrar Browne, born in 1834, was one of its most famous practitioners, writing under the pseudonym Artemus Ward. The genre was extremely popular: homespun wit and down-to-earth sentiments were expressed in a style which seemed to reflect the sounds of local speech and with words often deliberately misspelled. There's no specific accent or dialect underlying his style, and as a consequence his brand of humour went down well on both sides of the Atlantic.

In the summer of 1866 Browne visited London. In addition to lecture performances, all delivered in a mock-serious, deadpan manner, he wrote a series of letters for *Punch* magazine. Here's an extract from 'A Visit to the British Museum', which was his last published work, as he died from tuberculosis the following year.

> I first visited the stuffed animals, of which the gorillers interested me most. These simple-minded monsters live in Afriky, and are believed to be human beins to a slight extent, altho' they are not allowed to vote. In this department is one or two superior giraffes. I never woulded I were a bird, but I've sometimes wished I was a giraffe, on account of the long distance of his mouth to his stummuck. Hence, if he loved beer, one mugful would give him as much enjoyment while goin down as 40 mugfulls would ordinary persons.

And a little later...

> I enjoyed myself very much lookin at the Egyptian mummys, the Greek vasis, etc, but it occurred to me there was rayther too many 'Roman antiquitys of a uncertain date'. Now, I like the British Mooseum, as I said afore, but when I see a lot of erthen jugs and pots stuck up on shelves, and all 'of a uncertin date,' I'm at a loss to 'zackly determin whether they are a thousand years old or was bought recent. I can cry like a child over a jug one thousand years of age, especially if it is a Roman jug; but a jug of a uncertin date doesn't overwhelm me with emotion.

Alexander Graham Bell Day

Rather than remember his birth (in Scotland, 3 March 1847) or death (in Nova Scotia, Canada, 2 August 1922), this day commemorates the granting in 1876 of an American patent for the device that would soon be called the telephone. Headed 'Improvement in Telegraphy', it begins:

> Be it known that I, Alexander Graham Bell, of Salem, Massachusetts, have invented certain new and useful Improvements in Telegraphy, of which the following is a specification...

A 2,830-word technical description follows, of a 'method of, and apparatus for, transmitting vocal or other sounds telegraphically ... by causing electrical undulations, similar in form to the vibrations of the air accompanying the said vocal or other sound'.

Three days later he used a transmitter to speak the now famous words to his assistant in the next room: 'Mr. Watson, come here, I want to see you.' The words were heard, and telephone communication began. Within a year the first telephone exchange was built in Connecticut, and the Bell Telephone Company was created in July 1877.

The linguistic consequences were immediate. What conventions should be used to announce yourself or to acknowledge a call? Callers had to have a way of starting a conversation, and recipients had to let callers know they were there, especially when using a line where the connection was always open. Suggestions included 'Are you there?', 'Do I get you?', 'Are you ready? and even the nautical 'Ahoy!' The winner, of course was 'Hello', recommended by Thomas Edison when he developed Bell's system.

This wasn't the first time *hello* had been used. During the previous fifty years there are many recorded instances of the way people had used it in informal settings to attract attention, to express surprise, and to greet someone. But the telephone gave it a new lease of life, and a new level of formality (SEE 21 NOVEMBER). Within a decade the women employed as the first telephone operators were being called 'hello girls'.

National Proofreading Day

This day was created in the United States in 2012 by corporate trainer Judy Beaver. She chose it because it was her mother's birthday, and she wanted to honour a lady who was evidently a stickler for correctness in written expression. There's a professional body: the American Copy Editors Society, founded in 1997. The UK equivalent is the Chartered Institute of Editing and Proofreading, formed in 1988. All such organizations have the same aim: to promote excellence in language editing. They set and demonstrate editorial standards, provide training courses, and act as a support network for editorial professionals.

Proofreading is an essential part of the concern to make text accurate, clear, consistent and fit for purpose. The alternative can be ambiguity, embarrassment or a serious outcome, as when something goes wrong in safety instructions, or a word like *not* is inadvertently omitted from a directive. The famous case of the 'Wicked' Bible' of 1631 comes to mind:: 'Thou shalt commit adultery'.

At an everyday level, basic proofreading techniques are well worth acquiring for anyone writing formally or publicly. They can be something as simple as taking time to read over a piece of writing before submitting it. Reading aloud what you've written can help. So can reading a line or a page backwards. It's surprising how many typos are spotted when we break our habit of reading silently and at speed.

In the computer world, proofreading awareness means not totally relying on an autocorrect function to do the job. Helpful as this can be, such systems may ignore missing or duplicated words, punctuation errors and wrong alternatives – not correcting *plane* if you mean *plain*, for example. It's remarkable, too, how errors can be missed when reading a text on screen – errrors that are spotted immediately when the text is printed out. But nothing can beat the value of having a second pair of eyes – and the more professional those eyes are the better.

How good were you at proofreading this page? Did you spot the two deliberate errors? (SEE APPENDIX, if needed)

William Cobbett was born in 1763

Cobbett is chiefly remembered today for his literary and political writing, but he also wrote a dictionary, a speller and three grammars. *A Grammar of the English Language* (1818) was a series of letters to his teenage son, James Paul. It was hugely successful. By the time of his death in 1835 over 100,000 copies had been sold.

This grammar differs from the other prescriptive grammars of the time in its educational and political aims. His prescriptivism was a means to an end. In *Advice to Young Men*, he wrote: 'The possession of this branch of knowledge raises you in your own esteem, gives just confidence in yourself, and prevents you from being the willing slave of the rich and titled parts of the community.' And his subtitle reinforces this aspiration: *Intended for the Use of Schools and of Young Persons in General; but more especially for the Use of Soldiers, Sailors, Apprentices and Plough-Boys.*

In places he's strikingly modern. These sentiments, expressed in his Introduction, wouldn't be out of place in any modern textbook: 'grammar teaches us how to make use of words'; 'innumerable are the paths [to knowledge], and Grammar is the gate of entrance to them all'. And he acknowledges the role of usage: in noting the replacement of *thou* by *you*, he writes in Letter 6: 'what a whole people adopts and universally practises must, in such cases, be deemed correct, and to be a superseding of ancient rule and custom.'

And this must be one of the most remarkable stories in the history of grammar, when he writes in a memoir about his time in the army:

> I procured me a Lowth's grammar and applied myself to the study of it with unceasing assiduity and not without some profit ... The pains I took cannot be described: I wrote the whole grammar out two or three times. I got it by heart; I repeated it every morning and every evening, and, when on guard, I imposed on myself the task of saying it all over once every time I was posted sentinel.

Hallie Quinn Brown was born in 1850

She was a professor of elocution, public lecturer and civil rights activist during the end of the nineteenth century and well into the twentieth (she died in 1949). 'Lecturer' is too weak: 'performer' is better, for she was recognized in America and Europe for her speaking, singing and reciting, in a voice a contemporary described as having 'wonderful magnetism and great compass'. She holds a major place as part of the civil rights movement at the turn of the century, her achievements including the founding of the Colored Woman's League of Washington DC in 1894. But for this book my focus is on her notable contribution as a writer and practitioner in the field of elocution.

Her instructional texts and anthologies continue to be relevant, as they provide a corrective to the still widely held view that elocution is only a matter of clear articulation or replacing a regional accent. For her, elocution embraced rhetoric, acting and phonetics. More importantly, it showed how the art of oratory has an empowering social and political role, enabling people who have no public voice to be given the opportunity of effective political participation.

It was a lifetime skill that she began to develop as a child. Born in Pennsylvania, in 1864 she moved with her parents to a farm in Canada. From Faustin Delany's edition of Brown's *Bits and Odds: A Choice Selection of Recitations for School, Lyceum, and Parlor Entertainments* I especially love this account of her morning routine at her home:

> She jumps upon a stump or log and delivers an address to the audience of cows, sheep, birds, etc. Neither knowing nor caring what she says; she goes through her harangue, earnestly emphasizing by arm gesture and occasionally by a stamp of the foot. She has a separate speech for the larger animals, and special addresses to the lambs, ducklings and any other juvenile auditors that happen to be near. Having exhausted her vocabulary, she begins a conversation in the language of the horse, cow, sheep, goose, rooster, or bird, until each is imitated … This is her daily morning program.

An unusual but evidently effective training for a professor of elocution.

England's first daily newspaper was published in 1702

This was *The Daily Courant*. It appeared every morning except Sundays, consisting of a single sheet with two columns, news on the front and advertisements on the back. Its front page that day consisted of items taken from other European publications in Haarlem, Amsterdam and Paris. Here's the beginning of the first report in the launch issue:

Naples, Feb. 22.
On Wednesday last, our New Viceroy, the Duke of Escalona, arriv'd here with a Squadron of the Galleys of Sicily. He made his Entrance drest in a French habit; and to give us the greater Hopes of the King's coming hither, went to Lodge in one of the little palaces, leaving the Royal one for his Majesty.

The first issue also contained an advertisement on the front page written by the editor:

the Author has taken Care to be duly furnish'd with all that comes from Abroad in any Language. And for an Assurance that he will not, under Pretence of having Private intelligence, impose any Additions of feign'd Circumstances to an Action, but give his Extracts fairly and impartially; at the beginning of each Article he will quote the Foreign Paper from whence 'tis taken, that the Publick, seeing from what Country a piece of News comes with the Allowance of that Government, may, be better able to judge of the Credibility and Fairness of the relation: Nor will he take upon him to give any Comments or Conjectures of his own, but will relate only Matter of Fact; supposing other People to have Sense enough to make Reflections for themselves.

A long lost insight! At the bottom we read:

London. Sold by E. Mallet, next Door to the King's-Arms Tavern at Fleet-Bridge.

It all seems innocent enough, until we realize that *E* stands for *Elizabeth*, who called herself 'he' in the advertisement, to avoid the inevitable criticism of her time, that a woman would dare to carry out such a task.

Tim Berners-Lee submitted a proposal for an information management system in 1989

We know it now as the World Wide Web. The proposal was made to the European Organization for Nuclear Research, known as CERN from its French name: Conseil Européen pour la Recherche Nucléaire. Berners-Lee (born in 1955) had worked there as a consultant in 1980, later joining it full-time. Faced with the huge complexity of the operation, his thought was to develop a hypertext system that would enable anyone to find out who was working on which project using which software on which computers. His initial idea was called simply 'Information management: a proposal'. Its opening paragraph is nicely informal:

> Many of the discussions of the future at CERN and the LHC [Large Hadron Collider] era end with the question – 'Yes, but how will we ever keep track of such a large project?' This proposal provides an answer to such questions.

Linked information systems was the solution. In his 1999 memoir, *Weaving the Web*, he sums up his vision succinctly in the opening chapter: it was 'about anything being potentially connected with anything'.

The proposal contains a reference to the image of 'a "web" of notes with links (like references) between them ... like a diagram of circles and arrows, where circles and arrows can stand for anything'. From a linguistic point of view, especially notable is the way the Web has increased the expressive range of individual languages through the emergence of new stylistic varieties and provided new opportunities for multilingual presence – a boon for minority and endangered languages.

When the British Council celebrated its 80th anniversary in 2014, it asked a panel of twenty-five scientists, technologists, academics, artists, writers, broadcasters and world leaders to choose their most significant moments of the past eighty years. It then asked 10,000 people around the world to vote to rank the list. Interestingly, the spread of English as a global language came out at no. 11. But the creation of the World Wide Web was no. 1.

John Barbour died in 1395

Barbour was born in about 1320. Little is known of his early life, but he's recorded as becoming archdeacon of Aberdeen, an auditor of the Scottish exchequer and a royal pensioner. He holds a position in Scots literature similar to Chaucer in England, thanks to his long historical verse romance *The Brus* – the story of the hero Robert Bruce and his champion, James Douglas, and their role in the first war of Scottish independence, with its central episode the Battle of Bannockburn (1314). It was written in 1375 and is linguistically important for its use of the dialect 'Inglis', as Barbour calls it – a name for the variety of English emerging in southern Scotland that continued in use until the sixteenth century, when it gradually came to be replaced by 'Scots'. It's organized into twenty books, a total of 13,546 lines of rhyming couplets, each line containing eight syllables, with the occasional extra unstressed syllable.

The growing distinctiveness of Scots as a new language variety is evident in the spellings, which clearly reflect a pronunciation that is still there today, such as *nocht* and *richt*. Barbour calls his epic a romance, but emphasizes in his opening lines the importance of historical accuracy.

Storys to rede ar delatibill	*Stories to read are delightful*
Suppos that thai be nocht bot fabill:	*Even if they be nothing but fable*
Than suld storys that suthfast wer,	*Then should stories that true were*
And thai war said on gud maner	*And they were said in a good way*
Hawe doubill plesance in heryng:	*Have double pleasure in hearing.*
The fyrst plesance is the carpyng,	*The first pleasure is the narration*
And the tothir the suthfastnes,	*And the other the truth*
That schawys the thing rycht as it wes.	*That shows the thing right as it was*

And later in the poem we see such dialect forms as *gang* 'go', *stane* 'stone' and *mekill* 'much', as well as distinctive northern spellings such as *quhar* 'where' and *quhill* 'while'.

International Ask a Question Day

Why on this day? It's the birthday of Albert Einstein, born in 1879, who asked some of the biggest questions ever. Many people might be puzzled by the reason for such a day, but it begins to make sense if we remember how often people don't get a chance to ask a question, or are scared to ask one for fear of social sanction, or forget to ask one at the right time. Questions do more than simply enquire after information. They can build or break relationships, assert identity, create antagonism ('Are you looking at me?'), help to get thoughts in order, and much more.

But most questions are driven by a sense of curiosity and the need to learn; and this was the motivation behind two fascinating books published in 2012 and 2013. Thousands of schoolkids aged 4–12 were asked to send in questions about anything, and Gemma Elwin Harris asked experts to answer them. Her first collection was called *Big Questions from Little People – Answered by Some Very Big People*. The sequel was, more mysteriously, called *Does My Goldfish Know Who I Am?*

Here are the language-related questions that came up in 2012.

— Why do we speak English?* — Who wrote the first book ever?
— How did we first learn to write? — Who named all the cities?
— Why do we have an alphabet? — Why can't animals talk like us?
(answered by Noam Chomsky)

The sequel contained more:

— How many languages are there in the world?* — How do we learn to speak?
— Do animals like cows and sheep have accents? — Is silence a sound?
— Do babies think in words or their own language? — Do spiders speak?
— If oranges are called oranges, why aren't bananas called yellows?
— If you shouted in space would you hear anything?
— Why do cats 'miaow', cows 'moo' and sheep 'baa'?

* I was asked to answer these. I was described as 'a mixture of Gandalf and Dumbledore, thanks to his big white beard'. I hope that helped.

The first Internet domain name was registered in 1985

This was *symbolics.com*, the name of a computer company that developed software in the artificial intelligence laboratory at the Massachusetts Institute of Technology. An earlier name, *nic.nordu.net*, had been created at the beginning of that year by a Scandinavian research team to serve as the identifier of the first root server; but *symbolics.com* was the first name to be registered through the DNS (Domain Name System) process.

The system had a slow start, as at the time the Internet wasn't being thought of as a commercial medium – more as a tool for academic and military purposes. Only five other companies registered a domain name in 1985: *bbn.com*, *think.com*, *mcc.com*, *dec.com* and *northrop.com*. Today, according to VeriSign, the global provider of domain name registry services, there are (end of September 2022) 349.9 million domain name registrations across all top-level domains. The most popular name base is *.com*, with 160.9 million registrations.

Many linguistic issues arise in connection with domain names. There are technical criteria to be met: keeping within the number of units (1–63) in the English character set (A–Z, 0–9), allowing dashes (but not at the beginning or end, or in the third or fourth string positions), and disallowing spaces between characters. Languages that have writing systems using non-Latin scripts faced a problem for several years, largely solved by the development of Unicode.

There are also pragmatic issues. It helps if the name includes keywords that can enable search engines to find the site – or, these days, keyword combinations, as most single-word keywords are already taken. Deliberate misspellings of everyday words can extend the options, but these are more difficult to remember and are more likely to generate typing errors. Spellings with double or triple letters are especially prone to typos, as are names including hyphens. The easy pronounceability of a name is important too, especially now that speech-to-text systems are more sophisticated. And there are all the issues surrounding sensitivity, within and across languages.

Day of the Book Smugglers in Lithuania

To feel the force of this day, we have to imagine a situation in which
an external agency introduced a law in an English-speaking country
banning all books written in the Latin alphabet and requiring everything
to be printed in a different orthographic system. Within a generation,
Shakespeare and English literature would be a distant memory.

This was the situation in Russian-occupied Lithuania in 1866, when
Tsar Alexander II banned the use of Lithuanian and all manifestations of
national culture. Jonas Stepšis (the son of one of the smugglers) describes
it in a memoir for the *Draugas News* in 2004:

> He installed a Governor General, one Mikhail Nikolaevich Muravyov,
> with instructions to produce a Lithuania 'with nothing Lithuanian in it'.
> Muravyov began his implementation of the Tsar's orders by proclaiming
> a complete ban on the Lithuanian press, the usage of the Latin alphabet
> and the Lithuanian language – only the Cyrillic alphabet and Russian
> language were to be used and taught. In essence everything Lithuanian
> – language, culture, religion – was proscribed, and so severe were the
> penalties for contravention that, during his time as Governor-General (till
> March 1865) Muravyov became known as the 'Hangman of Lithuania'.

The ban lasted until 1904, when political circumstances changed. The
prohibition became known in Lithuania as the 'Forty Years of Darkness'.

This day – *Knygnešio diena* in Lithuanian – recognizes the birthday
of Jurgis Bielinis (1846–1918), a newspaperman who created a secret
network for getting Lithuanian books, journals and newspapers into the
country and distributing them. His Garšviai Book Smuggling Society
was one of several organizations that would buy Lithuanian literature in
East Prussia or further afield and bring it in surreptitiously. Historians
of the period suggest that over 5 million items were transported in this
way. It was a dangerous business, with a perpetual risk of being shot,
imprisoned or exiled to Siberia, and many suffered in this way. Bielinis
himself managed to evade capture, gaining a reputation as a folk hero,
and later attracting the informal sobriquet 'King of the Book Smugglers'.

TESOL was founded in 1966

The acronym (pronounced *T-sol*) stands for Teaching or Teachers of English to Speakers of Other Languages, and specifically identifies an American organization founded on this day at a conference in New York, after a series of pilot meetings going back to 1963, along with two national conferences. It grew out of a concern that there was no single all-inclusive organization that would bring together professionals – administrators as well as teachers – from all educational levels to promote the quality of English language teaching (ELT) through research, professional development, the establishment of standards, and public advocacy. The founders avoided using such words as 'American' or 'National' in the name because they wanted it to be a truly international institution, and so it has proved to be. In 2021 it had become the world's largest ELT organization, with over 12,000 members in 156 countries.

The field of ELT has developed enormously since 1966, and any newcomer to it has to cope with a bewildering number of acronyms, reflecting different aims and student constituencies (SEE ALSO 20 FEBRUARY). If ELT is taking place in a country or for students where English has some sort of official standing, and is thus the language most likely to be learned after the mother tongue, the acronym TESL is often used: Teaching English as a Second Language. In other countries, where English has no special status, but is simply a 'foreign language' taught in schools, the acronym is TEFL: Teaching English as a Foreign Language. But then we also encounter EAL: English as an Additional Language, for learners who are multilingual, and for whom English might be their third or fourth (or more) language. In practice, TEFL and TESL are often used interchangeably, and some countries don't bother with the 'second language' distinction at all.

Within the TEFL world, there are several focused domains. The two most often encountered are TEAP and TESP. A course in Teaching English for Academic Purposes would be aimed at students in higher education. One in Teaching English for Specific Purposes would be designed for professionals, such as doctors or bankers.

John Walker was born in 1732

At the end of the eighteenth century, John Walker achieved for his work on pronunciation the same kind of fame that Samuel Johnson had achieved for vocabulary and Robert Lowth for grammar (SEE 15 MAY, 8 FEBRUARY). His name became a household word after his death in 1806, so that any reference to 'Walker' would get immediate recognition as, say, 'Fowler' would in the twentieth century with his *Dictionary of Modern English Usage*. He was also called 'Elocution Walker', for this was his profession as a writer and lecturer, after an earlier period as an actor.

Following in the footsteps of Johnson's *Dictionary*, and aware of its weaknesses in its treatment of pronunciation, Walker devised an ambitious project in 1774: 'A General Idea of a Pronouncing Dictionary of the English Language, on a Plan Entirely New'. It took him seventeen years to complete – the delay largely caused by being sidetracked into other books. In 1775 he published a very successful *Rhyming Dictionary*, and in the 1780s three books on elocution and related topics.

His groundbreaking dictionary eventually appeared in 1791, with the title *A Critical Pronouncing Dictionary and Expositor of the English Language*. At the time, *critical* meant 'exercising careful judgement' and 'fault-finding', and both traits are evident in his entries, which are a wonderful mix of acute observation – invaluable to the present-day student of eighteenth-century pronunciation – and social disapproval. The title continues: *Rules to be observed by the Natives of Scotland, Ireland and London for avoiding their respective peculiarities*.

By the natives of London, he meant of course working-class cockneys, not cultured and educated citizens. For him, as for virtually everyone at the time, London upper-class speech provided the ideal model for speakers wherever they lived, because it was 'more generally received' – he means, from the court and other influential social institutions, such as the Church and the universities. It's an early use of the adjective that today is found in the term *Received Pronunciation* for the regionally neutral accents of British educated society, and widely recognized in the world of English language teaching.

National Let's Laugh Day

I can find no reference to this day before 2017, or who first floated the idea, but it's been given quite a lot of recognition in the United States. To some extent it's been overtaken by World Laughter Day – the first Sunday in May – created in 1998 by Dr Madan Kataria, who founded the worldwide Laughter Yoga movement, in which muscles of the face, abdomen and lungs are engaged in the core exercise. The physiological effects have now been demonstrated: laughter reduces stress by releasing endorphins and lowering cortisol. The phenomenon has its own science: gelotology (from the Greek word for 'laughter') – the *g* pronounced as in *George* – but the beneficial effects of laughing have long been expressed proverbially: 'Laughter is the best medicine.'

Laughing is usually associated with humour. It occurs when we find something funny, or when something is *thought* to be funny – this point being necessary to allow for the 'laugh tracks' inserted by television programme makers. These were first introduced regularly into comedies by sound engineer Charley Douglass in the 1950s, using his 'laff box' – a process which came to be called 'sweetening'. But when we analyse the way laughing is used in everyday conversation, we find that most instances are nothing to do with humour.

In a study I made some years ago of a corpus of informal chat, virtually every recording was punctuated by laughs, but hardly any were the result of someone telling a joke. People laughed to show appreciation of vivid phrasing, to express sympathy or recognition, to acknowledge an emotive or sensitive word, or a self-criticism, or to show appreciation of an unexpected piece of precision. Today, online *LOL* ('laughing out loud') is more often used to express rapport than to signal a real laugh. It can be a marker of amusement, but also an expression of irony or sarcasm. So when it became necessary to say that a message had indeed made the receiver laugh out loud, a new convention had to emerge. Some people repeat the letters: *LOLOL*. Some gloss it: *actual lol*.

World Storytelling Day

The art of telling a story is celebrated at the March equinox. The idea is to give as many people as possible the opportunity to hear a story — orally spontaneous or read aloud — in as many languages and places as possible. Events range from public gatherings in festivals and theatres with professional storytellers to private settings in homes and care-giving situations, where the teller can be a parent or a carer. From a professional point of view, the day forges links between storytellers from different countries or parts of a country, who usually have little opportunity to get together. And it fosters a greater appreciation of oral storytelling as an art form, and of the diversity of practices. The important point is that these are events for people of all ages and backgrounds. Everyone loves a story.

There have long been storytelling festivals in many countries of the world, and special occasions when stories would be told, often by 'official' tellers, such as the Anglo-Saxon *scops* or West African *griots*. The modern movement seems to have started in Sweden in 1991, when this day was chosen as 'All Storytellers Day'. Storytelling groups in some other countries used the same date, and in the early 2000s the day became global, with social media fostering international collaboration. A different theme is chosen for each year to provide a focus and to stimulate fresh creativity. The first in 2004 was Birds, and since then there have been explorations of Bridges, the Moon, the Wanderer, Dreams, Neighbours, Light and Shadow, Water, Trees, Fortune and Fate, Monsters and Dragons, Wishes, Strong Women, Transformation, Wise Fools, Myths and Legends, Voyages, New Beginnings, Lost and Found, and (2023) Together We Can.

The value of a story goes well beyond the art form. It can become a part of a larger narrative, such as a lecture, sermon or marketing pitch. The people at TEDx (Technology, Education, Design) know this. As Carmine Gallo says, in her book *Talk Like TED*, which emphazises the importance of a good story in gaining rapport with an audience: 'Storytelling is not something we do. Storytelling is who we are.'

World Poetry Day

Some countries have celebrated their own poetry day for many years. Often it was in October – the 15th, in several places, chosen because this was the date traditionally recognized as the birthday of Virgil. Some chose the third Saturday in October. In the UK it's the first Thursday. But UNESCO went for this date, decided in Paris in 1999. The purpose of the day is given a powerful statement on the UN website:

> Poetry celebrates one of humanity's most treasured forms of cultural and linguistic expression and identity. Practiced throughout history – in every culture and on every continent – poetry speaks to our common humanity and our shared values, transforming the simplest of poems into a powerful catalyst for dialogue and peace.

A multiplicity of more focused aims follows:

> The observance of World Poetry Day is also meant to encourage a return to the oral tradition of poetry recitals, to promote the teaching of poetry, to restore a dialogue between poetry and the other arts such as theatre, dance, music and painting, and to support small publishers and create an attractive image of poetry in the media, so that the art of poetry will no longer be considered an outdated form of art, but one which enables society as a whole to regain and assert its identity.

And it adds yet another purpose:

> to support linguistic diversity through poetic expression and to offer endangered languages the opportunity to be heard within their communities.

Today has an obvious connection to Poetry Break Day (13 JANUARY), where the message is one of personal creativity: 'there's a poem in everyone'. World Poetry Day has a complementary and broader set of aspirations: to appreciate the poetry in everyone else, through listening, reading and teaching; to give poets the honour that is their due; and to move beyond a personal level of aesthetic satisfaction towards the recognition of its potential – like music – as a way of bringing nations and peoples together and keeping cultures alive.

Talk Like William Shatner Day

It was the success of *Star Trek* that caused it. Aficionados began to introduce expressions from their favourite characters into their everyday conversation; and it was a fruitful source for professional impressionists. American voice artist Maurice LaMarche voiced William Shatner for several animated films, and found the character so appealing that he inaugurated this day in 2009. The following year he was joined by stand-up comedian Kevin Pollak, whose impressions of Shatner and other *Star Trek* characters were a big part of his act. There's a nice YouTube video of the two of them celebrating Shatner's 90th birthday in 2021.

As with all impressionists, the effect is gained by exaggerating a selection of notable features. In Shatner's case the — pausing in unexpected — places, and thesuddenspeedingup of bits of sentences. And some idiosyncratic word stress. They spend some moments riffing on Shatner's pronunciation of *sabotage*.

It's something everyone does, from time to time. A mutually recognized spoken quotation from a favourite film or television series — or, in older times, from radio — brings rapport and humour into a conversation. LaMarche chose Shatner for this day. It might have been… just anybody. Journalist John Walsh devoted an entire book to the practice: *Are You Talking To Me?* — its subtitle, *A Life Through the Movies* — in which he explores the occasions when films seen as a child have shaped his consciousness, and when words from those films unexpectedly pop into his mind or mouth. His title is one such quotation, from Martin Scorsese's 1976 film *Taxi Driver*, when Travis Bickle (Robert de Niro) speaks to himself in front of his bedroom mirror.

The borrowing applies to writing as much as speech. Indeed, parody is a well-recognized literary genre. And many authors include a favourite movie quotation or two to reach out to their readership. I'm no different. For me, it's *The Third Man*. I hide a phrase or two from that film in my writing every now and again. There's one on this page. And also from *The Prisoner* television series. Be seeing you. (SEE APPENDIX for answers, if needed.)

OK Day

It's certainly unusual to see a day celebrating an individual word. This one was proposed in 2011 by Allan Metcalf, author of *OK: The Improbable Story of America's Greatest Word*. Why today? The date of its first recorded written use, in the Saturday edition of the *Boston Morning Post* in 1839. The editor, Charles Gordon Greene, wrote a jocular article about an Anti-Bell Ringing Society, responding to a piece in the *Providence Journal*, and added *o.k.* with a gloss. The sentence reads:

> The 'Chairman of the Committee on Charity Lecture Bells' is one of the deputation, and perhaps if he should return to Boston, via Providence, he of the Journal, and his *train*-band [militia], would have the 'contribution box,' et ceteras, *o.k.* – all correct – and cause the corks to fly, like *sparks*, upward.

Its origin has sparked many theories. From Scottish *och aye*. From French *au quai* (goods arriving 'at the quayside'). From Choctaw *oke* ('it is') or Wolof *okeh* ('yes'). From a mis-spelled Latin *omnis korrecta* ('all correct', written by schoolmasters on homework). From Greek letters *omega* + *khi* (an incantation against fleas). From Obediah Kelly, a railwayman who authorized freight movements with his initials.

The Boston newspaper citation is now accepted as the correct etymology. There was at the time a vogue for creating humorous abbreviations using initials. *KY*, for example, for *know yuse* (= 'no use'). Nobody uses this any more, but *OK* received a boost when in 1840 it was used as a slogan during the US elections – the shortened form of *Old Kinderhook*, the nickname of President Martin Van Buren. Kinderhook was the name of his hometown in New York State.

OK became an interjection meaning 'all right, good', and other senses soon developed, such as 'fashionable' ('the OK thing to do'), 'trustworthy' ('He's OK'), and 'comfortable' ('Are you OK with that?'). In British English, it received huge graffiti exposure during the 1970s, when the fad to say that someone or something 'rules OK' was seen on walls everywhere. And today it's a default online dialogue response.

Olive Schreiner was born in 1855

Any global history of English must include this writer and political activist, born in Cape Colony (present-day Lesotho). *Story of an African Farm* (1883) was the first novel to come out of South Africa, and its portrait of a strong, independent-minded female protagonist greatly impressed the early women's movement. From a linguistic viewpoint, the novel is of special interest for the way it unapologetically presents the local landscape and culture, while acknowledging the linguistic limitations of her readers abroad through a short glossary. Her opening chapter has this evocative paragraph:

> The plain was a weary flat of loose-red sand, sparsely covered by the dry karoo bushes, that cracked beneath the tread like tinder, and showed the red earth everywhere. Here and there a milk-bush lifted its pale-coloured rods, and in every direction the ants and beetles ran about in the blazing sand. The red walls of the farmhouse, the zinc roofs of the outbuildings, the stone walls of the kraals, all reflected the fierce sunlight, till the eye ached and blenched. No tree or shrub was to be seen far or near. The two sunflowers that stood before the door, out-stared by the sun, drooped their brazen faces to the sand; and the little cicada-like insects cried aloud among the stones of the kopje.

The glossary adds:

> *Karoo* – The wide sandy plains in some parts of South Africa.
> *Kopje* – A small hillock, or 'little head'.
> *Kraal* – The space surrounded by a stone wall or hedged with thorn branches, into which sheep or cattle are driven at night.

She spent several years in England and Europe, and died in South Africa in 1920. Her letters include some prescient comments about language. To Havelock Ellis she writes (20 May 1913):

> What a farce to spend time gaining a little dry smattering of the grammar of a foreign language and to know nothing of its literature or the history of the nation! Language should not be taught through grammar, but through reading and speaking and hearing it; grammar should be studied as a science apart, comparative grammar.

Anna Seward died in 1809

The 'Swan of Lichfield', as she came to be called, was born in Derbyshire in 1742, and gained a reputation as a poet and literary figure. Six volumes of her extensive correspondence, often showing heavily revised versions, were published soon after her death – only 'a twelfth part of my epistolary writing', as she wrote to her publisher. Her letters reveal not only a deep knowledge of English literature but much about the literary world of her time, not least its leading personalities. James Boswell wrote to her when compiling his biography of Samuel Johnson, though some of her frank opinions about Johnson's personality and literary weaknesses never – as the modern idiom has it – made the cut.

Her elegant epistolary style can be seen in a letter to James Boswell (25 March 1785):

> I have often thought, that we never rise from any composition by the pen of the illustrious, with exactly the same degree of respect for the talents of the author with which we sat down to peruse it; our mass of admiration is either increased or diminished. If it is but by a single grain, that grain is something.

And a letter to a Dr S—— (7 June 1785) provides a further illustration, as well as showing her readiness to argue a stylistic point:

> As for your dislike to imperfect rhymes, which you would not allow, except in passages which express conflicting emotions, I will venture to assert, that, in general, whoever looks on poetry with the painter's eye, will find himself as little disposed to quarrel with his author for an imperfect rhyme in a passage of scenic description, as in one that conveys the struggles of impassioned affection. All our best writers continually give us precedents for their usage. A poet will lose much more on the side of sense, and grace of expression, then he will gain on the side of jingle, by narrowing his scale of rhymes in the pursuit of imaginary perfection, which, when attained, cloys the very ear by its sameness.

William Caxton finished his translation of *Aesop's Fables*

This is one of the many books that Caxton personally translated and printed, and thus made available to an English-speaking readership for the first time. In addition to the actual text, he often added a preface or epilogue, in which he explains his reasons for choosing the books for publication, comments on the difficulties he had to face, tells us about his literary interests, and identifies some of the linguistic problems he encountered. His remarks about language are an obligatory feature of any detailed account of the history of English, most famously those in the Preface to his translation of Virgil's *Eneydos* (*Aeneid*), made five years later.

The Aesop translation brings to light an interesting historical detail. At the beginning of his text, he says he translated it in 1483:

> Here begynneth the book of the subtyl historyes and fables of Esope, whiche were translated out of Frensshe into Englysshe by Wylliam Caxton at Westmynstre in the yere of Oure Lorde MCCCClxxxiii.

That is, 1483. But at the end the colophon gives a different year: 1484.

> And herewith I fynysshe this book translated and emprynted by me William Caxton at Westmynstre in thabbey, and fynysshed the xxvi daye of Marche the yere of Oure Lord MCCCClxxxiiii and the fyrst yere of the regne of Kyng Rychard the Thyrdde.

Why the difference? It's a consequence of the old style of dating: 26 March is the day following Lady Day (in Catholic tradition, the feast of the Annunciation). In the Julian calendar this marked the beginning of a new civil and legal year. Turning this into modern terms: it is as if he began the translation on 31 December and finished it on 1 January.

The last sentence of the colophon is worth a moment's reflection. Caxton started his press in 1476, while Edward IV was king. Richard seized the throne in 1483, but was killed at the Battle of Bosworth two years later. Not the best of times to be finding the right political patrons for a business start-up, but he managed it.

World Theatre Day

The day was first held in 1962, the initiative of the International Theatre Institute. Its primary aim is easily stated: to promote the value and practice of theatre in all its forms around the world, so that governments and institutions recognize this value and support it. On the day, special events in many countries demonstrate the joyful nature of the theatre experience. And there is an International Message, in which language is often mentioned. These extracts are adapted from the message in 1966 by the then director-general of UNESCO, René Maheu:

> On this stage, where nothing being real, everything is being imbued with meaning, all things, credible or absurd, because none is true, are marvellously possible. Here which is everywhere, this evening which is timeless, the whole world and the whole story of yesterday and tomorrow, of now and of never, are set before us for our fancy's exploration. Let me hail the theatre as the stuff of all dreams. ...
>
> What power lies, too, in the communion thus established among people, which transcends the divisions and boundaries of nature and society, and even of culture? Unlike other assemblies, the theatre audience is not a collection of individuals in isolation; it is a community seeking its soul and, from time to time, finding it – never thereafter to forget it.
>
> Power, too, of speech, which is essential to the theatre. Speech, that is thought. These words, which use expressive voices and features so as to enable us to gaze into our own deep secrets; words incarnate in living forms, frail and lovely, guiding them through the conflicts, the lures, the disputes and the snares to the culmination or extinction – splendid, pathetic or ludicrous as may be – of love or death, of the grotesque or the superb; their meaning takes me beyond what I see. Through them my beliefs become clear to me and I appraise them. It is thus that I shall leave this hall of illusions with an understanding of reality, which I can apply to my own life.

Virginia Woolf died in 1941

The acclaimed novels of Virginia Woolf, who was born in London in 1882, have somewhat overshadowed her prolific output of talks and essays, some of which had an insightful focus on language. In a BBC talk on 29 April 1937 for the series *Words Fail Me*, she spoke of the power of suggestion in words.

> Words, English words, are full of echoes, of memories, of associations – naturally. They have been out and about, on people's lips, in their houses, in the streets, in the fields, for so many centuries. And that is one of the chief difficulties in writing them today – that they are so stored with meanings, with memories, that they have contracted so many famous marriages.
>
> The splendid word 'incarnadine', for example – who can use it without remembering also 'multitudinous seas'? In the old days, of course, when English was a new language, writers could invent new words and use them. Nowadays it is easy enough to invent new words – they spring to the lips whenever we see a new sight or feel a new sensation – but we cannot use them because the language is old. You cannot use a brand new word in an old language because of the very obvious yet mysterious fact that a word is not a single and separate entity, but part of other words. It is not a word indeed until it is part of a sentence.
>
> Words belong to each other, although, of course, only a great writer knows that the word 'incarnadine' belongs to 'multitudinous seas'. To combine new words with old words is fatal to the constitution of the sentence. In order to use new words properly you would have to invent a new language; and that, though no doubt we shall come to it, is not at the moment our business. Our business is to see what we can do with the English language as it is. How can we combine the old words in new orders so that they survive, so that they create beauty, so that they tell the truth? That is the question.

John Gumperz died in 2013

It's good to have the opportunity to recognize the subject of sociolinguistics in the first few months of this book, through the work of one of its leading practitioners. Born in 1922 in Germany, Gumperz left the country in the 1930s, and after some time in Europe entered the United State in 1939, where he trained as a linguist. In 1956 he joined the faculty at the University of California, Berkeley. There, along with Dell Hymes (SEE 13 NOVEMBER), he became a leading proponent of a field that came to be called the 'ethnography of communication', and his research focused particularly on the nature of interaction.

It's an approach that studies in minute detail the way people use language when they talk to each other, and how breakdowns in communication can occur. Probably the most famous example is the time Gumperz went to Heathrow Airport to investigate a culture clash between newly hired cafeteria staff from India and Pakistan and the baggage handlers who were eating there. The handlers said the new staff were being rude, while the cafe people felt the handlers were being discriminatory, as no complaint was being made against the older British cafe staff. Both sides were puzzled by the situation, and wanted it resolved.

Gumperz recorded the conversations, and found a tiny but profound difference between the way the two groups of cafe staff spoke to customers. The word *gravy* was the prime example. When offering it to customers, the British staff said it with a high rising intonation, as would be normal for their accent – 'Gravy?' The new staff used a falling intonation – 'Gravy!' It was the contrast between 'Are you asking me or telling me?' To British ears, the latter would sound like 'This is gravy' and was evidently being interpreted as a rude 'Take it or leave it!', when the intention was only to be polite. It's when cultural differences of this kind are explained that social tensions can be resolved, and this is one of the benefits of the subject Gumperz pioneered: interactional sociolinguistics.

National Pencil Day

The day is celebrated in the United States, remembering American manufacturer Hyman Lipman (1817–1893), who in 1858 received a patent for a pencil with a rubber eraser at one end, thereby replacing the previous option of needing two separate implements. It's not known who started the day – very likely a pencil company – but it certainly sparked fresh interest in the history and diverse uses of pencils, from everyday writing and drawing to sophisticated artistry and technical applications. They play a critical role as the starting point in the development of children's ability to draw and write, with its erasable feature especially attractive.

'Pencil' is derived from Old French *pincel* 'small paint brush', and this is how the word was first used in English. In Shakespeare's *King John* (3.1.236), King Philip talks about people 'besmeared and overstained / With slaughter's pencil, where revenge did paint / The fearful difference of incensed kings.' The French word comes from the Latin for 'brush', *peniculus*, which in turn comes from the word for 'tail', *penis* – a little-known etymological connection, but one joyously exploited in early-twentieth-century slang.

The modern sense came into use during Shakespeare's lifetime, following the discovery of a large black-metal deposit at Borrowdale in Cumbria the year he was born, 1564. People thought it was lead ore (*plumbago*), so early pencils came to be described as *black lead*, and later as *lead pencils* – even though there's no lead in them at all. The term *graphite* entered the language a century later.

Modern pencils are a mixture of graphite and clay, the ratio governing the level of hardness, giving rise to widely recognized but often little understood systems of pencil abbreviations. In the HB scale, B = *black*, a relatively soft pencil, which increases the blackness of a mark. H = *hard*. So HB = *hard black* – that is, 'medium-hard'. A further grade, F = *firm*, for a pencil that sharpens to a fine point. Degrees of each are shown by a number, from 1 to 9: the higher the number, the harder or blacker the pencil.

International Hug a Medievalist Day

Interest in the medieval period has grown enormously in recent years, thanks partly to the popularity of films and television series based in the Middle Ages, such as *Game of Thrones*. Its range is usually from the fifth to the fifteenth centuries CE. So as far as the English language is concerned, that includes all the writing that has survived from Old English and Middle English.

The idea for this day began on Facebook, where 'hugging a' somebody or something has been a trend, to the extent that a digital hug reaction was rolled out in 2020: a smiling emoji hugging a heart. This particular day was introduced in 2011 by a medieval literature student at Oxford, Sarah Laseke, and attracted a lot of publicity.

Medievalists were, I suspect, somewhat taken aback by the interest. On the whole, those who study the language and literature of the Middle Ages work alone and out of sight in libraries, museums and public record offices. Increasingly they are at home or in a university office, as so much medieval material is now available online. I'm not sure what would be the reaction if someone actually offered such individuals a hug – whether physical or virtual – but I'm sure it would be appreciated. And the intention of the day has certainly to be applauded, to develop public awareness of the painstaking work that goes into medieval research, and of its value in providing insights into our past that far exceed the pastiches encountered in television series.

In studying the history of English, I've often found myself standing on the shoulders of scholars of the Middle Ages, with all the specialisms they have to offer – especially palaeography, the study of handwriting in manuscripts and the character of ancient inscriptions. But the hugs need to spread more widely, as linguistic history should never be divorced from the study of history in general, or from its sister-discipline, archaeology. The most illuminating introductions to the medieval period are always those in which the linguistic dimension is thoroughly integrated within the culture of its time. Hug 'em all!

All Fools' Day

Linguists have spent little time creating language hoaxes for this day, perhaps because they are too likely to be taken seriously. In 1996 David Pesetsky made a 1 April announcement, purporting to come from MIT Press, that Noam Chomsky's new book *The Minimalist Program* was being subjected to a product recall on grounds of low quality. It began:

> Unfortunately, it has been brought to our attention that the book contains mistakes, including (but not limited to):
> 1. Faulty use of the Greek letters 'alpha', 'xi' and 'zed'.
> 2. Extensive misspellings in Faroese and Bantu data.
> 3. Picture of unplayable cello on the cover (broken C, G, D and A strings). [there was indeed a cello-like stringless human outline]

The MIT Press bookstore started getting requests from people wanting to return their copies, and had to send out an explanation, referring them to the name of the message sender: A. Paul Fuhl

I had a similar experience. On 1 April 2016 I published a book for the tenth anniversary of Shakespeare's Globe called *The Unbelievable Hamlet Discovery*, in which I reported the finding of a previously unknown manuscript of *Hamlet* showing conclusively that Shakespeare suffered from octoliteraphilia – a little-known psychiatric disorder that manifests itself in an obsession with the letter *H*. The manuscript is an early version of the play in which every word begins with that letter. As an illustration, here is the opening of its most famous speech:

> Halt hara-kiri? Have hara-kiri? Hmm.
> Headache. Heartstop halts heartaches,
> Hardships. However... hazardous haviour.
> Hereafter hintless. Hindsight hidden,
> Humans hesitate.

The whole text is available through my website. But beware. Not long after, I got an email request from a foreign student wanting me to supervise him in a PhD on the manuscript. He was serious. Presumably 1 April had no cultural meaning in his country.

2 APRIL

International Children's Book Day

The day was inaugurated in 1967 by the International Board on Books for Young People (IBBY), a non-profit organization founded in Zurich in 1953, and today composed of eighty National Sections worldwide. Its website has a powerful mission statement:

— to promote international understanding through children's books
— to give children everywhere the opportunity to have access to books with high literary and artistic standards
— to encourage the publication and distribution of quality children's books, especially in developing countries
— to provide support and training for those involved with children and children's literature
— to stimulate research and scholarly works in the field of children's literature
— to protect and uphold the Rights of the Child according to the UN Convention on the Rights of the Child.

They chose this day because it was the birthday of Danish author Hans Christian Andersen in 1805, whose fairy tales – 156 in all, with many other stories listed in the archive at the H.C. Andersen Centre in Odense, Denmark – have never been surpassed. And in two cases their linguistic impact has gone far beyond their intended readership: the idiomatic use of *ugly duckling* and *emperor's new clothes* in contexts far removed from their original stories.

   The aim of the day is to inspire a love of reading and to call attention to children's books. Families, schools and libraries are encouraged to create special reading events. Each year a different National Section becomes the international sponsor of the day. It chooses a theme, invites a well-known illustrator to design a poster, and asks one of its leading authors to write a message to the children of the world. Recent themes and sponsors illustrate the scope and scale of the initiative:

Stories are wings that help you to soar every day (Canada, 2022)
The music of words (USA, 2021)
A hunger for words (Slovenia, 2020)
Books help us slow down (Lithuania, 2019)
The small is big in a book (Latvia, 2018)

Ruth Prawer Jhabvala died in 2013

Born in Germany in 1927, Jhabvala lived in India, Britain and the United States, and famously described herself as 'always a refugee'. Her writing sits at the intersection between the language of books and the language of films, whose relationship is such an important part of media studies. She's the only person to have been awarded the Booker Prize (for *Heat and Dust* in 1975) and an Oscar for Best Adapted Screenplay (for *A Room with a View* in 1987 and *Howards End* in 1993). She was famously self-critical about her screenwriting, calling it her 'hobby', but was nonetheless respectful of both, and would often comment on the contrast: 'One sentence in a film is like 15 or 20 in a book.' In an interview for *New York Times Magazine* (11 September 1983) she expanded on her view. She describes how 'writing films scripts is so much easier than working on a novel', and goes on:

> In a novel you have to do it all yourself, you have to make the characters real. You have to show not only what they say, but the way they say it, the gestures, the turn of voice, everything the actor does. You have to describe everything, which is what the camera does. You have to hold everything together, which is what the director will do. You even have to supply the music. In a film, you present the blueprint, which the other people fill in.

She wrote 23 scripts out of the 44 films that came from producer Ismail Merchant and director James Ivory. Her name is often missing from the branding, but her role was so fundamental that, in a 2019 British Film Institute piece about her work, she's described as being 'one part of the "three-headed god" that made up Merchant Ivory'.

I've seen several of her films. My favourite is the one about an English acting company touring India, *Shakespeare Wallah*, which from a language point of view is a fine exemplar of how to blend a multiplicity of Englishes into an artistically seamless production.

Isidore of Seville died in 636

For many people, this seventh-century Spanish archbishop, born around 560, is the (unofficial) patron saint of the Internet, because of his vast encyclopedia. His *Etymologiae* ('Etymologies'), also known as the *Origines* ('Origins'), is a compendium of linked extracts and paraphrases of texts from Greek, Roman and Christian writers. In the invaluable translation of the entire work, published in 2006 (and available online), the editors say: 'It was arguably the most influential book, after the Bible, in the learned world of the Latin West for nearly a thousand years'.

Its encyclopedic character can be seen from its topical arrangement into twenty 'books': Grammar; Rhetoric and dialectic; Mathematics, music, astronomy; Medicine; Laws and times; Books and ecclesiastical offices; God, angels and saints; The Church and sects; Languages, nations, reigns, the military, citizens, family relationships; Vocabulary; The human being and portents; Animals; The cosmos and its parts; The earth and its parts; Buildings and fields; Stones and metals; Rural matters; War and games; Ships, buildings and clothing; Provisions and various implements.

An etymological character permeates the whole:

> The knowledge of a word's etymology often has an indispensable usefulness for interpreting the word, for when you have seen whence a word has originated, you understand its force more quickly.

So we find thousands of examples of the kind 'Wine (*vinum*) is so called because it replenishes the veins (*vena*) with blood.' Most of his etymologies are spurious, and today linguists call the principle the 'etymological fallacy', for there's no necessary connection between the meaning of a modern word and what it originally meant.

But any linguist reading the language-related books can't fail to be impressed by the range and depth of Isidore's compilation. The opening book entitled 'Grammar' is actually an entire introduction to language, including orthography, phonetics, parts of speech, syllables, metre, prosody, punctuation, abbreviations, signing, spelling, etymology, borrowing, figures of speech, genres, and more.

Swinburne was born in 1837

Part of the intrigue of poetry is to see how creative a writer can be within a self-imposed linguistic discipline. The sonnet, haiku, clerihew and limerick are well-known examples. Less familiar is the creation of the poet Algernon Charles Swinburne, born in London, who devised a variation on an earlier French model to create the *roundel*. It was one of those spontaneous moments, halfway through his poetic life (he died in 1909). He says in relation to his collection *A Century of Roundels*, published in 1883, that he had 'taken a fancy to the form and went on scribbling in it' until he reached a hundred, all composed within just two or three months. In a letter he wrote in April 1883 he describes his 'tiny new book of songs or songlets, in one form and all manner of metres'. Critics have been divided over their merit in comparison with his other work, but there are not many examples in poetic literature of this kind of stylistic innovation.

Unlike the sonnet, with its linear pattern, the roundel is circular, its final line taking us back to the words with which it begins. It has three stanzas, each of three lines, with the refrain repeated at the end of the first and third stanzas. Considerable discipline is imposed by the rhyme scheme – *ABAB, BAB, ABAB* – as can be seen in this example, called simply 'The Roundel' (number 63 in the book).

A roundel is wrought as a ring or a starbright sphere,
With craft of delight and with cunning of sound unsought,
That the heart of the hearer may smile if to pleasure his ear
    A roundel is wrought.

Its jewel of music is carven of all or of aught –
Love, laughter, or mourning – remembrance of rapture or fear –
That fancy may fashion to hang in the ear of thought.

As a bird's quick song runs round, and the hearts in us hear
Pause answer to pause, and again the same strain caught,
So moves the device whence, round as a pearl or tear,
    A roundel is wrought.

Isaac Asimov died in 1992

Asimov's fame as a science-fiction writer has rather eclipsed his prodigious writings in other genres. He was born in Russia in 1920, moved with his parents to the USA in 1923, began writing in his late teens, and by the time he died had published over 500 books, and so many other items that I haven't tried to count them, in the interests of completing this book. He had something to say about everything, and language themes turn up repeatedly in his essays on writing, in the editorials he wrote for his *Science Fiction* magazine, and in his introductions to anthologies. He wrote books of limericks, some for children, and some very definitely for adults. His introduction to Shakespeare is a massive 700+ pages.

Out of all this, for this book I choose four of my favourite language-related quotations.

Writing is my only interest. Even speaking is an interruption.

Thinking is the activity I love best, and writing to me is simply thinking through my fingers. I can write up to 18 hours a day. Typing 90 words a minute, I've done better than 50 pages a day. Nothing interferes with my concentration. You could put an orgy in my office and I wouldn't look up – well, maybe once.

I have an informal style, which means I tend to use short words and simple sentence structure, to say nothing of occasional colloquialisms. This grates on people who like things that are poetic, weighty, complex, and, above all, obscure. On the other hand, the informal style pleases people who enjoy the sensation of reading an essay without being aware that they are reading and of feeling that ideas are flowing from the writer's brain into their own without mental friction.

What do you call that nice, shiny white metal they use to make sidings and airplanes out of? Aluminum, right? Aluminum, pronounced 'uh-LOO-mih-num', right? Anybody knows that! But do you know how the British spell it? 'Aluminium', pronounced 'Al-yoo-MIH-nee-um'. Ever hear anything so ridiculous? The French and Germans spell it 'aluminium', too, but they're foreigners who don't speak Earth-standard. You'd think the British, however, using our language, would be more careful!

Yvonne Vera died in 2005

She was born in Bulawayo in 1964 – at the time southern Rhodesia, now Zimbabwe, and her experience of living through the war of independence in the 1970s permeates her writing. She emigrated to Canada in 1987, though returned to her home country for a period as director of the National Gallery in Bulawayo. Her novels, praised for their strong female characters and her courageous addressing of taboo subjects, such as infanticide and incest, are written in a poetically allusive style, with short sentences and an abundance of surrealistic metaphor that has sometimes been criticized for obscuring her narrative. But her physical imaging of the way language expresses thought has been widely acclaimed, in such books as *Without a Name* (1994) and *Under the Tongue* (1996).

Her writing is infused with a focus on the power of words and names to fight against the silence surrounding her difficult subject matter, and to foster relationships, as in this extract from chapter 11 of *Under the Tongue*:

> Grandmother pulls a word from her mouth and places it under my tongue. I feel fingers reach beneath my tongue. Grandmother's word grows and her mouth trembles with the word she has taken from it that she remembers.
>
> Grandmother touches my forehead with her tongue.
>
> I touch my forehead and find the word Grandmother has given to me. I carry the word between my fingers. I know she has given me a word from long ago, a word that she has retrieved from an anthill. The word is covered with ancient soil, with all her memory. Grandmother buried a word in an anthill before I was born. It is a word that brings all our birth. It is a word filled with water. She buried it after rain had fallen for many mornings and nights. She buried the word to ease her suffering. When she had buried it she returned to the world and gave birth to my mother. Grandmother's arms are heavy. Her arms carry many words. A word is like a wound that has dried, she says.

International Romani Day

The day was inaugurated in 1990 during the fourth World Romani Congress of the International Romani Union, held in Poland. It remembers the first major international meeting of Romani representatives, held in 1971 in the UK. Its aim is to celebrate Romani culture and raise awareness of the issues facing its people.

The Romani language is Indo-Aryan in origin, and found worldwide. In Europe there could be as many as 5 million speakers, making it the most widely used minority language on the continent, probably present in every country. Its spread is reflected in loan words in many European languages. English has several borrowings, mainly used in informal settings, such as *pal* (from *phral* 'brother'), *chav* (from *chavo* 'unmarried Romani man'), *nark* (from *nok* 'nose') and *lollipop* (from *loli phabai* 'red apple').

To give a brief illustration of the language, here's a riddle – a popular genre among the Roma, along with other forms of language play. There's a proverbial expression: *dž/ivipen džal lokeder pherasenca* 'life goes forward more easily with jokes': it deserves to be universally known.

činel sar čhuri,	*it can cut like a knife,*
sastarel o jilo,	*it can cure the heart,*
anel tut pro lačho drom,	*it can take you on the right way,*
šaj tut marel pal o drom tele.	*and it can take you away from the right way.*

The answer? *o lav*, 'the word'.

More about the structure and uses of the language can be found in the best introduction to the language I've seen: a joint publication in 2000 by the Centre de recherches tsiganes (Gypsy Research Centre) at the Université René Descartes in Paris and the University of Hertfordshire: *What is the Romani Language?* The Patrin Web Journal is the go-to online source for Romani culture and history. They gloss their name thus: 'Marker used by traveling Roma to tell others of directions, also used for passing on news using prearranged signals. Also, a leaf or page.' Excellent choice of name, for a website.

The first known recording
of an audible human voice in 1860

The recording was made by French inventor Édouard-Léon Scott de Martinville (1817–1879) on what he called a *phonautogram*. His device (a phonautograph) created a visual image of the sound – a combination of horn and diaphragm causing vibrations that made a stylus mark a moving surface covered in a black pigment. It didn't have the ability to play back the recording (unlike Edison's device some years later). He hoped to make a kind of 'speech to text' process that would allow people to read it. This never proved possible, but in 2008 a way was found to play the few surviving recordings. A muffled, scratchy rendition of the first few bars of the French song 'Au clair de la lune' can be heard (they're available online).

He submitted his proposal to the French Academy of Sciences in 1857, and received a patent. His opening statement was vivid and prescient:

Is there a possibility of reaching, in the case of sound, a result analogous to that attained at present for light by photographic processes? Can it be hoped that the day is near when the musical phrase, escaped from the singer's lips, will be written by itself and as if without the musician's knowledge on a docile paper and leave an imperishable trace of those fugitive melodies which the memory no longer finds when it seeks them? Will one be able, between two men brought together in a silent room, to cause to intervene an automatic stenographer that preserves the discussion in its minutest details while adapting to the speed of the conversation? Will one be able to preserve for the future generation some features of the diction of one of those eminent actors, those grand artists who die without leaving behind them the faintest trace of their genius? Will the improvisation of the writer, when it emerges in the middle of the night, be able to be recovered the next day with its freedom, this complete independence from the pen, an instrument so slow to represent a thought always cooled in its struggle with written expression?

I believe so.

Nugi Garimara died in 2014

This was her Aboriginal name; her English name was Doris Pilkington. Born in 1937, she became known for *Follow the Rabbit-Proof Fence* (1996), a novel based on the true story of three Aboriginal girls from the northern part of Western Australia, among them her mother Molly, who had been forcibly taken from their families as part of the government campaign to integrate mixed-race children into white society. The girls were taken to a settlement near Perth, and almost immediately decided to escape and make their way home, using as a guide a fence built the length of Australia from north to south in the (failed) hope that it would protect farmland from hordes of rabbits. It's that journey of over a thousand miles that's told in the novel.

The feel of their mother tongue, Mardujara, is present throughout – a language they were not allowed to speak. It was another official policy, as this extract illustrates. The girls have just arrived at the settlement.

> Back at the dormitory the girls were trying to snuggle down in their cold, uninviting beds. Molly, Daisy and Gracie began to talk normally amongst themselves, not whispering but speaking in their own relaxed manner.
>
> 'You girls can't talk blackfulla language here, you know,' came the warning from the other side of the dorm. 'You gotta forget it and talk English all the time.'
>
> The girls were dumbfounded, they couldn't say anything but stare at the speaker.
>
> 'That's true,' said Martha in support. 'I had to do the same. They tell everybody that when they come here and go to school for the first time.' Molly couldn't believe what they had just heard. 'We can't talk our old wangka,' she whispered. 'That's awful.'

Wangka is 'language'. The gloss is given at the end of the book in a fifty-word glossary, listing the Mardujara words used. It includes conversational words such as *youay* 'yes' and *indi* 'isn't it', domestic words such as *dgudu* 'older sister', *worru* 'fire', and *mundu* 'meat', and words for the fauna encountered on their journey, such as *dgundu* 'dog' and *girdi girdi* 'hill kangaroo'.

The first performance of Shaw's *Pygmalion* in 1914

Why, out of the thousands of first performances in theatre history, is this one worth recalling? Because on this day it made a series of linguistic headlines, such as this one in the London *Daily Sketch*:

'PYGMALION' MAY CAUSE SENSATION TO-NIGHT.
Mr. Shaw Introduces a Forbidden Word.
WILL 'MRS PAT' SPEAK IT?
Has The Censor Stepped In, Or
Will The Phrase Spread?

George Bernard Shaw had given Mrs Patrick Campbell, in the character of Eliza Doolittle, the line: 'Not bloody likely.' The writer continues:

> If the Censor has not interfered the audience will either laugh immoderately or – well, anything may happen.
> Is an expression which hitherto no respectable newspaper has dared to print permissible when uttered on the stage?

And, indeed, the entire article doesn't print the word once.

In the event, the audience loved it. Next-day newspapers reported that there was a gasp of surprise, then everyone roared with laughter for over a minute. The effect lasted for some years. People would talk about 'the Shavian adjective', or say 'not pygmalion likely'.

It was a curious situation. *Bloody* developed its intensifying force of 'very' towards the end of the seventeenth century, and was used by all social classes. Jonathan Swift, for example, had no difficulty in using it in a letter to a woman – several times, in fact, usually in relation to the weather. In the middle of a long letter to Stella (27 April 1711) he writes: 'It was bloody hot walking to day.' But during the eighteenth century the sensitive ears of the 'polite' classes turned against it, probably because of its associations with rowdiness and rough behaviour. Aristocratic rowdies were known as *bloods*, so to be *bloody drunk* was to be 'drunk as a blood'. When Johnson described it in his *Dictionary* of 1755 as 'very vulgar' its fate was sealed.

Drop Everything and Read Day

The sentiment is self-explanatory: make reading a priority for the day – and beyond. DEAR day, as it's usually called, became a national celebration in the United States as a result of a single children's book. *Ramona Quimby, Age 8* was published in 1981 by children's author Beverly Cleary, born on this day in 1916 – one of a bestselling series (in the USA) about this little girl and her family and friends (and enemies). In chapter 2 Ramona's teacher tells her class that they're going to have 'sustained silent reading' every day.

> This means that every day after lunch we are going to sit at our desks and read silently to ourselves any book we choose in the library.

And they wouldn't have to write it up as a task in a book report! To make it sound more fun, she decides to call it DEAR.

The idea caught on, and a day highlighting the importance of reading has been widely celebrated in American schools ever since the book came out. It received especial publicity in 2021, following the author's death two weeks before. A large group of interested parties is involved in its celebration each year, including the publisher HarperCollins, the Association for Library Service to Children, the National Education Association, the Newspaper Association of America Foundation, and several other agencies involved with early reading.

Cleary got the idea from the experience of her own children participating in this practice in their school. As Ramona's teacher says, it's called 'sustained silent reading' – also known as 'free voluntary reading'. Students read silently in a designated time period every day in school. The practice has been studied by, among others, educational researcher Stephen Krashen – a name well known in the field of Teaching English as a Foreign Language – who reviewed many studies and found that it led to gains in reading comprehension, vocabulary, spelling and other aspects of literacy. But perhaps the best effect is the long-term one. Many who experienced the approach have said it instilled in them a habit of reading that never went away.

National Scrabble Day

Today is the birthday of American architect Alfred Mosher Butts (1899–1993), who invented the game in 1933 during a period of unemployment after the Great Depression. He was an enthusiast for language play, and the influence of such word games as anagram-finding and crossword puzzles clearly influenced his thinking. According to the Hasbro history of the game, he felt 'there is one thing that keeps word games from being as popular as card games: they have no score'. It took a while for the name to emerge. He originally called it Lexiko, then Criss-Cross Words. The modern name was finally settled when it became the trademark of the American toy and game manufacturer Hasbro in 1948.

Butts' linguistic acumen can be seen in several features of the game. Its fundamental principle, the letter value, was evidently the result of an analysis of the frequency with which letters turned up on a front page of the *New York Times* – an analysis that stands up well in the light of later letter-frequency counts. The procedure was similar to that used by Samuel Morse (SEE 27 APRIL), when he devised his code based on the number of letters used in a box of printers' type. At a more specific level we see his language awareness in the restriction of *S* tiles to four, being aware that to have more would weaken the game by allowing too many plural-noun and third-person verb forms.

The biggest problem, of course, is how to keep the official word list up to date, given the rapidity of lexical change. Official word lists also differ – not least because of the differences between American and British spelling. The recognition of abbreviations, slang words, dialect variations, proper names and offensive words regularly present the authorities and individual players with problematic issues. As I write this entry, my wife and her mother are playing a game, and most of the conversation surrounds the question of whether a particular word is 'allowed'. At national and international levels, such disputes can make tennis champion John McEnroe's outbursts on court seem mild by comparison!

Anne Sullivan was born in 1866

Anne Sullivan is best known for being the teacher, governess and companion (until her death in 1936) of deaf–blind Helen Keller (1880–1968). Born in Massachusetts, she had personal experience of vision problems, having contracted an eye disease at age 5, and received most of her education at the Perkins School for the Blind in her state. When the school was contacted for help by Helen's father, Anne was recommended, and she met Helen in 1887. She used a technique of spelling words out onto Helen's palm – a method that allowed the young girl to learn, within a year, hundreds of words, as well as Braille.

Later, Helen learned speech by 'lip-reading with fingers' – the thumb lightly placed against the speaker's lips and the fingers on the jaw and neck, thereby sensing airflow from mouth and nose, articulatory movements and vocal fold vibration. Her oral fluency developed to the extent that she was able to speak French and German, as well as English, and her writing skills led to many books and articles. Helen's autobiography, available online, is a must-read for anyone who wants to gain insight into her condition and Anne's methods: *The Story of My Life*. Here's a short extract:

> We walked down the path to the well-house, attracted by the fragrance of the honeysuckle with which it was covered. Some one was drawing water and my teacher placed my hand under the spout. As the cool stream gushed over one hand she spelled into the other the word water, first slowly, then rapidly. I stood still, my whole attention fixed upon the motions of her fingers. Suddenly I felt a misty consciousness as of something forgotten – a thrill of returning thought; and somehow the mystery of language was revealed to me. I knew then that 'w-a-t-e-r' meant the wonderful cool something that was flowing over my hand. That living world awakened my soul, gave it light, hope, joy, set it free! There were barriers still, it is true, but barriers that could in time be swept away.

Since 2006 Helen Keller Day has been celebrated on 27 June, her birthday.

Vigdís Finnbogadóttir was born in 1930

Born in Reykjavik, Finnbogadóttir became a politician who served as the fourth president of Iceland for three terms from 1980 to 1996 – the first woman in the world to be democratically elected as a constitutional head of state. Earlier she studied French and English, became a teacher of French, and developed a lifelong enthusiasm for languages. In 1998 she was appointed UNESCO's Goodwill Ambassador for Languages, and in 2000 UN Goodwill Ambassador in the fight against Racism and Xenophobia. The Vigdís Finnbogadóttir Institute for Foreign Languages was established at the University of Iceland in 2002.

Her main legacy for this book is the successful completion of a major project in Reykjavik to celebrate and promote language and languages. The Veröld – House of Vigdís was formally opened in April 2017: the Vigdís International Centre for Multilingualism and Intercultural Understanding. Its aims, as stated on its website, are:

— to promote multilingualism in order to further understanding, exchange and respect between cultures and nations;
— to raise awareness of the importance of language as a core element of the cultural heritage of mankind;
— to promote translation and translation studies and the observation, analysis and statistics of translation flow;
— to work at the preservation of languages and to create awareness of language policies and control of languages, with multilingualism as a guiding light;
— to promote research and education in foreign languages and cultures;
— to support and promote research into mother tongues, regarding them as a basic element of human rights.

It was the linguistic success story of the decade – a decade in which other projects for 'houses of languages' had failed for a combination of political and financial reasons. There's no better statement of aims, and my hope is that more countries will see the importance and relevance of creating public spaces where languages can be heard, seen, explored and celebrated, and follow Iceland's lead (SEE 18 MAY).

World Voice Day

The voice is taken for granted – until we lose it, for whatever reason. Sometimes it's the result of disease, but it can also be a consequence of overuse or a poor speaking technique. When a problem occurs, it's often dismissed as something that will go away – except that often it doesn't, and more serious problems develop. 'Loss' doesn't mean only silence. 'Voice' technically refers to the buzzing noise produced by the vibration of the vocal folds. When these fail to function normally, the result can be a whispery, breathy, creaky or husky voice quality that in speech pathology is labelled *dysphonia*. A total loss would be *aphonia*.

World Voice Day was established to increase public awareness of the importance of the voice and its underlying physiology, and thus facilitate the identification and prevention of voice problems. It acknowledges a sentiment expressed, for example, by composer Richard Strauss: 'The human voice is the most beautiful instrument of all, but it is the most difficult to play.' First celebrated nationally in Brazil in 1999, the initiative was soon taken up by other countries, and in 2002 a global day was recognized. Each year a theme is addressed: in 2021 it was 'One World, Many Voices'; in 2022 'Lift Your Voice'.

The day raises the profile of those involved in voice research, training, intervention and rehabilitation, for the wide range of professions is often not appreciated. In the medical domain they are primarily otolaryngologists – physicians and surgeons who specialize in ENT ('ear, nose and throat') disorders. The remedial side of a medical condition is chiefly the responsibility of speech pathologists and therapists. Psychologists may also be involved, as a voice problem can affect a person's mental and emotional well-being in many ways. A great deal of research is carried on by phoneticians and acoustic physicists. And a cadre of speech trainers play an important role in the world of theatre, public speaking and music – for the singing voice is in many ways even more at risk than the speaking voice because of the greater pitch range and intensity of its production (SEE 15 OCTOBER).

Blah Blah Blah Day

Blah is clearly an imitative word, like *babble* and *bubble*, and probably an informal development of *blab*, known in English since the sixteenth century in a range of meanings, including 'talking too much' or 'without care'. As a spoken colloquialism, never written down, it has probably been in use for a long time, but its first recorded usage as a single word isn't until 1918 in the United States. It soon duplicated and then tripled, and in theory there's no limit to the number of times it might be repeated. But there's a stylistic pressure in many languages to 'speak in threes', and this has shaped usage since – and the name of this day. A similar development is seen on 23 July.

Blah is traditionally used with negative meanings. The *Oxford English Dictionary* defines it as 'meaningless, insincere, or pretentious talk or writing; nonsense, bunkum. Also used as a derisive interjection.' But there's more to it than that. In many settings, the triple *blah* is simply an economy measure, when someone is explaining a point and realizing it's unnecessary to go into everything in detail because they know their listeners will understand what's being taken for granted. It's a corrective to wordiness.

By contrast, the aim of this day is to increase meaningful communication, to appreciate the value of everyday conversation, and to foster achievement. It was created in 2006 by Ruth and Thomas Roy of Wellcat Holidays and Herbs with a very positive set of intentions. As one of the 'on this day' websites puts it: 'It's about listening to those nagging words and putting them to action. Whether they're telling you to clean your home, apply for jobs, or quit smoking. People also take the time to listen to others in their daily lives joining together for a simple talk.'

And, in a further contrast, today is also International Haiku Poetry Day, an initiative of the Haiku Foundation. In English a haiku usually takes the form of three lines with a 5–7–5 syllable structure.

Language on this day
A moment for blah blah blah
And gentle haiku

Leonard Bloomfield died in 1949

As an undergraduate encountering linguistics for the first time in 1959, there was one book that was obligatory reading above all others: *Language*, by Leonard Bloomfield, published in 1933. This American linguist was the most influential expounder of structural linguistics in the United States until the late 1950s, when Noam Chomsky changed the direction of the subject. But in 1959 I had never heard of Chomsky.

Language introduced me to a world of languages that I never knew existed. Bloomfield was born in Chicago in 1887, at a time when comparative philology was a major academic force, and this proved to be a considerable influence on his early work. He studied Indo-European languages in the USA and Europe, and specialized in Germanic. But later he carried out fieldwork on American Indian languages, especially on four members of the Algonquian family: Fox, Cree, Menominee and Ojibwe. He also studied Tagalog, a language of the Philippines. In all cases his concern was to provide a description of these languages in their own terms, rejecting the traditional assumption that everything could be described using a model derived from Latin.

I especially appreciated his synthesis of contemporary thinking about the structure of language into a single 'Bloomfieldian method'. Many of his ideas and methods would become outmoded in the second half of the century, but his emphasis on the scientific basis of linguistics remains as valid today as it ever was. So does his insistence on treating linguistics – a subject 'only in its beginnings' – as a discipline that exists independently of other domains where language is a focus. At the beginning of chapter 2 of his book, he writes:

> The most difficult step in the study of language is the first step. Again and again, scholarship has approached the study of language without actually entering upon it. Linguistic science arose from relatively practical preoccupations, such as the use of writing, the study of literature and especially of older records, and the prescription of elegant speech, but people can spend any amount of time on these things without actually entering into linguistic study.

Byron died in 1824

Baron George Gordon Byron, known universally as Lord Byron (born in London in 1788), made many references to language in his poems, and wasn't averse to introducing the occasional linguistic observation. One of my favourites is this one, from *Don Juan* (canto 7, stanza 42), when he's describing the battle between the Russians and the Turks:

> ... few are slow
> In thinking that their enemy is beat
> (Or beaten, if you insist on grammar, though
> I never think about it in a heat) ...

In his prose writing he gives some striking language-related accounts. Here is one from his *Detached Thoughts* (1821), a commonplace book of observations about anything that came into his mind. He opens it thus:

> Amongst various journals, memoranda, diaries, &c., which I have kept in the course of my living, I began one about three months ago, and carried it on till I had filled one paper book (thinnish), and two sheets or so of another. I then left off...

Item number 53–4 is about the literary people he finds difficult to talk to, and he recalls one marvel:

> I do not remember a man amongst them, whom I ever wished to see twice, except perhaps Mezzophanti, who is a Monster of Languages, the Briareus of parts of Speech, a walking Polyglott and more, who ought to have existed at the time of the tower of Babel as universal Interpreter. He is indeed a Marvel-unassuming also: I tried him in all the tongues of which I knew a single oath (or adjuration to the Gods against Postboys, Lawyers, Tartars, boatmen, Sailors, pilots, Gondoliers, Muleteers, Camel-drivers, Vetturini [coach-drivers], Postmasters, post-horses, posthouses, post-everything), and Egad! he astounded me even to my English.
>   Three Swedes came to Bologna, knowing no tongue but Swedish. The inhabitants in despair presented them to Mezzophanti. Mezzophanti (though a great Linguist) knew no more Swedish than the Inhabitants. But in two days, by dint of dictionary, he talked with them fluently and freely, so that they were astonished, and every body else, at his acquisition of another tongue in forty eight hours.

Chinese Language Day

Chinese is one of the six official languages of the United Nations. The day was established by the UN in 2010 (on 12 November) as part of the general policy to 'celebrate multilingualism and cultural diversity as well as to promote equal use of all six of its official working languages throughout the organization'. It was moved to this day in April the following year. Each year a theme is chosen to give some focus to the range of events that take place. In 2021 it was 'highlighting pictographs', using three types of script associated with three different Chinese cultures and World Heritage Sites. In 2022 it was 'China Chic'.

The date was chosen to honour Cangjie, a legendary figure who is said to have invented Chinese characters 5,000 years ago. He observed the distinctive marks left by beasts on the ground, and extended the idea to all visible things. The demons however were unimpressed, as they knew that, once humans learned to write, it would be much more difficult to deceive them.

The day is the beginning of a period in the Chinese year called *Guyu*, the sixth of the twenty-four terms that make up the calendar. The name means 'rain of millet', as, according to legend, when Cangjie invented the characters, the gods wept tears of joy and the sky rained millet. In the Gregorian calendar the period begins around this day and ends around 5 May.

The impact of Chinese on other languages has been substantial. Hundreds of words and expressions have entered English, either directly or indirectly (such as from Japanese, Korean or other European languages). The best known are food-related, such as *chopsticks*, *chop suey*, *chow*, *chow mein*, *dim sum*, *ketchup*, *lychee*, *wok*, *cha* [tea] and *foo yung*. Then there are the names of games, beliefs and rituals, such as *go*, *kung fu*, *mahjong*, *tai chi*, *butoh*, *feng shui*, *qi* and *tao*. But the widespread nature of contact with Chinese culture over the centuries is the dominant impression, reflected in such borrowings as *bonsai*, *kaolin*, *kowtow*, *monsoon*, *pidgin*, *rickshaw*, *sampan* and *typhoon*.

World Creativity and Innovation Day

A day for this theme had been celebrated in many countries since 2002, but it was only in 2017 that the United Nations passed a formal resolution recognizing it. The day is the culmination of a week devoted to creative events beginning on 15 April, the birthday of Leonardo da Vinci, often referred to as the world's greatest ever artist and innovator.

The range of the day is spelled out on the UN website in terms of the 'creative economy – which includes audiovisual products, design, new media, performing arts, publishing and visual arts' (SEE ALSO 30 MAY). It's considered to be

> a highly transformative sector of the world economy in terms of income generation, job creation and export earnings ... At the same time, creativity and culture have a significant non-monetary value that contributes to inclusive social development, to dialogue and understanding between peoples.

Language, of course, takes its place within several of these domains. Linguistic creativity is at the heart of any understanding of literature, all forms of language play, and child language acquisition. At a deeper level it's the force underlying our ability to speak, write and sign that linguistic theory aims to explain: how we create new sentences and discourses. Any notion of innovation also has a linguistic dimension, for attempts to solve old problems in new ways are likely to involve a critique of the way we talk about them.

It isn't so far from here to another event celebrated by some on this date: Big Word Day. It's not clear how this day developed, but several websites now recognize it. Evidently the motivation is to celebrate – and possibly use – words outside one's normal vocabulary range. Most of the online examples I've seen are of the extreme kind, such as citing the longest word in the language, or playful creations such as *supercallifrag...*. There's also an unwelcome suggestion that it's a day when people should use big words for their own sake, just to impress others. That would be an unfortunate outcome of a day that has great potential as a motivation for vocabulary building.

Vladimir Nabokov was born in 1899

Born in Russia, from 1918 Nabokov lived in England, Germany and France, fleeing to the United States in 1940, and working there as a college lecturer until a final move to Switzerland in 1961, where he stayed until his death in 1977. His first works were in Russian, and he also wrote in French, but his fame grew after he switched to English following his US move, and especially after the success of his novel *Lolita* (1955). His mixed linguistic background is expressed in his often-quoted remark: 'My head speaks English, my heart speaks Russian, and my ear speaks French.'

The distinction comes to the surface in the closing paragraph of a contribution he made in a 1957 article, 'On a Book Entitled *Lolita*':

> My private tragedy, which cannot, and indeed should not, be anybody's concern, is that I had to abandon my natural idiom, my untrammelled, rich, and infinitely docile Russian tongue for a second-rate brand of English, devoid of any of those apparatuses – the baffling mirror, the black velvet backdrop, the implied associations and traditions – which the native illusionist, frac-tails flying, can magically use to transcend the heritage in his own way.

This seriously understates his mastery of English, and especially his ability to use the language in a metaphorical and ludic way, as that quotation itself illustrates. Few native speakers would be able to define *frac-tails*, for example – a design of equestrian tailcoat. He also carried out one of the most difficult translation tasks presented by English literature: *Alice in Wonderland* into Russian.

An interesting footnote to any account of Nabokov's language interests relates to an interview he gave to the *New York Times* in 1969. He was asked about how he would rate his standing in the literary world. He evaded the issue, instead responding:

> I often think there should exist a special typographical sign for a smile – some sort of concave mark, a supine round bracket, which I would now like to trace in reply to your question.

We now call this 'supine round bracket' a smiley :-)

World Book Day

In fact, today any language enthusiast is spoilt for choice. World Book Day is probably the most widely recognized event, organized by UNESCO to promote reading, publishing and copyright. It began in 1995, developing a previously celebrated Day of the Book (*Dia del llibre*) in Catalonia, held on this day, which is also the feast day of St George. In the UK and Ireland a related event is held in early March.

A second initiative was introduced in 2010, when each of the UN's official languages was given its special day. This date was chosen for English because it was the traditional birthday in 1564 (and deathday in 1616) of Shakespeare in the New Style calendar introduced into England in 1652. However, a linguistically more motivated English Language Day is celebrated later in the year (SEE 13 OCTOBER). An alternative would be to celebrate Spanish Language Day instead, for this date was also the one chosen by the UN in honour of Cervantes, whose birthday was close by, 22 April.

Shakespeare comes into his own in a different connection. In 2009 the Shakespeare Theater in Chicago introduced a Talk Like Shakespeare Day, to help break down the impression of difficulty many people have about the language of the plays and poems. The aim, as its website says, is 'to celebrate Shakespeare's birthday by bringing the spoken words of the playwright into their daily lives', with the longer-term aspiration that this will increase motivation to see or read the plays. It makes several suggestions, such as replacing *you* and *your* by *thou*, *thee* and *thy*, and using such verb endings as *-est* and *-eth* (*makest*, *maketh*). Friends might be addressed as *coz* or *cousin*, men as *sirrah*, women as *mistress*. Discourse markers such as *methinks* and *forsooth* could be introduced. And conversationalists might look out for idioms from Shakespeare that are used without a second thought, such as *to the manner born* and *seen better days*. Nor would the occasional quotation go amiss – as long, of course, as the speaker respects the maxim that brevity is the soul of wit.

Anthony Trollope was born in 1815

In his autobiography, published in 1883, the year after his death,
Trollope makes an interesting comment on style – interesting because
of its rarity. The nineteenth century was the heyday of grammatical
prescriptivism, when the strict rules governing how sentences should be
formed were instilled into children in school, often with great force. He
says he remembers little about his lessons, but the evidence of English
prescriptive teaching is there when he reflects on style. And this is what's
interesting. Novelists don't usually admit to following grammarians
so scrupulously, in the way he describes. Nor, for that matter, do they
follow their admission with such vivacious analogies.

> An author can hardly hope to be popular unless he can use popular
> language. That is quite true; but then comes the question of achieving a
> popular – in other words, I may say, a good and lucid style. How may an
> author best acquire a mode of writing which shall be agreeable and easily
> intelligible to the reader?
>
> He must be correct, because without correctness he can be neither
> agreeable nor intelligible. Readers will expect him to obey those rules
> which they, consciously or unconsciously, have been taught to regard
> as binding on language; and unless he does obey them, he will disgust.
> Without much labour, no writer will achieve such a style. He has very
> much to learn; and, when he has learned that much, he has to acquire the
> habit of using what he has learned with ease. But all this must be learned
> and acquired, – not while he is writing that which shall please, but long
> before.
>
> His language must come from him as music comes from the rapid touch
> of the great performer's fingers; as words come from the mouth of the
> indignant orator; as letters fly from the fingers of the trained compositor;
> as the syllables tinkled out by little bells form themselves to the ear of the
> telegraphist. A man who thinks much of his words as he writes them will
> generally leave behind him work that smells of oil.

License Plates Day

Vehicle registration plates have been known since 1893, when France became the first country to introduce them. This date, however, received its label in the United States – hence the American spelling – recalling the first time a state required one: New York in 1901. How many people recognize the day isn't at all clear. I've found no mention of its origins; it gets hardly any mention on websites; and it seems to be virtually unknown outside the USA. Its motivation, nonetheless, is understandable, for these plates have long held a fascination, not least among youngsters who (at least in times past – me being one) collected car numbers assiduously – clearly an early attempt at corpus linguistics.

Amongst adults, the fascination continues, though now plates are often seen as desirable markers of social or personal identity, over and above the requirements for unique legal identification. Several linguistic issues arise, such as the need to maintain legibility and avoid ambiguity, with some symbols posing particular problems (such as *0* vs *O*, or *I* and *1*). Then there are problems arising from real-word recognition. Licensing agencies can withhold certain sequences, such as *ARS* in English. The UK Licensing Authority states on its website:

> Such numbers are withheld if they are likely to cause offence or embarrassment to the general population in this country on the grounds of political, racial and religious sensitivities or simply because they are in poor taste when displayed correctly on a number plate.

The problem, of course, is how to interpret 'poor taste' and how to regulate 'offence' when plates are personalized. The same issues occur that can bedevil the notion of offensive language generally. So, for example, in 2017 a car owner in Manitoba, Canada, devised a plate with a *Star Trek* allusion: ASIMIL8. To any Trekkie, the reference is clearly to the cyborg bad guys who would shout 'you will be assimilated!' at their enemies. But there were complaints that it was offensive to indigenous people, for whom the memory of threatened assimilation was all too real. The plate had to be withdrawn.

Alien Day

The search for UFOs intensifies on World UFO Day, which has a double identity. For some it's 24 June, the date in 1947 of the first reported UFO in the United States; for others it's 2 July, the date of the alleged spacecraft crash at Roswell, New Mexico. Alien Day is of a different order: an annual event organized since 2016 by 20th Century Fox to promote the *Alien* franchise – the 1979 blockbuster film and its five sequels. The date is a reference to the name of the moon where the aliens were first discovered: LV-426.

How to communicate with aliens is a recurring theme in literature and cinema. Several extraterrestrial languages have now been created, such as Klingon in the *Star Trek* series and Na'vi for the film *Avatar*, and in *Arrival* we see how a language investigation might actually work. The field of study goes by various names: exolinguistics, xenolinguistics, astrolinguistics.

Alien languages have a long history. For many writers the extraterrestrial visitors just happen to speak an Earth language, such as English, but with an accent – as with the monotone syllabic speech of the Daleks in *Doctor Who* (SEE 8 AUGUST). For others it's a different language, using sounds, symbols, signs or other sensory media. One of the earliest accounts is the story of an imaginary journey to the Moon written in the 1620s by Bishop Francis Godwin, and published in 1638 – a very popular book in its day. He describes the language spoken by the people his traveller meets there, the Lunars:

> Their Language is very difficult, since it hath no Affinity with any other I ever heard, and consists not so much of Words and Letters, as Tunes and strange Sounds which no Letters can express, for there are few Words but signify several Things, and are distinguished only by their Sounds, which are sung as it were in uttering; yea many Words consist of Tunes only, without Words.

The thought that it was possible to have a musical language was common at the time, and reinforced by travellers' accounts of the tones of Chinese.

Morse Code Day

The day remembers the birth of American painter and inventor Samuel Morse (1791–1872). Along with his assistant Alford Vail and other collaborators he began to explore the potential of the new electric telegraph to transmit messages using a system of electrical pulses and silences. The first public demonstration was in January 1838 at the Speedwell Ironworks in New Jersey, when a message was sent across 2 miles of wire: 'A patient waiter is no loser' – an ironic reflection on the long and troublesome time (there had been rival claims for the invention of the telegraph) it had taken Morse to get his scheme to this stage. Later that year he demonstrated his system at the Capitol building in Washington, sending from the Supreme Court room to Vail in Baltimore a message (taken from the Bible) that would become famous: 'What hath God wrought.'

The efficiency of the system was due to its linguistic awareness, as well as its ability to operate through sound or light. Morse correlated the length of a letter in the code with the frequency with which it appeared in print – using as evidence the quantities of movable type in the type cases of a local newspaper. So, the most frequent letter in English, E, was given a single dot, the next most frequent, T, a single dash; and so on, until we reach four-unit strings for such letters as Q (- - - -) and Z (- - · ·). In 1851 an international code was developed, to allow for non-English letters, numerals and a few other symbols.

There have been several attempts to popularize the code, notably Learn Your Name in Morse Code Day, created in 2015 by Sheila Cicchi from Virginia. She chose 11 January, the date of that first demonstration of the system in 1838. So, in the spirit of that day, this is me, signing off:

- - · · · - · · · · - · · - · · - · · - · · · - · · · · - · · · · · · · - · - · · - · · · ·

National Great Poetry Reading Day

In 1996 the Academy of American Poets launched a National Poetry
Month in April, and this day motivates a special focus on the great names
in the poetic world. There are similar days in many countries. In the
UK, National Poetry Day is the first Thursday in October, but that's
no help for this book, as the date changes each year. So today has to be
an American poet, and one who says something about poetry and about
language. Emily Dickinson (SEE 10 DECEMBER) ticks both boxes: the first
was written in about 1864, the second in about 1872. Her poems need
their space to breathe.

> The Poets light but Lamps –
> Themselves – go out –
> The Wicks they stimulate –
> If vital light
>
> Inhere as do the Suns –
> Each Age a Lens
> Disseminating their
> Circumference –

> A word is dead
> When it is said,
>   Some say.
> I say it just
> Begins to live
>   That day.

Alfred Hitchcock died in 1980

Why remember this film director, born in London in 1899, in a daybook on language? Because he often drew parallels between film-making and literature, and had a lot to say in interviews about the balance between the visual and the textual. The biggest fault, he felt, was to rely on dialogue to tell a story: 'If it's a good movie, the sound could go off and the audience would still have a perfectly clear idea of what was going on.' This was not to belittle the script: 'To make a great film you need three things – the script, the script, and the script.' But when actually making the film, 'I don't look at the script while I'm shooting. I know it off by heart, just as an orchestra conductor needs not look at the score.'

He liked to draw a contrast with the novel:

> The screenwriter does not have the same leisure as the novelist to build up his characters. He must do this side by side with the unfolding of the first part of the narrative. However, by way of compensation, he has other resources not available to the novelist or the dramatist, in particular the use of things. This is one of the ingredients of true cinema. To put things together visually; to tell the story visually; to embody the action in the juxtaposition of images that have their own specific language and emotional impact – that is cinema.

So were there for him any literary forms that closely resemble film? He cited one, in an interview for *Cinema* (1963):

> Construction to me, it's like music. You start with your allegro, your andante and you build up. Don't forget even a symphony breaks itself into movements, but a motion picture doesn't. The nearest form to it is the short story. You've got to take it in at one sitting. A play you break into three acts. A book you pick up and put down again. A short story, you read through from beginning to end. That's why the motion picture is the nearest in its shape to the short story.

Otto Jespersen died in 1943

Born in Denmark in 1860, Jespersen was the most famous of a group
of European linguists who introduced the descriptive study of English
grammar – in his case, a massive seven-volume *Modern English Grammar
on Historical Principles*, published between 1909 and 1949. His greatest
general work was *Language: Its Nature, Development and Origin* (1922),
which includes one of the earliest studies of child language; and he
anticipated present-day sociolinguistics in *Mankind, Nation and Individual*
(1925). His lively approach is well illustrated by this chapter opening:

> The individual in his use of the language has constantly to improvise. He
> continually finds himself in new situations and has things to express which
> he has never before met in exactly the same shape. He is like a chess-
> player who at every move is faced with a position of the pieces which he
> has never seen, but who makes his move as he has done before in similar
> positions.

And he supplements this in an extended analogy with musical
improvisation.

He was the first linguist I know to publish a full autobiography, an
invaluable memoir of the development of language studies at the time.
All the famous linguists of the early twentieth century are there, and his
anecdotes and recollections of them are as interesting as the reflections
on his own writing. Published in 1938, *A Linguist's Life* is a large work,
over 300 pages in translation. From it I select this paragraph from a
chapter titled 'Retrospect'. It's a good model for any aspiring linguist.

> I am above all an observer; I quite simply cannot help making
> linguistic observations. In conversations at home and abroad, in railway
> compartments, when passing people in the street and on the road, I
> am constantly noticing oddities of pronunciation, forms, and sentence
> constructions – but more in my younger days than now, when much of
> what was then striking is familiar to me. I have jotted down much of what
> I have picked up in that way and have developed quite a skill in catching
> language subtleties on the wing.

The Great Exhibition opened in London in 1851

The *Great Exhibition of the Works of Industry of All Nations* took place in a specially designed glass-clad building (the 'crystal palace') in Hyde Park, and continued until 15 October. It was the first of what would later be called 'world fairs'. The *Official Descriptive and Illustrated Catalogue* of over 1,400 pages listed the objects on display, the enormous range suggested by the opening entries in its index:

absynthium	accumulator
accident detector	acetic acid
accordions	acolyte
accordion-stand	aconite and its preparations
account books	acorns
accoutrements, military	aelodian

From a linguistic point of view, it's the terminological proliferation that's so striking. Not only the objects, but the lexical items, were a source of wonder. Dozens of new formations are listed – over thirty entries for types of *steam* equipment, over fifty to do with *railways*. The *Catalogue* sometimes provides the first recorded use of an item, such as *sulphurator* (an apparatus for sprinkling plants with sulphur) or *Tahiti cane* (sugar cane). The toileting system installed by George Jennings – his so-called 'monkey closets' – gave rise to a new idiom. Visitors had to pay a penny fee to use them, hence the (now archaic) expression 'to spend a penny'.

A large literature grew out of the *Exhibition*. Many poems were written about it, and there were alphabet books, new guide books to London, satirical articles in *Punch* and several kinds of memorial. Some were multilingual, such as *A Memorial of the Great Industrial Exhibition of All Nations in London, 1851: Consisting of a Sentence from Holy Writ in Above One Hundred Languages*. The sentence was from the Acts of the Apostles: 'God hath made of one blood all nations of men.' As the author of the *Alphabetical Epitome of the Great Exhibition* put it, at his letter *E*:

E's th' Exhibition! Twas worthy the name
Of the nation that called to the nations that came!

123

The traditional publication date of the King James Bible in 1611

'Traditional' is important. Gordon Campbell explains in *Bible: The Story of the King James Version 1611–2011*, published for the 400th anniversary:

> Because the KJV was classified as a revision rather than a fresh translation, it does not appear in the register of new books known as the Stationers' Register. In the absence of a dated entry in the register, we are left without any knowledge of when in 1611 the KJV began to be sold. The popular notion that it was published on 2 May is often repeated, but is a myth: there was no such thing as a publication date in the seventeenth century.

On the other hand, the KJV does need to be present in any book representing important moments in the history of English, so I continue with this date, for want of a better.

The linguistic influence hasn't been in relation to vocabulary. Only twenty-seven words have a first recorded usage in the KJV (according to the *Oxford English Dictionary* in 2022), most with specialized meanings:

backsliding	gopher	nose-jewel
battering-ram	Hamathite	palmchrist
Benjamite	Laodicean	peaceable kingdom
confessing	light-minded	pruning hook
dissolver	maneh	shittah
escaper	miscarrying	skewed
exactress	Nazariteship	waymark
expansion	needleworker	whosoever
Galilean	nighthawk	withdrawing

It's in the area of idiom that the KJV has had its main impact. A significant number of expressions can be traced back to it – either because it originated them or because it was the conduit through which they came into the language. An expression such as *thorn in the flesh* is unique to the KJV, but *salt of the earth* is found in many earlier Bible translations. How many are in use today, though rarely recognized as being biblical in origin? For the book I wrote for the 2011 anniversary year – *Begat: The King James Bible and the English Language* – I found 257.

National Wordsmith Day

This is one of those 'days' about which it seems nothing is known, apart from the fact that it exists. After a lengthy search of online sources, I could find no information about who began the day, or when, or where. 'Why' it began is easy to answer, for there has long been a readiness to acknowledge skilled users or makers of words, and there are several online sites with this name, all claiming to be able to improve our linguistic skills. It also turns up a lot heading a games or puzzles page in newspapers and magazines.

Wordsmith as a coinage is quite recent: a first recorded usage is in 1873. It built on a tradition of *-smith* words that goes right back to Old English – or indeed before, for *smith* was a common Germanic word for a skilled worker in metal. A family of words developed, in which the skill became attached to other materials, such as *goldsmiths*, *tinsmiths* and *silversmiths*, then to objects, as in *locksmith*, then to abilities, as in *songsmith* and *jokesmith*, and most recently to online sites. There's a software package of search tools for work in corpus linguistics: it's called *WordSmith*.

In the seventeenth century the skilled user of words was acknowledged, but by a different suffix: a *wordman*. We see it in Henry Cockeram's *The English dictionarie; or, An interpreter of hard English words* (1623): 'A great Word man, *grandiloquus*'. *Worder* was also in use. The nineteenth century added a variant: *wordsman*, and we also find *word-painter*. Then there's twentieth-century *wordster* and *wordnik*.

If we go back to the sixteenth century we see *wordmonger*, which initially had a pejorative tone, referring to people who used lots of words but in an esoteric or pedantic way. Today usage is mixed: for some there's very little difference to being called a *wordmonger* or a *wordsmith*. For others it still retains a nuance of pretentious or careless usage – but not enough evidently to put off makers of apps and games, as in *Wordmonger*.

Star Wars Day

It would be difficult to find a day-related pun to beat this one. There can be few English-speaking people unaware of the catchphrase from the *Star Wars* films: 'May the force be with you', and the attraction of 'May the fourth' was evident soon after the first film was released in 1977. As the number of films in the series grew, so did the interest in using this day as a focus for fans, and in 2011 the informal celebrations began to be replaced by more formal publicity events organized by the film companies. As is the way with puns, enthusiasts looked for other instances. So we find 5 May and 6 May both used to remember the third episode of the series: 'Revenge of the Sith'. Which you choose depends on whether you think *fifth* or *sixth* is the better pun.

The association of 4 May with the catchphrase extended well beyond the world of cinema. In the UK it's most famously associated with the day Margaret Thatcher took office as prime minister on 4 May 1979. A Conservative Party ad in the *Evening News* congratulated her: 'May The Fourth Be With You, Maggie'. But all one has to do is arrange an event for this day – a recital, a race... – and the pun will almost certainly be made.

For linguists the series is a treasure trove – partly for the range of new alien languages devised for various characters, but also for the stylistic originality of the dialogue, notably the inverted word order in the way the Jedi master Yoda speaks, which has echoes of the syntax of Old English. Phrases that would normally go at the end of a sentence are brought forward to front position, as in this example of a double inversion in *The Return of the Jedi*: 'When nine hundred years old you reach, look as good you will not.' Yoda's speech isn't consistent, but there are enough instances of this device to give listeners the overall impression of someone who comes from a different linguistic world.

Portuguese Language Day

The day was officially established in 2009 by the Community of Portuguese-speaking Countries, and in 2019 UNESCO made it a world day – the first time such a status had been given to a language that isn't an official medium at the United Nations. The case was supported by two facts: Portuguese is the most widely spoken language in the southern hemisphere, notably in Brazil; and it was a leading language during the first wave of globalization, introducing loan words into many languages.

It's actually problematic deciding how many words have come into English from Portuguese, whether European or Brazilian, as it's often unclear whether the words arrived via Spanish or some other language. But there are several clear etymologies – musical names such as *samba* and *bossa nova*; fauna such as *cobra* and *piranha*; food and drink such as *mango, marmalade, caipirinha* and *cachaça*.

The loan words dramatically increase when talking or writing about a cultural event in one of the Portuguese-speaking cultures. I built up quite a large vocabulary during visits to Brazil, often in February when the Rio carnival was taking place. An English conversation with Brazilian teachers would regularly include such expressions as the *escolas de samba* ('samba schools') that would be taking part in *Carnaval* (note the spelling) in the *desfile* (dess-*fee*-lay, 'parade') at the *Sambadrome* – the specially built venue, opened in 1984. There would be talk about the amazing *fantasias* ('costumes') and *mascaras* ('masks') the *passistas* ('dancers') would be wearing – and about the *enredos* (the theme chosen by each school) and the *bateria* (ba-tuh-*ree*-a, the drum section that drives the dancing along, containing a diverse array of percussion).

The conversations could become very technical, as people named *bateria* instruments, such as the *surdo* ('bass drum'), the *caixa* (*ky*-sha, a small snare drum) and the highly distinctive *cuica* (*kwee*-ka, a single-headed drum that produces voice-like high-pitched tones as the fingers rub an internal stick hanging down from the centre of the drum skin). After a while, I lost track of whether I was speaking English or Portuguese.

Henry David Thoreau died in 1862

This American philosopher, poet and environmentalist, born
in Massachusetts in 1817, is best known for his book *Walden*, a
memoir describing his two-year experiment in simple living in
natural surroundings: *Walden; or, Life in the Woods* (1854). Perhaps
unexpectedly, this contains several reflections on language: there are
sections on Reading, Sounds, and – less obviously – Visitors, but the
reason is quickly apparent, as he explains:

> One inconvenience I sometimes experienced in so small a house, the
> difficulty of getting to a sufficient distance from my guest when we began
> to utter the big thoughts in big words. You want room for your thoughts
> to get into sailing trim and run a course or two before they make their
> port. The bullet of your thought must have overcome its lateral and
> ricochet motion and fallen into its last and steady course before it reaches
> the ear of the hearer, else it may plough out again through the side of his
> head. Also, our sentences wanted room to unfold and form their columns
> in the interval. Individuals, like nations, must have suitable broad and
> natural boundaries, even a considerable neutral ground, between them. I
> have found it a singular luxury to talk across the pond to a companion on
> the opposite side.

It's in his *Journals* that we see the most diverse set of linguistic
reflections, such as this one from 1845:

> There is a memorable interval between the written and the spoken
> language, the language read and the language heard. The one is transient,
> a sound, a tongue, a dialect, and all men learn it of their mothers. It is
> loquacious, fragmentary, – raw material. The other is a reserved, select,
> matured expression, a deliberate word addressed to the ear of nations and
> generations.

Or this eminently quotable observation from 1840:

> A word is wiser than any man, than any series of words. In its present
> received sense it may be false, but in its inner sense by descent and
> analogy it approves itself. Language is the most perfect work of art in the
> world. The chisel of a thousand years retouches it.

Kate Swift died in 2011

This is a day that needs to be shared. Born in New York in 1923, Swift was an American writer and editor who introduced a groundbreaking feminist perspective into English in the 1970s. But she didn't do it alone. She worked with her companion Casey Miller (1919–1997). Together they formed an editorial partnership in 1970, and it was when they were asked to copy-edit a sex-education manual for junior high-school students that it dawned on them how the male writer's message was being obscured by the language. As Swift put it in a 1994 interview:

> We suddenly realized what was keeping his message – his good message – from getting across, and it hit us like a bombshell. It was the pronouns! They were overwhelmingly masculine gendered. We turned in the manuscript with our suggestions such as putting singular sexist pronouns into plural gender-free ones, avoiding pronouns wherever possible, and changing word order so that girls or women sometimes preceded rather than always followed boys or men. The publisher accepted some suggestions and not others as always happens. But we had been revolutionized.

Today, when people are so aware of the pronoun problem, it's easy to forget that the movement to introduce gender-neutral expression had a beginning. Two important articles followed: 'Desexing the English Language' in the inaugural issue of *Ms.* magazine, and 'One Small Step for Genkind' in the *New York Times Magazine*. And then the book which first alerted me to them: *Words and Women: New Language in New Times* (1976, revised 1991). It was followed by their influential *The Handbook of Nonsexist Writing: For Writers, Editors, and Speakers* (1980). Not all their suggestions were taken up. Their proposal to replace the *he/her/his* series by *tey/ter/tem* joined a host of later coinages that have never received general acceptance. But the work of these two far-sighted women influenced many people at the time – including me. The first edition of my Penguin *Linguistics* was published in 1971, and it was full of male pronouns. I got rid of them for the second edition a decade later.

Allen Mawer was born in 1879

A philologist, born in London, Mawer is remembered for his work in the early decades of the twentieth century on the Vikings in Britain, and then more generally on English place-names, founding in 1923 the English Place-Name Society. Its aim was to conduct a county-by-county survey of the place names of England. The first one, of Buckinghamshire, appeared in 1925. Meanwhile Mawer had published two important books: *Introduction to the Survey of English Place-Names* (with Frank Stenton), and *Chief Elements used in English Place-Names*. By the time of his death in 1942, the Society had published many volumes, and to date almost all the counties have been surveyed to some degree, with over ninety volumes in their list.

When I arrived at University College London in 1959, it was to enter a place-name world, as at the time this was the headquarters of the Society, under the direction of Hugh Smith. In 1972 it moved to the University of Nottingham, where it remains. I learned that far more was involved than simply the names of villages, towns, cities and counties. There were fieldwork trips into the countryside, where local people would be asked about the origin of the names of fields, hills, streets, streams, rivers and other notable geographical features.

It's a hundred years since Mawer made his important statement, in a 1922 lecture on 'Place-names and history':

> It is only within the last twenty years or so ... that the great truth has been established which lies at the base of all place-name study, viz., that it is impossible to place any satisfactory interpretation upon the history of a name until we have traced it as far back as the records will allow, and that in many cases, unless the records go a good way back, speculations upon its meaning are worse than useless.

He was writing at the beginning of a scientific revolution in place-name study, in which records became increasingly accessible and searchable. Since the end of the nineteenth century the subject has a recognized technical name – or, rather, set of names: *toponomy*, *toponymics* or *toponomastics*.

Freya Stark died in 1993

She was an explorer and travel writer, born in Paris in 1893, whose
journeys throughout the Middle East and Afghanistan led to several
acclaimed books, beginning with *The Valleys of the Assassins* (1934). Her
language skills, especially Arabic and Persian, gave her opportunities for
close interaction with the people, and she provides illuminating accounts
of local culture, customs and behaviour which often have a linguistic
dimension, as in this extract from an interview she gave in 1977. She was
asked what it was like to be in a nomad camp:

> They have certain manners that I think are delightful. One is that you
> don't have to talk all the time. If you have something to say, you say it.
> But they don't mind a circle of ten or twelve or twenty people, quite quiet
> and silent, who haven't anything much to say. And then, if someone *has*,
> they say it. These pleasant pauses are so agreeable that one is inclined to
> get into the habit, and it isn't the thing at all in a European drawing room.

And she adds: 'Conversation is a whole art which, I have a theory, comes
from the fact that the lighting in their tents has never been good enough
for reading. You can't really do anything except sit and talk.'

She makes general observations too, such as this excursus on science
and art in the diary section of *A Winter in Arabia* (1940) – the quotation
is from Milton:

> The scientist simply *states*, the artist *evokes*. Instead of relying on words
> alone, he lets the reader's mind fill in the meaning, and, in the measure
> of his magnanimity, will trust to what his reader can supply. It is
> collaboration, as between player and instrument.
>
> 'Avenge oh Lord thy slaughtered saints whose bones
> Lie scattered on the Alpine mountains *cold*.'

In the language of science, the adjective merely applies to the rocks of the
hillside; but the poet knows that in the mind of his readers it awakens the
vision of the cold and stiffened bodies of dead men.

Thomas Young died in 1829

Born in Somerset in 1773, Young became a physician, and was widely regarded as the greatest polymath of his age, best known today for his innovative work in physics. Linguists respect him for laying the foundations of the approach that eventually enabled Jean-François Champollion to decipher Egyptian hieroglyphics using the Rosetta Stone. His other claim to a place in the history of linguistics appeared in 1813, when he wrote a hugely detailed 42-page review of a general history of languages by a German philologist, Johann Cristoph Adelung. It includes these words:

> Another ancient and extensive class of languages, united by a greater number of resemblances than can well be altogether accidental, may be denominated the Indoeuropean, comprehending the Indian, the West Asiatic, and almost all the European languages. If we chose to assign a geographical situation to the common parent of this class, we should place it to the south and west of the supposed origin of the human race.

This is the first recorded use of the label *Indo-European*.

His views were surprisingly modern. Many of his observations wouldn't be out of place in any present-day introduction to socio-linguistics. For example, his review includes one of the earliest presentations of the problem, much addressed in the twentieth century, of the distinction between a dialect and a language:

> It appears to be most convenient to consider as separate languages, or as distinct species in a systematic classification, all those which require to be separately studied in order to be readily understood, and which have their distinct grammatical flexions and constructions; and to regard, as varieties only, those dialects which are confessedly local and partial diversities of a language manifestly identical. It is however absolutely impossible to fix a correct and positive criterion of the degree of variation which is to constitute in this sense a distinct language: for instance, whether Danish and Swedish are two languages or two dialects of one, and whether the modern Romaic is Greek or not, might be disputed without end, but could never be absolutely decided.

Douglas Adams died in 2001

He was a writer of comedic science fiction, born in Cambridge in 1952, and best known for the radio and television series *The Hitchhiker's Guide to the Galaxy*, which led to a variety of books and spin-offs. Observations about language are scattered throughout his writing, and some of his imaginings have had a life outside his novels, such as the *Babel fish*, 'small, yellow and leechlike': 'If you stick a Babel fish in your ear you can instantly understand anything said to you in any form of language.' It was used for a while as the name of an online translator, and still has currency when alluding to automatic translation.

Then there are comments like this one, from *The Hitchhiker's Guide*:

> One of the things Ford Prefect had always found hardest to understand about humans was their habit of continually stating and repeating the very very obvious, as in *It's a nice day*, or *You're very tall*, or *Oh dear you seem to have fallen down a thirty-foot well, are you all right?* At first Ford had formed a theory to account for this strange behaviour. If human beings don't keep exercising their lips, he thought, their mouths probably seize up. After a few months' consideration and observation he abandoned this theory in favour of a new one. If they don't keep exercising their lips, he thought, their brains start working.

A more explicit linguistically oriented book is *The Meaning of Liff* (1983), co-written with John Lloyd, in which place names are given a new definition, such as *Aynho* in England, glossed as a verb: 'Of waiters, never to have a pen'. The preface to the first edition explains:

> The world is littered with thousands of spare words which spend their time doing nothing but loafing about on signposts pointing at places. Our job, as we see it, is to get these words down off the signposts and into the mouths of babes and sucklings and so on, where they can start earning their keep in everyday conversation and make a more positive contribution to society.

National Limerick Day

Writer and illustrator Edward Lear was born on this day in 1812. He's best known for *A Book of Nonsense* (1846), containing 112 poems, each accompanied by a comedic drawing. The poems had a rhyming pattern of *AABBA*, with the two *B* rhymes on one line. This is the opener:

> There was an Old Man with a nose,
> Who said, 'If you choose to suppose
> That my nose is too long, you are certainly wrong!'
> That remarkable Man with a nose.

The third line was later split into two, resulting in the familiar five-line form now called the limerick. The last word in the final line would also usually be different from the last word in the first. But the content stayed, with the opening line introducing a person and with attributes.

Where did the name come from? Lear died in 1888, and didn't use the term. It's first recorded in 1896 in a letter by artist Aubrey Beardsley. There was a tradition of improvised nonsense singing in Ireland among soldiers' gatherings which had a chorus 'Will you come up to Limerick?' A likely theory is that the name was an allusion by writers of the Irish Literary Revival, such as Yeats, to the Maigue Poets, an eighteenth-century bardic school who met in and around Croom on the River Maigue, just south of Limerick. A verse inscription outside a tavern there offered a free drink to any passing poet – a custom sadly lost today.

Lear didn't invent the limerick. Shakespeare, for example, has a drinking song in *Othello* (a *canakin* was a small can of ale):

> And let me the canakin clink, clink;
> And let me the canakin clink;
> A soldier's a man
> O, man's life's but a span;
> Why, then, let a soldier drink.

There's even a Latin example in the writing of the medieval theologian Thomas Aquinas. But Lear was certainly the one who brought this poetic form to the attention of a wide public.

Feast day of Mother Julian of Norwich

She wrote the first book in English that we know was authored by a woman. Julian may have been her real name (it was used for both men and women in the Middle Ages), or it could have been given to her because she was a parishioner of St Julian's church in the city. She was an anchoress – a woman who retreated from the world into a closed cell to live a life of prayer and meditation. Little is known about her, other than occasional contemporary mentions and a few personal details in her book *Revelations of Divine Love* – a series of visions she received in May 1373 when, aged 30, she was seriously ill. It isn't known when she died. The last reference to her is dated 1416.

One sentence from her work has become widely known, often quoted in this form: 'And all shall be well and All manner of thing shall be well.' It appears in her account of the thirteenth revelation, and is often repeated in later chapters. To capture the flavour of her writing, here is one instance of it, from chapter 32, in the semi-modern translation by Grace Warrack in 1901:

> One time our good Lord said: *All thing shall be well*; and another time he said: *Thou shalt see thyself that all* MANNER *thing shall be well*; and in these two the soul took sundry understandings.
>
> One was that He willeth we know that not only He taketh heed to noble things and to great, but also to little and to small, to low and to simple, to one and to other. And so meaneth He in that He saith: All manner of things *shall be well*. For He willeth we know that the least thing shall not be forgotten.

And she concludes:

> And thus in these same five words aforesaid: *I may make all things well*, etc., I understand a mighty comfort of all the works of our Lord God that are yet to come.

International Dylan Thomas Day

The day was launched at Swansea University in 2015 as a celebration of the life and work of the Welsh poet, born in Swansea in 1914. It was chosen to commemorate the first time his play *Under Milk Wood* was read in 1953 at 92Y The Poetry Center, New York, during one of his American tours. He died in New York during a further tour later that year.

Thomas is often cited in linguistic approaches to English style for his distinctive poetic prose and the daring way in which he breaks normal collocation expectations, as in such phrases as *a grief ago* and *all the sun long*, his capturing of the rhythms and intonations of the speech of his Welsh characters, and his exploitation of the phonaesthetic power of individual sounds and words. His letters frequently include comments on his language likes and dislikes, as in a long letter to writer Pamela Hansford Johnson in December 1933, in which he tells her about his favourite words:

> The greatest single word I know is 'drome', which, for some reason, nearly opens the doors of heaven for me. Say it yourself, out aloud, and see if you hear the golden gates swing backward as the last, long sound of the 'm' fades away. 'Drome', 'bone', 'dome, doom', 'province', 'dwell', 'prove', 'dolomite' – these are only a few of my favourite words, which are insufferably beautiful to me. The first four words are visionary: God moves in a long 'o'.

His many letters, not as well known as *Under Milk Wood* or his short stories and poems, have been collected in an anthology edited by Paul Harris. They are full of novel metaphorical word associations, often combined into single sentences – such as this one, from another letter to Pamela in May 1934:

> And does the oneeyed ferryman, who cannot read a printed word, row over a river of words, where the syllables of the fish dart out & are caught on his rhyming hook, or feel himself a total ghost in a world that's as matter-of-fact as a stone?

First use in 1907 of the word *blurb*

It's a rare event when a word's birthday can be identified, so this one deserves its celebratory day. It happened when American humourist and illustrator Gelett Burgess (1866–1951) spoke at the annual dinner of the American Booksellers Association in New York. The guests had received a limited edition of *Are You a Bromide?* that had been published in 1906. A special dust jacket had been printed for the occasion, and above the title were these words in bold print:

YES, this is a 'BLURB'!
All the Other Publishers commit them. Why Shouldn't We?

Beneath was a picture in an oval frame of a woman shouting something. To the left was her name: 'Miss Belinda Blurb'. To the right: 'in the act of blurbing'. Further down was a puff from the publisher, full of high-blown praise. Two of its sentences illustrate the tone:

> We consider that this man Burgess has got Henry James locked into the coal-bin, asking for 'Information'. ... When you've READ this masterpiece, you'll know what a BOOK is.

The next day the *New York Times* reported on the dinner, giving us the word's first public usage. It caught on. Any testimonial for a book, on front or back covers, was soon being called a blurb. In his *New Dictionary of Words You Have Always Needed* (1914), Burgess defined his term:

> NOUN 1 A flamboyant advertisement; an inspired testimonial.
>   2 Fulsome praise; a sound like a publisher.
> VERB To flatter from interested motives; to compliment oneself.

Usually all we can say about the origins of a word is that it appeared 'in the late sixteenth century' or 'in the early 1990s'. The unabridged online *Oxford English Dictionary* gives citations for the first recorded usage of all its words; but in most cases a word will have been in use for some unknown years in speech before it ever came to be written down. We don't know the exact moment that Burgess coined the word, but the New York dinner event is certainly when he announced it.

National Biographer's Day

The day was chosen to commemorate the first meeting between Samuel Johnson and the man who would become his biographer, James Boswell. It took place in Thomas Davies's bookshop in Covent Garden, London, and we have Boswell's precise dating for it in his *Life of Samuel Johnson*. It illustrates the perils that can accompany any would-be biographer.

> At last, on Monday the 16th of May, when I was sitting in Mr. Davies's back-parlour, after having drunk tea with him and Mrs. Davies, Johnson unexpectedly came into the shop; and Mr. Davies having perceived him through the glass-door in the room in which we were sitting, advancing towards us, – he announced his aweful approach to me, somewhat in the manner of an actor in the part of Horatio, when he addresses Hamlet on the appearance of his father's ghost, 'Look, my Lord, it comes.' ...
>
> Mr. Davies mentioned my name, and respectfully introduced me to him. I was much agitated; and recollecting his prejudice against the Scotch, of which I had heard much, I said to Davies, 'Don't tell where I come from.' – 'From Scotland,' cried Davies roguishly. 'Mr. Johnson, (said I) I do indeed come from Scotland, but I cannot help it.' ... this speech was somewhat unlucky; for with that quickness of wit for which he was so remarkable, he seized the expression 'come from Scotland,' which I used in the sense of being of that country; and, as if I had said that I had come away from it, or left it, retorted, 'That, Sir, I find, is what a very great many of your countrymen cannot help.' This stroke stunned me a good deal; and when we had sat down, I felt myself not a little embarrassed ...

After a second put-down, he thinks his chances of a further meeting are over. 'And, in truth, had not my ardour been uncommonly strong, and my resolution uncommonly persevering, so rough a reception might have deterred me for ever from making any further attempts.' But the two struck up a friendship, and the biography was published in 1791.

Anna Brownell Jameson was born in 1894

Born in Dublin, Jameson moved to London as a child, and became well known as a writer in several fields, including Shakespeare, travel, women's education and suffrage, and especially art history and appreciation, notably in her six-volume series *The Poetry of Sacred and Legendary Art*, the final two books published after her death in 1860. She made several observations about language in *A Commonplace Book of Thoughts, Memories and Fancies* (1855), such as this:

> It is one of the most serious mistakes in Education that we are not sufficiently careful to habituate children to the accurate use of words. Accuracy of language is one of the bulwarks of truth. If we looked into the matter we should probably find that all the varieties and modifications of conscious and unconscious lying – as exaggeration, equivocation, evasion, misrepresentation – might be traced to the early misuse of words; therefore the contemptuous, careless tone in which people say sometimes 'words – words – mere words!' is unthinking and unwise.

Her Preface includes an insightful justification of the commonplace book as a literary genre, and offers a stimulus to others, who might never have thought of doing such a thing, to go and do likewise.

> For many years I have been accustomed to make a memorandum of any thought which might come across me – (if pen and paper were at hand), and to mark (and *remark*) any passage in a book which excited either a sympathetic or an antagonistic feeling. This collection of notes accumulated insensibly from day to day.… A book so supremely egotistical and subjective can do good only in one way. It may, like conversation with a friend, open up sources of sympathy and reflection; excite to argument, agreement, or disagreement; and, like every spontaneous utterance of thought out of an earnest mind, suggest far higher and better thoughts than any to be found here to higher and more productive minds. If I had not the humble hope of such a possible result, instead of sending these memoranda to the printer, I should have thrown them into the fire …

International Museum Day

The day was created in 1946–7 by the International Council of Museums, an organization whose mission, as stated on its website, is a commitment 'to the research, conservation, continuation and communication to society of the world's natural and cultural heritage, present and future, tangible and intangible'. The day has been recognized since 1977, its aim being to raise awareness about the importance of museums as a means of cultural exchange, enrichment of cultures, and development of peace among peoples.

There are very few museums or 'houses' dedicated to language around the world (SEE ALSO 15 APRIL). The largest, opened in 2020, is Planet Word in Washington. One of the smallest is Mundolingua in Paris. In between, several cities have museums devoted to the national language of a country or to local linguistic diversity, such as the Canadian Language Museum, but places devoted to language in general, and to all the languages of the world, are still few and far between – certainly compared with the coverage given to such areas as art, science and natural history. There have been some ingenious ideas, such as the World of Languages pop-up museum devised at the University of Cambridge in 2019, which travelled around before being curtailed by the pandemic. And at a local level, schools, libraries and community centres have developed exhibitions, competitions and other initiatives.

Proposals to create permanent institutions have sometimes been made – in London in the 1990s, in Barcelona in the 2000s, and elsewhere – but they fell through for a combination of political and financial reasons. The Internet has helped fill the gap. There are some online presences now, such as the National Language Museum, based in Maryland, USA, founded in 2008. One of the fullest accounts of the world situation is also available online, produced by the Centre for Norwegian Language and Literature, and edited by Ottar Grepstad. But nothing replaces the experience of being in a building, interacting with the exhibits, and sharing the enthusiasm and excitement of other visitors.

John Betjeman died in 1984

Born in London in 1906, Betjeman became a journalist and broadcaster, well known for his guidebooks on church architecture; he was best known as a poet, becoming the British Poet Laureate in 1972 until his death. He doesn't comment on language often in his poems, but when he does it's sharp observation about social issues, most famously in 'How to Get on in Society', where he parodies class-related speech habits:

> Phone for the fish knives, Norman
> As cook is a little unnerved;
> You kiddies have crumpled the serviettes
> And I must have things daintily served.

The lexical choices are sensitive: *phone* for *telephone*, *serviettes* for *napkins*, and the distant *cook* instead of a proper name.

There's an explicit sociolinguistic comment in 'Beside the Seaside', where he describes the behaviour of families at the beach:

> A single topic occupies our minds.
> 'Tis hinted at or boldly blazoned in
> Our accents, clothes and ways of eating fish,
> And being introduced and taking leave,
> 'Farewell', 'So long', 'Bunghosky', 'Cheeribye' –
> That topic all-absorbing, as it was,
> Is now and ever shall be, to us – CLASS.

Bunghosky is now long obsolete. It was an early-twentieth-century affectation to attach *-ski* to words, in a humorous imitation of Russian – added here to *bung-ho*, used as a drinking toast (*bung* being a stopper in a bottle) or when leaving.

He makes just one reference to language, in *High and Low* (1966):

> The English language has such range,
> Such rhymes and half-rhymes, rhythms strange,
> And such variety of tone,
> It has a music of its own. ...
> For endless changes can be rung
> On church-bells of the English tongue.

A Comprehensive Grammar of the
English Language was published in 1985

The twentieth century was a period when the study of English grammar
broke free from the prescriptive approach to the language, which
had been the norm since the eighteenth century, characterized by the
imposition of inauthentic rules governing how the language should
and should not be used. In its place evolved a descriptive approach,
aiming to provide an account of English in all its reality and diversity.
Early works included Otto Jespersen's *Modern English Grammar on
Historical Principles* (SEE 30 APRIL), but this, along with other grammars
written during the first half of the century, was illustrated mainly
from the written language. The study of spoken English had to await
technological developments, in the form of tape recorders, that would
enable samples of speech to be subjected to the same kind of rigorous
analysis as had traditionally been devoted to writing. These began to be
commercially available only after the 1930s.

Enter, in 1959, the Survey of English Usage, founded by Randolph
Quirk (SEE 12 JULY), and based in the English department at University
College London. This was the first attempt to provide a systematic survey
of spoken and written English grammar, with speech samples being taken
from everyday conversation as well as special settings such as sports commentary, sermons, lectures, speeches and broadcast talks programmes.
Careful attention was paid to the intonation, tones of voice and pauses
that provide the 'punctuation of speech', within which grammar operates.

Over a decade later the first fruits of the approach were published
as *A Grammar of Contemporary English* (1972) by the team of Randolph
Quirk, Sidney Greenbaum, Geoffrey Leech and Jan Svartvik. Then,
after a further decade of research, came this much larger work from
the same team, far more comprehensive in scope, as its title suggests,
with the addition of an index compiled by me. Its publication led to a
number of derivative works for use in teaching contexts, such as my own
Rediscover Grammar; and the approach continues to be influential, as seen
in the online grammar resource enticingly named *Englicious*.

World Day for Cultural Diversity for Dialogue and Development

UNESCO adopted its Universal Declaration on Cultural Diversity in 2001, and the following year the UN General Assembly inaugurated this day. Its aim is to acknowledge the world's cultural diversity and affirm the contribution of culture to sustainable development. The notion of dialogue is critical. As the UN website puts it:

> Equitable exchange and dialogue among civilizations, cultures and peoples, based on mutual understanding and respect and the equal dignity of all cultures, is the essential prerequisite for constructing social cohesion, reconciliation among peoples and peace among nations. ...
>
> Within the larger framework of intercultural dialogue, which also encompasses interreligious dialogue, special focus is placed on a series of good practices to encourage cultural pluralism at the local, regional and national level as well as regional and sub-regional initiatives aimed at discouraging all expressions of extremism and fanaticism and highlighting values and principles that bring people together. ...
>
> Development is inseparable from culture. In this regard, the major challenge is to convince political decision-makers and local, national and international social actors to integrate the principles of cultural diversity and the values of cultural pluralism into all public policies, mechanisms and practices, particularly through public/private partnerships.

A linguistic dimension is implicit in all these statements, and explicit in the notion of 'equitable dialogue'. That requires a recognition of the two main forces that underlie any use of language: the need for intelligibility and the need for identity. We need to make ourselves understood without feeling it necessary to defend the individual way we speak, such as in our choice of accent, dialect or language; and we need to adopt the same perspective when listening to what others are saying. It's a difficult balance to achieve, and the fact that it has so often failed is one of the motivations behind this day.

Arthur Conan Doyle was born in 1859

The fame of this Edinburgh-born writer and physician, who died in 1930, rests almost entirely on his crime novels and short stories – hence the alternative name for today: Sherlock Holmes Day. I haven't found linguistic topics discussed in his writing, apart from passing references, but he had a great deal to say about the role of literature and the value of reading.

In 1894 he wrote a series of articles which he turned into a memoir, *Through the Magic Door*, serialized in 1906–7. The 'magic door' is the entrance into literature, as its opening paragraph reveals. His style is of its age, and we have to ignore present-day feelings of discomfort over the use of 'man' to appreciate the underlying sentiment. Replace it by 'writer' or 'author', and choose pronouns to suit.

> I care not how humble your bookshelf may be, nor how lowly the room which it adorns. Close the door of that room behind you, shut off with it all the cares of the outer world, plunge back into the soothing company of the great dead, and then you are through the magic portal into that fair land whither worry and vexation can follow you no more. You have left all that is vulgar and all that is sordid behind you. There stand your noble, silent comrades, waiting in their ranks. Pass your eye down their files. Choose your man. And then you have but to hold up your hand to him and away you go together into dreamland. Surely there would be something eerie about a line of books were it not that familiarity has deadened our sense of it. Each is a mummified soul embalmed in cere-cloth and natron of leather and printer's ink. Each cover of a true book enfolds the concentrated essence of a man. The personalities of the writers have faded into the thinnest shadows, as their bodies into impalpable dust, yet here are their very spirits at your command.

The books on the shelves described in his memoir are his own. The invitation to explore is for everyone.

Eric Partridge's *Dictionary of Slang* is given a glowing review in the *New York Times* in 1937

It might seem unusual to devote a day to a rave review of a book, but this was a very unusual book, and nobody – least of all the author – had expected it. Its full title was: *A Dictionary of Slang and Unconventional English* – with the further explanation on the jacket: 'from the Fifteenth Century to the Present Day', and underneath the title we read:

> Slang and Colloquialisms
> Vulgarisms and Solecisms
> Language of the Underworld
> Nicknames and Catch-Phrases
> Inclusive of Naturalized Americanisms

The review was by Dilworth Faber, who was himself planning a dictionary of American slang. And in his opening words he homes in on the issue that was causing such a furore in Britain.

> The lost words of the language have finally come to roost.
> The unmentionables are mentioned.

At the time this book was published, British obscenity laws prohibited any words deemed to be vulgar to be printed in full. Asterisks replaced the vowels in such words as *f*ck*. This wasn't enough to satisfy the sensibilities of the time, and for many years the *Dictionary* was not to be found on the open shelves of libraries.

In the Preface to his first edition, he notes that previous dictionaries had either omitted vulgarisms or been judiciously selective. He states categorically: 'I have given them all.' And adds:

> My rule, in the matter of unpleasant terms, has been to deal with them as briefly, as astringently, as aseptically as was consistent with clarity and adequacy; in a few instances, I had to force myself to overcome an instinctive repugnance; for these I ask the indulgence of my readers.

The asterisks were dropped in due course, and the book emerged from library back rooms. By the time he died, in 1979 at the age of 85, the *Dictionary* had become a landmark in the history of lexicography.

The first printed catalogue of
library holdings was published in 1595

It happened at Leiden University in the Netherlands. The library was
founded in 1587, with just a few books in a small room, but within
a few years the collection needed to move into larger premises. The
catalogue had the Latin title *Nomenclator autorum omnium, quorum
libri vel manuscripti, vel typis expressi exstant in Bibliotheca Academiae
Lugduno-Batavae* – 'List of all authors whose books, whether manuscript
or printed, are available in Leiden University Library'.

This was the first attempt at a public catalogue for any institutional
library. A contemporary print shows large folio volumes laid out on
twenty-two shelves, and grouped into themes: theology, literature,
philosophy, mathematics, history, medicine and law. Each book was
chained to a rod above a slanting shelf, so that readers were able to tilt
them out, consult them, but not remove them.

Anyone who has used a library will be familiar with the idea of classification, whether through simple headings on shelves or a comprehensive
hierarchy such as Melvil Dewey's numerical system, though the extent
of the differences between the many approaches is often not appreciated. A classification system, or taxonomy, isn't an easy thing to create.
Hundreds of decisions have to be made, and these will reflect cultural,
political and intellectual preoccupations. Should Crafts be part of Arts or
separate? Which countries should go under 'Middle East'?

The number of subdivisions within a category is frequently
contentious, and it can be some time before they're universally
accepted, as with the families of natural history. A subclassification
is always influenced by the theoretical stance of the classifier. In the
field of language: is phonetics part of linguistics or a separate science?
is morphology (the study of word structure) a separate area within
grammar, or should we see it as a part of syntax (the 'syntax of the
word')? and where should we place a 'compound' topic such as the
'psychology of language'? Decisions have to be made, and the more we
understand the taxonomy, the easier it will be to find what we want.

Bede died in 735

Saint Bede – *Bæda* in Old English – was born in about 672, and became a monk at Jarrow in north-east England. He wrote over sixty works on history, geography and science, as well as biblical commentaries, lives of the saints, hymns and poems. His account of the origins of English in the *Historia Ecclesiastica Gentis Anglorum* ('The Ecclesiastical History of the English People') is an essential part of English language history, as it's the earliest literary source we have for the events which shaped the linguistic character of the nation. In his opening chapter he tells us:

> This island at present ... contains five nations, the English, Britons, Scots, Picts and Latins, each in its own peculiar dialect cultivating the sublime study of Divine truth. The Latin tongue is, by the study of the Scriptures, become common to all the rest.

He reports the arrival of the Anglo-Saxons in 449, and gives us an account of where they came from:

> Those who came over were of the three most powerful nations of Germany – Saxons, Angles and Jutes. From the Jutes are descended the people of Kent, and of the Isle of Wight, and those also in the province of the West-Saxons who are to this day called Jutes, seated opposite to the Isle of Wight. From the Saxons, that is, the country which is now called Old Saxony, came the East-Saxons, the South-Saxons, and the West-Saxons. From the Angles, that is, the country which is called Anglia, and which is said, from that time, to remain desert to this day, between the provinces of the Jutes and the Saxons, are descended the East-Angles, the Midland-Angles, Mercians, all the race of the Northumbrians, that is, of those nations that dwell on the north side of the river Humber, and the other nations of the English.

Even though there are problems interpreting exactly what Bede meant, it's clear that Britain was multi-ethnic and multilingual – or, at the very least, multidialectal – from the outset.

Samuel Pepys died in 1703

Born in London in 1633, Pepys was a leading member of London society after the restoration of the monarchy in 1660, rising to become chief secretary to the Admiralty. From 1660 for nearly a decade he kept a daily diary, written in shorthand, and shown to nobody during his lifetime, but carefully preserved. It was deciphered and published in the nineteenth century, when it was found to be one of the best sources of information about life and times during that decade – of especial interest because of his coverage of the Great Plague of 1665 and the Great Fire of London in 1666. Failing eyesight caused him to stop writing in 1669.

His entries on the Plague have particular resonance during a pandemic:

> 16th August 1665, after going to his office: Thence to the Exchange, where I have not been a great while. But, Lord! how sad a sight it is to see the streets empty of people, and very few upon the 'Change. Jealous [suspiciously watchful] of every door that one sees shut up, lest it should be the plague; and about us two shops in three, if not more, generally shut up.

Apart from the linguistic interest in his system of shorthand, and the multilingual code-switching when he talks about his amorous adventures ('she was to my thinking at this time une de plus pretty mohers that ever I did voir in my vida, and God forgive me my mind did run sobre elle all the vespre and night and la day suivants'), the diaries contain numerous insights into the literary world, such as this visit to see a Shakespeare play:

> 9 August 1667: we saw 'The Tameing of a Shrew,' which hath some very good pieces in it, but generally is but a mean play; and the best part, 'Sawny,' done by Lacy, hath not half its life, by reason of the words, I suppose, not being understood, at least by me.

The play was called *Sawney the Scot, or the Taming of a Shrew* – an adaptation of Shakespeare (by John Lacy), which was a common practice at the time.

'An Act to restrain abuses of players' came into force in 1606

Political and religious concern about the way plays were being written and performed led to this parliamentary bill:

> For the preuenting and auoyding of the great abuse of the holy Name of God in Stage-playes, Interludes, Maygames, Shews and such like, Be it enacted by our Soueraigne Lord the Kings Maiestie, and by the Lords Spirituall and Temporall, and Commons in this present Parliament assembled, and by the Authoritie of the same, That if at any time or times after the end of this present Session of Parliament, any person or persons, doe or shall in any Stage-play, Interlude, Shew, Maygame, or Pageant, iestingly, and prophanely speake, or vse the holy Name of God, or of Christ Iesus, or of the holy Ghost, or of the Trinitie, which are not to bee spoken but with feare and reuerence, Shall forfeit for euery such offence by him or them committed tenne Pounds.

The Act applied only to performances, so the extent to which it influenced printed texts is debatable. But its effect on Shakespeare's plays is significant, and there are many differences between quarto editions pre-1606 and the First Folio of 1623. Over a hundred expressions were affected, such as *ʒounds* ('God's wounds'), *'sdeath* ('God's death') and *before God*. But more was affected than the simple removal of a swear word. In *Richard III*, a popular play that had four quarto editions before 1606, Buckingham tells Richard he'll no longer make his case to the people, and we read the following exchange:

> *Buckingham* Come citizens. Zounds. I'll entreat no more.
> *Richard* O, do not swear, my Lord of Buckingham.
> *Catesby* Call him again…

In the First Folio we read:

> *Buckingham* Come Citizens, we will entreat no more.
> *Catesby* Call him againe…

A whole line disappears, along with a nice piece of Ricardian irony.

Maya Angelou died in 2014

Born in Missouri in 1928, Angelou achieved fame as a poet and memoirist, and was an important figure in the American civil rights movement. Observations about language frequently occur in her autobiographies, a fascination she explained in a 1999 interview:

> For about six years, from when I was seven to thirteen, I was a mute. And I loved to hear people speak. I still do. I've heard things they said which were painful, but I've never heard a voice, a human voice, that didn't please me – never. I used to think I could make my whole body an ear. And I could walk into a room and absorb sound. I've been able to speak ten, eleven, twelve languages; I can get around in six or seven now. It's really because I love to hear human beings talk and sing that I've listened so assiduously, and out of that came the love of language.

There were some specific influences: 'If I had not studied Latin in school, I wouldn't have found it as easy to comprehend the structure of language.' And that awareness appears in insightful comments about the realities of language use, and the power and validity of the personal voice – especially valuable because they come from personal experience, as opposed to the detached descriptions of the observing sociolinguist. Here's an example from chapter 29 of her first memoir, the acclaimed *I Know Why the Caged Bird Sings* (1969):

> My education and that of our Black associates were quite different from the education of our white schoolmates. In the classroom we all learned past participles, but in the streets and in our homes the Blacks learned to drop *s*'s from plurals and suffixes from past-tense verbs. We were alert to the gap separating the written word from the colloquial. We learned to slide out of one language and into another without being conscious of the effort. At school, in a given situation, we might respond with 'That's not unusual'. But in the street, meeting the same situation, we easily said 'It be's like that sometimes'.

The trademark 'ESCALATOR' was registered in 1900

Charles Seeberger worked for the Otis Elevator Company, and he registered this name for the world's first moving-step machine when it was demonstrated at a Paris trade fair in 1900. The use of capital letters and inverted commas shows the word's special status. However, fifty years later, Otis lost its rights to the mark 'ESCALATOR', in a case known as *Haughton Elevator Co.* v. *Seeberger.* The court decided that the word had become generic. A crucial piece of the evidence was the way Otis itself was using it, in such advertisements as

> To thousands of building owners and managers, the Otis trademark means the utmost in safe, efficient economical elevator and escalator operation.

The company was clearly using the word in a general sense alongside *elevator*, which had never been a trademark.

Trademark law is complex, not least because the status of a word can vary among countries. Dozens of other words have had – or are currently going through – a similar transformation, such as *cashpoint, cellophane, heroin, hoover, launderette, linoleum, sellotape, trampoline, videotape* and *yo-yo*. Legal cases are common.

Words vary in their ability to act as a trademark, depending on how unique they are. The strongest ones are called *fanciful* – made-up words that have no other existence in a language. *Arbitrary* marks are those where a word from one semantic field is used uniquely in another, such as *Apple* for computers and not fruit. It isn't possible to take a normal generic word, such as *computer* or *fruit*, and trademark it, because it's in general usage. Trademark disputes thus usually revolve around the question of the extent to which a word has in fact become general – a linguistic issue. When a trademarked word begins to be used in different grammatical ways – a noun becoming an adjective or a verb, for instance, as in someone *googling* or *ʒooming* – it's a sign that a process of genericization is under way.

National Creativity Day

The day was founded in 2018 by American film producer Hal Croasmun, the president of ScreenwritingU, a company that provides screenwriting courses and helps screenwriters to break into the industry. The stated aim is 'to celebrate the imaginative spirits everywhere and to encourage them to keep creating'. The operative word is 'everywhere'. The day isn't only for 'professional' creators – authors, artists, musicians, craftworkers... – but to acknowledge the creative potential in everyone (SEE ALSO 21 APRIL). The domain of creativity is limitless – gardening, decorating, walking, visiting, cooking, or simply sorting out something we've 'always been meaning to do'.

Linguistic creativity isn't usually acknowledged in all this, other than in relation to recognized verbal art forms such as poetry. But it has become a commonplace in linguistics to affirm its fundamental role in everyday speech and writing. The vast majority of the sentences I've written in this book, for example, have never been used before. And everyday conversation is a mixture of the familiar and the novel. Once a language has been learned, users are very ready to manipulate it in original ways, making jokes and puns, coining new words, creating riddles, and introducing all kinds of fresh and ingenious interactions. And in writing, there are initiatives such as beginning a diary or an online blog, or, more ambitiously, a mini-autobiography.

The writer Robert Graves (SEE 24 JULY) once put it succinctly, with reference to poetry, that a poet should 'master the main grammatical rules before daring to bend or break them'. His point can be generalized, for we can bend and break the rules of any aspect of language, not just grammar. We can play with pronunciation, spelling, punctuation, vocabulary, and any other aspect of language in order to create novel effects. And this is something humans seem to do instinctively. Studies of young children's acquisition of language have shown the way they begin to play with sounds and words almost as soon as they learn them. And caretakers reinforce the process through nursery rhymes, songs, adopting character voices in storytelling, and many other ways.

Walt Whitman was born in 1819

One of America's greatest poets – some say *the* greatest – Whitman
had a great deal to say about language, being a lifelong observer and
collector of usage. It's a theme he addressed in the preface to his best-
known collection, *Leaves of Grass* (1855), and the power and variety
of words are recurring themes in his poetry. An essay titled 'Slang in
America', published in 1885, illustrates his linguistic insight. It was his
last prose account of language (he died in 1892). The article is much
broader in scope than its title suggests, including neologisms, etymology,
nicknames, place names and general observations. The flavour of his
spirited poetic prose can be seen from his opening words:

> View'd freely, the English language is the accretion and growth
> of every dialect, race, and range of time, and is both the free and
> compacted composition of all. From this point of view, it stands for
> Language in the largest sense, and is really the greatest of studies. It
> involves so much; is indeed a sort of universal absorber, combiner, and
> conqueror. The scope of its etymologies is the scope not only of man
> and civilization, but the history of Nature in all departments, and of
> the organic Universe, brought up to date; for all are comprehended in
> words, and their backgrounds. This is when words become vitaliz'd,
> and stand for things, as they unerringly and soon come to do, in
> the mind that enters on their study with fitting spirit, grasp, and
> appreciation.

It's difficult to top such a powerful affirmation, but he does so later in the
essay:

> Language, be it remember'd, is not an abstract construction of the
> learn'd, or of dictionary-makers, but is something arising out of
> the work, needs, ties, joys, affections, tastes, of long generations of
> humanity, and has its bases broad and low, close to the ground. Its final
> decisions are made by the masses, people nearest the concrete, having
> most to do with actual land and sea. It impermeates all, the Past as well
> as the Present, and is the grandest triumph of the human intellect.

National Say Something Nice Day

It's a shame that people felt it was necessary to create such a day, but the perceived growth of racial violence in the USA, among other factors, led a group of people in South Carolina to establish this day in 2006. The prime mover was Mitch Carnell, president of the Charleston Speech and Hearing Center, and the author of several books on communication, including *Say Something Nice: Be a Lifter @ Work* (2012). Other supporters of the initiative included the South Baptist Convention and the Charleston-Atlantic Presbytery, and the day was officially proclaimed by the mayor of North Charleston.

It doesn't seem to have had much recognition in other countries, but the sentiment is so important that it ought to have done. Since 2006 there has been a notable increase in online abuse on social media, largely fuelled by the mask of anonymity. And the kind of workplace behaviour acknowledged in Carnell's book doubtless has parallels everywhere:

> Today's workplace is very toxic with harsh words and unrelenting criticism from managers, supervisors and fellow employees. The verbal poison has reached an alarming level. This must change. The present level of hostility is both harmful to one's health and costly to the employer. It takes everyone to turn things around. Use these words to create a positive working environment. Lead your workplace to observe Say Something Nice Day on June first and practice positive speech every day. Become an army of one to challenge the verbal abuse.

The book encourages people to be 'lifters'. The notion is one of 'lifting others up' rather than 'putting them down'. It has a long history in this sense, with a first recorded usage in Coverdale's translation of the biblical psalms in 1535: 'But thou, O Lord, art my defender: thou art my worship, and the lifter up of my head' (Psalm 3:3). It was later used in a wide range of metaphorical contexts, such as by a seventeenth-century author who writes that music is 'a lifter of Dead, Drowsie and Melancholly Spirits'.

Adelaide Casely Hayford was born in 1868

She was born in Freetown, British Sierra Leone, to parents who were
part of the elite sector of the Creole community. *Creole* here refers to
much more than a language variety. Adelaide M. Cromwell, in her 2004
biography, *An African Victorian Feminist*, characterizes it as 'a cultural
mixture of Settler, English and African, and the acceptance of a public
life style, at least, which is represented by England and things English'.
Hayford went to school in England. After the break-up of her marriage
she returned to Sierra Leone, becoming a pioneer of women's education
there, founding a Girls' Vocational School in Freetown in 1923.

In her writing, under the name of A. Hayford, she uses standard
British English, but in her short stories her characters sometimes speak
in the local variety. 'Kobina (A little African Boy)' was published in
the *Sierra Leone Weekly News* in 1949. Kobbie, aged 4, has been left in
charge of his mother's luggage at a station, while she takes a train to
go shopping. When she misses her return train, she arranges with the
officials to put Kobbie on a train to get to her, but when they take the
luggage away to put it in the luggage van he's distraught, as he thinks
caring for it is his duty. He's screaming as he's being put into a passenger
compartment. An old woman tries to comfort him:

> 'Hush yah lillie bobo! Hush yah! Noting go do you. We go take care of
> you!' To which Kobbie responded with an adroit blow on her withered
> cheek from his little clenched fist. This fanned her smoldering fire into
> flame.
>
> 'Guard!' she yelled. 'Carry am go! Make e no stop here! We no want
> am!'

He gets his way, and ends up happily in the luggage van on top of his
mother's things. The railway staff are very impressed with his sense of
responsibility.

Sierra Leonian Creole, or Krio, is widely spoken as a lingua franca in
the country today. Hayford died in 1960. Her daughter Gladys became
known as a pioneering writer of Krio poetry.

National Repeat Day

This is probably the most bizarre idea for a day to come out of the USA, though it does have some strong competitors for this title (22 MARCH, for instance). One of the holiday websites explains: 'followers seek out activities and experiences they love so much that they want to do them over and over again'. Another illustrates some of the options:

> Wash the dishes twice.
> Make the same meal for lunch as you do for supper.
> Say 'thank you' twice.
> Proofread your emails twice.
> Play your favorite song twice.
> Watch the same movie twice, especially *Groundhog Day*.

Well, if you've got nothing better to do…

But the day does at least provide a motivation to reflect on the nature of repetition in language. In writing, style guides sometimes dismiss it as 'tautology', and cite examples like 'repeat again', 'free gift' and 'please RSVP'. But most repetition has a point. It's the usual way of adding emphasis to an utterance: 'It was very very cold', 'More and more people came'. It's important in dialogue, where it has such functions as clarification, reinforcement, mockery and excitement. 'I've passed my exam!', says A. 'You've passed your exam?' says B. 'Yes, I've passed my exam!!', says A, with extra emphasis. And more repetitions might follow.

In language acquisition, it's used by caretakers as a way of showing children the linguistic journey they have to make. 'There car', says the child. 'Yes, there's a car', says the parent, thereby illustrating the grammatical expansion needed to acquire the adult norm. There's also a little understood speech disorder called *echolalia*, in which someone automatically repeats something, typically without appreciating the meaning. It's often encountered in psychological or neurological contexts such as dementia, autistic spectrum conditions, and aphasia. It's the kind of thing anyone might do, as when A says 'It's a puzzle' and B says thoughtfully 'It's a puzzle alright'. The difference is that in echolalia the repetition isn't under control, and interferes with communication.

Chester Nez died in 2014

Few people will have heard of this American veteran of World War II, born in New Mexico in 1921, but he earns a place in any linguistic history as the last surviving Navajo code talker, one of the 'first 29' recruited by the US Marine Corps in 1942. Code talkers are military personnel who speak a language that an enemy is unlikely to know, which is then used as a means of secret communication. In some cases words from the language are used as a cipher, replacing letters of the English alphabet. In the Navajo cipher, *A* 'ant' was *wol-la-chee*, *B* 'bear' *shush*, *C* 'cat' *moasi*, and so on. An alternative method used everyday conversation, with indigenous expressions replacing entities not known in the home culture. Examples of Navajo substitutions were *gini* 'chicken hawk' for a dive bomber, *besh-lo* 'iron fish' for a submarine, and *ca-lo* 'shark' for a destroyer. Sally McClain's book *Navajo Weapon* (1994) tells the whole story. This is one of her examples, showing a Navajo message as it would be in English:

> *Original* Request artillery and tank fire at 123B, Company E move 50 yards left flank of Company D
> *Coded* Ask for many big guns and tortoise fire at 123 Bear tail drop Mexican ear mouse owl victor elk 50 yards left flank ocean fish Mexican deer

Navajo is the most famous case, but other Amerindian languages have performed this function, including Hopi, Mohawk and Tlingit in World War II and – the earliest known use of this strategy in modern times – Choctaw, Cherokee and Comanche in World War I. Canadian forces used Cree in a similar way. The practice has been employed again in more recent conflicts, such as Nubian by the Egyptians in the 1973 Arab–Israeli war. And during the Yugoslavian civil war of the 1990s, the Royal Welch Fusiliers, part of the UN peace-keeping operation, used Welsh in their radio transmissions.

The Navajo and other code talkers remained unrecognized for many years, but their story was finally declassified in 1968, and surviving speakers in the USA were given medals of honour.

Margaret Drabble was born in 1939

Born in Yorkshire, she became known primarily for her novels and biographies, as well as her critical and editorial work. Her 1979 pictorial journey around Britain raised some interesting issues to do with language. It was titled *A Writer's Britain*, with the subtitle *Landscape in Literature*, and reveals an image of the country – a love of place – as expressed by writers from Anglo-Saxon times to the present day. In her foreword she makes an interesting point:

> The desire to turn landscape into art seems a natural one, though it is hard to say precisely why painters and writers should labour to reproduce in paint or words what each of us can see with our own eyes. But we all see differently, and every writer's work is a record both of himself and of the age in which he lives, as well as of the particular places he describes. The appreciation of landscape has evolved over the years, and fashions in viewing scenery have changed; in recent years much has been written about the painter's attitude to landscape, but less about the writer's, though writers have been affected by and have helped to create the same fashions, the same new awareness.

She then draws attention to something I hadn't noticed before, and adds an intriguing remark.

> The word 'landscape' itself is relatively new, dating from the end of the sixteenth century: the word 'scenery' is even more recent, dating from the late eighteenth century. Both are so familiar that it is hard to imagine how writers managed without them. Perhaps, as some believe, the ability to enjoy scenery for its own sake is as recent as the language we use to describe it.

She's right about the recency, though the latest *OED* research has found instances a little earlier, but still only as far back as 1712. We might think that *scenery* (in the sense of the items on a stage) derives from the general sense meaning the picturesque appearance of the landscape. In fact it's the other way round. *Scenery* first turns up in the theatre world.

Russian Language Day

One of the six official languages of the United Nations, the day was established by the UN in 2010 (on 12 November) as part of the general policy to 'celebrate multilingualism and cultural diversity as well as to promote equal use of all six of its official working languages throughout the organization'. It recognizes Russia's most famous poet, Alexander Pushkin, born on this day in 1799. A line from his poem 'Sleeplessness' has achieved a wide online presence in this translation: 'I want to understand you, I study your obscure language.' Its impact has gone well beyond the context of the original poem, turning up in settings as diverse as personal relationships and endangered languages.

Loanwords from Russian came into English relatively late, compared with the massive influx from European languages during the Middle Ages and the Renaissance. The sixteenth century saw the arrival of *czar* (in various spellings), but most borrowings took place during the late nineteenth century and into the twentieth, especially after the emergence of the Soviet Union. Many related to political or social developments, such as *agitprop*, *apparatchik*, *bolshevik* (and its diminutive *bolshie*), *commissar*, *glasnost*, *gulag*, *intelligentsia*, *perestroika*, *politburo*, *samizdat* and *soviet*; but there were also several cultural and domestic words, such as *balaclava*, *balalaika*, *borsch*, *borzoi*, *dacha* and *mazurka*. The world of nature gave us *beluga* and *tundra*. Russian progress in space gave us *cosmonaut*.

The most fruitful loan from Russian (with support from Yiddish) has undoubtedly been the suffix -*nik*, used to denote a supporter of a cause or a member of a particular group, as in one of its earliest uses, *beatnik*. Later usage tended to be humorous or dismissive, as with *peacenik*, *protestnik*, *conferencenik*, *computernik* and *refusenik*. It's less productive today, but it was especially popular in the years following the launch of the Russian satellite, *Sputnik*, in 1957. When a subsequent launch by the USA failed, the papers went into overdrive with such terms as *flopnik*, *oopsnik* and *dudnik*.

Lindley Murray was born in 1745

Undoubtedly the most famous English grammar of the nineteenth century was written by Lindley Murray. It was published in 1795, and by 1850 had sold nearly 2 million copies. He was born in Pennsylvania, became a lawyer and merchant, and moved to England in 1785, eventually settling in York, where he lived until his death in 1826. There he helped to establish a boarding school for young teenage girls, and it was a request in 1794 from teachers there – 'having suffered great inconvenience from the want of a complete English Grammer [*sic*] with examples & Rules annexed, proper for this and similar Institutions' – that led him to write his book.

He emphasized that it wouldn't be original, but merely a compilation that he hoped would improve on existing grammars. Long sections were copied from earlier grammars, especially the one written by Robert Lowth (SEE 8 FEBRUARY). But his formula worked. The demand was such that he then wrote a book of exercises, a separate book of answers, an *English Reader*, a spelling book, and various abridged and introductory texts. It's been estimated that their combined sales amounted to around 14 million copies worldwide, with strong sales in America as well as Britain. By the end of the nineteenth century he was being referred to as 'the father of English grammar', and talking about 'Murray' would need no further detail, much as people in the twentieth century talked of 'Fowler'. His name appeared on commercial products, such as cigar tins and matchbox holders. There was even a ludo-like board game produced in 1857 called *A Journey to Lindley Murray*.

Not everyone appreciated his prescriptivism, and the artificiality of many of his exercises and rules led to serious as well as comic criticism. Charles Dickens, in *The Old Curiosity Shop*, tells how Mrs Jarley in her waxworks exhibition altered 'the face and costume of Mr Grimaldi as clown to represent Mr Lindley Murray as he appeared when engaged in the composition of his English Grammar'. And he's mentioned in novels by George Eliot, Mark Twain, Charlotte Brontë, Harriet Beecher Stowe and others.

Danes attack Lindisfarne in 793

The *Anglo-Saxon Chronicle* described the event: 'the harrying of the heathen miserably destroyed God's church in Lindisfarne by plunder and slaughter'. It was one of the earliest attacks by the Danes. Many more followed, and by the end of the ninth century Danish settlement was established throughout north-east Britain, and soon after in a broad swathe of eastern England running roughly from Cheshire to Essex which became known as the Danelaw. The result was a wave of linguistic influence from their language, now called Old Norse. Over 2,000 Scandinavian place names are found throughout the area – hundreds ending in *-by* ('farmstead' or 'town'), *-thorpe* ('village, outlying farm'), *-thwaite* ('clearing'), or *-toft* ('homestead'), as seen in *Rugby*, *Althorp*, *Braithwaite* and *Sandtoft*.

It took a while for Old Norse words to become a noticeable feature of English speech and writing. A few early ones reflect the imposition of Danish law and administration throughout the region, but influence is sporadic until the early Middle English period. The surviving literature, from around 1200, shows a huge number of loanwords in texts such as *Orrmulum* and *Havelock the Dane*, with many illustrating the impact of Old Norse on everyday life, as can be seen in this small sample:

> anger, awkward, cake, crooked, dirt, dregs, egg, fog,
> freckle, get, kid, leg, lurk, meek, neck, seem, sister,
> skill, skirt, smile, take, Thursday, window

More surprising is the way Old Norse made a permanent impact on English grammar, through the introduction of a new set of third-person-plural pronouns, *they*, *them* and *their*, which eventually replaced Old English inflected forms such as *hie*, *heom* and *heora*. There were verb changes too, notably the *-s* ending of the third-person-singular present-tense form of a verb (as in *walks* – replacing *walketh*) and the use of *are* as the third-person plural of *be*. The negative response word, *nay*, still common in many regional dialects, is also Old Norse in origin (*nei*). And when we say *to and fro* we're linking an Old English word and a Norse one.

International Archives Day

The International Council on Archives (ICA) was founded at a meeting in Paris in 1948, and established this day in 2007. It defines the domain in this way:

> They are the documentary by-product of human activity retained for their long-term value, and as such are an irreplaceable witness to past events, underpinning democracy, the identity of individuals and communities, and human rights. But they are also fragile and vulnerable. The ICA strives to protect and ensure access to archives through advocacy, setting standards, professional development, and enabling dialogue between archivists, policy makers, creators and users of archives.

The records can be in any medium – audio, written (on paper or screen), photographic, moving image… but whatever the medium, language is an essential part of the process, in making the context of the archive explicit and clear (who created it, how, when, where and why) and in providing efficient captioning and interrogating tools.

To be of value an archive has to be 'a trusted resource'. The ICA gives four criteria, which they define as follows:

> *Authentic* – the record is what it claims to be, created at the time documented, and by the people or organization cited.
> *Reliable* – it accurately represents the events to be captured, though it will be through the view of those creating the document.
> *Integrated* – the content is a complete and coherent account of the events.
> *Usable* – the archive must be in an accessible location and in a usable condition.

In relation to usability, mention is made of earthquakes, hurricanes and war as factors that can make archives useless. But a more universal problem is that storage media become out of date very quickly. Those old enough to recall tape recorders, floppy discs, Betamax videotapes, and other cutting-edge and now defunct techniques from the late twentieth century are well aware of the issue of inaccessibility. Transferring data to a new technology is time-consuming and costly, and who knows how long the latest technology will last?

National Ballpoint Pen Day

Any book on language needs to acknowledge the devices that make handwritten text possible. Pencils are one such technology (SEE 30 MARCH), but nothing has matched the universal appeal of the ballpoint pen – or *biro*, as it's more commonly known in British English, named for the Hungarian brothers László and György Bíró, who developed the technology when refugees in Argentina. Their design was patented in the USA on this day in 1943. They solved the problem that had plagued previous inventors, with the ink either running too quickly and making smudges, or being of the wrong consistency, thereby clogging up the point and making smudges. Their solution was inspired by the fast-drying viscous inks used by the printing industry. The new pens soon became the dominant writing implement, providing a cleaner, easier and cheaper alternative to dip pens and fountain pens.

Several authors have testified to the way the biro has altered writing behaviour. Quills and dip pens were the most constraining of previous methods, requiring a writer to stay in one place, usually at a desk with inkpots, blotting paper and the like readily to hand. Even fountain pens, although portable, had to stay in routine proximity to an ink source. The biro allowed writing to take place in virtually any environment, and the range of qualities and colours that eventually developed offered new creative opportunities.

The fame of the implement was acknowledged when Douglas Adams paid tribute to it in chapter 21 of *The Hitchhiker's Guide to the Galaxy*. It reports how a young student of ancient philology, among other things, 'became increasingly obsessed with the problem of what happened to all the biros he'd bought over the past few years'. He theorized that somewhere in the cosmos there was

> a planet entirely giving over to biro life forms. And it was to this planet that unattended biros would make their way, slipping away quietly through wormholes in space to a world where they knew they could enjoy a uniquely biroid life-style, responding to highly biro-oriented stimuli, and generally leading the biro equivalent of the good life.

Ben Jonson was born in 1572

Known primarily for his plays and poetry, Jonson also wrote an
English grammar and kept a collection of observations titled *Timber,
or Discoveries made upon men and matter*, with the subtitle: *as they have
flowed out of his daily readings, or had their reflux* [return flow] *to his
peculiar* [personal] *notion of the times*. *Timber* alludes to the multiplicity
of trees in a wood. No manuscript survives: it was incorporated into the
edition of his collected work published in 1641 four years after his death.
Many entries are about language, style, rhetoric and the nature of poetry.
These three extracts capture the aphoristic character of his anthology:

> A wise tongue should not be licentious and wandering; but moved and,
> as it were, governed with certain reins from the heart and bottom of the
> breast: and it was excellently said of that philosopher, that there was a
> wall or parapet of teeth set in our mouth, to restrain the petulancy of our
> words; that the rashness of talking should not only be retarded by the
> guard and watch of our heart, but be fenced in and defended by certain
> strengths placed in the mouth itself, and within the lips.

> How much better is it to be silent, or at least to speak sparingly! for
> it is not enough to speak good, but timely things. If a man be asked a
> question, to answer; but to repeat the question before he answer is well,
> that he be sure to understand it, to avoid absurdity; for it is less dishonour
> to hear imperfectly than to speak imperfectly. The ears are excused, the
> understanding is not.

> Language most shows a man: Speak, that I may see thee. It springs out
> of the most retired and inmost parts of us, and is the image of the parent
> of it, the mind. No glass renders a man's form or likeness so true as
> his speech. Nay, it is likened to a man; and as we consider feature and
> composition in a man, so words in language; in the greatness, aptness,
> sound structure, and harmony of it.

This, of course, is 'man' in the generic sense of 'person'. The insight
applies to us all.

Probable opening of the Globe theatre in 1599

Shakespeare's Globe is in London, situated on the south bank of the River Thames. It is a reconstruction of the first Globe playhouse, built on a nearby site in 1599, and this day was chosen for its formal opening in 1997. There has been a great deal of debate about the actual date of the original opening, but the Globe management was persuaded by research which suggested that the choice of day would have been influenced by several factors, notably the date of the summer solstice that year – 12 June in the old-style Julian calendar which was still in use at the time.

The commitment to raising a theatre that replicated the original building – in so far as records and research would allow – had significant consequences for performance. Early productions at the new Globe explored a range of original practices, notably in voice projection, costume, music, lighting, movement and audience interaction. Then in June 2004 the Globe added a linguistic dimension, presenting a play in original pronunciation (OP): a weekend of performances of *Romeo and Juliet*, mounted in the middle of a run in which the play was being performed in present-day English. The success of that event led to a further production, of *Troilus and Cressida*, in 2005. And since then some twenty (in 2023) of Shakespeare's plays have been given OP performances, in various parts of the world, as well as plays by other authors, prose writers and song composers of the Elizabethan era.

Reconstructing the OP of any period is a sophisticated linguistic operation. For this time, Early Modern English, it involves a detailed analysis of the rhymes and puns where pronunciation has since changed (Shakespeare would have rhymed *wars* and *stars*, for example), the spellings (which reflected pronunciation more closely than happens today), and the many commentaries about English sounds that were published at the time, often in relation to the contentious question of whether the English spelling system should be reformed. An introduction to the OP of Early Modern English can be found on a dedicated website: www.originalpronunciation.com.

Fanny Burney was born in 1752

This is the name usually used for Frances Burney, known as Madame d'Arblay after her marriage in 1793, one of the best commentators of the social scene in the late eighteenth and early nineteenth centuries. Born in Norfolk, she moved with her family to London in 1760. She came to fame through her first novel, *Evelina* (1778), written in an epistolary style. In over seventy years of journal writing, she describes the personalities and events of her day, adding a personal perspective. She died in 1840.

The flavour of her journalistic style, with a remarkable ability to reconstruct naturalistic dialogue, can be seen in this extract on a linguistic point, written on Saturday, 28 January 1783, in which an Italian friend makes a visit:

> While Mr. George Cambridge was here Pacchierotti called – very grave, but very sweet. Mr. G.C. asked if he spoke English.
>
> 'O, very well,' cried I, 'pray try him; he is very amiable, and I fancy you will like him.'
>
> Pacchierotti began with complaining of the variable weather.
>
> 'I cannot,' he said, 'be well such an inconsistent day.'
>
> We laughed at the word 'inconsistent,' and Mr. Cambridge said, –
>
> 'It is curious to see what new modes all languages may take in the hands of foreigners. The natives dare not try such experiments; and, therefore, we all talk pretty much alike; but a foreigner is obliged to hazard new expressions, and very often he shews us a force and power in our words, by an unusual adaptation of them, that we were not ourselves aware they would admit.'
>
> And then, to draw Pacchierotti out, he began a dispute, of the different merits of Italy and England; defending his own country merely to make him abuse it, while Pacchierotti most eagerly took up the gauntlet on the part of Italy.
>
> 'This is a climate,' said Pacchierotti, 'never in the same case for half an hour at a time; it shall be fair, and wet, and dry, and humid, forty times in a morning in the least. I am tired to be so played with, sir, by your climate.'

Alexander Ellis was born in 1814

Born in Middlesex, Ellis first trained as a mathematician, but linguists know him for his many writings on phonetics, a subject then in its earliest stages of development. His five-book *Early English Pronunciation* is full of perceptive observations about the methodology needed to describe speech accurately, and he added a historical dimension, providing the first detailed account of the pronunciation used by Chaucer and Shakespeare. He died in 1890.

Ellis influenced later phoneticians in his use of the term 'received pronunciation', and anticipated one of the most important notions in modern phonetics: 'When a stranger goes among the country people, they immediately begin to "speak fine," or in some way to accommodate their pronunciation to his.' And these extracts from chapter 21 of Book 4 (published in 1875) illustrate his modern thinking:

> It is indeed remarkable how unconscious the greater number of persons appear to be that any one in ordinary society pronounces differently from themselves. If there is something very uncommon, it may strike them that the speaker spoke 'strangely' or 'curiously', that 'there was something odd about his pronunciation', but to point to the singularity, to determine in what respects the new sound differs from their own, baffles most people.

His comment on observation is prescient: 'The only safe method is to listen to the natural speaking of some one who does not know that he is observed.' And he adds a note of caution about 'educated speakers, who are mostly fanciful in their pronunciation'. He goes on:

> It is never safe to ask such people how they pronounce a given word. Not only are they immediately tempted to 'correct' their usual pronunciation, to tell the questioner how they think the word ought to be pronounced, and perhaps to deny that they ever pronounced it otherwise; but the fact of the removal of the word from its context, from its notional and phonetic relation to preceding and following sounds, alters the feeling of the speaker, so that he has as much difficulty in uttering the word naturally, as a witness has in signing his name, when solemnly told to sign in his usual handwriting.

Magna Carta was sealed in 1215.

The 'Great Charter of Freedoms' (*Magna Carta Libertatum*) has huge symbolic standing in English history as a charter of rights agreed between King John and his barons. It concludes:

> Given by our hand in the meadow that is called Runnymede, between Windsor and Staines, on the fifteenth day of June in the seventeenth year of our reign

The original is written in medieval Latin, as was normal for official documents at the time, and authorized by a large royal seal.

One of its interesting linguistic features is the frequent use of abbreviations – an important space-saving convention for a text written on expensive parchment. Words were reduced to their initial letters, their first two or three letters, a selection of letters, or substituted by a simple symbol. There would be a diacritic or other mark to show that something had been omitted. For example, in Magna Carta *and* was written as a dash with a small tail, *per* ('of') could appear as a letter *p* with a crossbar on the descender, and *nostra* ('our) was written *nra* with a horizontal line above.

Scribal abbreviations can be found in manuscripts from the earliest period of English writing. A symbol that looked like the numeral *7* was very frequent in Anglo-Saxon texts as a replacement for *and*: it derives from the symbol used in classical Latin for *et* ('and') by Cicero's scribe, Marcus Tullius Tiro (and thus often called the 'Tironian *et*'). It can still sometimes be seen in modern Irish Gaelic notices as a replacement for *agus* 'and'. The modern English equivalent is the ampersand *&*, which derives from the linking of the two letters of *et*.

A horizontal or wavy bar above a letter showed that a following *n* or *m* was omitted. A stroke through the ascender of letter thorn (*þ*) represented the word *þæt* 'that'. The influence of Latin is pervasive, and abbreviations from that language are still with us, such as *i.e.* (*id est* 'that is'), *e.g.* (*exempli gratia* 'for the sake of example'), and *etc.* (*et cetera* 'and the others').

Bloomsday

The day celebrates the life and writing of Irish author James Joyce
(1882–1941), chiefly by retracing the route through Dublin taken by
Leonard Bloom, the central character in *Ulysses*, published in 1922.
The novel is a modern parallel to the *Odyssey* of Homer, and Bloom
represents Ulysses on his long journey. The difference is that the action
of the novel takes place entirely on a single day: 16 June 1904, which
was also the day Joyce first went out with Nora Barnacle, whom he later
married. Each year there's a Bloomsday Festival, beginning at 8 o'clock
in the morning. Some begin with a Bloomsday Breakfast, with the same
fry-up (including liver and kidneys) eaten by Bloom in the novel. People
often dress up in costumes from the period, such as wearing a straw
boater hat. Readings and performances accompany visits to the places
mentioned in the book – and not just in Dublin, for the novel continues
to attract an enthusiastic readership all over the world.

To do justice to Joyce's innovative achievement, especially in *Ulysses*
and *Finnegans Wake* (1939), requires a combination of linguistic, literary
and creative writing perspectives, and we find all three in the masterly
exposition by Anthony Burgess (SEE 25 NOVEMBER), *Joysprick: An
Introduction to the Language of James Joyce* (1973). In his opening chapter
he discusses one of the central questions: is Joycean writing to be heard
or to be read?

> In his approach to language, Joyce seems to have set himself up a
> kind of implied continuum in which, in the middle, groups of letters
> signify ordinary words but, on the one side, shade into non-linguistic
> symbols – arithmetical, algebraic, cabbalistic, essentially visual – and,
> on the other, into attempts at representing inarticulate noise. *Finnegans
> Wake*, considered, after *Paradise Lost*, the most auditory of all works
> of literature, cannot be well understood by the ear alone. To take two
> simple examples: such coinages as 'clapplaud' make auditory sense, but
> the charmingly simple metathesis 'cropse', which is a small poem of
> death and resurrection, has to be seen to be appreciated.

J.R. Firth was born in 1890

Known always by his first-name initials, John Rupert Firth was the most influential British linguist in the 1940s and 1950s, becoming professor of general linguistics in the University of London. He died in 1960. Several linguists who introduced the subject in other British universities were his students or colleagues, such as Frank Palmer, who set up departments of linguistics at Bangor and Reading, and who gave me the opportunity to develop my own career in the subject.

In chapter 10 of a small book Firth wrote in 1937, *The Tongues of Men*, he introduces a theoretical concept which influenced a great deal of linguistic thinking thereafter: the notion of a 'context of situation' for the study of language.

> Most people, I suppose, regard the meaning of a word as something at the back of their minds which they can express and communicate. But the force and cogency of most language behaviour derives from the firm grip it has on the ever-recurrent typical situations in the life of social groups, and the normal social behaviour of the human animals living together in those groups. Speech is the telephone network, the nervous system of our society much more than the vehicle for the lyrical outbursts of the individual soul. It is a network of bonds and obligations. A common language is a sort of social switchboard which commands the power grid of the driving forces of the society. The meaning of a great deal of speech behaviour is just the combined personal and social forces it can mobilize and direct.

He illustrates from a simple expression: 'Say when!' and he comments:

> What do the words mean? They mean what they do. ... A Martian visitor would best understand this 'meaning' by watching what happened before, during, and after the words were spoken, by noticing the part played by the words in what was going on. The people, the relevant furniture, bottles and glasses, the 'set', the specific behaviour of the companions, and the words are all component terms in what may be called the context of situation.

Samuel Butler died in 1902

Born in Nottinghamshire in 1835, he became well known after the publication of his satirical novel *Erewhon* (1872), an anagram of *nowhere*, the story of a journey to an unknown country and the strange society he found there. Less known are his notebooks, kept throughout his life, and edited by his friend and literary assistant Henry Festing Jones in 1912. As Butler put it: 'One's thoughts fly so fast that one must shoot them.' Several contain observations about aspects of language, such as these aphoristic remarks that come from a section compiled by Jones titled 'Thought and Word'.

The mere fact that a thought or idea can be expressed articulately in words involves that it is still open to question; and the mere fact that a difficulty can be definitely conceived involves that it is open to solution.

We want words to do more than they can. We try to do with them what comes to very much like trying to mend a watch with a pickaxe or to paint a miniature with a mop; we expect them to help us to grip and dissect that which in ultimate essence is as ungrippable as shadow. Nevertheless there they are; we have got to live with them, and the wise course is to treat them as we do our neighbours, and make the best and not the worst of them. But they are parvenu people as compared with thought and action. What we should read is not the words but the man whom we feel to be behind the words.

Words impede and either kill, or are killed by, perfect thought; but they are, as a scaffolding, useful, if not indispensable, for the building up of imperfect thought and helping to perfect it.

All words are juggles. To call a thing a juggle of words is often a bigger juggle than the juggle it is intended to complain of. The question is whether it is a greater juggle than is generally considered fair trading.

Words are like money; there is nothing so useless, unless when in actual use.

Juneteenth Day

It's not often that a lexical blend becomes an official name, and never has one achieved such prominence as this one in the USA. It began in Texas as a celebration of the day when African-American slaves there were finally emancipated in 1865, and spread throughout the southern states. It became a federal holiday in 2021 when President Biden signed the Juneteenth National Independence Day Act.

Blends are in fact a very popular means of lexical creation these days, and several types of blend are identified in linguistic descriptions. This one is sometimes called a *partial* blend, as a complete word is joined to a word-part – *June* + *nineteenth* – a pattern also seen in *mansplain* (*man* + *explain*) and *fanzine* (*fan* + *magazine*). A more central category is where both elements are word-parts, as in *brunch* (*breakfast* + *lunch*) and *slithy* – a word from 'Jabberwocky' that puzzles Alice in Lewis Carroll's *Through the Looking Glass*. She asks Humpty Dumpty what it means:

> Well, 'slithy' means 'lithe and slimy'. 'Lithe' is the same as 'active'. You see it's like a portmanteau – there are two meanings packed up into one word.

And *portmanteau* has since named this kind of lexical coinage.

Blending became increasingly common during the twentieth century, though there are several earlier instances, such as *foolosophy* (sixteenth century) and *foolocracy* (nineteenth century). They provided a convenient means of generating new trade names, as in *Microsoft* (*microcomputer* + *software*), *Natwest* (*National* + *Westminster*) and *Instagram* (*instant* + *telegram*). They were especially prominent during the early stages of the 2019 pandemic, when people coined playful expressions – a way of linguistically laughing in the face of adversity. Several types of blend occurred. We saw two word-parts joined in *quarantini* (*quarantine* + *martini*) and the Juneteenth pattern is seen in *staycation* (*stay* + *vacation*). *Quarantine* was especially productive, with many coinages, such as *quarantedium*, *quaranteetotal* and *quaranteenager*. *Covid* itself led to many *overlapping* blends where the two elements share common sounds, such as *covidodging, covigilant* and *covidiot*.

John Evelyn's letter of 1665 proposing an English academy

A leading diarist of the seventeenth century, writing for over sixty years, Evelyn (1620–1706) was one of the founders of the Royal Society in 1660. A few years later some of the members formed themselves into a committee 'to consider of the improvement of the English tongue', along the lines of the French Academy established in 1635. Evelyn was part of it, but he couldn't make its meetings, which were held on a Tuesday afternoon. So he wrote an apologetic letter to the chairman, Sir Peter Wiche, and summarized the linguistic situation as he saw it. In a dozen recommendations, he says what has to be done:

— a grammar to lay down rules
— a reformed orthography
— a guide to the pronunciation of sentences and tone of voice in recitation
— a lexicon of 'pure English-Words'
— a collection of technical terms
— an encyclopedic element (such as weights and measures)
— a catalogue of exotic words with glosses
— an account of 'what particular Dialects, Idiomes and Proverbs were in use in every several Country of England'
— a catalogue of courtly expressions
— a listing of new and outdated words
— a selection of the best words in other languages.

The last point in his letter is about the qualifications required for academicians. They would need a 'stock of reputation gain'd by some publiq writings and compositions ... so that others may not thinke it dishonor to come under the test, or accept them for judges and approbators'.

Nothing happened. Apart from one brief mention, the Committee isn't further acknowledged by the Society, probably because the members felt that its work fell outside its scientific and technological aims, and were doubtless put off by the enormous scope of the proposal and the problem of choosing judges. There would be several other such proposals over the next century (SEE 22 FEBRUARY). None succeeded, and the idea of an Academy gradually faded from view.

Release of *Jaws* in 1975

The last time I heard the threatening low-pitched two-note sequence from the 1975 film *Jaws* was not on a screen. It was in a conversation, where one of the speakers wanted to warn the others that a mock-dangerous situation was looming. It was a jocular musical quotation, which the speaker knew the other participants would recognize. Of course, if the listeners had never seen *Jaws*, they would have no idea what was going on. But that's not how musical quotations are used. They are introduced where the speakers know each other well enough to be able to rely on mutual recognition. They are markers of solidarity.

Musical quotations have been very little studied, and it's unclear how they would be transcribed phonetically. They don't turn up very often, which is why they've been neglected, but they are remarkably diverse. Another example is the opening word in Handel's 'Hallelujah Chorus' from *Messiah*, as an expression of delight or relief, but sung not spoken – or perhaps 'intoned' would be a better description, as no care is taken to replicate the original tune. An out-of-tune pastiche is all that's required to gain recognizability.

Films and television are the primary sources for musical quotations, such as a snatch from *Doctor Who*, the alien tone-sequence in *Close Encounters of the Third Kind*, or the whistling motif from Clint Eastwood's spaghetti westerns. But classical music has its place too, such as the opening four notes of Beethoven's Fifth Symphony, as does popular music. Aficionados of the Beatles are likely to incorporate such fragments as 'Help, I need somebody' from time to time. Young people will introduce allusions that are totally opaque to older generations.

Some allusions lack a specific source, such as the 'Ta-daa' fanfare that accompanies an arrival. The origin might be a circus, a racecourse, or simply an imagined fanfare. There are stylized tunes, such as children's catcalls ('*na*-na-*na*-na *nah*-nah'). And there are intonational idioms, such as the call to eat: 'Come and ge-e-et it'. It all adds up to a musical dimension to speech.

William Chester Minor was born in 1834

He was an American army surgeon, who served in the Civil War. A deteriorating mental condition led to hospitalization in Washington and eventual army discharge. In 1871 he went to London, hoping that the change would help, but his paranoia worsened, and in 1872 he fatally shot a man he mistakenly believed was an intruder. Found not guilty by reason of insanity, he was sent to the Broadmoor asylum in Crowthorne, Berkshire, where he stayed until 1910. A campaign to release him led to deportation back to the USA, where he continued to be in care until his death in 1920.

The campaign was a consequence of his fame as a lexicographer. While in Broadmoor he had relatively comfortable quarters, in which he accumulated a library of antiquarian books, thanks to a generous army pension. When he learned of an appeal for volunteers to help find quotations of word usage for the future *Oxford English Dictionary* (SEE 15 FEBRUARY), he wrote to the editor, James Murray, offering his services. He became the dictionary's leading contributor, sending in a huge number of citations, neatly written on slips of paper following Murray's method. The target word would be written at the top on the left, with the date below it, along with the name of the author and the exact source, and then, below that, the quotation itself. Murray was so impressed that he gave him special mention in his talks, such as one to the Philological Society in 1897:

> So enormous have been Dr Minor's contributions during the past 17 or 18 years, that we could easily illustrate the last four centuries from his quotations alone.

Murray made several visits to Broadmoor, and developed a friendship that continued until his death in 1915. The full story is told in Simon Winchester's *The Surgeon of Crowthorne* (1998). It was published in the USA as *The Professor and the Madman*, and this was the title when the story was filmed in 2019, starring Mel Gibson as Murray and Sean Penn as Minor. It's rare indeed to see lexicography given such publicity.

International Typewriter Day

For those who know only the modern computer keyboard, it perhaps
needs to be explained that a typewriter was a portable mechanical device
that allowed users to type directly onto a sheet of paper. The concept
had a long history. An English engineer, Henry Mill, had patented
it as early as 1714: 'an artificial machine or method for impressing or
transcribing of letters, one after another, as in writing, whereby all
writing whatsoever may be engrossed in paper or parchment so neat
and exact as not to be distinguished from print.' No trace of this exists,
if it was ever produced. Today's date remembers the granting of a US
patent to Christopher Latham Sholes and Carlos Glidden in 1868, who
produced the first commercially successful machine. The earliest devices
could type only capital letters, but it wasn't long before both upper and
lower case became available.

It's difficult to appreciate today the revolutionary impact of the
'type-writer' (as it was first spelled). An 1874 advertisement began:
'This Machine is to the Pen what the Sewing Machine is to the Needle'.
It was expensive: $125 from one production company – the equivalent
in purchasing power of over $3,000 today. But that didn't stop a rapid
take-up, and enthusiastic letters of support were used by manufacturers,
such as this one from a William Hemstreet, in 1874:

> I willingly state your type-writer furnishes me most splendid aid, and
> has, from the hour I received it, entirely superseded the pen in official and
> professional work, and, in fact, in correspondence, memoranda, and all
> matters of record. ... I rank it next to my wife; enthusiastic over it, and
> regard it as an invention that is to be as universally adopted as the sewing
> machine, the steam engine, or the printing press.

A fine array of typewriter memorabilia, including this ad, has been
lovingly collected by Janine Vangool for her book *The Typewriter: A
Graphic History of the Beloved Machine* (2015). And everyone who uses
a computer with a *QWERTY* keyboard layout is paying unconscious
homage to the typewriter.

Ambrose Bierce was born in 1842

Born in Ohio, Bierce became a journalist, short-story writer, poet and critic, known for his social criticism and – especially relevant for this book – his satirical *The Devil's Dictionary*. This was originally a series of newspaper pieces, collected in 1906 under its first title *The Cynic's Word Book*. Another claim to fame is his unknown death: he disappeared while travelling in Mexico in 1913, and – despite many theories – what happened to him remains a mystery.

The character of his humour can be seen in this selection of his shorter entries to do with language (which he defines as 'the music with which we charm the serpents guarding another's treasure'):

APOLOGIZE *v.t.* To lay the foundation for a future offence.

COMMENDATION *n.* The tribute that we pay to achievements that resemble, but do not equal, our own.

CONGRATULATION *n.* The civility of envy.

CONVERSATION *n.* A fair for the display of the minor mental commodities, each exhibitor being too intent upon the arrangement of his own wares to observe those of his neighbor.

DICTIONARY *n.* A malevolent literary device for cramping the growth of a language and making it hard and inelastic. This dictionary, however, is a most useful book.

ELOQUENCE *n.* The art of orally persuading fools that white is the color that it appears to be. It includes the gift of making any color appear white.

GRAMMAR *n.* A system of pitfalls thoughtfully prepared for the feet of the self-made man, along the path by which he advances to distinction.

QUOTATION *n.* The art of repeating erroneously the words of another. The words erroneously repeated.

TELEPHONE *n.* An invention of the devil which abrogates some of the advantages of making a disagreeable person keep his distance.

I wonder where this lexicographical impulse came from? Possibly relevant is the fact that his father gave all thirteen of his children names beginning with A: Abigail, Amelia, Ann, Addison, Aurelius, Augustus, Almeda, Andrew, Albert, Ambrose, Arthur, Adelia and Aurelia.

Judith Wright died in 2000

Born in 1915 in New South Wales, Australia, Wright wrote in many literary genres, and was especially recognized for her several books of poetry. She brought these together in *Collected Poems 1942 to 1985*, first published in 1993 and issued in an updated edition in 2016. In her later years she became well known as an environmentalist and campaigner for the land rights of Aboriginal peoples, her contributions including *The Coral Battleground* on the conservation of the Great Barrier Reef, and *We Call for a Treaty* on the work of the Aboriginal Treaty Committee.

She focuses on language in several poems, especially in her last collection, *Phantom Dwelling* (1985). It includes 'Words, Roses, Stars', whose final stanza is a memorable affirmation:

> If I could give a rose to you, and you,
> It would be language; sight and touch and scent
> join in the symbol. Yet the word is true,
> plucked by a path where human vision went.

Later in the same collection we find 'Brevity', in which she thinks back over her previous four decades of poetic choices:

> Old Rhythm, old Metre
> these days I don't draw
> very deep breaths. There isn't
> much left to say.
>
> I used to love Keats, Blake.
> Now I try haiku
> for its honed brevities,
> its inclusive silences.
>
> Rhyme, my old cymbal,
> I don't clash you as often,
> or trust your old promises
> of music and unison.
>
> Issa. Shiki. Buson. Bashō.
> Few words and with no rhetoric.
> Enclosed by silence
> as is the thrush's call.

She's referring to four of the greatest Japanese writers of haiku: Kobayashi Issa (1763–1828), Masaoka Shiki (1867–1902), Yosa Buson (1716–1784) and Matsuo Bashō (1644–1694). I especially like her second stanza: 'music and unison' perfectly summarizes the two linguistic functions of rhyme.

UK publication of *Harry Potter and the Philosopher's Stone* in 1997

Why should the publication date of this book by J.K. Rowling deserve a place in a Language on This Day? Because of what happened next. It was published in the USA in 1998 under a different title: *Harry Potter and the Sorcerer's Stone*. When the two editions are placed side by side over seventy changes can be seen. Words and expressions felt to be 'too British' are turned into American rough equivalents. So this day can act as a testimony to the differences that still separate the two varieties.

We mustn't exaggerate, though: if someone were to add up all the words and idioms that distinguish British from American English in their standard forms (that is, excluding regional variations) the figure would be less than 1 per cent of the English lexicon. But when we read a book such as this, the number seems larger because most of the distinctive vocabulary is domestic, and thus likely to be encountered in a novel.

So what kinds of changes were made? Here are twenty examples:

UK	USA	UK	USA
cooker	stove	mummy	mommy
crumpets	English muffins	packet of crisps	bag of chips
dustbin	trashcan	queuing	lining up
football	soccer	roundabout	carousel
fringe	bangs	rounders	baseball
ice lolly	ice pop	sellotape	scotch tape
jelly	jell-O	set books	course books
jumper	sweater	sweet-boxes	candy-boxes
letter-box	mail slot	toilet	bathroom
motorway	highway	trainers	sneakers

There are also points of grammatical and idiomatic difference, such as (British > American) *next day > the next day*.

Other books in the series show similar alterations in grammar and idiom. My favourite switch is in chapter 2 of *The Chamber of Secrets*. 'Bit rich coming from you!' says British Harry to British Ron. 'You should talk!' says American Harry to American Ron.

Robert Cawdrey finishes his
Table Alphabeticall in 1604

This is the date ending the Preface to an innovative publication by schoolteacher Robert Cawdrey, assisted by his schoolteacher son, Thomas. It was such a new idea that he had to explain in his introduction how his *Table Alphabeticall* should be used:

> If thou be desirous (gentle Reader) rightly and readily to understand, and to profit by this Table, and such like, then thou must learn the alphabet, to wit, the order of the Letters as they stand, perfectly without book, and where every Letter standeth: as b near the beginning, n about the middest, and t toward the end.

We can easily forget that there was a time when the notion of alphabetical order was novel. And this was the first time readers had available an English word list with English-only (as opposed to bilingual) definitions arranged in this way.

It wasn't a dictionary of the kind we know today. It wasn't very large, containing only 2,449 defined items. And, as the description on his title page says, it contained only 'hard words', many of which had only recently entered the language:

> A Table Alphabeticall, conteyning and teaching the true writing, and
> vnderstanding of hard vsuall English wordes, borrowed
> from the Hebrew, Greeke, Latine, or French, &c.
> With the interpretation thereof by plaine English words, gathered
> for the benefit & helpe of Ladies, Gentlewomen, or any other
> unskilfull persons.
> Whereby they may the more easilie and better vnderstand many hard
> English wordes, which they shall heare or read in Scriptures, Sermons,
> or elswhere, and also be made able to vse the same aptly themselues.

(*Unskilfull persons* would be anyone – men or women – who lacked a high level of education, especially in the classical languages.)

The book did include many 'hard' words, such as *dilacerate* and *ebulliated*, but there were also more everyday words, such as *alarum* and *idiot*. Cawdrey's *Table* gave English lexicography a new direction.

Pierre Paul Broca was born in 1824

He was a French physician, anatomist and anthropologist, who made many contributions to medical science, but for language enthusiasts he's remembered for providing the first anatomical proof of the localization of speech in the brain. He died in 1880. In an 1865 paper, 'Sur le siège de la faculté du langage articulé' ('On the site of the faculty of articulated speech') he refers to his earlier work: 'I had localized the capacity of speech in the left third frontal convolution'. He'd carried out an autopsy on a man who had been unable to say anything except the word *tan* (pronounced as in French *temps*), usually said twice, regardless of the context. (The hospital staff used it as a nickname, calling him Monsieur Tan.) Broca found a large lesion in that part of the brain. He then followed it up with similar studies. Later research on Tan's brain (which is still preserved) has shown that the lesion was more extensive than Broca suspected, but his basic conclusion was robust.

He gives an update, in an attractively informal style, captured in this translation, using the term *aphémie* to describe the loss of speech – what would later be called *expressive aphasia*:

> You remember, no doubt, that in all the cases I mentioned in 1863, the lesion was located on the left. I remarked on this fact without coming to any conclusions, and I added that, before groping for the implications of a finding so strange, one has to wait for new findings. Since then the facts have presented themselves in great numbers, and almost all have pointed in the same direction.

Towards the end of his paper he provides a signpost that has been followed by generations of speech and language therapists:

> I am convinced that considerable results can be obtained with restoring to *aphémiques* the part of their intellect that perished with a part of their brain. These results can be achieved by exercising sufficient perseverance, by treating them with the tireless patience of the mother who teaches her son how to speak.

The region of the brain is now known as 'Broca's area'.

First National Educational Association spelling bee held in the USA in 1908

Spelling bees are a familiar event these days, at least in English-speaking countries, where the irregularity of the English spelling system and the sheer scale of its lexicon makes for a challenging competition. Languages where the orthography is predictable tend not to run such events, though they aren't unknown (there's one in Dutch, for example). They're especially popular in the USA. Annual contests are held locally, and winners can then compete at higher levels, with the top level being the National Spelling Bee, which has run since 1925, now called the Scripps National Spelling Bee. The event attracts huge national interest, to the extent that in 2002 a 97-minute documentary, *Spellbound*, followed eight of the contestants in the 1999 national competition – as dramatic as any thriller, and a challenge to those watching to match themselves against the finalists.

The level of difficulty can be illustrated by some of the words presented in the 2019 championship: *erysipelas*, *bougainvillea*, *cernuous*, *odylic*, *pendeloque*. There needs to be a reference standard, as there's a great deal of spelling variation in English, especially between British and American varieties, and this is provided for US competitions by *Webster's Third New International Dictionary*.

Spelling isn't the only topic to motivate bees. Any gathering of people with a shared purpose might attract the name, especially if the aim is for people in a community to get together to help one of its members. This was the original sense, recorded since the eighteenth century, and we find *quilting bees*, *sewing bees*, *apple bees*, and many others. The spelling competition emerged somewhat later, in the nineteenth century.

It's the communal quality of the events that led to the thought that *bee* derived from the name of the insect, known for its social behaviour. In fact the origin is less vivid, but not entirely clear. There are dialect usages of *been*, from Middle English *bene* 'prayer, petition', with the meaning of 'neighbourly help'; *boon* is a related word. But if *bee* does derive from *been*, the reason it lost its final -*n* is a mystery.

World Social Media Day

The day was introduced by the entertainment and multi-platform digital media business Mashable in 2010 to recognize and celebrate the impact of social media on global communication. These media are now so universally routine that it would hardly seem to need the attention that a special day affords. But days do more than draw attention; they provide a moment to take stock. And there are certainly many issues that would benefit from regular scrutiny, such as fake news, hate speech, and the other unanticipated negative outcomes of these platforms. This day provides an opportunity to debate such matters more fully.

It also provides an opportunity for linguistic reflection. The social media phenomenon is so recent, diverse and changeable that it's difficult to arrive at reliable statements about the language of any one platform, let alone generalizing about the medium as a whole. The recency is clear from the launch dates. The first social media platform, Sixdegrees, was launched in 1997 (closing in 2001). Then we have Friends Reunited (2000), Friendster (2002), LinkedIn (2003), MySpace and Facebook (2004), YouTube (2005), Twitter (2006), Instagram (2010), Snapchat (2011), Tiktok (2016), and a host of others, each with a linguistic character uniquely reflecting its individual technological and marketing aims. Nor is the genre easy to define because of the way it overlaps with messaging and gaming services, such as WhatsApp and Minecraft.

The speed of change is also a complicating factor for linguists. Twitter is a good example (SEE 15 JULY). Its self-imposed constraint as a short messaging service, with a limited number of characters, made it a promising domain for identifying distinctive stylistic features. But the switch from the prompt 'what are you doing?' to 'what's happening?' in 2009 motivated a new set of linguistic preferences – such as a wider range of tense forms and personal pronouns – and the later increase in the character count offered fresh options for sentence construction. But, despite the difficulties, this domain offers new generations of linguists an enticing and apparently limitless set of opportunities for original linguistic enquiry.

Harriet Beecher Stowe died in 1896

Born in 1811 in Connecticut, Beecher Stowe became a prolific author of novels, stories, articles and letters, and achieved international recognition as a leading abolitionist. The fame of her anti-slavery novel *Uncle Tom's Cabin* (1852) has to some extent taken attention away from her other writing, which contains many vivid and memorable pictures of life and times. Language is often a focus, not only in her realistic depiction of the way people spoke, but in the way she steps back to comment, often with great humour, about linguistic attitudes and practices. Here's an instance from the memoir of Horace Holyoke, as told in *Oldtown Folks* (1869): chapter 33 describes 'School-life in Cloudland', capturing the ethos of school grammar competitions.

> Bless me, how we did study everything in that school! English grammar, for instance. The whole school was divided into a certain number of classes, each under a leader, and at the close of every term came on a great examination, which was like a tournament or passage at arms in matters of the English language. To beat in this great contest of knowledge was what excited all our energies. Mr. Rossiter searched out the most difficult specimens of English literature for us to parse, and we were given to understand that he was laying up all the most abstruse problems of grammar to propound to us. All that might be raked out from the coarse print and the fine print of grammar was to be brought to bear on us; and the division that knew the most – the division that could not be puzzled by any subtlety that had anticipated every possible question, and was prepared with an answer – would be the victorious division, and would be crowned with laurels as glorious in our eyes as those of the old Olympic games. For a week we talked, spoke, and dreamed of nothing but English grammar. Each division sat in solemn, mysterious conclave, afraid lest one of its mighty secrets of wisdom should possibly take wing and be plundered by some of the outlying scouts of another division.

Freedom from Fear of Speaking Day

I've been unable to establish who started this day or when, but why it was started is acknowledged on many a website. The focus is not on speaking in general but on the anxiety felt by many people when asked to speak to an audience on a public occasion, with advice being offered about how to overcome it.

The first step is to acknowledge our natural speaking ability. Clinical conditions aside, everyone is naturally eloquent. The spontaneous volubility of children as they reach age 5 or so is well recognized, and this transfers into a natural storytelling ability, shown by the way people readily tell a joke, describe what happened on a holiday, or bring others up to date on an episode of a television programme. When I was writing *The Gift of the Gab: How Eloquence Works* I encountered many who denied they were eloquent, but who then went on to give an eloquent explanation of why they weren't. They were proficient speakers, easily holding their own in conversations and contributing humour and originality to them. Clearly, they had no fear when talking informally to a group of people they knew. It was the prospect of talking on a formal occasion to a group of people they didn't know, or didn't usually talk to, that scared them.

The self-help books and sites are full of advice. They point out that nervousness is normal; it's panic that has to be avoided. First and foremost: know your subject, and care about it. You must *want* to tell people about it. Then, get organized, with notes and other aids. Use technology judiciously, and never rely on it to work. Practise (repeatedly) with people you know, and get the timing right. Ease yourself into a speech by an off-topic remark at the outset, so that you get used to how you sound and the audience gets used to your voice. If possible, visit the place where the speech will be held and become familiar with its facilities and atmosphere. And, as the moment arrives, deep breathing before starting always helps.

Daniel Jones's first public presentation of Shakespeare in original pronunciation in 1909

During the second half of the nineteenth century, interest steadily grew in reconstructing the English accents of earlier times. Scholars such as Alexander Ellis (SEE 14 JUNE) began to make phonetic transcriptions of texts, and by the time Daniel Jones (SEE 4 DECEMBER) joined the phonetics department at University College London, an impressive body of knowledge had accumulated. Jones, unlike his predecessors, was prepared to put the theory into theatrical practice. Ellis had shied away from such a prospect, writing in 1871 that 'it is, of course, not to be thought of that Shakespeare's plays should now be publicly read or performed in this pronunciation'. It was a time when the only acceptable accent for dramatic performance was received pronunciation (RP).

RP still ruled the stage in 1909, so it was quite daring of Jones to make a public presentation of original pronunciation (OP) on this day, taking scenes from *The Tempest* and *Twelfth Night*, himself playing Prospero and Andrew Aguecheek. It was evidently a success, judging by the review in the next day's *Observer*: 'The effect of the old pronunciation on the ear was very pleasing.' And the day was immortalized in a phonetics journal the following year:

> Saturday, 3 July, 1909, marks an epoch in the history of Elizabethan representations of Shakespeare. On that date people living in the twentieth century heard some of Shakespeare's work in the pronunciation which may be safely accepted as that used by the poet himself.

The appeal of the event is also suggested by the fact that he repeated it in Wimbledon (where he lived) in December 1909, this time including some madrigals from the period.

He would, I believe, be delighted at the way OP has become a movement attracting global interest, being taken up in 2004 by London's Shakespeare's Globe (SEE 12 JUNE) for a production of *Romeo and Juliet*, and since then for a host of other plays and songs. The development of the practice can be found at www.originalpronunciation.com.

United States Independence Day

The day commemorates the US Declaration of Independence in 1776. The event had linguistic as well as political consequences, for many thought a new nation needed a new language. It was Noah Webster (SEE 16 OCTOBER) who made the clearest statement, in a book written a decade later: *Dissertations on the English Language*. In his opening chapter he presents his case:

> As an independent nation, our honor requires us to have a system of our own, in language as well as government. Great Britain, whose children we are, and whose language we speak, should no longer be *our* standard … she is at too great a distance to be our model, and to instruct us in the principles of our own tongue.

There is no better time, he believes:

> We have therefore the fairest opportunity of establishing a national language, and of giving it uniformity and perspicuity, in North America, that ever presented itself to mankind. Now is the time to begin the plan. The minds of the Americans are roused by the events of a revolution.

And he draws a contrast with European countries:

> America, placed at a distance from those nations, will feel, in a much less degree, the influence of the assimilating causes; at the same time, numerous local causes, such as a new country, new associations of people, new combinations of ideas in arts and science, and some intercourse with tribes wholly unknown in Europe, will introduce new words into the American tongue. These causes will produce, in a course of time, a language in North America, as different from the future language of England, as the modern Dutch, Danish and Swedish are from the German, or from one another: Like remote branches of a tree springing from the same stock; or rays of light, shot from the same center, and diverging from each other, in proportion to their distance from the point of separation.

His prediction was wrong: British and American English are not so different. But distinctiveness there certainly is, and much of it is due to Webster's own innovations, especially in spelling.

Alice Masak French died in 2013

She was born in 1930 in Baillie-Hamilton Island in the Nunavut region of Canada, and became especially known for her two autobiographies describing her Inuit heritage, and the difficulties in maintaining it: *My Name is Masak* (1977) and *The Restless Nomad* (1992). She explained her linguistic background during an interview in *Canadian Literature* in 2000:

> Our language is called the Inuvialuit language. The Eastern Arctic is Inuktitun, so there's a few sets of language. But then there's a lot of little dialects in between, such as Siglit, Ummarmiut, and Kangiryourmuit dialects. Any little settlement has its own dialect so it's very hard to say that everybody has the same language.

She's asked if there are many speakers left:

> Yes, there are quite a lot. Especially in the Eastern Arctic. They have kept their language alive through all these years. I don't know how they did it, but they've kept it alive much more than we have in the Western Arctic. We have lost a lot. But we've got a lot of good Inuvialuit teachers coming into the schools to teach the language, which is good.

Asked why she used English in her books, her answer well illustrates some of the practical issues that any author of an endangered or minority language has to deal with:

> Well, I stuck to English mainly because it was easier for me to keep it flowing. If I used Inuvialuit terms, I would have to stop and explain all the time and so it would get disjointed. And the other reason was that my children didn't know their language and they would have to forever come to me and say, 'What does this mean?' or 'Does this really explain what that is?' So it was mainly easier for my own work to use English. I tried in one chapter to use Inuvialuit terms, but I got so muddled because I'd have to explain what it was and then try to get back my train of thought when I was there and to get back to it.

William Faulkner died in 1962

He was born in Mississippi in 1897, and became the author of such
acclaimed novels as *The Sound and the Fury* (1929), *As I Lay Dying* (1930)
and the sequence later called the Yoknapatawpha saga, beginning with
Light in August (1932). He was awarded the Nobel Prize for Literature
in 1949. An interview in *The Paris Review* for 1956 provides some
memorable moments.

Asked how he thinks of himself as a writer:

> If I had not existed, someone else would have written me, Hemingway,
> Dostoyevsky, all of us. Proof of that is that there are about three
> candidates for the authorship of Shakespeare's plays. But what is important
> is *Hamlet* and *A Midsummer Night's Dream*, not who wrote them, but that
> somebody did. The artist is of no importance. Only what he creates is
> important, since there is nothing new to be said.

Is there any possible formula to follow in order to be a good novelist?

> Ninety-nine percent talent ... ninety-nine percent discipline ... ninety-
> nine percent work. He must never be satisfied with what he does. It never
> is as good as it can be done. Always dream and shoot higher than you
> know you can do. Don't bother just to be better than your contemporaries
> or predecessors. Try to be better than yourself. An artist is a creature
> driven by demons. He don't know why they choose him and he's usually
> too busy to wonder why. He is completely amoral in that he will rob,
> borrow, beg, or steal from anybody and everybody to get the work done.

Do you mean the writer should be completely ruthless?

> The writer's only responsibility is to his art. He will be completely
> ruthless if he is a good one. He has a dream. It anguishes him so much
> he must get rid of it. He has no peace until then. Everything goes by the
> board: honor, pride, decency, security, happiness, all, to get the book
> written. If a writer has to rob his mother, he will not hesitate; the 'Ode on
> a Grecian Urn' is worth any number of old ladies.

Richard Brinsley Sheridan died in 1816

Born in Dublin in 1751, Sheridan became a theatre owner and Member of Parliament, but is best known for his satirical plays such as *The Rivals* (1775), *The School for Scandal* (1777) and – of special relevance for this book – *The Critic* (1779), a parody of theatre writing and practices. It is linguistically memorable for the character of Mr Puff, who describes himself as 'a practitioner in panegyric, or, to speak more plainly, a professor of the art of puffing, at your service'.

A *puff* was a piece of inflated or unmerited praise, used to advertise a product or (in this case) to publicize a play. Widely used in the eighteenth century, it retained its usefulness, and exponents of the art have been variously called *puff-masters*, *puff-purveyors* and *puff-merchants*. Mr Puff describes a catalogue of the types of puff he employs in his profession, and Sheridan doesn't pull any punches in identifying the leading puff-masters of his day, such as those who conduct auctions:

> Even the auctioneers now – the auctioneers, I say – though the rogues have lately got some credit for their language – not an article of the merit theirs: take them out of their pulpits, and they are as dull as catalogues! – No, sir; 'twas I first enriched their style – 'twas I first taught them to crowd their advertisements with panegyrical superlatives, each epithet rising above the other, like the bidders in their own auction rooms! From me they learned to inlay their phraseology with variegated chips of exotic metaphor: by me too their inventive faculties were called forth: – yes, sir, by me they were instructed to clothe ideal walls with gratuitous fruits – to insinuate obsequious rivulets into visionary groves – to teach courteous shrubs to nod their approbation of the grateful soil; or on emergencies to raise upstart oaks, where there never had been an acorn; to create a delightful vicinage [neighbourhood] without the assistance of a neighbour; or fix the temple of Hygeia [the Greek goddess of health] in the fens of Lincolnshire!

Raja Rao died in 2006

Born in 1908 in Karnataka (formerly Mysore) in India into a Kannada-speaking family, he became known for his novels such as *Kanthapura* (1938) and *The Serpent and the Rope* (1960). Kanthapura has a famous foreword describing the challenge of telling a story about his village.

> The telling has not been easy. One has to convey in a language that is not one's own; the spirit that is one's own. One has to convey the various shades and omissions of a certain thought-movement that looks maltreated in an alien language. I use the word 'alien', yet English is not really an alien language to us. It is the language of our intellectual make-up, like Sanskrit or Persian was before, but not of our emotional make-up. We are all instinctively bilingual, many of us writing in our own language and in English. We cannot write like the English. We should not. We cannot write only as Indians. We have grown to look at the large world as part of us. Our method of expression therefore has to be a dialect which will some day prove to be as distinctive and colorful as the Irish or the American. Time alone will justify it.

He adds a comment about style.

> The tempo of Indian life must be infused into our English expression, even as the tempo of American or Irish life has gone into the making of theirs. We, in India, think quickly, we talk quickly, and when we move we move quickly. There must be something in the sun of India that makes us rush and tumble and run on. And our paths are paths interminable. ... Episode follows episode, and when our thoughts stop our breath stops, and we move on to another thought. This was and still is the ordinary style of our story-telling. I have tried to follow it myself in this story.

The linguist Braj Kachru (SEE 29 JULY) wrote in *World Literature Today* (1988): 'I do not believe that before Rao the questions of linguistic innovations and new identities of English had been addressed with this precision and conviction.'

Franz Boas was born in 1858

Often called 'the father of American anthropology', Boas was born in Germany, and emigrated to the USA in 1887, becoming professor of anthropology at Columbia University, and remaining there until his death in 1942. He might equally be called the father of American linguistics, as he published many descriptions of American Indian languages, and made the relationship between language, culture and thought a central topic of study.

He also brought a fresh perspective to the theoretical issues that arise when classifying languages, and his detailed illustrations of Amerindian grammatical features were an eye-opener to European linguists, whose mindset was largely conditioned by Latin and Greek – notions such as singular vs plural, or masculine, feminine and neuter. Even today, people who know only the languages of Europe find it difficult to think outside of these categories.

Here are two illustrations from the introduction he wrote to the *Handbook of American Indian Languages* (1911). Tense is traditionally seen as a category of the verb, but nouns can have tenses too:

> As we may speak of *a future husband* or of *our late friend*, thus many Indian languages express in every noun its existence in present, past, or future, which they require as much for clearness of expression as we require the distinction of singular and plural.

Gender was also presented in a new way:

> In the languages of the world, gender is not by any means a fundamental category, and nouns may not be divided into classes at all, or the point of view of classification may be an entirely different one... The Algonquian of North America classify nouns as animate and inanimate, without, however, adhering strictly to the natural classification implied in these terms. Thus the small animals may be classified as inanimate, while certain plants may appear as animate. ... The Iroquois distinguish strictly between nouns designating men and other nouns. ... The Uchee distinguish between members of the tribe and other human beings. In America, true gender is on the whole rare.

National Clerihew Day

The day is recognized chiefly in the United States, commemorating the birthday of Edmund Clerihew Bentley (1875–1956). Born in London, he became a journalist, and then a writer of popular whodunnits, especially involving the amateur detective Philip Trent, beginning with *Trent's Last Case* (1912), published in the USA as *The Woman in Black*. He achieved greater fame as a humorous poet, creating (at age 16) the whimsical four-line verse named after him.

Its first line is a famous person's name, the second adds a biographical note, and the concluding two lines say something humorous, usually absurd or anachronistic. It follows a strict rhyme scheme of AABB, but the lines are irregular in length. In tone they are a pseudo-eulogy, never unpleasantly satirical or abusive. The effect depends largely on the way an ingenious rhyme can be found for the subject's surname.

His first collection was called *Biography for Beginners* (1905), with the title page explaining: *being a collection of miscellaneous examples for the use of upper forms*. Each item had an illustration by G.K. Chesterton. Here are two examples from a later book, *Baseless Biography* (1939):

Lewis Carroll
Bought sumptuous apparel
And built an enormous palace
Out of the profits of *Alice*.

Although Machiavelli
Was extremely fond of jelly,
He stuck religiously to mince
While he was writing *The Prince*.

It's an infectious genre. And there's no shortage of linguists whose surnames are a challenge:

Randolph Quirk
Was never one to shirk.
He employed a hammer
To subdue English grammar.

I leave you, dear reader, to find one for Noam Chomsky.

Bowdler's Day

Thomas Bowdler was born in Bath on this day in 1754; he died in 1825. He trained as a physician, but became known as the author of *The Family Shakespeare*, though his sister Harriet actually did most of the editing – an event that at the time was considered improper for a woman, but acceptable for a doctor. It was published in 1807, initially with just twenty plays, and became famous for its editorial principle explained in the subtitle: *in which nothing is added to the original text; but those words and expressions are omitted which cannot with propriety be read aloud in a family*. The verb *bowdlerize* soon began to be used to mean 'expurgate passages considered indecent or offensive'.

He writes in his Preface:

> Many words and expressions occur which are of so indecent a nature as to render it highly desirable that they should be erased. Of these, the greater part are evidently introduced to gratify the bad taste or the age in which he lived, and the rest may be ascribed to his own unbridled fancy. But neither the vicious taste of the age, nor the most brilliant effusions of wit, can afford an excuse for profaneness or obscenity; and if these could be obliterated, the transcendent genius of the poet would undoubtedly shine with more unclouded lustre. To banish every thing of this nature from the writings of Shakespeare is the object of the present undertaking.

So, for example, the Porter scene in *Macbeth* goes because of its drunkenness. So does the scene in *Henry V* between the French princess and her maid, learning English words for parts of the body. The prostitute Doll Tearsheet is omitted from *Henry IV*. Hamlet's suggestive remarks to Ophelia go, such as 'Lady, shall I lie in your lap?' Religious references are adapted: Polonius's 'name of God' becomes 'name of heaven'. His decisions have been widely condemned as a form of unnecessary censorship; but at the time they received much praise because his editions, reasonably priced, attracted a much wider readership among children than had ever been possible before.

The issues are still with us, as the controversy in 2023 over the editing of Roald Dahl's books illustrates.

New Conversations Day

The day was inaugurated in 2017 by the online company Awkward Silence. The website founder Steven Benbow writes:

> Conversation is so valuable yet so under-valued. I believe conversation is where friendship comes alive. I believe conversation is where ideas bloom. I believe conversation is the life-blood of relationships. Talk with someone and you will be fascinated, valued, challenged and enlightened. You gain new perspective. You grow bonds. You discover yourself.

It's a subject that has attracted a great deal of linguistic research under such headings as *conversation analysis* or *discourse analysis*. It was a relatively late developing field in linguistics, mainly because of the difficulty of obtaining reliable recordings of natural conversation of good acoustic quality. It's much easier today, with modern recording technology, and younger people are more used to having their speech recorded than were their parents and grandparents. But, despite all the academic work, the linguistic character of everyday chat is still not widely appreciated, which is why I wrote my own *Let's Talk: How English Conversation Works* (2020).

This day is also the birthday of Randolph Quirk (1920–2017), professor of English language at University College London for many years, and founder of the Survey of English Usage in 1959, which was one of the first serious attempts to describe the grammatical features of informal conversation (SEE 20 MAY). It brought to light features that had never been mentioned in grammar books, such as the 'comment clauses' that are frequent in conversation (*you know, you see, I mean, mind you...*), and showed that they have a grammar of their own and play an important role in helping an informal interaction to operate smoothly.

Several of the more widely spoken modern languages have received some conversation analysis, but there are many that have received no linguistic description at all, and there's still a great deal to be explored even in English, such as differences in conversational style that may distinguish social and ethnic groups.

Wole Soyinka was born in 1934

This Nigerian playwright, novelist, poet and essayist was awarded the Nobel Prize for Literature in 1986. He was born in Abeokuta, in the Yoruba-speaking part of the country, and while his works reflect this cultural background, he writes in English – an inevitable consequence of developing a literary presence in multilingual Nigeria, with its hundreds of languages, where English was the colonial lingua franca. Language – and especially the abuse of language by political leaders – is a recurring theme in his many talks and interviews, along with an affirmation of the critical role played by culture, as in this 2018 interview for Turning Page:

> All cultures are related to one another in some way. I am an African playwright, and I can use a play written by Brecht and adapt it with African classics. ... Culture generally is comparative, which is where the joy lies. There is joy when you can relate and connect another culture with yours and feel a certain air to them all.

The importance of freedom of speech is another theme, powerfully expressed in an interview for Index on Censorship in 2012:

> There are many cultures on the African continent where days are set aside, days of irreverence where you can say anything you want about an all-powerful monarch or chief. It's a safety valve. It's a recognition of freedom of expression, which perhaps has not been exercised, and bottled up grievances; this is the day when you express your grievances in society. So there is no society, really, which does not boast some form or measure of freedom of expression. Now, it's true that freedom of expression carries with it an immense responsibility. Well that is why laws of libel exist – that when you carry things too far, you can be hauled up before the community, and judged to see whether you are right to call somebody a thief, or a hypocrite, and damage his reputation. But unless you establish that principle of freedom of expression, we might all just go around with a padlock on our lips.

Richard Taverner died in 1575

He was born in Norfolk in 1505, became a lawyer, and made one of the early translations of the Bible into English, published in 1535. Four years later he carried out another major translation: 'Proverbes or adagies [adages] with newe addicions gathered out of the Chiliades [thousands] of Erasmus'. The figure was not an exaggeration: Erasmus had made the largest collection of Latin proverbs to date – over 4,000 of them. Many have entered the lexicon of modern languages, such as 'call a spade a spade'. This is Taverner's entry (I've expanded his abbreviations):

> *Veritas simplex oratio.*
> Trouthes tale is simple, he that meaneth good fayth, goeth not aboute to glose hys communicacion wyth painted wordes. Plaine and homely men call a fygge [fig], a fygge, & a spade a spade. Rhetorike and colorynge of spech proueth many tymes a mans mater [matter] to be naught.

That is a typical example of his method: take a Latin aphorism, give a literal translation, and then expand it with examples. All kinds of subjects are treated in his selection of 169 entries, supplemented by a further selection from Pythagoras and Publius. Here are some more on language:

> *Non est eiusdem & multa et oportuna dicere.*
> It is not for one man to speake both many wordes and apte wordes. This prouerbe teacheth vs to eschue [avoid] much talke, for asmuche as for moost parte, he must nedes fayle in hys speche that loueth to haue many wordes. To thys agreeth the wyse man in hys prouerbes, where he sayeth, y^t [that] vnto much speakynge is synne annexed.

> *Qui quae uult dicit, quae non uult audiet.*
> He that speaketh what he woll [will], shall heare what he woll not. Let men beware howe they rayle.

> *Dicendo dicere discunt.*
> By speakynge men lerne to speake, by wrytynge men lerne to wryte, by syngynge to synge, briefly euery science is gotten by lernynge of the same.

> *Qualis uir talis oratio.*
> As the man is, so is hys talke. The talke of honest men is honesty, the talke of knaues is knauerye.

Launch of Twitter in 2006

Originally *Twttr*, the name changed to its present form a few months later. It was conceived as a short-messaging service allowing users to share short status updates with followers by sending a text to a single number. The messages were limited to 140 characters, a figure determined by the maximum size of text messages at the time. Texts by phone allowed 160 characters, but when messages were posted online 20 were reserved to capture user identity. Described as a 'microblogging' service, it became one of the fastest growing social networking platforms.

The linguistic character of early tweets was constrained by the 'what are you doing?' prompt, which motivated the use of the present tense and first-person pronouns. A company launch-day blog post drew attention to this aspect:

> Twttr is a new mobile service that helps groups of friends bounce random thoughts around with SMS. When we showed it to Jason Goldman (product manager of Blogger) he called it 'present tense blogging.' That's a great way to describe it. It's fun to use because it strips social blogging down to its essence and makes it immediate.

When the prompt changed in 2009 to 'what's happening?' a much more diverse set of tense forms appeared, as users talked about what had just taken place or was about to happen. Similarly the range of third-person references increased, as users talked about what was going on around them. The content also diversified, with tweets increasingly being used for news reporting, advertising, and other information services.

There was a belief at the time that a limit of 140 characters would result in a grammatically simplified usage that could over time have negative consequences for people's expressive language ability. In fact, although many tweets use short sentences and abbreviated forms, 140 characters still offers a great deal of grammatical choice. In English, that allows sentences of some 20 or even 30 words, which is more than enough to permit some quite complex constructions. And grammatical options became even more flexible when the character limit was increased to 280 characters in 2017.

Mari Evans was born in 1919

Mari Evans was born in Toledo, Ohio. Her birth year was affirmed at her funeral in 2017 by relatives, for many sources give this as 1923. She became known for her writing in several genres, and especially for her poetry, such as *I Am a Black Woman* (1970). The power of language is a recurrent theme in her critical essays, notably in *Clarity as Concept: A Poet's Perspective* (2006), and especially the way language in general – and African-American idiom in particular – can be used as a means of creating identity: 'I try for a poetic language that says, this is who we are, where we have been, where we are. This is where we must go. And this is what we must do.'

She relates this to the first-person pronoun in a 2016 interview, describing three phases of 'I' usage when becoming a writer. The earliest is 'letting people know who I am'. Then:

> The second phase is when you start to look around you and talk about the people around you and who they are. Then there's a third phase when you talk about yourself *and* the people around you. The third phase is when you have a political point of view – that's when the 'I's become important.

The neglected subject of listening is given a powerful expression in 'How We Speak':

> Listening is a special art. It is a fine art developed by practice. One hears the unexpressed as clearly as if it had been verbalized. One hears silence screaming in clarion tones. Ninety decibels. Hears tears, unshed, falling. Hears hunger gnawing at the back of spines; hears aching feet pushed past that one more step. Hears the repressed hurt of incest, hears the anguish of spousal abuse. Hears it all. Clearly, listening is a fine art. It can translate an obscure text into reality that walks, weeps and carries its own odor. Listening can decode a stranger's eye and hear autobiography. Listening can watch a listless babe and understand the absence of future, the improbability, in fact, of possibility. Listening, more often than not, is a crushing experience.

World Emoji Day

The day was created in 2014 by the founder of emojipedia, Jeremy Burge, to promote the use and enjoyment of emojis. This was the date that Apple unveiled its iCal app in 2002, and it became the standard display on iPhones, now called Apple Calendar. Since 2017, Apple has used the day to announce the latest extension to the emoji set.

There have always been some non-alphabetic symbols in English (and other languages), as shown on any keyboard (&, %, £, etc.), but something different happened in the 1980s with the arrival of smileys and emoticons. The first efforts used keyboard characters which, viewed sideways in English settings, were intended to convey an emotional feeling or tone. As the original name suggested, the emotion was one of pleasure or humour, expressed typically by :), but this was soon followed by variations that expressed other meanings. Feelings were supplemented by creative combinations to represent real-world characters and events.

The technology evolved to replace keyboard symbols with more realistic faces – yellow and homogeneous at first, and now representing different skin colours and genders, recognizing the need to respect social diversity. Emojis were introduced in 1999, a more sophisticated option than emoticons that took advantage of technological developments in social media platforms. The increase in use has been dramatic, with new directions appearing, such as the emoji + anime blend that has emerged in the past decade in the form of stickers; but there have been problems.

The symbols were introduced to avoid a perceived limitation in the graphic character of electronic communication, which lacked facial expressions, bodily gestures and the prosody of speech. The belief was that the symbols would express emotional intentions unambiguously. Some emojis, such as objects and animals, are indeed more likely to elicit a uniform response, but others produce uncertain reactions. A joined-hands emoji, for example, has been variously interpreted as 'prayer', 'clap hands', 'appeal', 'thanks', and more. It remains to be seen just how serious the interpretation problem is for the development of the medium. In the meantime, research is needed into their function and distribution.

John Hart became Chester Herald in 1567

There are few biographical facts known about John Hart. His birth year was about 1501, and he died in 1574, but the date he became an officer-of-arms in Chester is recorded. He was one of the first generation of sixteenth-century spelling reformers, and his books are unequalled for their phonetic detail. In 1569 he published *An orthographie, conteyning the due order and reason, howe to write or paint thimage of mannes voice, most like to the life of nature.* He advocated radical reform, believing that only a phonic approach – one sound, one letter – would rid the language of its several 'vices and corruptions'.

In the Preface to his *Orthography*, he explains why reform is needed. This is his first reason:

> I will nowe signifie unto such as have not wilfully professed themselves to be obstinate in their custome, that the use and experience of thorder of this following English Orthographie, shall bring their commodities [advantages] following. First it shall cause the naturall English [person] knowing no letter, to be able to learne to decerne and easily to reade (whatsoever he may see before him so written or printed) so soone as he were able to learne readily, and perfectly to know and name, the number of figures or members of the bodie and substance of our voice and speach, & so observing the new or straunge order hereafter written, the learned man may instruct any naturall English reasonable creature, to read English, in one quarter of the time that ever any other hath heretofore bene taught to reade, by any former maner. And in what lesse time, and how much more easie and readie, it will be for the writer or printer, reader and hearer, I will not write, but leave it to the judgement of the reader, of the sayd following treatise, and to the experience it selfe as occasion shall serve.

That opening lengthy sentence contains an intriguing hint: how best to reform spelling was a controversial and hotly debated topic at the time. The final sentence is a nice piece of marketing: just try it!

Alan Lomax died in 2002

Born in Austin, Texas, in 1915, Lomax became known primarily as
an ethnomusicologist, recording and describing folk-music traditions
in the USA, Britain and other parts of Europe, many of which would
have been lost without his efforts at preservation and publication. His
combined focus on music and language makes his work of special interest
to linguists, and his comments on folk music in 'An Appeal for Cultural
Equity' echo those made by researchers into endangered languages:

> Scientific study of cultures, notably of their languages and their musics,
> shows that all are equally expressive and equally communicative, even
> though they may symbolize technologies of different levels... With
> the disappearance of each of these systems, the human species not
> only loses a way of viewing, thinking, and feeling but also a way of
> adjusting to some zone on the planet which fits it and makes it livable;
> not only that, but we throw away a system of interaction, of fantasy
> and symbolizing which, in the future, the human race may sorely need.

In an essay titled 'Song Structure and Social Structure', published in
1962, he recommended that 'ethnomusicology should turn aside, for a
time, from the study of music in purely musical terms to a study of music
in context, as a form of human behavior.' He devised a method to locate
sets of musical phenomena cross-culturally which he called *cantometrics* –
thirty-seven criteria that classified songs on the basis of such features as
the size, structure and location of the music-making group, and the vocal
organization and embellishments heard in sung performance.

In a category titled 'words to nonsense' he rated the relative importance
of meaningful words as against nonsense syllables: words important and
dominant; words less important; words with some nonsense; nonsense
more important than words; and nonsense only (as in a song consisting
only of scat singing). Other language-related parameters were volume,
glissando, tremulo, vocal register, nasality, raspiness, forcefulness and
consonant enunciation. The only thing missing, to my mind, was regional
accent.

Deborah Schiffrin died in 2017

Born in Philadelphia in 1951, Schiffrin became known for her work in sociolinguistics and pragmatics, and specifically in the field of discourse analysis. The cover of one of her influential books, *Discourse Markers* (1987), illustrates the kind of topic involved: a collage of the particles *well*, *oh*, *now*, *then*, *I mean* and *y'know*, and the connecting words *so*, *because*, *and*, *but* and *or*. Words like these were among the least studied features of conversation, yet they're crucial to maintaining the smoothness of speech, reinforcing a mutually supportive interaction between participants, and fostering their social relationships. The range of factors that explain their use surprised her:

> I didn't expect to have to describe my informants' positions on controversial issues, their views of themselves in relation to each other, to their social groups, and to the larger society and culture, or their means of socializing with each other through arguments and stories.

A traditional analysis of a word like *now*, for example, would say simply that it was an adverb of time, as in *I'm on the bus now*. But when used in conversation it often has a much wider range of functions. It can introduce a comparison with a point just made, as in *now where else did we go?* It can soften a disagreement, as in *now, that isn't so hard*. It can show a shift in the way someone is speaking, as in *now why was that?* It can suggest resistance to a suggestion, as in *now look here…* In these and other such contexts there's one thing in common: the word isn't given a main stress, as it does in *I'm on the bus now*.

This is tricky research to do, as it depends on building a corpus of recordings that maintain the natural and unselfconscious flow of a conversation. It needs to be of good acoustic quality, so that discourse markers, often rapidly and quietly spoken, aren't missed. And it needs an interdisciplinary approach, in which sociological and psychological factors are taken into account, alongside the insights obtained through linguistics.

Jonathan Miller was born in 1934

Born in London, Miller trained as a physician, but his career moved in a different direction following his early performances in the Cambridge revue *Beyond the Fringe*. He became known as a theatre and opera director, and achieved a public presence through many television programmes and series, including directing six plays for the BBC Shakespeare Project (1978–85) and in 1990 a four-part series *Born Talking: A Personal Inquiry into Language*, exploring child language acquisition, language disorders, sign language and the nature of conversation. He always maintained the medical strand in his life, both as a writer and researcher, notably in writing and presenting the television series *The Body in Question* (1978). He died in 2019.

This extract from the 'Healing and Helping' chapter of the book *The Body in Question* illustrates the wide range of his interests, especially his unique ability to bring together aspects of medical science, anthropology and linguistics:

> One of the most consistent features of a magical performance is the ritual use of words and slogans – something which is conspicuous by its absence from procedures which are obviously technical in character. Surgical operations are not usually performed to the accompaniment of rhymes or ditties: if a surgeon hums to himself or recites bawdy limericks under his breath, he does so to steady his nerves, and if he says anything else it is because he is trying to communicate with his staff. When the magician speaks, however, he is addressing neither himself nor his assistants: he is talking to, or rather at, his materials. In fact, the language of magical spells is deliberately uncommunicative. The incantations are mumbled or muttered and, even when they can be overheard, they usually sound nonsensical – words may be spoken backwards or they may, as in the familiar 'abracadabra', just be salads of syllables. This is partly because magic is a secret art, and because some of its power depends on mystification. But it is also because language is being put to a totally different use: not to convey meaning, but to bring about effects. Spells are not communiqués, they are gestures.

22 JULY

Spooner's Day

William Archibald Spooner was born in London on this day in 1844; he died in 1930. He became a fellow of New College Oxford in 1867, taught ancient history, philosophy and divinity, and eventually became warden from 1903 to 1924. He was highly regarded, intellectually, administratively and socially – contemporaries describe many instances of kind-heartedness towards students as well as the disadvantaged in the wider community. He succeeded despite his physical disabilities – very poor eyesight (a consequence of albinism) and a little-understood neurological condition which gave him (what he called) 'transpositions of thought' that led to errors both in speech and in writing.

In writing he made anticipatory errors – writing a word that would be needed later in a sentence, then crossing it out and replacing it with the correct word when he realized the error. He would perseverate, inappropriately repeating a word already written. And there were blends, such as 'buried *in the grace*' ('grave + place'). In speech, the problem surfaced as one commonly described as 'slips of the tongue' (SEE 19 JANUARY), where sounds or syllables are unintentionally transposed, as in *kinquering congs*. They were sporadic and infrequent, but very noticeable on public occasions, causing humour or embarrassment, and this is what led to his name being associated with the phenomenon. The term *spoonerism* began to emerge during the 1880s.

Very few instances can be attributed with certainty to Spooner himself – less than a dozen in speech. The majority of famous cases, such as 'is the bean dizzy?', were probably undergraduate creations. And certainly today the phenomenon is usually viewed as a source of humour or literary ingenuity rather than as a disability – which is presumably what gave rise to this day. Spooner himself made hardly any reference to it in his diaries, but regretted that he had become 'better known for his defects than for any merits'. He didn't like his reputation. In William Hayter's 1977 biography we read of him adding wrily, after a speech: 'And now I suppose you will expect me to say one of those things.'

Yada Yada Yada Day

It's sometimes called International Yada Yada Yada Day, but whether you'd recognize the allusion outside the USA would depend on whether you were a fan of the sitcom *Seinfeld*, which was hugely popular on American television between 1989 and 1998. Episode 153 (aired on 24 April 1997) was called 'The Yada Yada', because of the way the phrase was used by the characters. The expression has the same function as *blah blah blah* (SEE 17 APRIL) — a way of telling a listener that the remainder of an utterance doesn't need to be said because it's uninteresting, unimportant or irrelevant. It might be glossed as 'and so on and so forth' or 'etcetera'. The humour in the episode lay in the way things can go wrong when the omitted information turns out to be very important.

As with several other words from the series, it became a catchphrase, especially in the USA. But its use long predates its television fame, and it's often heard in British English and elsewhere. The first recorded use in the *Oxford English Dictionary* is by the comedian Lenny Bruce in 1967. Its origin isn't certain. It could be simply a modern imitation of the imagined sound of rapid speech. But it could also be an adaptation of *yatter*, meaning 'talk idly, chatter' which dates from the early nineteenth century, and is found chiefly in Scotland. That in turn may be a blend of *yammer* and *chatter*. *Yammer* is medieval, meaning 'lament, wail' and related to *yomer* 'sorrowful', which takes us right back to Old English *geomor*. There's no sign of *yada yada* in Anglo-Saxon texts, though.

It's not entirely clear what one might do on the day, which has been recognized since 2015, other than watch or rewatch the *Seinfeld* episode. Or perhaps read Jerry Seinfeld's book on humour, *Seinlanguage*, published in 1993. I imagine using the phrase as often as possible in conversation, as some websites recommend, could easily pall, other than among the most steadfast of Seinfelders. But you never know, yada yada yada…

Robert Graves was born in 1895

Born in London, Graves became a poet and novelist, known especially for his wartime autobiography *Goodbye To All That* (1929) and his novels about ancient Rome, *I Claudius* (1934) and its sequel, filmed for BBC television in the 1970s. He died in 1985.

He also wrote a great deal on the nature of language and style. He gave the first of his Oxford Chair of Poetry Lectures in 1961, entitled 'The Dedicated Poet'. Buried deep within it is a short observation which I've found invaluable as an insight into the nature of stylistic explanation:

> I believe that every English poet should read our English Classics, master the main grammatical rules before daring to bend or break them...

The observation can be extended to all aspects of language. Whether we're talking about pronunciation, orthography, vocabulary, discourse, or any other domain of linguistic enquiry, what the poet – or any language innovator – does is 'bend and break' the rules. That is the basis of linguistic originality (SEE 30 MAY). The lines were slightly misquoted in a *Time* article later that year, and in one form or another have become part of language lore. This is the original phrasing in his anthology *Oxford Addresses on Poetry* (1962).

In *On English Poetry* (1922) he makes an observation that anticipates psycholinguistic studies of memory spans in language. Talking about rhyme and alliteration:

> The best effects seem to have been attained in more recent poetry by precisely (if unconsciously) gauging the memory length of a reader's mental ear and planting the second alliterative word at a point where the memory of the first is just beginning to blur; but has not quite faded.
> ... So with internal and ordinary rhyme; but the memory length for the internal rhyme appears somewhat longer than memory for alliteration, and for ordinary rhyme, longer still.

Samuel Taylor Coleridge died in 1834

Born in 1772 in Devon, Coleridge achieved fame as a poet and literary critic, one of the founders of the Romantic literary movement in English poetry, as seen in such major works as 'The Rime of the Ancient Mariner' and 'Kubla Khan', and his *Biographia Literaria* was influential in literary criticism. For a linguist, and especially a stylistician, of special note is his criticism of Wordsworth's claim to be using everyday language in his poetry (SEE 15 SEPTEMBER), drawing attention to the crucial distinctive role of metre and rhyme. His 'translation' of some of Wordsworth's lines into 'rustic' speech, in chapter 18 of the *Biographia*, is especially apt, but perceptive observations about language are scattered throughout that book, as well as in his *Table Talk*.

Here's one such comment from *Table Talk* (3 July 1833):

> The definition of good prose is – proper words in their proper places; – of good verse – the most proper words in their proper places. The propriety is in either case relative. The words in prose ought to express the intended meaning, and no more; if they attract attention to themselves, it is, in general, a fault. In the very best styles, as Southey's, you read page after page, understanding the author perfectly, without once taking notice of the medium of communication; – it is as if he had been speaking to you all the while. But in verse you must do more; – there the words, the *media*, must be beautiful, and ought to attract your notice – yet not so much and so perpetually as to destroy the unity which ought to result from the whole poem.

And a linguistic temperament shows in this extract (27 May 1830). He has been talking about lexical variety in Greek:

> We are not behindhand in English. Fancy my calling you, upon a fitting occasion, – Fool, sot, silly, simpleton, dunce, blockhead, jolterhead, clumsy-pate, dullard, ninny, nincompoop, lackwit, numpskull, ass, owl, loggerhead, coxcomb, monkey, shallow-brain, addle-head, tony, zany, fop, fop-doodle; a maggot-pated, hare-brained, muddle-pated, muddle-headed, Jackan-apes! Why I could go on for a minute more!

Esperanto Day

This was the day the first Esperanto teaching manual was published in 1887, the public launch of a language that its creator, Ludwik Lejzer Zamenhof (1859–1917) had begun to devise while still a schoolboy. It was first published in Russian with the title *International Language*, but later became known as *Unua Libro* (First Book), as a second book (*Dua Libro*) came out the following year. It was translated into many languages, an English translation appearing in 1889 as *Dr. Esperanto's International Language*. Zamenhof had used this pseudonym ('Doctor One Who Hopes'), and the name soon came to be applied to the language. There is now a Zamenhof Day on 15 December, his birthday.

He knew his proposal would be greeted with scepticism, as other artificial languages were being created, and international languages were widely used. In *Unua Libro* he explains his aims, and these are recapitulated by the Universal Esperanto Association on its website:

> We propose that the world should celebrate the 26th of July as a day of linguistic justice and therefore of just and fair relations among ethnic groups, cultures, and peoples.

By 'fairness' they mean that no speaker has an advantage in using a mother tongue in international communication when other participants have to use it as a second language – an issue routinely encountered, of course, in relation to English.

To illustrate the character of Esperanto, here are the opening lines of Hamlet's soliloquy, 'To be or not to be':

> Ĉu esti aŭ ne esti, – tiel staras
> Nun la demando: ĉu pli noble estas
> Elporti ĉiujn batojn, ĉiujn sagojn
> De la kolera sorto, aŭ sin armi
> Kontraŭ la tuta maro da mizeroj
> Kaj per la kontraŭstaro ilin fini?

Hilaire Belloc was born in 1870

Born in France, Belloc grew up in England, and became known as
a writer in many genres, a controversial speaker, and at one point
a Member of Parliament. His *Cautionary Tales for Children* (1907)
included poems that would become very well known, such as 'Matilda
(who told lies, and was burned to death)'. He died in 1953. From his
many humorous essays I select 'A Guide to Boring' (1931), in which
he describes the 'science and practice' lying behind the active 'Art of
Boredom: informing such of us (and I am one) as desire to inflict it upon
our enemies'. As far as I know, boring speech has never been given a
linguistic or semiotic description. Here are two of his recommendations.

> The first sign is an attention in the eye of the bored person to
> something trivial other than yourself. If while you are talking to him
> his eye is directed to a person aiming a gun at him, that is not a sign of
> boredom. But if you see it directed to a little bird, or a passing cloud,
> that is a symptom, as the doctor said. Another symptom is occasional
> interjections which have nothing to do with what you are saying.
> A third, and very much stronger, symptom which should especially
> delight you as proof of triumph is the bored one's breaking out into
> conversation with somebody else in the middle of your speech.

He gives a series of tips for aspiring borers, and concludes:

> Lastly, let me urge on you two private recipes of my own. One is
> spells of silence in the intervals of boring – it's a paradoxical truth that
> they add vastly to the effect. They must not be so long as to let the
> victim take up a book, but just long enough to break his nerve. Watch
> his face, observe its gradual relaxation, and time yourself exactly for
> the renewal of the agony. The other is talking half incomprehensibly,
> mumbling, and the rest of it – then, when the boree impatiently asks
> you to repeat, do it still less clearly. It never fails.

Gerard Manley Hopkins was born in 1844

Hopkins was an English priest and poet, born in Essex. When he decided to become a Jesuit in 1868, he burned all his early poetry, which he felt was unfitting for his new profession, but in 1875 took up his pen again at his religious superior's request. The result was 'The Wreck of the Deutschland' (1875), the first of many poems introducing an innovative rhythm, with echoes of Anglo-Saxon and Welsh writing. He explained it in a letter to a friend (6 October 1878):

> I had long had haunting my ear the echo of a new rhythm which now I realised on paper. To speak shortly, it consists in scanning by accents or stresses alone, without any account of the number of syllables, so that a foot may be but one strong syllable or it may be many light and one strong. I do not say the idea is altogether new; there are hints of it in music, in nursery rhymes and popular jingles, in the poets themselves, and, since then, I have seen it talked about as a thing possible in critics. Here are instances – '*Díng, dóng, béll;* Pússy's ín the wéll; *Whó pút* her ín? Líttle Jóhnny Thín. *Whó púlled* her óut? Líttle Jóhnny Stóut.' For if each line has three stresses or three feet it follows that some of the feet are of one syllable only. So too '*Óne, twó*, Búckle my shóe' *passim*. ... But no one has professedly used it and made it the principle throughout, that I know of. Nevertheless to me it appears, I own, to be a better and more natural principle than the ordinary system, much more flexible, and capable of much greater effects.

He goes on to say that the marking of the stresses and other 'oddnesses' dismayed magazine editors, who rejected his submissions. It put him off, to the extent that he says: 'even the impulse to write is wanting, for I have no thought of publishing'. And indeed his surviving poems weren't published until 1918, long after his death in 1889.

Braj Kachru died in 2016

He was born in Kashmir in 1932, studied linguistics in Edinburgh, then moved to the USA, where he had a fifty-year career at the University of Illinois at Urbana-Champaign, becoming head of the Department of Linguistics, then of the Division of English as an International Language, and finally the Center for Advanced Study. His thinking about the way English has become a global language proved to be hugely influential. This is how he first described it in a conference paper in 1985:

> The spread of English may be viewed in terms of three concentric circles representing the types of spread, the patterns of acquisition and the functional domains in which English is used across cultures and languages. I have tentatively labelled these: the *inner* circle, the *outer* circle (or *extended* circle), and the *expanding* circle.
>
> In terms of the users, the inner circle refers to the traditional bases of English – the regions where it is the primary language [he lists the UK, USA, Canada, Australia, New Zealand].
>
> The outer circle needs a historical explanation: it involves the earlier phases of the spread of English and its institutionalization in non-native contexts [he illustrates from Nigeria, Zambia, Singapore, India].
>
> The expanding circle brings to English yet another dimension. Understanding the function of English in this circle requires a recognition of the fact that English is an international language... The geographical regions characterized as the expanding circle do not necessarily have a history of colonization by the users of the inner circle [he illustrates from China, Indonesia, Greece, Israel, Japan, Korea, Nepal, Saudi Arabia, Taiwan, Zimbabwe]. ...
>
> These three circles, then, bring to English a unique cultural pluralism, and a linguistic heterogeneity and diversity which are unrecorded to this extent in human history.

The statistical dimension shows what he meant by 'extent'. Current estimates suggest that there are about 2.3 billion users of English worldwide. Of these, only around 400 million belong to the inner circle. For every one native speaker, there are now five non-native speakers. The centre of gravity of the language has indeed moved far from its historical origins.

Jean Arasanayagam died in 2019

She was born in Kandy, Sri Lanka, in 1931, and became a writer, known chiefly for her poetry. She wrote especially about the ethnic troubles in her country, and about her identity as a Dutch Burgher – the Dutch arrived in Ceylon in 1638, hence the name *burgher* 'citizen' for their descendants. Her maiden name was Solomons, and she married into a Tamil family; her surname means 'king [*rasa*] of the city [*nayagam*]'. In a 1988 interview with LeRoy Robinson about her heritage, and her links with other Sinhalese writers, she replied:

> We share a language. English. We wrote, we write, in English. The influences in literature were largely European and British. Most of the Burgher writers wrote in a style almost indistinguishable from that of those to whom English was a native language. ... Some of the first poets here to write in English were Burghers. They used language creatively. A language that was alien, non-native. First introduced as the language of bureaucracy. That was interesting. I find we have a connection there, English being the first language of the Burghers here. We generally used Standard English. It was part of our education in a colonial set-up. I now find myself beginning to look at this language differently, with the awareness of the new Englishes that are appearing in the post-colonial context.

We can see her mixed cultural heritage in the first stanza of 'The Ruined Gopuram' (a monumental tower at the entrance to a Hindu temple):

Somewhere lost landscape
White sands and palmyrah fronds
Freakishly black,
All evening the pyres burn
Beside the broken walls,
The ruined gopuram.
Caves darkened in the evening light,
The turquoise seas bright with morning sun
Dimmed and went black.
Unknown goddess, guardian
Of the freshwater spring
Is silent.

Denis Diderot died in 1784

Born in France in 1713, Diderot was a philosopher, novelist, and a leading intellectual of his day, becoming especially known as editor-in-chief of the *Encyclopédie*, its full title translating as *a Systematic Dictionary of the Sciences, Arts and Crafts*. It was published between 1751 and 1772 in seventeen volumes of text and eleven volumes of plates. It was the first encyclopedia to include contributions from different writers, though Diderot wrote thousands of articles himself.

He had something to say about everything, including language, notably in his 1751 *Lettre sur les sourds et muets* ('Letter on the Deaf and Dumb'). The title is misleadingly specific. His focus on gesture broadens to include the functions and origins of language, the grammatical properties of different languages, the possibility of translation, the nature of painting and poetry, and other aesthetic considerations. His liveliness of temperament is well illustrated by this personal anecdote about how he came to appreciate the power of gesture:

> I used to frequent the theatre, and I knew by heart most of our best plays. On the days when I meant to examine actions and gestures I would climb to the gallery, for the further I was from the actors the better. As soon as the curtain was raised, and the rest of the audience disposed themselves to listen, I put my fingers in my ears, much to the astonishment of my neighbours; not knowing my motives, they looked on me as a madman who only came to the play to miss it. I paid no attention to their remarks, and kept my fingers obstinately in my ears as long as the gestures and actions of the actor corresponded with the dialogue which I remembered. When I was puzzled by the gestures I took my fingers from my ears and listened; Ah, how few actors there are who can stand such a test, and how humiliated the majority would be if I were to give the world my criticisms! But judge of my neighbours' surprise when they saw me shed tears at the pathetic passages, though I had my fingers in my ears.

1 AUGUST

Yorkshire Day

The day was inaugurated in 1975 by the Yorkshire Ridings Society as a protest against local government reorganization in 1974, which did away with many traditional country boundaries and names in Britain. The date originally recognized a military event – the role of the Yorkshire Light Infantry at the Battle of Minden in 1759. It was also the anniversary of the success in 1834 of Yorkshire MP William Wilberforce's campaign for the emancipation of slaves in the British Empire.

County identity is linguistically recognized by dialect societies. The Yorkshire Dialect Society was established in 1897, and is the oldest surviving such society in England. It grew out of a committee brought together by Joseph Wright (SEE 27 FEBRUARY), who had been collecting material for what would become his *English Dialect Dictionary*. An English Dialect Society had been founded in 1873 with that aim, and once it had been achieved it was wound up.

Several other counties have founded dialect societies or similar organizations. A Lakeland Society dates from 1939, recognizing the dialects of the old counties of Westmorland and Cumberland (present-day Cumbria). A Lancashire Dialect Society flourished between 1951 and 1992. Northumberland and adjacent areas have the Northumbrian Dialect Society, founded in 1983.

Many books, journals, newsletters, recordings and now websites have presented dialect word lists, poems, stories and translations. As a brief illustration, here are the opening sentences of Arnold Kellett's *Ee By Gum, Lord! The Gospels in Broad Yorkshire* (1996). The chapter is headed 'T' Babby Born in a Mistal' – a cowshed:

> 'As-ta ivver thowt abaht why it wor in t' little tahn o' Bethle'em wheeare it all started? Well, it come abaht this rooad...

Yorkshire is by no means alone. Several other counties have their special day too, such as Sussex Day (16 June) and St Piran's Day in Cornwall (5 March). And the aim of remembering, documenting and where possible revitalizing local dialects remains a worthy aspiration.

William S. Burroughs died in 1997

Born in 1914 in Missouri, Burroughs became a writer of novels, short stories and essays, known especially for his experimental writing, seen initially in his novel *The Naked Lunch*, written in a nonlinear way, with flashbacks and other features breaking the chronological sequence of the story. More radical was what came to be called the 'cut-up' technique, in which a text is cut up into sections and rearranged to create a new text. He explained it in a interview:

> The cut-up method brings to writers the collage which has been used by painters for fifty years. And used by the moving and still camera. In fact all street shots from movie or still cameras are by the unpredictable factors of passers by and juxtaposition cut-ups. And photographers will tell you that often their best shots are accidents ... writers will tell you the same. The best writing seems to be done almost by accident, but writers until the cut-up method was made explicit had no way to produce the accident of spontaneity.

He thought the technique brought the result closer to the process of human perception: 'Every time you look out the window or walk down the street, your consciousness is cut by random, seemingly random events.' His conclusion: 'Life is a cut-up.'

The immediate stimulus for the approach was painter and writer Brion Gysin, who would cut newspaper articles into sections and rearrange them at random. The result would sometimes resemble nonsense and sometimes suggest unexpected meanings. But the notion has a long history. In a poem of advice to new poets, Lewis Carroll once wrote: 'For first you write a sentence, / And then you chop it small; / Then mix the bits, and sort them out / Just as they chance to fall: / The order of the phrases makes / No difference at all.'

There have been many applications. Political speeches have had the words alphabetized and rearranged to make a point. Satirists have exploited the 'hidden' meanings in a text. And digital techniques continue to offer a new world of cut-and-paste possibilities.

P.D. James was born in 1920

Born in Oxford, her full name was Phyllis Dorothy James, known for her series of crime novels featuring the English police commander Adam Dalgliesh. She died in 2014. In an interview during a US tour in 1998 she talked about the crucial stylistic features of the mystery genre, and especially about the way it offers the novelist a built-in structure: the unravelling of a crime.

> If you wanted to set out to be a novelist, this was a form that could teach you how to do it. You may remain in it, you may go outside of it, but if you tried to do it well, you'd really learn so much, largely because it has to be so carefully structured. You have to have credible characters, the setting has to come alive and you have to produce narrative thrust and your ingenious plot. It is a wonderful training. ... I've often said it's just as absurd to say you can't write a good novel within the form of a mystery as it is to say, how could you possibly write great poetry in the sonnet form? After all, you've only got 14 lines and you've got to have a strict rhyming sequence. I think many writers find that the discipline and conventions of the detective novel are in fact liberating.

All writers are at some point asked where their ideas come from. This was her reply:

> My books begin with a place, the feeling I want to set a book there, whether it's an empty stretch of beach or a community of people.

Or, she added (talking at the Ucheldre Centre in Holyhead in 1991, a former convent chapel now a community arts centre), in a place like this. I had introduced her talk, and was sitting at the side of the stage ready to field questions from the audience. She looked up and around the imposing building. A dramatic pause. Then: 'And next I need to find an interesting victim or murderer.' Another dramatic pause. The audience roared. She had turned and was looking judiciously at me.

Percy Bysshe Shelley was born in 1792

Born in Sussex, Shelley became one of the leading Romantic poets of his era, though much of his writing wasn't appreciated until well after his death, in a boating accident, in 1822. Several of his poems are now widely anthologized, and his prose essays on radical political and ethical subjects influenced several later writers. He was also an early stylistician, analysing lines in detail. For example, in an article that appeared in 1830 he takes a line of Shakespeare, 'How sweet the moonlight sleeps upon this bank', and gives it a quasi-phonetic analysis:

> Now, examining this line, we perceive that all the parts are formed in relation to one another, and that it is consequently a whole. 'Sleep', we see, is a reduplication of the pure and gentle sound of 'sweet'; and as the beginning of the former symphonizes with the beginning *s* of the latter, so also the *l* in 'moonlight' prepares one for the *l* in 'sleep', and glides gently into it; and in the conclusion one may perceive that the word 'bank' is determined by the preceding words, and that the *b* which it begins with is but a deeper intonation of the two *p*'s which come before it; 'sleeps upon this slope' would have been effeminate; 'sleeps upon this rise' would have been harsh and inharmonious.

His impressionistic vocabulary would in the twentieth century be replaced by phonetic terminology, but the intent is the same, which he summarized in his essay *A Defence of Poetry* (1821, published in 1840): 'the language of poets has ever effected a certain uniform and harmonious recurrence of sound, without which it were not poetry'. In its emphasis on formal patterning, his approach anticipates twentieth-century phonology, but with additional perspectives that relate to modern thinking in semantics and sound symbolism. His essay is full of memorable observations: 'Poetry is connate with the origin of man' ... 'Poetry is the record of the best and happiest moments of the happiest and best minds' ... 'Poetry turns all things to loveliness' ... and his closing sentence: 'Poets are the unacknowledged legislators of the world.'

Toni Morrison died in 2019

Born in 1931 in Ohio, Morrison became a university teacher and an acclaimed novelist, writing chiefly on racial themes in such powerful works as *Song of Solomon* (1977) and *Beloved* (1987). As an editor for Random House, she played an important role in enabling several African-American writers to be published. In 1993 she was awarded the Nobel Prize for Literature, the first black woman of any nationality to receive it. In her Nobel lecture in December that year she told a story about the power of storytelling, and the generational gap between old and young. The theme of language as a tool of oppression emerges in passionate words:

> The systematic looting of language can be recognized by the tendency of its users to forgo its nuanced, complex, mid-wifery properties for menace and subjugation. Oppressive language does more than represent violence; it is violence; does more than represent the limits of knowledge; it limits knowledge. Whether it is obscuring state language or the faux-language of mindless media; whether it is the proud but calcified language of the academy or the commodity driven language of science; whether it is the malign language of law-without-ethics, or language designed for the estrangement of minorities, hiding its racist plunder in its literary cheek – it must be rejected, altered and exposed. It is the language that drinks blood, laps vulnerabilities, tucks its fascist boots under crinolines of respectability and patriotism as it moves relentlessly toward the bottom line and the bottomed-out mind. Sexist language, racist language, theistic language – all are typical of the policing languages of mastery, and cannot, do not permit new knowledge or encourage the mutual exchange of ideas.

She makes a strong affirmation about the old woman in the story:

> Word-work is sublime, she thinks, because it is generative; it makes meaning that secures our difference, our human difference – the way in which we are like no other life.

And she ends with a note of optimism, with a meeting of minds between the woman and the youngsters who come to tease her, as they each explain their feelings: 'How lovely it is, this thing we have done – together.'

National Gossip Day

The day is recognized in the USA as the anniversary of the birth of American movie columnist Louella Parsons (1881–1972), the 'Queen of Hollywood gossip'. She was the first of an era of 'gossip columnists' whose aim was to provide revelations about celebrities – the more dramatic and scandalous the better. As a result, the word *gossip* began to acquire a stronger set of negative associations, to the extent that some websites define gossip only as a harmful behaviour, and refer to this day as an opportunity to cease using it. Others see it as a day to celebrate the genre and to engage in it at a personal level.

Gossip was originally a religious notion: it referred to someone who acted as a sponsor at a baptism. By the sixteenth century it had developed the sense of a person who delights in idle talk; and in the nineteenth century we begin to see opposed senses emerge – easy and unrestrained chat among people who know each other, and talk about groundless rumours, often spiteful or malicious. Today the collocations of the word reflect this divergence. People talk about having a 'nice' or 'lovely' gossip as well as dismissing something they've heard as 'silly', 'nasty' or 'just gossip'.

Whatever the attitudes involved, the fact remains that gossip in the sense of inconsequential, unverified talk about people and events forms a huge part of everyday conversation. This inevitably raises the question: why do people engage in it so much? An evolutionary answer was argued by anthropologist Robin Dunbar in his book *Grooming, Gossip and the Evolution of Language* (1997), who saw it as a mechanism for bonding in a social group. Its origins, he argued, can be related to the importance of social grooming among primates. Gossip in this context is a form of 'vocal grooming'. As one of the blurbs for his book says: 'It seems there is nothing idle about idle chatter. Having a good gossip ensures that a dynamic group – of hunter-gatherers, soldiers, workmates – remains cohesive.'

Professional Speakers Day

Many people have an anxiety about speaking in public, and this is recognized by a different day (SEE 2 JULY). What's less often appreciated is that professional speakers have concerns too. These are people who earn their living by public speaking, or where public speaking plays an important role in their professional life – toastmasters, after-dinner speakers, lecturers, schoolteachers, debaters, religious ministers, politicians, television pundits, and many others. I've not been able to find out who launched this day, or when, but its aim is clear. As one website puts it: 'to recognize the importance of those who stand up in front of us and share their knowledge and insight on an endless range of topics'.

The speakers themselves have done a great deal to grow their professionalism. In 1973 an American public-speaking champion, Cavett Robert (1907–1997), founded a National Speakers Association. This grew into the International Federation for Professional Speakers, launched in 1998 by Australia, Canada, New Zealand and the United States. In 2009 the name was changed to the Global Speakers Federation (GSF), which today comprises seventeen independent associations.

The mission of the GSF is 'to support and provide resources to help develop and grow associations of professional speakers worldwide'. On its website it expands this aspiration into three aims:

— Strengthen worldwide recognition of professional speaking within the meetings industry.
— Provide support to member associations on forming, managing, and leading associations, including sharing best practices.
— Build a global community of like-minded people to encourage alliances, connections, and support networks.

The desirability of sharing ideas and information about best practice was highlighted during the Covid pandemic, when individuals and organizations had to rethink many of their traditional methods of presentation. Public speaking via Zoom and similar platforms raises a fresh and challenging set of issues, and part of the solution must be the sharing of initiatives among countries and among professional speakers.

Terry Nation was born in 1930

Born in Cardiff, Wales, Nation became a screenwriter and novelist. He was best known for his contributions to the BBC 1970s' television science-fiction series *Blake's 7* and *Survivors*, and most famously to *Dr Who* in the 1960s, for which he created the Daleks and then their creator Davros. He died in 1997.

In a series of interviews in the 1980s he talked about the way he imagined the Daleks speaking: 'It had to be mechanical and broken down into syllables all the time', and he made an interesting point about their lack of connected speech and his solution:

> The Daleks, when they have to make any kind of speech, are immensely boring characters. You can't have a Dalek doing four or five sentences in a row, so I wanted someone to speak for the Daleks. This thing that was half-man and half-Dalek [Davros] was a perfect example of this, and I made sure that he was not killed in that series …. He became a very good plot piece, and anyway, any crazy old mad professor is wonderful to have around.

Unfriendly life forms pose a linguistic challenge to their creators (SEE 26 APRIL). They need to have pronunciations that are very different from present-day educated standards, but also different from recognizable regional norms. At the same time, these beings have to be intelligible, if viewers are going to understand them. The solution lies in the distinction between the segments (the vowels and consonants) and the tones of voice in everyday speech. Segments convey the basic meaning of a sentence; tones of voice add emotion. So, if we want to create an intelligible but evil alien, all we have to do is use normal vowels, consonants and syllables, and replace normal patterns of pitch, loudness, rate, rhythm and timbre with abnormal tones of voice. In the case of the Daleks this was a loud monotone, with abnormal rising lilts, a staccato, syllable-timed rhythm, often with lengthened syllables, and an acoustically generated voice quality. Such a voice is definitely not on our side.

International Day of the World's Indigenous Peoples

The day was established by the UN General Assembly in 1994, the date being that of the first meeting in 1982 of a UN Working Group on Indigenous Populations. Each year a theme is chosen to provide a focus for events. In 2022 it was 'The role of indigenous women in the preservation and transmission of traditional knowledge' and in 2021 'Leaving no one behind: indigenous peoples and the call for a new social contract'. In 2018 the theme was 'Indigenous languages', highlighting the need to revitalize, preserve and promote these languages.

The UN website summarizes the world situation:

There are over 476 million indigenous peoples living in 90 countries across the world, accounting for 6.2 per cent of the global population. Indigenous peoples are the holders of a vast diversity of unique cultures, traditions, languages and knowledge systems. ... Although numerous indigenous peoples worldwide are self-governing and some have been successful in establishing autonomy in varying forms, many indigenous peoples still come under the ultimate authority of central governments who exercise control over their lands, territories and resources.

The linguistic situation is especially serious, with at least 40 per cent of the world's languages at some level of endangerment (SEE 21 FEBRUARY). At the closing event of the Year of Indigenous Languages in 2019, held in Los Pinos, Mexico City, a formal declaration established a Decade of Indigenous Languages, 2022–2032. The UN website identifies the main issues:

the Los Pinos Declaration emphasizes indigenous peoples' rights to freedom of expression, to an education in their mother tongue and to participation in public life using their languages, as prerequisites for the survival of indigenous languages many of which are currently on the verge of extinction. With regard to participation in public life, the Declaration highlights the importance of enabling the use of indigenous languages in justice systems, the media, labour and health programmes. It also points to the potential of digital technologies in supporting the use and preservation of those languages.

Julia Mood Peterkin died in 1961

Born in 1880 in South Carolina, Peterkin became known for her novels and short stories, *Scarlet Sister Mary* winning the Pulitzer Prize for the Novel in 1929. Her writing focused on the people of the plantation South, and is notable for its realistic presentation of the Gullah language used in the region. Here's an example from the first three stanzas of 'The Wind', published in *Poetry* magazine in 1923.

> De win' mek me laugh –
> E duh do so much mischeevous ting!
>
> E put e mout' to de crack an' blow;
> Den e run roun' de house
> An' mek strange noise.
> De smoke een de chimney git so f'aid
> E run clean back down to de fire!
> Dem big ol' tree trimble an' moan!
>
> De win' tell decloes on de line
> Dey is people.
> People!
> Dey puff dey-se'f out
> An' try fo' step roun' …
> Try fo' dance, my Gawd!
> Some wouldn' stop
> Tell dey jump clean down
> On de groun'!

Gullah is a creole spoken by African Americans living in the coastal plain and islands in the south-eastern USA. Its lexicon is notable for retaining a great deal of its African heritage, and several features of its culture have become widely known, such as *gumbo* stew. Loanwords are heard from several African languages, such as *wanga* 'charm' from Temne, *kome* 'gather' from Mende, and *defu* 'rice flour' from Vai, all spoken in Sierra Leone. The African substrate has altered the pronunciation of most English words, and influenced the grammar in several ways, as the poem illustrates.

Geoff Nunberg died in 2020

Born in 1945 in New York City, Nunberg became an academic linguist, his research focusing on English grammar and usage, and on the way language is used in technology, culture and politics. He became well known outside academia for his lively writing aimed at a general readership, as well as for frequent radio contributions. *Talking Right* was chosen as one of the ten best nonfiction books of 2006. Its subtitle was probably record-breaking for its length: 'Conservatives Turned Liberalism into a Tax-Raising, Latte-Drinking, Sushi-Eating, Volvo-Driving, New York Times-reading, Body-Piercing, Hollywood-Loving, Left-Wing Freak Show.'

It's difficult to choose one example from his extensive portfolio, but this extract from a 2011 interview illustrates his informal style, clarity of explanation – and tough talking. He has been asked about possible negative effects of the Internet on language.

> There's a kind of observer effect here – it isn't that the state of English has gotten any worse, but that we're seeing a broader slice of it. People are always pointing out the beauty of the Internet is that anyone can set down his or her thoughts and reach a vast potential audience, so it shouldn't be surprising that a great number of the participants in the new electronic discourse are people whose grasp of English orthography and grammar was always a little shaky. Take a word that's tough to spell, like *accommodate*. In the press, it's misspelled a bit more than one percent of the time; in the Google newsgroups it's misspelled over 60 percent of the time. But that error rate on *accommodate* has probably always been about right for the mass of people who write without benefit of a copy editor – the only difference is that before now, their spelling errors were visible only on the notes they left on their refrigerator doors. Still, it provides grist for the language police – really we should call them the minutemen, the sorts of people whose sense of self-worth rests on having mastered the rules for using the apostrophe in seventh grade. And you can blame the Internet for making them more visible, too.

Paule Marshall died in 2019

She was born in New York City in 1929, and became a writer, best known for her first acclaimed novel *Brown Girl, Brownstones* (1959). Language is a major theme, arising out of the combination of cultures that formed her background – parents from Barbados now living in a mixed white American and African-American setting, thus exposing her to standard English, Bajan Creole and Black English Vernacular. She saw this as a strength. Asked in an interview in 1990 if she was an American or a Caribbean writer, she said:

> I like to think of myself as a kind of bridge that joins the great wings of the black diaspora in this part of the world. ... there is a certain advantage in being neither fish nor fowl; perhaps it gives me a unique angle from which to view the two communities ... [adding a much-quoted punchline] All o' we is one.

She explains in a 1983 essay, 'From the Poets in the Kitchen', how her fascination with language originated – listening as a child to her mother's conversations:

> There was no way for me to understand it at that time, but the talk that filled the kitchen those afternoons was highly functional. It served as therapy, the cheapest kind available to my mother and her friends. Not only did it help them recover from the long wait on the corner that morning and the bargaining over their labor, it restored them to a sense of themselves and reaffirmed their self-worth. Through language they were able to overcome the humiliations of the work-day. ... Finding themselves permanently separated from the world they had known, they took refuge in language.

She quotes Nobel laureate Czesław Miłosz, 'Language is the only homeland', and adds:

> This is what it became for the women at the kitchen table. They had taken the standard English taught them in the primary schools of Barbados and transformed it into an idiom, an instrument that more adequately described them – changing around the syntax and imposing their own rhythm and accent so that the sentences were more pleasing to their ears.

13 AUGUST

Joyce Carol Thomas died in 2016

Born in 1938 in Oklahoma, Thomas became a poet, playwright and writer of many children's books, as well as a teacher in US colleges and an acclaimed campus motivational speaker on such topics as African-American issues, the art of storytelling, developing self-esteem, and writing techniques. In various interviews she gave an account of her background, in which language and languages played an important role. After her family resettled in rural California, she worked alongside Mexican migrant workers harvesting crops.

Her fascination with stories she attributed to her home setting:

Every year when we went out to pick cotton in Red Rock, the women told stories at night to entertain us. My mother, who was the lead teller, specialized in really scary stories.

She became known as a poet in the 1970s, writing mainly about the African-American experience in California. She also wrote many books for children, such as the award-winning *The Blacker the Berry* (2008). This is her title poem:

'The blacker the berry
The sweeter the juice.'

I am midnight and berries
I call the silver stars at dusk
By moonrise they appear
And we turn berries into nectar

Because I am dark the moon and stars shine brighter
Because berries are dark the juice is sweeter

Day couldn't dawn without the night
Colors, without black, couldn't sparkle quite as bright

'The blacker the berry
The sweeter the juice.'

I am midnight and berries

Thomas Sheridan died in 1788

Born in 1718 in Dublin, Sheridan became an actor and theatre manager, but spent most of his life developing ideas about public spoken delivery – an enterprise which he claimed was seriously neglected by speakers in all walks of life, and particularly 'in the pulpit, the senate-house, or at the bar'. Those words come from his *Discourse* introducing his 'Course of lectures on elocution and the English language'. He passionately believed that a revival in the art of speaking would benefit religion, morality and constitutional government.

He first presented the lecture course in 1758–9 and continued to do so into the 1780s. The talks attracted great crowds, as this report of a visit to Scotland illustrates, published in the *Scots Magazine* (July 1761):

> *Edinburgh, June* 16.1761. Mr Sheridan proposes to read two courses of LECTURES; the first, on ELOCUTION, the second, on the ENGLISH TONGUE; consisting of eight lectures each.
>
> In the first, he will treat of every thing necessary to a GOOD DELIVERY, under the following heads: ARTICULATION, PRONUNCIATION, ACCENT, EMPHASIS, PAUSES or STOPS, PITCH and MANAGEMENT of the VOICE, TONES, and GESTURE.
>
> In the second, he will examine the whole state and constitution of the English Tongue, so far as relates to sound; in which he will point out its peculiar genius and properties, and specific difference from others, both antient and modern.

It was a hugely profitable venture. It cost a guinea to attend both courses – 21 shillings in old money, equivalent (in purchasing power) to around £250 today. The report says over 300 gentlemen attended, 'the most eminent in this country for their rank and abilities'. They could also buy his book if they subscribed at the time, for half a guinea.

The course lasted a month, and he then presented a shorter course – again at a guinea a time – and 'the house was crouded with ladies and gentlemen'. His Edinburgh talks must have earned him, in today's money, at least £150,000. And that was just one of many such events. There was evidently money to be made in elocution.

E. Nesbit was born in 1858

Born in Surrey, E. Nesbit (the E is for Edith) became the best-known children's writer of her generation, producing such long-lasting favourites as *The Wouldbegoods* (1901) and *The Railway Children* (1906, filmed 1970). She also wrote adult novels and short stories, some under the pseudonym Fabian Bland. She died in 1924.

Her nonfiction writing has been less widely read. She has little to say directly about language, but there are some interesting observations in *Wings and the Child* (1913), including this excursus about the teaching of reading. She evidently supported a 'look and say' approach, leaving phonics until later.

> A child should be taught to read almost as soon as it has learned to speak. I can remember my fourth birthday, but I cannot remember a time when I could not read. Without going into details as to the merits of different methods of teaching, I may say that a good many words may be taught before it is necessary to teach the letters – that reading should precede spelling – that CAT should be presented whole, as the symbol of Cat – and that the dissection of it into C.A.T. should come later. I believe that children taught in this way, and taught young, will not in after life be tortured by the difficulties of spelling. They will spell naturally, as they speak or walk. ...
>
> For a child from ten onwards it is no bad thing to give the run of a good general library. When he has exhausted the story books he will read the ballads, the histories and the travels, and may even nibble at science, poetry, or philosophy. ... I do not mean that absolutely every book is fit for a child's reading, but if you allow the reading of the Old Testament it is mere imbecility to insist that all the rest of your child's reading shall ignore the facts of life. You can always have a locked book-case if you choose: only see to it that the doors are not of glass, for the forbidden is always the desired.

National Tell a Joke Day

There are in fact two days assigned to this theme, both coming out of the USA. The other is 1 July, International Joke Day, though how far it's genuinely international is unclear. It was selected by American author and illustrator Wayne Reinagel in 1994 as promotion for his two books of jokes published at the time. The choice of date was a good one: 1 July is halfway through the year, and the thought was that if the first half has been going badly, a joke or two will help give the second half a good start. I haven't been able to find a reason for the choice of 16 August, or whose idea it was.

Either way, the focus on the joke is a good moment to reflect on the way language is used in humour. Unlike most other forms of conversational interaction, a joke needs to be mutually agreed before it's told. People use various alerting techniques, such as 'Have you heard the one about...?' or 'That reminds me of a joke...' Failing to do this can result in miscommunication, and lead to an explanation or apology: 'I'm only joking.'

As with the traditional two-mask symbol of theatre – one crying, the other laughing – jokes provide a valuable counter to gloom and tragedy. But social attitudes about what is acceptable humour are always subject to change. Traditional joke-telling relies greatly on stereotypes ('There's an Englishman, an Irishman...', 'Two X's walk into a bar...' – where X refers to any social group), and it's easy for a comedian to cause offence – especially these days, when there's a great sense of caution in the public humour business. Some high-profile showbiz events no longer use comedians as their hosts, for fear of offending groups who might send aggressive responses. Headlines about 'the death of comedy' are often seen in the press, accordingly, and there's a growing debate about the optimal balance between freedom of speech and social responsibility. At the same time, many continue to recognize the potential of joke-telling as a desirable vehicle of radical thought.

Meaning of 'is' Day

This is a day whose origins are perfectly clear, but what we're supposed to do with it is totally obscure. It all began in 1998 when Bill Clinton became the first president to testify before the Office of the Independent Counsel and a grand jury, as part of an investigation into his conduct during an alleged affair with Monica Lewinsky. He was eventually impeached by the House of Representatives, and then acquitted by the Senate.

The exchange between one of the prosecutors and Clinton provides the context for the day.

> *Prosecutor* ... the statement that there was 'no sex of any kind in any manner, shape or form, with President Clinton,' was an utterly false statement. Is that correct?
>
> *Clinton* It depends on what the meaning of the word 'is' is. If the – if he – if 'is' means is and never has been, that is not – that is one thing. If it means there is none, that was a completely true statement.

A few seconds later he repeated the grammatical point:

> Now, if someone had asked me on that day, are you having any kind of sexual relations with Ms Lewinsky, that is, asked me a question in the present tense, I would have said no. And it would have been completely true.

Upon being further pressed on the point, he repeated it again, drawing attention to the broad time frame that the present tense can express:

> anyone generally speaking in the present tense, saying there is not an improper relationship, would be telling the truth if that person said there was not, in the present tense; the present tense encompassing many months.

I suppose we could salvage something out of all this by seeing it as an opportunity to explore the verb *be* in English. It's something I did for a book called *The Story of Be* (2017). It has a greater range of meanings, uses and regional forms than any other English word – over 1,800 so far recorded by the *OED* lexicographers. But it would take more than a day to go through them all.

Virginia Dare was born in 1587

She was the first English child born in a New World colony. The event is recorded in *The Generall Historie of Virginia, New England, and the Summer Isles* – compiled in 1624 by 'Captaine John Smith sometymes Governour in those Countryes & Admirall of New England'. It's also recorded in John White's diary for 1587, which begins: 'The fourth voyage made to Virginia, with three shippes, in the yeere, 1587. Wherein was transported the second Colonie.' This is White's entry:

> The 18. [of August] Elenora, daughter to the Governour, and wife to Ananias Dare, one of the Assistants, was delivered of a daughter in Roanoak, and the same was christened there the Sunday following, and because this child was the first Christian borne in Virginia, she was named Virginia. By this time our shippes had unlanded the goods and victuals of the planters, and began to take in wood, and fresh water, and to newe calke and trimme them for England: the planters also prepared their letters, and tokens, to send backe into England.

White had been a member of the first attempt to colonize Roanoke island in 1585, serving as artist and map-maker. He returned in 1587 as governor of the colony, with his daughter and her husband among the settlers. He was obliged to go back to England later that year to get fresh supplies, but there was a long delay caused by the war with Spain (the Spanish Armada event in 1588), and when he eventually returned the colonists had disappeared. He never discovered what happened to his daughter and her family.

The 'lost colony', as it came to be called, became the subject of many imaginative treatments, and Virginia herself a prominent figure in American folklore, especially in North Carolina. Roanoke itself became an area of special linguistic interest, as the isolation of those who eventually settled there led to a dialect and accent of a more conservative character than those on the mainland. However, the belief that it preserved the speech of Elizabethan England – and thus of Shakespeare – has no linguistic foundation.

Ogden Nash was born in 1902

Born in New York, Nash moved to Baltimore in 1931 – as he wrote:
'I could have loved New York had I not loved Balti-more' – where he
lived until his death in 1971. He tried various professions, including
advertising and editing, before his first book of humorous verse, *Hard
Lines*, was published in 1931. Many more followed, all characterized
by unconventional rhymes, often using long words that would seem to
defy rhyming, and joyfully incorporating puns, misspellings, playful
pronunciations and nonstandard English. Is there a rhyme in English
for *adverb*? Of course there is. In a poem on current usage (1957), he
comments:

> I guess an adjective is the same as an adverb
> And 'to parse' is a bad verb.

What about *Avenue? Havenue* (haven't you). *Insouciance? Nousiance*
(nuisance). He explained in an interview: 'I think in terms of rhyme, and
have since I was six years old.'

Several of his poems are wry reflections on language, and even
linguistics gets a mention in one of the pieces in his last collection, *The
Old Dog Barks Backwards* (1972): 'What do you want, a meaningful
dialogue, or a satisfactory talk?' He's reflecting on what he believes are
deteriorating language standards, and these are the concluding lines:

> Just as bad money drives the good beyond our reach,
> So has the jargon of the hippie, the huckster and the bureaucrat debased
>   the sterling of our once lucid speech.
> What's worse, it has induced the amnesia by which I am faced;
> I can't recall the original phraseology which the jargon has replaced.
> Would that I had the memory of a computer or an elephant!
> What used I to say instead of uptight, clout and thrust and relevant?
> Linguistics becomes an even eerier area, like I feel like I'm in Oz,
> Just trying to tell it like it was.

20 AUGUST

Voyager 2 was launched by the USA in 1977

The spacecraft was carrying a 'Golden Record' containing sounds and images selected to show the human form and the diversity of life and culture on Earth. The selection was made by a team led by American astronomer Carl Sagan, and included a wide variety of spoken, written, musical, visual and audio content.

The linguistic component comprised written or spoken messages in fifty-five languages, in the order shown below, and there were further instances of communicative behaviour in other parts of the disk, including Esperanto, laughter, Morse Code, and animal communication.

> Sumerian, Ancient Greek, Portuguese, Cantonese, Akkadian, Russian, Thai, Arabic, Romanian, French, Burmese, Hebrew, Spanish, Indonesian, Quechua, Punjabi, Hittite, Bengali, Latin, Aramaic, Dutch, German, Urdu, Vietnamese, Turkish, Japanese, Hindi, Welsh, Italian, Sinhala, Zulu, Sotho, Wu, Armenian, Korean, Polish, Nepali, Mandarin, Ila, Swedish, Nyanja, Gujarati, Ukrainian, Persian, Serbian, Oriya, Ganda, Marathi, Amoy, Hungarian, Telugu, Czech, Kannada, Rajasthani, English

Each message was very short – some just a single word, such as 'Peace'. The English message was 'Hello from the children of planet Earth.'

The whole exercise assumes that any alien beings would have sensory systems like ours, so that they would be able to see and hear the recordings – and have the technology to play them. Many researchers in SETI (the search for extraterrestrial intelligence) think this to be highly unlikely. Organisms may respond to different acoustic frequencies, much as we already know some animal species do on our own planet; and the medium of transmission can affect the character of the acoustic information, as is known from the way ocean-dwelling creatures communicate. Who knows what atmospheric densities, temperatures and factors exist on other planets, which would affect the speed and character of sound? Improving our understanding of the semiotic systems used by our own world's species could be a more useful preparatory step anticipating – as the title of one recent science-fiction film put it – 'arrival'.

Lady Mary Wortley Montagu died in 1762

Born in Nottinghamshire in 1689 into an aristocratic family, she was
a voracious reader, and began writing poems, prose works and letters
in her teens, having already learned Latin from books in her father's
library. As an adult she's best known for her letters, especially about her
travels in Europe with her husband Edward, published after her death.
In 1716 Edward was appointed ambassador to the Turkish court in
Constantinople (modern Istanbul). They stayed for two years, and her
'Turkish Embassy Letters' became widely known.

In one (16 March 1718) she talks about her linguistic situation:

> I live in a place, that very well represents the tower of Babel: in Pera
> they speak Turkish, Greek, Hebrew, Armenian, Arabic, Persian,
> Russian, Sclavonian, Walachian, German, Dutch, French, English,
> Italian, Hungarian; and, what is worse, there are ten of these languages
> spoken in my own family. My grooms are Arabs; my footmen French,
> English, and Germans; my nurse an Armenian; my house-maids
> Russians; half a dozen other servants, Greeks; my steward an Italian;
> my janizaries Turks; so that I live in the perpetual hearing of this
> medley of sounds, which produces a very extraordinary effect upon the
> people that are born here; for they learn all these languages at the same
> time, and without knowing any of them well enough to write or read
> in it. There are very few men, women, or even children here, that have
> not the same compass of words in five or six of them. I know, myself,
> several infants of three or four years old, that speak Italian, French,
> Greek, Turkish, and Russian, which last they learn of their nurses, who
> are generally of that country. ...
>
> As I prefer English to all the rest, I am extremely mortified at the
> daily decay of it in my head, where I'll assure you (with grief of heart)
> it is reduced to such a small number of words, I cannot recollect any
> tolerable phrase to conclude my letter with, and am forced to tell your
> ladyship very bluntly, that I am, Your's, &c. &c.

Dorothy Parker was born in 1893

Born in New Jersey, Parker became a poet, short-story writer, screenwriter and literary critic, especially known for her witty ripostes, satirical observations and lethal put-downs. She died in 1967. A Dorothy Parker Society was founded in New York City in 1999, whose aims – apart from promoting her work and getting involved in service projects – include 'to have as much fun as possible'. In that spirit, here's a selection of her quips on subjects related to language.

> To me, the most beautiful word in the English language is 'cellar-door'. Isn't it wonderful? The ones I like, though, are 'cheque' and 'enclosed.'

> There's a hell of a distance between wise-cracking and wit. Wit has truth in it; wise-cracking is simply calisthenics with words.

> Of course I talk to myself. I like a good speaker, and I appreciate an intelligent audience.

> The first thing I do in the morning is brush my teeth and sharpen my tongue.

> The nowadays ruling that no word is unprintable has, I think, done nothing whatever for beautiful letters. … Obscenity is too valuable a commodity to chuck around all over the place; it should be taken out of the safe on special occasions only.

Several of her remarks were directed towards the business of writing for a living.

> The writer's way is rough and lonely, and who would choose it while there are vacancies in more gracious professions, such as, say, cleaning out ferryboats?

> There's life for you. Spend the best years of your life studying penmanship and rhetoric and syntax and Beowulf and George Eliot, and then somebody steals your pencil.

> I hate writing, I love having written.

With no heirs, she bequeathed her estate to Martin Luther King, and after his death to the National Association for the Advancement of Colored People, who now license her works.

Tom McArthur was born in 1938

Born in Glasgow, McArthur became a leading writer, lexicographer, editor and commentator on English, known to a global readership as the founding editor of the journal *English Today* and the magisterial *Oxford Companion to the English Language* (1992, 2nd edition 2018). In 1987 we collaborated in the production of an eighteen-part radio version of the acclaimed BBC television series *The Story of English*, and the memory of his lively, down-to-earth presentations remains with me. He died in 2020.

But of all his many contributions to English language studies, I would highlight the *Longman Lexicon of Contemporary English*, an eight-year project, published in 1981. This was the first thematic monolingual learner's dictionary, combining the insights of the dictionary and the thesaurus. This is how he describes it in his preface.

> Lexicography has traditionally used the alphabet as its principal means of organizing information about words. Indeed, most of us think about wordbooks as 'dictionaries', and dictionaries as, necessarily, having an alphabetical order.
>
> There has, however, been an alternative tradition, in which compilers have used groups of topics instead of the alphabet as their basis for organization. The alphabet, with all its virtues, places animals and zoos, uncles and aunts far apart in its scheme of things, whereas in the human mind such words go close together. The alphabetical dictionary has a logic, but it is not the logic of everyday life.

The *Lexicon* brings together around 15,000 items, grouping them into fourteen semantic fields – the body, people, food and drink, and so on. A 125-page alphabetical index at the back facilitates word search. So, if you want to find *uncle*, you can either look it up 'top down' in the contents, find the field to do with 'family relations' (numbered C15) within the broad category of 'People', and there it will be along with *aunt*, *nephew*, *niece* and *cousin*; or look in the index under *uncle*, and that will send you to C15 straight away. It was an ingenious breakthrough, which came to be called *index-to-system* lexicography.

Jorge Luis Borges was born in 1899

Language has often been called 'the infinite use of finite means'. In Noam Chomsky's conception of 'competence', speakers are able to produce an infinite number of novel sentences. The Argentinian writer and translator Jorge Luis Borges (who died in 1986) gave this thought a literary dimension in his short story 'The Library of Babel', published in 1941. It begins (in translation): 'The universe (which others call the Library) is composed of an indefinite, perhaps infinite number of hexagonal galleries.' All the books in it are 410 pages, and written using twenty-five characters (twenty-two letters, full stop, comma, space). The library contains every possible permutation, and thus contains everything that could possibly be expressed alphabetically in any language.

> For while the Library contains all verbal structures, all the variations allowed by the twenty-five orthographic symbols, it includes not a single absolute piece of nonsense. It would be pointless to observe that the finest volume of all the many hexagons that I myself administer is titled *Combed Thunder*, while another is titled *The Plaster Cramp*, and another, *Axaxaxas mlö*. Those phrases, at first apparently incoherent, are undoubtedly susceptible to cryptographic or allegorical 'reading'; that reading, that justification of the words' order and existence, is itself verbal and, *ex hypothesi*, already contained somewhere in the Library. There is no combination of characters one can make – *dhcmrlchtdj*, for example – that the divine Library has not foreseen and that in one or more of its secret tongues does not hide a terrible significance. There is no syllable one can speak that is not filled with tenderness and terror, that is not, in one of those languages, the mighty name of a god. To speak is to commit tautologies.

There's an old analogy: if monkeys had typewriters and infinite time, they'd eventually write all of Shakespeare. In Borges' library, this would be just one tiny fraction of the whole. It would include everything I've ever written, including this page, and the other pages I've yet to write. All I'd have to do is find the right place and choose it. It would save me an awful lot of time.

Thomas Dekker died in 1632

Few details of Dekker's early life are available. He was born in London around 1572, and became known for his plays, notably *The Shoemaker's Holiday* (1599), and a huge number of pamphlets about Elizabethan and Jacobethan life, including several on the London underworld of thieves and confidence tricksters. One of these was *The Bel-Man of London* (1608), with its subtitle *Discovering the most notable villanies now in the Kingdom*. A bellman was a sort of town crier – he would go around the streets making public announcements, and attract attention by ringing a bell.

The pamphlet introduces the vocabulary (or *cant*) used by the 'villains'. At one point he describes the way someone is initiated into the company of beggars. The aspirant kneels before the leader, his best clothes are removed and sold, a pot of ale is poured on his head, and these words are said:

> I – do stall [install] thée – to the *Rogue*, by vertue of this soveraigne English liquor, so that henceforth it shall bee lawfull for thée to *Cant*, (that is to say) to be a *Vagabond* and *Beg*, and to speake that pedlers French, or that *Canting language*, which is to be found among none but *Beggers...*

He's then instructed to learn the names of all the ranks within the company. It's a long list:

> We have amongst us some eighteen or nineteen severall offices for men, and about seven or eight for women: The *Chiefest* of us are called *Upright men* ... the next are *Rufflers*: then have we *Anglers*, but they seldome catch fish, till they go up *Westward* for *Flounders*: then are there *Roagues*: ... Next are *Wilde Rogues*, then *Priggers*: then *Palliardes*: then *Fraters*: then *Tom of Bedlams* band of madcaps, otherwise called *Poore Toms Flocke of Wilde-geese* ... and those *Wild-geese*, or *Hayre-braynes* are called *Abraham-men*: in the next Squadron march our brave *Whip-jacks*, at the taile of them come crawling our *Counterfeit Crankes...*

and so the list continues as Dekker completes the entire hierarchy, and gives each category a full description – a veritable gold mine for historical lexicographers.

Elizebeth Smith Friedman was born in 1892

The spelling of her first name is correct – a strategy by her mother, it's said, to avoid the shortened form *Eliza*. She has been called America's first female cryptologist, and she and her husband William (1891–1969) the nation's 'first cryptographic couple'. They spent a lifetime working for US government institutions, decoding thousands of hidden messages sent by foreign powers and illegal groups, during and between both world wars and into the 1960s. Her cryptographic successes were legendary, and a biography by Jason Fagone appeared in 2017: *The Woman Who Smashed Codes*. She died in 1980.

Born in Indiana, she was introduced to cryptology in 1916 when she joined Riverside Laboratories in Illinois as part of a project investigating the supposed messages enciphered into Shakespeare's plays that would show they were really written by Francis Bacon. The nineteenth century had created a frenzy of speculation on the subject, with anti-Shakespeare enthusiasts searching for the required evidence, assumed to be encoded within the plays and poems, and the Riverside initiative was set up to find it. Bacon was the preferred candidate for authorship, given that he had himself created a cryptographic system. But within the next fifty years many other candidates were put forward, and by 1950 over 4,000 books and articles had been published, supporting seventeen possible authors. The number of contenders has doubled since.

That statistic is taken from the Friedmans' book *The Shakespearean Ciphers Examined* (1957). This is its opening paragraph:

> Shakespearean scholars have often had to deal with arguments that Shakespeare did not have the birth, breeding or education necessary to write the plays. The evidence brought forward by both sides in this particular argument is necessarily conjectural, and must therefore always be inconclusive. On the other hand, claims based on cryptography can be scientifically examined, and proved or disproved. In this book we examine the cryptographic evidence used to support the thesis that someone other than Shakespeare wrote the plays.

In their dispassionate analysis, they found the evidence lacking.

Neville Alexander died in 2012

He was born in Eastern Cape, South Africa, in 1936, and became a
leading political activist during the apartheid years, co-founding the
National Liberation Front. In 1964 he began a ten-year imprisonment
on Robben Island, his time there coinciding with Nelson Mandela.
After the fall of apartheid, he was a pioneer in the field of language
policy, planning, and educational reform. At the University of Cape
Town he founded in 1992 the Project for the Study of Alternative
Education in South Africa, usually referred to as PRAESA, devoted
to literacy research and development in a multilingual environment.
Three years later he became chair of a Language Plan Task Group to
advise the government on measures to cope with the complex linguistic
situation in the country, where the constitution recognizes eleven official
languages. In 2008 he was awarded the annual Linguapax Prize for his
contributions to linguistic diversity and multilingual education.

He developed his approach to language planning in many papers,
reports and books, such as *Language Policy and National Unity in South
Africa/Azania* (1989) – Azania being the name proposed for the country
by an indigenous nationalist movement. In the book he explores the
notion of language planning, defining it as 'a deliberate and systematic
attempt to change a language itself or to change the function of a
language in a particular society'. He places this in a much wider context:

> Many people believe that one should not 'tamper' with language: they
> say it is best to 'leave your language alone'! However, in these days when
> almost nothing happens in modern industrial societies without some
> degree of planning, such views are simply outdated or at best quaint.
> When economic planning, town planning and even family planning are
> accepted by the majority of people in the world today as being necessary
> for a healthy and secure existence, there ought to be no objection in
> principle to language planning. The only proviso must be that such
> planning will at all times occur with the full participation and consent of
> all the people involved.

28 AUGUST

Paul Grice died in 1988

Philosopher of language Paul Grice was born in Britain in 1913, but moved to the USA in 1967, where he taught at the University of California at Berkeley. When he died, the branch of linguistics that his work would most influence had hardly begun to take shape. This was *pragmatics* – a subject with various definitions, depending on the way it's approached. For me, it's the study of the choices – appropriate or inappropriate – we make when we use language in different situations, the reasons for those choices, and the effects those choices convey. How do we address or greet each other? What forms of politeness do we use or avoid? The subject focuses on all the conventions and strategies we employ in talking, writing or signing to each other, and aims to explain why we use them.

Grice formulated a 'cooperative principle' to explain what goes on, and illustrated it from four 'maxims' that underlie the efficient collaborative use of language. His claim was that when people communicate with each other they normally behave according to these maxims. They try to keep what they say to the point (the maxim of *relevance*). They try to make their points in a clear, orderly and brief way (the maxim of *manner*). They try not to say too much or too little to make their points (the maxim of *quantity*). And they try to make their points truthfully and supported by evidence (the maxim of *quality*).

Of course people don't always follow these principles. In particular, Grice hadn't anticipated the Internet, where there's a great deal of uncooperativeness, as illustrated by trolling, spam, anonymous abuse, and all the other behaviours that can make online communication an unpleasant experience. Grice's point is that we nonetheless recognize the breaking of maxims when they occur, and judge utterances accordingly. We can challenge people who make false claims; call them back if they move away from the point; ask for clarification if they're being obscure; and tell them (politely or rudely) to shut up if they talk too much.

Sybil Marshall died in 2005

Born in 1913 in Cambridgeshire, Marshall became a primary-school teacher, working on her own in a small school, and later a university lecturer. She developed methods fostering child creativity, initially using art to integrate curriculum subjects. She describes these in the autobiographical *An Experiment in Education* (1963), illustrated with insightful anecdotes of classroom interaction. Here's part of her observations about English teaching.

> Children learn the English of their parents and their environment first and foremost, and will continue to use this sort of language, despite all efforts to overlay it with a veneer of 'correct English', whenever they are completely free from the shackles of conventional schoolroom education. This means that every class confronts its teacher with about 75 per cent of its members speaking 'the dialect of the tribe', and the other 25 per cent speaking 'good English' naturally. In the past, the general practice has been to attempt to teach the large majority what amounts to a completely new language by means of constant meaningless exercises, and the repetitive and frustrating correction of the worst mistakes in their natural speech.
>
> The exercises were a complete waste of time. I well remember one of the first English lessons I ever took. I had been given a new set of text-books supposedly suitable for the seven-to-nine age range. The first lesson was about subject and predicate. After explanation and examples, the children were given a list of jumbled subjects for which they had to sort out the right predicates from another jumbled list. At the end of an industrious half-hour I was in possession of a lot of new facts that had previously been left out of my own education.
>
> A policeman rises in the east. The sun has a large hump. Gratitude is a place full of trees. A camel wears a helmet. A forest means thankfulness.
>
> The result of this method of teaching has generally been to allow the poor children to fall neatly between two stools, never really grasping the niceties of grammar, but being only too much aware of certain things wrong with their native speech.

Many teachers today would say nothing much has changed.

30 AUGUST

John Kani was born in 1943

He is a South African actor, director and playwright, who became known following the anti-apartheid play by Athol Fugard, in which he and Winston Ntshona collaborated, *Sizwe Banzi is Dead* (1975). He has played many Shakespearean roles, notably as Othello in the 1987 production in South Africa, still under apartheid rule at the time, where his performance on stage, which involved kissing a white Desdemona, caused huge controversy and troubling times for both the actors involved. He has since become a leading voice for the arts in his country, founding a Theatre Foundation and a Theatre Laboratory.

He repeatedly emphasizes Shakespeare's universality and relevance, as in this 2019 interview: 'You can give me any of Shakespeare's plays and I'll tell you a parallel African folktale. You say *Macbeth*, I immediately remember Shaka Zulu in KwaZulu-Natal, who wanted to be King while his uncle was still reigning.' And in the CD series *Beyond Babel* (2001) he presents an intriguing reversal of linguistic perspectives:

> When we did *Othello*, Janet Suzman was directing and she kept talking about performances by Lord Olivier, a performance by Paul Robson, a brilliant performance by so and so and so and so. And I said, 'I can't find the reference for myself. I'm an African, a Xhosa tribesman. I have to translate this text into Xhosa for me so I understand it in Xhosa. Then I translate it back to English in order to understand what I'm doing. So I will be a little slower than the other actors whose first language is English, whose culture is English. I am not English. I am an African, I am a Xhosa man. So I see Othello as one of the great warriors that my grandfather used to tell us about who fought against Amakalukwe, Ongkela, Onchaba, Kokocalo, Kmomkaba Aday.

He sums it up in this way:

> I am actually speaking in Xhosa but for your benefit, because you're ignorant, you do not understand my language, I will speak in English but that English is Xhosa. It sounds English to you for your benefit.

244

We Love Memoirs Day

The day was created in 2013 as a Facebook group by two American writers of memoirs, Victoria Twead and Alan Parks, who wanted to create a place where readers and authors of this genre could come together and chat. What's interesting, looking at the various websites that talk about the day, is the uncertainty surrounding the notion, and especially over its relationship to autobiography.

Both genres are about the writer's life and personal experiences, and usually written in the first person (*I, me, my, mine*), though sometimes in the third (*he, she*, etc.), when (for whatever reason) writers want to distance themselves from their story. An example is *The Education of Henry Adams* (1905), written by – Henry Adams. We read sentences such as: 'He first found himself sitting on a yellow kitchen floor in strong sunlight. He was three years old when he took this earliest step in education; a lesson of color.'

There are several differences between the two genres. An autobiography presents the entire life of the writer, limited only by the fallibility of memory. A memoir is a more focused product, telling a particular aspect of the writer's story. It's much more selective. My own *Just a Phrase I'm Going Through* is a memoir, not an autobiography, as its subtitle indicates: *My Life in Language*. Another difference is that an autobiography typically tells a life story in chronological order, whereas a memoir can dart back and forth in time. And, crucially, the other characters that turn up in an autobiography are incidental to the main character, the writer; whereas a memoir can be about the writer's 'memoiries', as it were, of someone else.

There's also a difference from the reader's point of view. We read an autobiography because we're interested in the writer. We read a memoir because we're interested in the subject matter and/or the writer's background or standing in relation to it, or even for his/her style. Someone who did both was Winston Churchill: *My Early Life* vs *Memoirs of the Second World War*.

World Letter-Writing Day

It's easy to understand why this day was founded. Every website reporting it takes the same approach, regretting the 'lost art of letter-writing' – by which they mean handwritten letters (though not excluding typed ones) – in an age of electronic communication where most people use email, texting and social media. The day was created by Australian photographer Richard Simpkin in 2014. He writes on his website:

> I became interested in letters in the late 1990's when I started a project called Australian Legends. I wanted to meet, photograph & if I could, interview those whom I considered to be an Australian legend. I sent out proposal letters asking to meet a particular person to photograph them & hear about their amazing lives. I was always excited when I went to the letterbox & there was a letter addressed to me from one of the legends. Some were typed, the others were hand written, & at the bottom was the legend's signature which only they themselves could personally do.

He wasn't alone. A National Letter-Writing Day is celebrated in the USA on 7 December with the same general aims: to ensure the art isn't lost (SEE ALSO 9 OCTOBER).

The enthusiasts stress the value that comes from letter-writing. For writers, it's a medium making them think more carefully before they write, as there's no easy erase function. It also expresses their personality. As one website puts it: 'Handwriting is your DNA'. Then there's the artistic element: for every person who claims 'my handwriting is awful' there's another who has – or who tries to develop – an elegant hand. For readers, there's a sense of personal contact and intimacy that digital media lack. And the fact that it's an autograph – whether the whole letter or just a signature – turns letters into potential keepsakes and, in the case of famous writers, collectibles. There's also an appreciation of the accessories, from choosing paper and envelopes to stamp collecting.

Of course, whether letter-writing is a celebration depends very much on the type of letter it is. Tax collectors write letters too.

2 SEPTEMBER

Laura Riding died in 1991

She was born in New York City in 1901, and became a writer in several genres, in later life as Laura (Riding) Jackson, after marrying *Time* poetry critic Schuyler Jackson. She first became known as a poet, publishing *Collected Poems* in 1938, but fell out of love with the genre in the 1940s, and turned to exploring the nature of meaning, truth and the power of language, notably in her manifesto *The Telling* (1972). But a fascination with words was always present, as in these lines from 'Hospitality to Words':

> How mad for friendliness
> Creep words from where they shiver and starve,
> Small and far away in thought,
> Untalkative and outcast.

Her writing is full of intriguing and unconventional linguistic observations, such as 'Language is a form of laziness; the word is a compromise between what is possible to express and what is not possible to express' (1928).

The intensity of her 'falling out' with poetry is seen in many later writings, including several published after her death. The *London Review of Books* in 1995 gave one of her essays the cover title 'Twilight of the Poem', though the piece is actually entitled, more positively, 'The Promise of Words'. This extract well illustrates her depth of feeling:

> Between the poet as language-priest and the reading congregation there is an unwittingly unholy covenant to evade the intellectual, and therefore linguistic, final difficulties and yet by exploiting a certain 'way with words' – the poet leading, the congregation following – to transcend them, dissolve them, soar past them. There is a diabolical side to poetry, which adds overtones of angelic beauty to the din of ordinary parlance. This is its futility, its ministering to the vanities rather than to the needs of human beings in their dependence on words, its raising them to heights of illusion of linguistic felicity only to let them drop down to real speaking ground with no increase of capacity to make – or, rather, let – words carry full burden of meaning.

E.E. Cummings died in 1962

He was born in 1894 in Cambridge, Massachusetts, and became a writer
in several genres, especially known for his unconventional poems, in
which typography, syntax, spellings, punctuation, spacing and word
formation are manipulated in an innovative free-form poetry. Many of
his lines reverse word order or play with word classes, using them in
technically ungrammatical places, as with this untitled poem from 1940:

> anyone lived in a pretty how town
> (with up so floating many bells down)
> spring summer autumn winter
> he sang his didn't he danced his did.

His penchant for lower-case was extended to his initials by one of his
publishers, and the practice caught on, though he himself usually kept
the capitals. His name is often shown as *e e cummings*. The full form of
his first names isn't often used: Edward Estlin.

Cummings was also a painter, and the influence of the visual arts is
evident in his writing. A poem often consists of just a few words spaced
about a page in ways which look random but which convey contrasts in
meaning, and suggest variations in pace that often comes alive when the
poem is read aloud. The point is made explicit in an imaginary interview
he wrote in 1945, 'Forward to an Exhibit: II'. Here are its opening lines:

> Why do you paint?
> For exactly the same reason I breathe.
> That's not an answer.
> There isn't any answer.
> How long hasn't there been any answer?
> As long as I can remember.
> And how long have you written?
> As long as I can remember.
> I mean poetry.
> So do I.
> Tell me, doesn't your painting interfere with your writing?
> Quite the contrary: they love each other dearly.

First weather forecast
offered to *The Times* in 1860

Before 1860 the only way people in Britain would have been able to
hear about forthcoming weather was through the reports of individual
scientists and private observers, who inevitably would have been able to
supply information about only very limited areas of the country. It was
when the head of the Board of Trade, Rear Admiral Robert Fitzroy – the
former captain of HMS *Beagle*, the ship on which Charles Darwin sailed
– began to use the new telegraph system to gather reports from all over
the country that the possibility of a national system emerged. A similar
use of telegraphy took place in several other countries. Terms such as
weather-cast and *weather report* were being used in the 1860s, and weather
was described as being 'probable' or 'expected'. Then during the 1870s
Fitzroy's term *weather forecast* became the norm, as did the modern name:
the Meteorological Office.

The Board wrote to *The Times* offering to supply weather reports, and
Fitzroy wrote a reply on this day:

> The Proprietors of The Times are obliged to the Board of Trade for their
> offer to furnish certain meteorological returns for publication in The Times;
> & I beg on behalf of the Conductors of that paper to accept your offer.

The first one appeared in the paper two days later. It was headed simply
'The Weather: Meteorological Reports', and gave a listing of fourteen
locations in Britain and northern France with eight conditions for each,
such as temperature, wind direction and cloudiness, as reported on the
previous day. Below the technical information was another table giving
everyday terms, headed 'Wind and weather report at 8 o'clock yesterday
evening'. It started in the north of Scotland and covered twenty-five
towns and cities:

Inverness, S.W.; fine.	Dundee, calm; fine
Aberdeen, N.; dull	Edinburgh, W.; foggy

The initials referred to wind direction. It was 'calm' and 'cloudy' in
Holyhead that day. 'Dull' in Manchester. 'Very fine' in Jersey.

Lewis Nkosi died in 2010

Born in 1938 in KwaZulu-Natal, South Africa, Nkosi began as a journalist and essayist, and had his works banned in the apartheid era. He entered a thirty-year period of exile in 1961, studying, writing, broadcasting and teaching, chiefly in the USA and Britain. His writing covered several genres, and included essays on a wide range of themes. He had a lot to say about the difficulties of self-expression, especially in an essay that was published after his death in 2011, 'How I Write'. It begins:

> It is not so long ago that European modernists, especially in France, used to say that when we read literature, writing is everything. When we read books or listen to stories, we have access to the world through words or the word made flesh, as the Bible put it. The mystery, of course, is how something that seems as immaterial as words can be made flesh.

He then goes on to talk about two instances when his reading caused him to break down in tears. One was at the death of Anna in Tolstoy's *Anna Karenina*, and the other was Cleopatra's suicide in Shakespeare's *Antony and Cleopatra*. At the end of the essay he remembers those feelings as he summarizes his views in a statement whose first sentence is often quoted:

> For me, writing is primarily a struggle with language – words refusing to be made 'flesh'. When Shakespeare writes: 'Full fathom five thy father lies / Of his bones are corals made', while I know that English people in the sixteenth century did not really speak like this, I find the lines true because of their music: that alliteration of the 'f' sound convinces me that a certain man lay in the depths of the sea as truly as if his body had been detected by laser beams.
>
> What is Anna Karenina to me that I should weep for her? Why do I mourn Cleopatra?
>
> A lot of it has to do with how words are put together. The rest is a mystery.

First Puritans leave Plymouth
on the *Mayflower* in 1620

They arrived in November of that year. Prevented by storms from reaching Virginia, they landed at Cape Cod Bay, and established a settlement at Plimoth (now Plymouth, Massachusetts). Records show that there were 102 settlers in all: 35 members of the English Separatist Church, and 67 others.

The group – later called the 'Pilgrim Fathers' – was extremely mixed in their regional background. William Bradford, the first governor of the colony, came from Yorkshire; his wife, Alice, from Somerset. The first military leader of the colony, Myles Standish, came from the Isle of Man; his second wife, Barbara, from Lancashire (his first wife, Rose, didn't survive the first winter). But most of the settlers came from London or counties in the east of England, such as Norfolk, Suffolk and Essex. As a result, the accent that developed in this area differed from the one that was emerging further south in Virginia, and along the coastal islands, where many of the settlers came from the West Country of England. The most noticeable difference – still heard in New England accents today, especially in the east – was that *r* wasn't sounded after vowels. *Harvard*, for example, was pronounced 'Haava'd'.

William Bradford's journal, *Of Plimoth Plantation*, was written between 1630 and 1651. In Book 2 he records the first attempt at communication between the settlers and one of the indigenous people:

> about yᵉ 16. *of March* a certaine Indian came bouldly amongst them, and spoke to them in broken English, which they could well understand, but marvelled at it. At length they understood by discourse with him, that he was not of these parts, but belonged to yᵉ eastrene parts, wher some English-ships came to fhish, with whom he was aquainted, & could name sundrie of them by their names, amongst whom he had gott his language. … His name was *Samaset*; he tould them also of another Indian whos name was *Squanto*, a native of this place, who had been in England & could speake better English then him selfe.

I.A. Richards died in 1979

Born in Cheshire in 1893, Richards was professionally known by his initials, standing for Ivor Armstrong. He became an influential literary critic and theorist of rhetoric, but for linguists his major contribution was a book he wrote in collaboration with the linguist C.K. [Charles Kay] Ogden. This was *The Meaning of Meaning: A Study of the Influence of Language upon Thought and of the Science of Symbolism* (1923). It was universally known as 'Ogden and Richards', as I discovered when I found it was a set text as part of the first year of my English degree in 1959. It presented a three-cornered view of meaning – the 'semantic triangle' – in which symbols (typically, words) are related to real-world entities (referents) and mediated by their mental image (our thought, or reference).

It was, to say the least, an unnerving experience for someone who had never heard of semiotic theory, but the danger of becoming lost in a mass of abstraction was alleviated by a supplementary essay at the back of the book by the Polish anthropologist Bronisław Malinowski. He showed how the Ogden and Richards model could be applied to the eminently practical task of describing indigenous languages, illustrating from the Trobriand Islanders of Papua New Guinea. His approach explored the relationship between linguistics and ethnography, and showed how utterances have to be seen in their 'context of situation' to be understood (SEE ALSO 17 JUNE).

The essay was greatly influential, not least for the way it introduced everyone to what he called *phatic communion*. This referred to the way 'ties of union are created by a mere exchange of words' – the sort of thing that happens in English when we say 'How do you do?', 'Turned out nice again', and other such pleasantries (SEE ALSO 11 MAY). The purpose of these utterances is not to transmit information but to foster social relationships. The term caught on. It would be frequently referenced when, later in the century, there developed sociolinguistic, stylistic and pragmatic dimensions for the study of language.

International Literacy Day

The day was created by UNESCO, and first celebrated in 1967. Its aim is stated on the UN website:

> to remind the public of the importance of literacy as a matter of dignity and human rights, and to advance the literacy agenda towards a more literate and sustainable society. Despite progress made, literacy challenges persist, with at least 773 million young people and adults lacking basic literacy skills today.

That's about one in ten. The figures for 'poor literacy skills' are high in every country. Even in highly literate societies, such as Britain, government surveys indicate that one in six adults would fall into that category, defined as the level of a 6-year-old child at the very start of its literacy journey.

The figures are inevitably approximate, as 'basic' is difficult to define. To say that someone is illiterate can mean that the person has no ability at all to read and write. It also includes people who are seriously challenged – perhaps able to read some very basic situations, such as road signs or price labels, but unable to cope with anything more advanced. They certainly can't access arrays such as transport timetables, official forms, medical instructions or Internet URLs. Quality of life is seriously affected, as most jobs rely on literacy. Family life is impaired when parents are unable to help children with schoolwork. Society as a whole can be harmed. According to the UK's Literacy Trust, some 60 per cent of the prison population have basic literacy needs.

A small but important feature of literacy is the ability to handle different written forms, such as upper-case vs lower-case letters, font differences and non-alphabetic symbols – logograms such as £, + and &. So it's worth noting that today is also National Ampersand Day. It was created a few years ago by an American, Chaz DeSimone, the founder of AmperArt. He chose this day because it allowed him to play with the letters in 'September 8', substituting each one with a font variation of &. The little symbol certainly allows a remarkable amount of graphic manipulation.

First reported case of a computer bug in 1947

The use of *bug* to describe a computer malfunction was popularized by American computer pioneer Grace Hopper, who would tell the story of how a moth became stuck in a relay of the Mark II computer being developed at Harvard University. It was extracted and can still be seen – stuck into the log book for the day – in the National Museum of American History in Washington DC. Under the insect is the droll description: 'First actual case of bug being found'.

The Harvard engineers didn't coin the term, which has a fascinating history. It's first recorded in the sixteenth century, referring to any small insect considered a pest. By the eighteenth century it had been extended to refer to any person considered a pest. Then in the nineteenth century there was a further extension, to any part of a machine considered a pest. It took a while for the usage to become familiar, judging by this report by a writer in the *Pall Mall Gazette* in 1889, who felt he needed to explain it:

> Mr. Edison, I was informed, had been up the two previous nights discovering 'a bug' in his phonograph – an expression for solving a difficulty, and implying that some imaginary insect has secreted itself inside and is causing all the trouble.

The usage became widespread in engineering, along with *debug*, so it wasn't surprising that when computers arrived the engineers continued to use them, first for faults in the hardware, and then for programming issues in the software.

Not everyone likes these terms, though, because a sentence such as 'There's a bug' seems to distance the fault from the human causer of the fault. Many alternatives have been suggested, such as *mistake, error, fault, failure, defect, gremlin*, and – increasing in frequency these days – *glitch*, originally used in electrical engineering for an unexpected short-lived surge in voltage. That's a puzzling word. A possible association with *itch* is understandable, but where the *gl-* comes from is a mystery.

Mary Wollstonecraft died in 1797

Born in 1759 in London, Wollstonecraft became a writer and philosopher, known especially for her advocacy of women's rights, as in *A Vindication of the Rights of Woman* (1792), and a memoir on the French Revolution, which she experienced while living in France between 1792 and 1795. Earlier she had written *Thoughts on the Education of Daughters* (1787), with its title amplified as *Reflections on Female Conduct, in The more Important Duties of Life*. Speaking, reading and writing are all discussed, as these extracts illustrate, sometimes with a characteristic forthrightness which was little appreciated in her day.

> Children should be permitted to enter into conversation; but it requires great discernment to find out such subjects as will gradually improve them. Animals are the first objects which catch their attention; and I think little stories about them would not only amuse but instruct at the same time, and have the best effect in forming the temper and cultivating the good dispositions of the heart. ...
>
> Reading is the most rational employment, if people seek food for the understanding, and do not read merely to remember words; or with a view to quote celebrated authors, and to retail sentiments they do not understand or feel. ...
>
> I would have every one try to form an opinion of an author themselves, though modesty may restrain them from mentioning it. Many are so anxious to have the reputation of taste, that they only praise the authors whose merit is indisputable. I am sick of hearing of the sublimity of Milton, the elegance and harmony of Pope, and the original, untaught genius of Shakespear [*sic*]. These cursory remarks are made by some who know nothing of nature, and could not enter into the spirit of those authors, or understand them. ...
>
> A florid style mostly passes with the ignorant for fine writing; many sentences are admired that have no meaning in them, though they contain 'words of thundering sound,' and others that have nothing to recommend them but sweet and musical terminations.

Hannah Weiner died in 1997

Born in Rhode Island in 1928, Weiner began to write poetry in the 1960s, and became known for her highly personal, unconventional style, associated with the avant-garde group called the Language Poets, named for their magazine *L=A=N=G=U=A=G=E* (1978–81). An early work was *Code Poems*, using the International Code of Signals, in which flag names, represented as letters, combine to make sentences, such as this extract from the first meeting of Romeo and Juliet:

S L D	Romeo:	My name is
R		Romeo
E B Q	Juliet:	Your name is not on my list; spell it alphabetically
J G	Romeo:	I wish to have personal communication with you
I J	Juliet:	Unless your communication is very important,
		I must be excused

Some were performed at a 1968 poetry event in Central Park, New York, helped by US coastguards manipulating flags and lights.

Her idiosyncratic style, arising partly from a schizophrenic condition, reached its best-known expression in *The Clairvoyant Journal* (1978). She explained its origins in an interview with Charles Bernstein in 1995:

> I started to see words in August 1972. And I saw them for a year and they were all over the place, coming out of my hair and my toenails ... I bought a typewriter. And I looked at the words and said *you have three choices: caps, italics, and regular type*, and that settled it, that's all. The words settled down to three voices. ... The capital words, which give instructions, the italics, which make comments, and the ordinary type, which is me just trying to get through the day. And it was a quite wild thing to type.

Her 'prose poetry', as it was called, is also a 'wild' thing to read, with the three typefaces interweaving, along with irregular spacing and vertical typing. The opening lines of one piece give only a hint of its typographical complexity:

> You hear TYPE go downstairs to the *mother* typing room YOU AREN'T PER-MITTED HERE not true GO DOWN IT'S NOT THE GUILLOTINE you ask to type REFUSE see WORK you can type *a few minutes* and AT NIGHT LAUGH

H.L. Mencken was born in 1880

Henry Louis Mencken, born in Baltimore, Maryland, was professionally known by his initials. He became a journalist and essayist before producing the work for which he's best known, *The American Language*. Its first edition was published in 1919, but he continued to revise and expand it, so that by the time of its 4th edition in 1936, 'corrected, enlarged, and rewritten', two large supplements were in progress. The first appeared in 1945, adding to chapters 1–6 of the original book which focused on the history of English in the USA. The second appeared in 1948, adding to chapters 7–12 which dealt with structure – pronunciation, spelling, grammar, names and slang. It was an enormous work, by any standards, with each volume running to around 800 pages. He died in 1956.

His essays covered a wide range of subjects. Here are two short extracts. The first is from an essay entitled 'The Poet and His Art':

> Once, after plowing through sixty or seventy volumes of bad verse, I described myself as a poetry-hater. The epithet was and is absurd. The truth is that I enjoy poetry as much as the next man – when the mood is on me. But what mood? The mood, in a few words, of intellectual and spiritual fatigue, the mood of revolt against the insoluble riddle of existence, the mood of disgust and despair. Poetry, then, is a capital medicine.

The second shows how unwise it was to mess with H.L. Mencken. Here he is condemning President Harding's use of English:

> He writes the worst English that I have ever encountered. It reminds me of a string of wet sponges; it reminds me of tattered washing on the line; it reminds me of stale bean soup, of college yells, of dogs barking idiotically through endless nights. It is so bad that a sort of grandeur creeps into it. It drags itself out of the dark abysm of pish, and crawls insanely up the topmost pinnacle of posh. It is rumble and bumble. It is flap and doodle. It is balder and dash.

John Cheke died in 1557

He was born in Cambridge in 1514, and became a classical scholar, translator, tutor to Prince Edward and Princess Elizabeth, and statesman during the reign of Edward VI. Following the accession of Mary Tudor in 1553, religious conflict forced him into exile in Europe, and imprisonment in the Tower on his return, until a public recantation of his beliefs in 1556 gave him a period of renewed prosperity.

It was during this time that he wrote a letter that has become a famous part of English linguistic history. It was published as one of the prefaces to his friend Thomas Hoby's translation of *The Book of the Courtier* by Baldassare Castiglione, published in 1561, and makes an early statement of the view that English has no need of the many borrowings that were flooding into the language at the time – words such as *condisciple*, *magnifical* and *fecundity*. They were dismissively called 'inkhorn' words, because they took a lot of ink to write. Plain English is all that's needed:

> I am of this opinion that our own tung should be written cleane and pure, unmixt and unmangeled with borowing of other tunges, wherin if we take not heed by tijm, ever borowing and never payeng, she shall be fain to keep her house as bankrupt. For then doth our tung naturallie and praisablie utter her meaning, when she bouroweth no counterfeitness of other tunges to attire her self withall, but useth plainlie her own, with such shift, as nature, craft, experiens and folowing of other excellent doth lead her unto, and if she want at ani tijm (as being unperfight she must) yet let her borow with suche bashfulnes, that it mai appeer, that if either the mould of our own tung could serve us to fascion a woord of our own, or if the old denisoned wordes could content and ease this need, we wolde not boldly venture of unknowen wordes.

He wrote this in London just two months before his death, 'From my house in Woodstreete the 16 of July, 1557'.

Anne Stevenson died in 2020

She was born in Cambridge UK in 1933, when her father was studying philosophy at the university, grew up in various parts of the USA, and returned to the UK in the 1960s. She became known on both sides of the Atlantic as a poet, essayist and critic, and especially for her biography of Sylvia Plath in 1989. In her books and many interviews she talks a lot about the poetic process, and about the interaction between forms and meanings, as in these remarks in *The Cortland Review* in 2000:

> So writing a poem is like conducting an argument between your unconscious mind and your conscious self. You have to get unconsciousness and consciousness lined up in some way. I suspect that's why working to a form, achieving a stanza, and keeping to it – deciding that the first and third and fifth lines will have to rhyme, and that you're going to insist on so many stresses per line – oddly helps the poem to be born. That is, to free itself from you and your attentions to it and become a piece of art in itself. Heaven only knows where it comes from! I suppose working out a form diminishes the thousands of possibilities you face when you begin. And once you've cut down the possibilities, you can't swim off into the deep and drown. Well, it's a very, very strange process.

In reflecting on one of her own poems, she talks about the way sounds were 'echoing' and 'chiming'. Her interviewer asks why she doesn't use a more technical vocabulary.

> I rarely think of terms like alliteration, internal rhyme, et cetera. Either a poem sings or it doesn't. I am conscious of the line endings, yes, but I never analyze what is happening when I write. That comes later. As Elizabeth Bishop put it, it's too easy to talk the life out of poetry. My model is, anyway, music: that is, poems come to me in musical phrases or cadences. Some of my poems are probably just musical toys.

1800: Wordsworth promises to finish a Preface to the *Lyrical Ballads*

One of the most famous pieces of writing in the history of English poetic style is the Preface that William Wordsworth wrote to the second edition of the *Lyrical Ballad*s, a collection of poems, including some by Coleridge, which was published in January 1801. An expanded version appeared in the 3rd edition the following year, and is now seen as a manifesto of the Romantic movement.

Wordsworth was evidently under some pressure to get the text to his printer, Nathaniel Biggs. He writes to him on this day: 'The Preface shall certainly be sent off in four days at furthest.' That was a Monday, so he seems to have meant 'by the end of the week'. He was over-optimistic. He had started to write it two days previously, judging by an entry in his sister Dorothy's journal: 'William writing his Preface'; but it wasn't finished until the 30th, when – in her role as copyist – she writes again: 'I wrote the last sheet of Notes and Preface'.

The paragraph most often quoted about language begins:

> The principal object, then, proposed in these Poems was to choose incidents and situations from common life, and to relate or describe them, throughout, as far as was possible in a selection of language really used by men, and, at the same time, to throw over them a certain colouring of imagination, whereby ordinary things should be presented to the mind in an unusual aspect … Humble and rustic life was generally chosen, because, in that condition, the essential passions of the heart find a better soil in which they can attain their maturity, are less under restraint, and speak a plainer and more emphatic language.

'Really used' was almost immediately a source of contention. The language was certainly a great deal 'plainer' than the crafted elegance of many previous writers, but it was still some way from everyday rustic domestic speech, as pointed out by Coleridge in his *Biographia Literaria* (SEE 25 JULY) a few years later.

Papua New Guinea
gains independence in 1975

Why, out of the many countries that gained their independence in the second half of the twentieth century, should Papua New Guinea be singled out? Because it's thought to be the most linguistically diverse country in the world, with over 800 known languages, and several more probably unknown, as it's believed there are still a few indigenous groups who have never been contacted. Most of the languages have very few speakers, and many are seriously endangered. English is the language of government and education, with Hiri Motu and Tok Pisin also official. The latter – etymologically from English 'talk pidgin', and often called New Guinea Pidgin – is the country's main lingua franca.

Pidgins are languages that have grown up among people who don't share a common tongue but who want to talk to each other for trading or other reasons. With so many languages in Papua New Guinea, the reason for the emergence of a pidgin is obvious. Originally the native language of no one, some – such as Tok Pisin – eventually become the first language of many speakers, and for them it's thus more accurately called a creole.

Pidgins mustn't be confused with the mock-pidgin talk, often portrayed in films, of the 'Me Tarzan' type. They do have a limited vocabulary, a reduced grammatical structure and a much narrower range of functions, compared to the languages which gave rise to them; but in the case of Tok Pisin, expansion has taken place to cope with all the demands placed upon it as a lingua franca. It's widely used in parliament, broadcasting, advertising and other everyday settings. Major literary works have been translated into it, and an indigenous literature has evolved. There's a national weekly newspaper, *Wantok* – a name that can be seen again in this illustration, the opening lines of Antony's famous speech in Shakespeare's *Julius Caesar*: 'Friends, Romans, countrymen, lend me your ears / I come to bury Caesar, not to praise him':

Pren, man bilong Rom, Wantok, harim nau.
Mi kam tasol long plantim Kaesar. Mi noken beiten longen.

The Third Man wins
the Grand Prix at Cannes in 1949

Carol Reed's film is an adaptation of a novella written by English writer Graham Greene (1904–1991). It's my favourite film, as another day in this book mentions (22 MARCH), and at a Graham Greene Festival in his birthplace of Berkhamsted a few years ago I presented a paper on his views about language. It was titled 'Going Especially Careful in *The Third Man*', alluding to a threat made to Holly Martins in the film.

It was a tricky assignment, as Greene hardly ever comments on language as a subject. I found just one remark in the whole of his letters, talking about the new language of Catholic liturgy:

> Words have a certain holiness; they should be able to represent truthfully a certain emotion as well as a certain belief and I do think the language of the seventeenth century succeeded in this better than the language of the twentieth century which is apt to date from one year to another.

But in the novels he has his characters repeatedly allude to languages. And whenever there's an explicit reference – to accent, words, grammar... – or to individual languages and dialects, it's a sign that trouble is brewing. This is especially so in *The Third Man*.

For those who don't know the film... A professional language user (a novelist) arrives in a country where he's unable to speak the language, to write some special language material (propaganda) for a friend. He encounters a situation where he has to rely on translation to find out anything at all, finds himself dealing with people who all have strange accents or names (that he sometimes gets wrong), and can't work out what's happening to him (in a taxi) or to others (with Anna, with a porter) because he doesn't understand the language. He ends up having to give a lecture on a subject he knows nothing about and loses his own language ability in the process: 'Well, yes. I suppose that is what I meant to say.' And so it continues, with over forty allusions. It's the most linguistically aware of all Graham Greene's works.

Samuel Johnson was born in 1705

Born in Lichfield, Johnson became a leading eighteenth-century figure, known for his writing, conversation and lexicography, publishing his great *Dictionary of the English Language* in 1755. He began his ambitious project with a small team of assistants in 1746, working in a room at the top of his house in Gough Square, near Fleet Street in London – today a Johnson museum, with a remarkable number of surviving artefacts. In 1747 he wrote a preliminary plan for the dictionary, which he sent to Lord Chesterfield, in which he admitted to being 'frighted at its extent'. It took him three years to read his source works and mark which bits were to be used. These were copied onto slips of paper and filed alphabetically. He then began to draft definitions. It was complete by 1754, and published in two large volumes.

The *Dictionary* portrayed the complexity of the English lexicon more fully than ever before: 42,773 entries in the first edition, with 140,871 definitions and 222,114 quotations. It was the first dictionary to use quotations in such an integrated and extensive way. Shakespeare, Dryden, Addison and Bacon provided over a third, but he cites over 500 authors in all. His citations began a practice that has informed high-quality English dictionaries ever since, though no longer restricted to the 'best' authors. Johnson saw four editions through the press, the last in 1773. He died in 1784.

But the quantities are only the starting point. As he wrote in his plan: 'The great labour is yet to come, the labour of interpreting these words and phrases with brevity, fulness and perspicuity'. In my anthology from the *Dictionary* for Penguin Classics for the 250th anniversary in 2005, I wrote about the definitions: 'They are the dictionary's primary strength, and its chief claim to fame.' I stand by that, and illustrate his three criteria with this perceptive definition of *sorry*:

Grieved for something past. It is generally used of slight or casual miscarriages or vexations, but sometimes of greater things. It does not imply any long continuance of grief.

International Talk Like a Pirate Day

It's not often that a private joke between friends becomes an international day, but that's what happened here. Apparently Americans John Baur and Mark Summer were playing racquetball when one injured himself, letting out an anguished 'aaarrr'. This being one of the utterances believed to be used by pirates of old, they cooked up the idea of having a day – they chose the birthday of Mark's ex-wife – in which people would dress up as pirates (eye patch, bandana, toy parrot…) and speak like they're imagined to do ('shiver my timbers, aye aye captain, avast me hearties…').

It was all good fun – notwithstanding the nasty realities of piracy today – and something many children and adults do, whose only experience of pirates is from films such as *Treasure Island*. I remember doing exactly the same thing myself, but at what age escapes me. The difference was that their fun project was picked up by the media in 2002 and rapidly spread. Today, it's an extra way of raising money for good causes.

The linguistics of the day involves both dialect and accent. Of course nobody knows how eighteenth-century pirates spoke. The impression most people have derives from Robert Louis Stevenson's *Treasure Island*, published in 1883, which brilliantly captures a plausible way of talking:

> 'I don't say nothing as to your being in our hands,' continued Silver, 'though there you are, and you may lay to it. I'm all for argyment; I never seen good come out o' threatening. If you like the service, well, you'll jine; and if you don't, Jim, why, you're free to answer no – free and welcome, shipmate; and if fairer can be said by mortal seaman, shiver my sides!'

The imagined accent, with its noticeable pronunciation of *r* after vowels, is influenced by Robert Newton's portrayal of Long John Silver in the 1950 Disney film. It's his West Country accent (born in Dorset, brought up in Cornwall and Devon) that fostered the stereotype of pirate speech – and probably not too far from the reality, as many buccaneers set sail from Bristol.

National Gibberish Day

This is an American day whose origins are obscure, and whose point – to talk nonsense to each other – isn't entirely clear. But it does prompt reflection on the phenomenon of speaking nonsense, which is more common than often realized. Websites about the day bring together two distinct notions: *gibberish*, which is unintelligible speech belonging to no known language, and *gobbledegook*, which is the use of jargon that the general public finds difficult or impossible to understand. Both are negative terms – behaviour to be avoided – which is presumably why someone with an anarchic spirit thought up this day originally.

Nonsense words and phrases do, however, have a small but useful role to play in everyday speech. They can help us out when we don't know what to call something, or have forgotten its name. And they're available when we feel that something is not worth a precise mention or we want to be deliberately vague. They've been recorded in English since the sixteenth century – many based on *what* (such as *whatchamacallit*, *whatsits*...) or *thing* (*thingummy*, *thingamajig*...). In the twentieth century a raft of *doo-* forms appeared, such as *doobry*, *doodad* and *doofer* for objects whose true name is forgotten or not known. 'Pass the doobery', one might say, referring to the device that changes television channels. Families often create such home slang.

Some people have turned nonsense into an art form, as in the scat singing used by Ella Fitzgerald and other jazz vocalists and folk singers (SEE 19 JULY), and the names of many popular songs, such Disney's 'Zip-a-dee-doo-dah', the Beatles' 'Ob-la-di, ob-la-da', the Crystals' (no relation) 'Da Doo Ron Ron', and innumerable variants of the *Sha-la-la*, *Shoo-be-doo* type. Australian singer Lisa Goddard often uses lyrics – if that's the right word – from no known language. Some poets have written nonsense verse (SEE 12 MAY). In linguistics, person-restricted speech goes by the name of *idioglossia* – as when young twins talk to each other idiosyncratically, religious people are inspired to 'speak in tongues' or magicians use words credited with special power (as in *abracadabra*).

Walter Scott died in 1832

Born in Edinburgh in 1771, Scott became Scotland's best-known historical novelist, as well as a prolific writer and editor of several other genres. He offers language enthusiasts so much that I've found it difficult to choose an extract for this book. He illustrated Scots dialogue with unprecedented realism, and gave many words their first recorded usage (over 400 in the *Oxford English Dictionary* – *bedazzled, cold shoulder, deferential, hilarious, password, uptake…*).

In the end I've opted for *Chronicles of the Canongate* (a street in central Edinburgh), his only collection of short stories, published in two volumes in 1827 and 1828, and the first work of fiction to which Scott put his own name – not on the title page, but in an autobiographical introduction. I choose it because of his description of the tale-teller, the fictional Mrs Martha Bethune Balliol, evidently based on a family friend, Mrs Anne Murray Keith. She's introduced by an old bankrupt – Scott himself had become insolvent the year before as a result of the country's financial crash – whose name appealed to me for obvious reasons: Chrystal Croftangry.

As Croftangry begins to describe Mrs Balliol's lodging, Scott writes: 'dearest reader, if you are tired, pray pass over the next four or five pages'. That would be a shame, as they would then miss an illuminating piece of sociolinguistic description of her dialect:

> It was Scottish – decidedly Scottish – often containing phrases and words little used in the present day. But then her tone and mode of pronunciation were as different from the usual accent of the ordinary Scotch PATOIS, as the accent of St. James's is from that of Billingsgate. … In short, it seemed to be the Scottish as spoken by the ancient Court of Scotland, to which no idea of vulgarity could be attached; and the lively manners and gestures with which it was accompanied were so completely in accord with the sound of the voice and the style of talking, that I cannot assign them a different origin.

First meeting of the proposed
East India Company in 1599

The minutes of the occasion list the 'adventurers' (today we'd call them 'investors') involved in the new scheme:

> The names of such persons as have written with their own hands, to venture in the pretended voyage to the East Indies (the which it may please the Lord to prosper), and the sums that they will adventure, the xxii. September 1599.

There followed 101 names of aldermen and merchants committing sums ranging from £3,000 to £100, and raising in total £30,133 6s 8d – which according to the Bank of England inflation index would be over £10 million today. The proposal was accepted by Queen Elizabeth in October, but the uncertain state of the peace negotiations with Spain caused a year's delay, and the company didn't receive its charter of incorporation until December the following year, by which time the number of adventurers had grown to 215.

The venture certainly did prosper. And as the Company grew in India and other territories, both commercially and politically, the impact of trade on English vocabulary was enormous. I read through many of the cargo lists of the main shipping lines, stored in the British Library, for its 'Evolving English' exhibition in 2010. One such list shows the items brought back to England from the Bay of Bengal and Fort St George by five ships on 14 July 1724. There's a picture of the list in my book of the exhibition: *Evolving English: One Language, Many Voices* (2010).

Most of the items are fabrics – mainly types of cotton, linen and silk – and most of the names are now obsolescent, familiar only to textile historians.

> Addaties, Alliballies, Allibannies, Baftaes, Bettellees Oringal, Carridarries, Chillaes, Chints, Coopees, Coffaes, Chowtars, Chucklaes, Cushtaes, Cuttannees, Doosooties, Doreas, Emerties, Ginghams Colour'd, Gurrahs, Humhums, Jamwars, Lacowries, Longcloth, Moorees, Mulmuls, Nillaes, Photaes, Romalls, Sallampores, Sannoes, Seerbands, Seerbettees, Seersuckers, Sooseys, Taffaties, Tanjeebs, Terrindams.

International Day of Sign Languages

This is a United Nations day, first celebrated in 2018. The proposal came from the World Federation of the Deaf. When it was accepted, the date chosen for the occasion was that of the establishment of the Federation in Rome in 1951. The WFD is an advocacy organization that 'promotes the preservation of sign languages and deaf culture as a prerequisite enabling deaf people to achieve a level of accessibility to life situations and policy-making decisions comparable to those offered to hearing people'. Through its national associations it represents over 70 million deaf people worldwide who collectively use around 300 different sign languages.

The UN resolution links the day to statements about the value of multilingualism, the International Covenant on Civil and Political Rights, and the Convention on the Rights of Persons with Disabilities. It emphasizes that sign languages are equal in status to spoken languages, and obligates states to facilitate the learning of sign and promote the linguistic identity of their deaf community. Using the traditional formal style of UN resolutions, we read that the General Assembly,

— *Affirming* that ensuring and promoting the full realization of all human rights relevant to matters of language and fundamental freedoms is a critical prerequisite to the full realization of human rights for deaf people,
— *Aware* that sign languages are fully fledged natural languages, structurally distinct from spoken languages, alongside which they coexist, and that, when working with deaf communities, the principle of 'nothing about us without us' must be considered and integrated,
— *Recalling* that early access to sign language and services in sign language, including quality education available in sign language, is vital to the growth and development of the deaf individual and critical to the achievement of the internationally agreed development goals,
— *Recognizing* the importance of preserving sign languages as part of linguistic and cultural diversity,

proclaimed the day, and encouraged all member states to take measures to raise public awareness of sign languages throughout society.

National Punctuation Day

The day was founded in 2004 by Jeff Rubin, an American consultant on writing and design, to increase public awareness of the importance of correct punctuation. It takes its place alongside other initiatives where individuals, concerned at what they perceive to be falling standards in written language, have formed organizations (such as the Apostrophe Protection Society), written books (such as Lynne Truss's *Eats, Shoots and Leaves*), arranged events, and gone out on campaigns to correct errors in public signs and notices – in most cases, the nonstandard use of apostrophes.

It's remarkable how punctuation – along with spelling – has achieved such an important role as an index of educability and stylistic mastery, and regrettable that educational systems have evidently failed to teach so many people the accepted rules. Part of the problem is that the English punctuation system isn't simple, as its evolution has resulted in many variations and exceptions. For example, the 'rule' that the apostrophe marks possession breaks down with pronouns, where we write *its*, *hers*, and so on. The 'rule' that there's no apostrophe in plural nouns breaks down in such cases as *the 1980's* and *dot your i's* (SEE 20 DECEMBER). There's a huge amount of usage variation sanctioned by tradition, such as *Earls Court* vs *Baron's Court* on the London Underground. And all of it is subject to change.

The famous case of the 'serial comma' shows how divided usage can be, with some publishing houses insisting there should be a comma before *and* in expressions like *tall, dark(,) and handsome* and some insisting that there shouldn't. Personal taste enters in, with some people using the marks to reflect pronunciation and some using them to reflect grammatical construction. And it's a fact of life that some of us like to use a lot of marks, while others avoid them except where they're essential to resolve written ambiguity and aid readability.

My feeling is that it would be more helpful, in the long term, to spend the day exploring the history of punctuation rather than going out with cameras to find errors, or with marker pens to correct them.

Joshua Steele dedicated his
Melody and Measure of Speech in 1775

He was born in Ireland in 1700, but spent his first eighty years (!) in London, where he became known as a writer with a special interest in music. In his later years he moved to Barbados, where he owned several estates, and was recognized for his efforts to improve living standards and treatment for the slave population. He died there in 1796.

Little is known of his time in London, but one clear fact is that on this day in 1775 he dedicated his major work to Sir John Pringle, the president of the Royal Society. This was *An essay towards establishing the melody and measure of speech to be expressed and perpetuated by peculiar* [special] *symbols*. He applied his musical knowledge to speech, and devised a transcription which included rising and falling pitch movements, variations in loudness and pause, and tempo changes such as largo and allegretto. The book is full of illustrations using an adapted five-line musical stave (USA: staff), including a complete transcription of himself speaking 'To be or not to be'.

He explains his motivation in an introduction:

Whilst almost every one perceives and admits singing to be performed by the ascent and descent of the voice through a variety of notes, as palpably and formally different from each other as the steps of a ladder; it seems, at first sight, somewhat extraordinary, that even men of science should not perceive the rapid slides of the voice, upwards and downwards, in common speech. ...

In traveling through a country, apparently level, how few people perceive the ascents and descents that would astonish them, if the man of art were to demonstrate them by his instrument, and to bring the sluggish stream to form a cascade! In like manner, when the modulation of the melody of speech shall be ripened into method by art, even the vulgar [common people] may be taught to know what the learned can now scarce comprehend.

His system is a remarkable anticipation of the way twentieth-century phoneticians developed the study of intonation and other features of speech prosody.

European Day of Languages

For Europeans, this has to be one of the most enticing days in the linguistic year. But the day has repercussions far beyond Europe, as its languages are spoken or taught, and recognized through the media, online and offline, on a global scale. The day was introduced in 2001, jointly organized by the Council of Europe and the European Union, and in 2021 had forty-six participating countries.

The aims of the day are summarized on the Council's website.

— Alerting the public to the importance of language learning and diversifying the range of languages learnt in order to increase plurilingualism and intercultural understanding;
— Promoting the rich linguistic and cultural diversity of Europe, which must be preserved and fostered;
— Encouraging lifelong language learning in and out of school, whether for study purposes, for professional needs, for purposes of mobility, or for pleasure and exchanges.

That website is also the place to go to see the remarkable range of innovative activities that can be used to celebrate the day – competitions, quizzes, games, displays, musical compositions, exhibitions, design themes for T-shirts or greetings cards, and a host of other events, all with a multilingual theme. Schools have an especially important role to play, as it's only by enthusing children to learn languages that a multilingual European future can be guaranteed. This future is already under serious threat in the UK, where the numbers of children studying a foreign language to examination levels, and the numbers of available foreign-language teachers, have drastically fallen over recent years.

The day needs to be exploited at all levels of government policy-making, as well as throughout the voluntary sector in non-governmental organizations, companies, charities and other private associations. Above all, the myth needs to be destroyed that language learning is only for children. On the contrary, it's a lifelong option offered by many local authorities, colleges and online companies.

William Safire died in 2009

Born in New York City in 1929, Safire became a journalist, presidential speech-writer, and political columnist for the *New York Times*, but for linguists he's best known for his 'On Language' column in the *New York Times Magazine*, which he began in 1979. It started as the usual kind of usage column, addressing traditional complaints, but he developed a witty style that gave him a general appeal. An indication of his tongue-in-cheek approach is seen in 1980, when he published a collection of his first year's pieces: *William Safire on Language*. Most authors accept what the blurb-writer has to say without comment. Not Safire, as the opening paragraph on the jacket illustrates:

> William Safire of *The New York Times* is the most widely read writer on language in America today. The new national word-watcher is catching our words on the wing in their regional migrations, their flights of fancy, and their nose-dives into pomposity and pretention. (*Note from W.S.: This metaphor has tired wings. 'Nose dive,' as a noun, should be two words, and only takes the hyphen when used as a verb.*)

For some reason he didn't pick on the spelling of *pretension*.

Over the years he became less prescriptive and more explanatory, reaching out to linguists as occasion demanded. I corresponded with him myself on occasional points of usage, when he wanted a British perspective. But a sociolinguistic awareness was there from the beginning, as this lively extract from the introduction to his 1980 book illustrates:

> English is a stretch language; one size fits all. That does not mean anything goes; in most instances, anything does not go. But the language, as it changes, conforms itself to special groups and occasions: There is a time for dialect, a place for slang, an occasion for literary form. What is correct on the sports page is out of place on the op-ed page; what is with-it on the street may well be without it in the classroom. The spoken language does not have the same standards as the written language – the tune you whistle is not the orchestra's score.

National Read a Child a Book You Like Day

The date was chosen to honour Kate Douglas Wiggin, American children's writer and educationalist, who founded kindergartens for poor children in California. She was born in Philadelphia on this day in 1856, and died in 1923. Internationally she became best known for her novel *Rebecca of Sunnybrook Farm* (1903), filmed in 1936.

I haven't been able to find when the day was created, but its aim is clear. Surveys by literacy organizations have repeatedly shown that many homes with children have few or no books, and the children have had little or no experience of being read to aloud. It's really valuable, then, when kindergartens and primary schools have regular story-reading periods, and even invite professional storytellers in. Some organizations, such as Bookstart in the UK, offer a package of free reading books to new parents.

The benefits that stem from reading aloud to children have been repeatedly demonstrated. In addition to the entertainment value, and the bonding it fosters between child and adult, the practice promotes cognitive skills. It assists the development of attention, memory and comprehension, and helps the acquisition of vocabulary and other aspects of spoken language, as the interaction presents many opportunities to have conversations about the way a story or topic unfolds.

These days the traditional model of parental reading has been supplemented by innovative digital reading experiences. Listen-and-read books, such as those provided by companies such as Pickatale, build a bridge between joint reading and solo reading. But they're a bridge that needs to be used well, to ensure that reading progress is made. Read-along books shouldn't be thought of as electronic babysitters, giving parents an easy time. Adults need to give them just as much energy as they would give when joint-reading a printed book. The narrator isn't a replacement for a parent or teacher, but a collaborator.

And of course the hope is that this day won't be seen as a one-off, but a prompt for every day. And with 'You' in the title replaced by 'They'.

Elizabeth Elstob was born in 1683

She was born in Newcastle upon Tyne. Unusually for women at the time, she learned several languages, becoming part of an antiquarian circle of scholars who were popularizing Anglo-Saxon. She died in 1756. She compiled the first Anglo-Saxon grammar written in English: *The Rudiments of Grammar for the English-Saxon Tongue* (1715). What makes it especially interesting is her preface, which she entitles 'An Apology for the Study of Northern Antiquities' – a forthright defence of the work of the scholars.

Her particular target is Jonathan Swift's *Proposal for Correcting, Improving and Ascertaining the English Tongue* (SEE 22 FEBRUARY). Not only do we see a female voice daring to speak out against a man of such high reputation, but we find a forceful and scholarly demolition of his views. As Charles Peake put it in an introduction to her work: 'There can be little doubt that Swift is decisively worsted in this argument.'

She makes a withering attack on those who have ignored the antiquarians, and then takes aim at Swift (I've modernized the typography):

> But to leave these Pedagogues to huff and swagger in the heighth of all their Arrogance. I cannot but think it great Pity, that in our Considerations, for Refinement of the English Tongue, so little Regard is had to Antiquity, and the Original of our present Language, which is the Saxon. This indeed is allow'd by an ingenious Person, who hath lately made some *Proposals for the Refinement of the English Tongue*, 'That the old Saxon, except in some few Variations in the Orthography, is the same in most original Words with our present English, as well as with the German and other Northern Dialects'; which makes it a little surprizing to me, to find the same Gentleman not long after to say, 'The other Languages of Europe I know nothing of, neither is there any occasion to consider them': because, as I have before observ'd, it must be very difficult to imagin, how a Man can judge of a thing he knoweth nothing of, whether there can be occasion or no to consider it.

International Translation Day

The day was inaugurated by the United Nations in 2017 to celebrate the role of language professionals. In the Resolution we read that the UN,

> *Recognizing* the practical contribution of language professionals, both in conference servicing and in the field, to furthering the cause of the United Nations ...
>
> *Affirms* that professional translation, as a trade and an art, plays an important role in upholding the purposes and principles of the Charter of the United Nations, bringing nations together, facilitating dialogue, understanding and cooperation, contributing to development and strengthening world peace and security.

The UN website summarizes the role of its many translators and interpreters, along with the associated editors, précis-writers, desktop publishers and verbatim reporters:

> Transposition of a literary or scientific work, including technical work, from one language into another language, professional translation, including translation proper, interpretation and terminology, is indispensable to preserving clarity, a positive climate and productiveness in international public discourse, and interpersonal communication.

A large team handles all kinds of documents, such as statements by Member States and reports prepared by expert bodies which cover every topic on the UN agenda.

This date was chosen as it's the feast day of Saint Jerome, who died in 420 CE, and who is remembered for translating most of the Bible into Latin from the Greek manuscripts of the New Testament, and parts of the Hebrew Gospel into Greek. He's also there in the UN St Jerome Translation Contest, held every year since 2005, which celebrates the best translations in Arabic, Chinese, English, French, Russian, Spanish and German. He is the patron saint of a wide range of people professionally involved in language – not only translators and interpreters, but also Bible scholars, archaeologists, archivists, librarians, military linguists, encyclopedists and students.

World Postcard Day

The day was launched in 2020 by Postcrossing, the website platform for physical postcard exchange, and the print production company Finepaper, following the 150th anniversary of the postcard in 2019. Their official website for the day explains how an Austro-Hungarian professor from Vienna wrote a newspaper article pointing out that the effort involved in writing a letter was out of proportion to the size of the message sent. He suggested that a more practical and cheaper method should be introduced for shorter communications. The Austrian Post put the idea into practice on this day in 1869.

There had been earlier proposals, but they never achieved much success. Postal services were concerned about the complexity and cost, and there was some public resistance to the thought of people being able to read private messages. But gradually there was international agreement about how to handle them, and more sophisticated photography and designs evolved. By the turn of the century they were everywhere, as reported in 1899 by London's *The Standard*:

> The illustrated postcard craze, like the influenza, has spread to these islands from the Continent, where it has been raging with considerable severity. Sporadic cases have occurred in Britain. Young ladies who have escaped the philatelic infection or wearied of collecting Christmas cards, have been known to fill albums with missives of this kind received from friends abroad; but now the cards are being sold in this country, and it will be like the letting out of waters.

The website comments that, with multiple daily pickups and deliveries, 'postcards were effectively the text messages of their time'. And, like texts, they developed their own style of language, with short and elliptical sentences, conventional expressions about weather, locality and travel, and lacking the traditional greeting and closing formulae of letters. But social media, texting and the price of stamps have recently hit the postcard industry hard – hence this day, which it's hoped will do something to help rejuvenate the medium.

National Name Your Car Day

The origins of this day are unknown, but the logic behind it is inescapable. People name their boats. Why not their cars? Boat-naming presumably began for practical reasons: to distinguish between many boats of a similar appearance in a harbour, or to identify individual boats on a voyage. Car licence plates have the same function, and they too can be personalized. But the aim behind this day is to go one step further, and to give your car a personal name. If the licence plate uses letters, that's often the motivation: FRD will obviously generate Fred, SLV will be Silvia. But the tendency to anthropomorphize a vehicle goes well beyond licence plates.

We only have to look at the famous car names from the worlds of cinema, television and video games: Kit from *Knight Rider*, Herbie from *Herbie the Love Bug*, General Lee from *Dukes of Hazzard*, Bandit from *Smokey and the Bandit*. Then there's Lightning McQueen and dozens more from the *Cars* game and its sequels. People often copy these names if they have a car of a similar make; but more often they introduce names reflecting their own interests or personalities. If you're into Shakespeare, there's a wide choice of male and female names waiting for you, though superstitiously minded owners might want to avoid the more tragic personalities. If you're stuck, there are online Name Your Car generators. You're asked a series of questions – usually about the car's colour, age or imagined gender, or which car movies or journeys you identify with, and up comes a suggestion.

Cars are not alone. People have anthropomorphized inanimate objects throughout history, when they have a special significance. In medieval times they named swords – most famously King Arthur's *Excalibur*. Gardeners might name their wheelbarrows, or their favourite plants. Geeks name their computers. And there's a growing body of social psychological research explaining why we do it. It seems we feel we understand our objects more and develop a warmer relationship with them if we give them a name.

SOS became the international maritime distress signal in 1906

The sequence of three dots + three dashes + three dots, with no spaces between each letter, had already been used by Germany as a distress signal, and it was adopted as a maritime standard at the first International Radiotelegraph Convention, which began on this day in Berlin. It was thought to be the most efficient sequence of pulses to signal an emergency – neither too short to be ambiguous nor too long to be unwieldy. It's technically a *prosign* (or procedural sign) – a single unit, not a letter sequence.

It wasn't the only suggestion. The Marconi company had already used *CQ* (from French *sécu*, short for *sécurité*) in land telegraphy, and adapted this as *CQD* for ships in distress – informally glossed in English as 'come quick danger'). But it fell out of use after the shorter *SOS* sequence became universal. Its use as an abbreviation in English for 'Save Our Souls' or 'Save our Ship' came later, as did its application in non-maritime settings for any urgent appeal for help.

The beauty of the Morse signal was its medium adaptability, visible using flashing lights as well as audible (SEE 27 APRIL). The downside was that it required skilled operators to send and interpret, as well as continual monitoring of the radio distress frequency. In 1979 it was replaced by an automatic means of alerting and locating ship emergencies, devised by the UN's International Maritime Organization: the Global Maritime Distress and Safety System. It's of especial value in situations where a radio operator might not have time or opportunity to send a written (*SOS*) or spoken (*MAYDAY* – from French *m'aidez*, 'help me') message.

SOS had one really useful linguistic feature: it's an ambigram – a word that can be read in the same way when flipped over. This helps when someone in trouble has traced out the letters in sand, for instance, or made the message from waste material. Search aircraft coming from opposite directions can read it easily. It's also simple to write and universally recognized, so its long-term future seems assured.

4 OCTOBER

Ten-Four Day

It's the fourth day of the tenth month, and thus the obvious choice to celebrate those who use citizen-band (CB) radio, where the brevity code 10-4 is used to mean an affirmative response – 'understood', 'message received'. The day was launched by the US telecommunications company Motorola in 1977, at a time when CB radio use was common among police forces, truckers and amateur radio enthusiasts. The technology has now largely been replaced by cell phones and other digital devices.

The CB system developed in the late 1930s in the Illinois police department, and became widespread when adopted for police communication by the Association of Public-Safety Communications Officials. Limitations of the new (at the time) radio technology motivated the use of short messages, and the need for clarity was paramount. Numbers to replace common phrases were thought to offer an ideal solution, but encountered a problem. When a message began with just a single number, such as '4', it would often be unheard, as it took a fraction of a second for the police-car radio transmitter to reach full power. Police officers were supposed to leave a short pause after turning on their microphone, but practice was erratic. The problem was solved by preceding each code with a '10'.

Around a hundred codes were devised, such as 10-6 (Busy), 10-9 (Repeat) and 10-28 (Check registration on...). Some became widely known, thanks to their use in television (such as *Highway Patrol*) and films, notably *Convoy* (1978), and passed into everyday slang. 'What's your twenty?' was a cool way of asking someone where they were (10-20).

Although ten-codes were intended to be a standardized system, variations were sporadically introduced by different police jurisdictions, leading to ambiguity or incomprehension. As a result, during the 2000s they began to be phased out across the USA, and replaced by everyday words. So 10-4 was replaced by *Roger*, 10-9 by *Say again*, 10-20 by *Location*, and so on. But the old system is still there, used by some truckers and radio hams, and especially useful if someone drives out of cell-phone range.

World Teachers' Day

The day was proclaimed by UNESCO in 1994. It commemorates the anniversary of the adoption in Paris in 1966 of a document, *Recommendation Concerning the Status of Teachers*, put together by UNESCO in association with the International Labour Organization. This proposed benchmarks for the rights and responsibilities of teachers, and standards for their initial preparation and further education, recruitment, employment and conditions.

Language teaching is well served by an international network of teaching associations. Other days in this book celebrate two of the main ones: the UK-based International Association of Teachers of English as a Foreign Language, universally known as IATEFL (SEE 20 FEBRUARY), and the US-based Teachers of English to Speakers of Other Languages, also universally known by an acronym, TESOL (SEE 17 MARCH). Australia has a national coordinating body called the Australian Council of TESOL Associations (ACTA). Canada has a similar federation for English as a Second Language (TESL Canada). And many other such associations exist. IATEFL, for example, has an international network of around a hundred associate language teaching organizations.

Several countries also have associations for teachers of English as a mother tongue, such as the National Association for the Teaching of English (NATE) and the English Association in the UK, the National Council of Teachers of English (NCTE) in the USA, and similar bodies in Australia, New Zealand, Canada and South Africa. Foreign-language teaching at all levels in the UK is represented by the Association for Language Learning (ALL).

These organizations have common aims, as indicated by the UN statements, and they're especially important nowadays as a means of sharing expertise and practices internationally – a need highlighted most recently by the challenging situations experienced during the 2020–21 pandemic. A common voice is also often needed, in addressing issues of national language policy, especially when language-learning opportunities are under threat.

Elizabeth Bishop ⸤

Born in 1911 in Massachusetts, Bishop ⸤
Poet Laureate Consultant to the Library o.
Pulitzer Prize winner a few years later (1956).
letters and conversations, I choose these reflectⁱ⸤
an interview in the *Christian Science Monitor* in 197⸤
for her, a poem begins with a sound, an image or an ⸤

> It differs with every single poem. Some poems begin as a
> that you aren't sure what they apply to, but eventually they ⸤
> and become lines, and then you see some pattern emerge. Som⸜
> an idea haunts me for a long time, though poems that start as ide⸜
> much harder to write. It's easier when they start out with a set of w⸜
> that sound nice and don't make much sense but eventually reveal their
> purpose. Again, the unconscious quality is very important. You don't
> ask a poem what it means, you have to let it tell you.

And then, asked how long she carries a poem in her head before
committing it to paper:

> From 10 minutes to 40 years. One of the few good qualities I think I
> have as a poet is patience. I have endless patience. Sometimes I feel I
> should be angry at myself for being willing to wait 20 years for a poem
> to get finished, but I don't think a good poet can afford to be in a rush.

Asked what one quality every poem should have, she replied:
'Surprise. The subject and the language which conveys it should surprise
you. You should be surprised at seeing something new and strangely
alive.' In that spirit, for this book, I close with the penultimate stanza
about her mentor poet (SEE 15 NOVEMBER), 'Invitation to Miss Marianne
Moore':

> With dynasties of negative constructions
> darkening and dying around you,
> with grammar that suddenly turns and shines
> like flocks of sandpipers flying,
> please come flying.

William Barnes died in 1886

n 1801 in the county of Dorset, Barnes became rector of the parish
Peter at Winterborne Came in 1862. He wrote over eight hundred
ms about his native county, becoming famous as 'the Dorset Poet'.
t he was also a keen amateur philologist, writing a grammar of Old
nglish, exploring the Germanic origins of the language, and strongly
advocating the replacement of all foreign loanwords in English by words
with Anglo-Saxon roots. He felt that if all non-Germanic words could be
removed from English, the language would immediately become much
more accessible and intelligible.

In his *fore-say* (preface) to his *Outline of English Speech-craft*
(grammar), he describes his book as a small contribution 'towards the
upholding of our strong old Anglo-Saxon speech'. We find *speech-lore*
(philology) and *book-lore* (literature), *thing-word* (noun) and *mark-word*
(adjective), *twin-words* (synonyms) and *wordlings* (particles). Ornithology
becomes *birdlore*. *Unfrienden* (alienate) anticipates social networking
(SEE 17 NOVEMBER).

His Anglo-Saxonisms had little permanent impact on the language as
a whole. But his return to the Anglo-Saxon roots of English influenced
several later writers, such as George Orwell. His dialect poetry is a
record of a rapidly disappearing rural culture, at times bright and light-
hearted, at times deeply nostalgic and moving. Here's the opening of
'False Friends-like':

> When I wer still a bwoy, an' mother's pride,
> A bigger bwoy spoke up to me so kind-like,
> 'If you do like, I'll treat ye wi' a ride
> In theäse wheel-barrow here.' Zoo I wer blind-like
> To what he had a-workèn in his mind-like,
> An' mounted vor a passenger inside;
> An' comèn to a puddle, perty wide,
> He tipp'd me in, a-grinnèn back behind-like.

Henry Fielding died in 1754

Born in Somerset in 1707, Fielding became well known for his plays and novels, especially *The History of Tom Jones, a Foundling* (1749). A few years previously, while working on his first major novel, *Joseph Andrews* (1742), he was writing a conduct booklet which he called *Essay on Conversation*, offering rules and advice on how actions and words contribute to a successful conversation.

His basic principle he calls 'good-breeding', by which he means 'the art of pleasing, or contributing as much as possible to the ease and happiness of those with whom you converse'. That means avoiding many pitfalls, which he describes at some length, such as this summary:

> A well-bred man, therefore, will not take more of the discourse than falls to his share; nor in this will he shew any violent impetuosity of temper, or exert any loudness of voice, even in arguing; for the information of the company, and the conviction of his antagonist, are to be his apparent motives; not the indulgence of his own pride, or an ambitious desire of victory; which latter, if a wise man should entertain, he will be sure to conceal with his utmost endeavour; since he must know, that to lay open his vanity in public, is no less absurd than to lay open his bosom to an enemy, whose drawn sword is pointed against it; for every man hath a dagger in his hand, ready to stab the vanity of another, wherever he perceives it.

Then there's this awful practice:

> discoursing on the mysteries of a particular profession, to which all the rest of the company, except one or two, are utter strangers. Lawyers are generally guilty of this fault, as they are more confined to the conversation of one another; and I have known a very agreeable company spoiled, where there have been two of these gentlemen present, who have seemed rather to think themselves in a court of justice, than in a mixed assembly of persons, met only for the entertainment of each other.

He was himself a lawyer.

World Post Day

The day was inaugurated at the 1969 Congress of the Universal Postal Union, held in Tokyo. The Union began on this day in 1874 in Bern, Switzerland – then known as the General Postal Union – and became an agency of the United Nations in 1948. Its aim, according to the UN website, is

> to create awareness of the role of the postal sector in people's and businesses' everyday lives and its contribution to the social and economic development of countries.

Every year, the UPU's 192 member countries celebrate the day using the event to introduce or promote new postal products and services. In many countries, philatelic exhibitions are organized, and new stamps and date cancellation marks are issued. There can be open days at post offices, mail centres and postal museums.

A theme is chosen for the year. In 2021, arising out of the pandemic, it was 'Innovate to Recover'. Covid-19 halted much of the international postal sector for significant periods. But, as a consequence, new social and economic postal services developed, along with creative ways of delivering mail. In 2022 the theme was 'Post for Planet'.

One of the most popular events is the annual International Letter-Writing Competition, which began in 1971, with the aim of promoting literacy through the art of letter-writing. Youngsters aged between 9 and 15 submit letters written on a given theme. It attracts well over a million global participants each year.

For linguists, the primary focus of attention is the language of addresses. Conventions change over the years, especially in layout, punctuation and abbreviation. I might find envelopes beginning like this, fifty years ago:

Mr. D. Crystal,   or   David Crystal, Esq.,
31, The Avenue,   31, The Avenue,

I wouldn't expect to see any such punctuation today.

R.K. Narayan was born in 1906

Born in Madras (modern Chennai), India, and professionally known by
his initials (for Rasipuram Krishnaswami), Narayan became famous for
his short stories and novels, many set in the fictional town of Malgudi in
the Tamil region, beginning with *Swami and Friends* (1935). He achieved
an international reputation as one of India's leading writers of English-
language fiction. His career was launched with the aid of Graham
Greene, who was greatly impressed by his characters and settings,
commenting that Narayan 'has offered me a second home. Without him I
could never have known what it is like to be Indian.' He died in 2001.

He wrote many essays and newspaper columns – short pieces in
a conversational style – several of which address local cultural and
linguistic issues, but often with a universal message. 'Street Names' is
a good example, published in a collection titled *Next Sunday* (1956), in
which he talks about 'the passion for changing names of streets, towns,
parks and squares' in India after independence, and warns:

> There must not be too much rationale in the naming of a street. This is
> just where members of municipal bodies and perfervid patriots go wrong.
> They attempt historical aptness or the righting of a historical wrong. This
> is generally seen in changing foreign names. Smith Lane, for instance, is
> always in danger of being attacked by righteous-minded persons. Someone
> will suddenly discover that Smith was an odious colonial administrator and
> transform the lane, with every pomp, to Jagadguru Lane.

A Jagadguru (a guru offering universal transformative influence) doesn't
need such an honour, he argues; nor is the change 'likely to make the
ghost of the old despot go pale with shame or remorse'. And he adds:

> On the contrary, the despot's name should be left untouched just to show
> how his despotism has proved futile in the long run.

His point cries out for consideration in a cultural climate where people
are ready to change (or 'cancel') geographical names for nationalistic or
ethnic reasons. Many Narayan essays are like that: they continue to have
a relevance outside of India and stand the test of time.

Alice Meynell was born in 1867

She was born in London, and became known as a poet, editor and essayist, and an important voice in the suffrage movement. Her poetic achievement made her a candidate for Poet Laureate on two occasions. Many of the essays in her several collections focus on language – indeed, it's unusual to read an essay which at some point doesn't make some remark about words. She pulled no punches in her criticism of poets and other writers who, she believed, had debased the language, and she had strong feelings about the loss of the linguistic past, as illustrated by an essay that gives one collection its title, 'The Second Person Singular' (1921), published a year before her death. It's a piece regretting the loss of *thou*, and its associated ending *-est*, which has left us with 'the modern monotony of "you"'.

At the same time, she celebrates aspects of language in a way that only a poet could. In 'The Little Language' (1909), mainly about Italian (she spent much of her youth in Italy), the essay opens memorably: 'Dialect is the elf rather than the genius of place, and a dwarfish master of the magic of local things.' And in the same collection there's one entitled 'Anima pellegrina', which she translates as 'pilgrim soul' – that leads her to generalize: 'Every language in the world has its own phrase, fresh for the stranger's fresh and alien sense of its signal significance; a phrase that is its own essential possession, and yet is dearer to the speaker of other tongues.' And her multilingual background – French too, from time in France and Switzerland – is reflected in an early essay, 'Composure' (1893):

> Speech is a school. Every language is a persuasion, an induced habit, an instrument which receives the note indeed but gives the tone. Every language imposes a quality, teaches a temper, proposes a way, bestows a tradition: this is the tone – the voice – of the instrument. Every language, by counter-change, replies to the writer's touch or breath his own intention, articulate: this is his note.

Machiavelli died in 2019

This was the professional name of British crossword compiler Joyce Cansfield (born in 1929) when she was writing puzzles for *The Listener*. She also compiled them for *The Times*, her final one (her 1,265th) appearing in 2011. Her lexical ingenuity was also illustrated by her prowess in language games: she was the 1980 UK national Scrabble champion (with 1,540 points) and the first series winner of the television show *Countdown*. Her non-ludic career was as a statistician.

Her choice of pseudonym reflects a fashion among crossword compilers to choose the names of people famous for plotting and torture. The most famous three in the UK, who wrote at various times for the *Observer*, were Edward Powys Mathers, Derrick Somerset Macnutt and Jonathan Crowther – respectively, *Torquemada*, *Ximenes* and *Azed* (*Deza* backwards), all members of the Spanish Inquisition. The choice reflects the aim of the compiler: to make life difficult for the solver.

There are now many different kinds of puzzle (SEE 21 DECEMBER), with the clues in cryptic crosswords providing the greatest source of fascination for the ludic linguist. They have a characteristic structure. Each cryptic clue has two parts – in effect, giving the answer twice: a synonym is followed by a piece of wordplay. A keyword (or phrase) tells the solver what to do. Bracketed numerals at the end show the answer structure. The four parts are separated by slashes in this example (solution, if needed, in the APPENDIX):

Men test-drive a / convertible to get / publicity. / (13)

This is a common clue-type: an anagram. Others include:

— bridgewords, where the last part of one word combines with the first part of the next: *October lingers in the city* (6)
— backwords, where a word is reversed: *Badly made cheese* (4)
— partwords, where a word hides within another: *Favourite in the competition* (3)

These examples are from Francois Greeff's *The Hidden Code of Cryptic Crosswords*, which illustrates dozens of structural and semantic types.

English Language Day

This is a day chosen by language enthusiasts rather than by UN politicians (SEE 23 APRIL). It's the creation of The English Project, an enterprise based in Winchester, UK, whose long-term aim is to establish a visitor attraction devoted to the English language in the city. It would be the first permanent exhibition space in the country presenting the history and present-day use of the language in a format that could be repeated globally, should other countries wish to create a similar thing.

Why this date? Because on this day in 1382 Sir Henry Green, the chief justice of the King's Bench, formally opened a new session of Parliament using English, instead of the traditional French. He stated the reasons for the assembly:

> That the King [Richard II) was desirous to know the Grievances of his Subjects; and particularly, that he might, by their Advice, redress any Wrongs that had been done to Holy Church; also, to reform all Enormities, especially about the Manner of exhibiting Petitions in Parliament.

The problem was that petitions had to be made in French, a language that most English people couldn't understand. So a statute was passed ordering that all pleas would thereafter be made in English. In the formal language of the time, the king

> hath ordained and stablished by the assent aforesaid that all pleas which shall be pleaded in his Courts whatsoever, or in his other places, or before any of his other Ministers whatsoever, or in the Courts and places of any other Lords whatsoever within the realm, shall be pleaded, showed, defended, answered, debated, and judged in the English tongue...

It came to be known as the Statute of Pleading. It took some time for it to be universally implemented, but by the turn of the century it had become the oral norm. When Henry IV was crowned in 1399, his speech was given in English – the first time that a monarch had done so. It took place on the feast of St Edward the Confessor – a nice reinforcement, as this was also 13 October.

national lowercase day

Many websites use capital letters to announce this day, illustrating the mental difficulty of breaking away from standard usage. I haven't been able to find who started it, but it's been recognized in the USA since at least 2011. Judging by the website accounts, it's aimed chiefly at people who overcapitalize in digital communication – SHOUTING ALL THE TIME. Messages entirely in capital letters do have an 'in your face' impact that many receivers find unpalatable, as there's usually no semantic reason for them. The day recommends that texters and others 'keep your fingers off the shift key' and send messages only in lower case. E.E. Cummings (SEE 3 SEPTEMBER) is considered a role model – or perhaps it should be archy (SEE 29 DECEMBER).

The day offers an opportunity to explore the history and use of *mixed case* in languages. The term originates in the way a printer's box of type (a *type case*) was used in the days of typesetting by hand. It would usually be placed on a slanting rack, with the capital letters in the upper section. If two boxes were used, the one containing capital letters would be above the other, so that the more commonly occurring letters would be easier to reach.

Mixed-case alphabets – those combining upper-case and lower-case letters – don't appear in the oldest European inscriptions and manuscripts, which used capital letters only. Lower-case writing, and then mixed case, gradually spread across Europe from the eighth century CE. Scribes and printers introduced rules governing usage, but these differed among languages, and altered over time. In the seventeenth century it was normal to capitalize all nouns in English; German still does. Days of the week begin with an upper-case letter in English, but a lower-case letter in French. And there's considerable stylistic and publishing variation – *moon* vs *Moon*, *president* vs *President*. Names in the internet (Internet) era have added to the variation, as with iPhones and PlayStation, captured by such terms as *bicaps* and *intercaps*, and picturesque names such as *CamelCase* (the capitals form the humps). All Very Interesting.

Cicely Berry died in 2018

Born in Hertfordshire in 1926, Berry became the best-known voice and text coach in the British theatre world, universally known as 'Cis'. She was the voice director at the Royal Shakespeare Company from 1969 to 2014, and then an advisory director. She also directed productions herself at the RSC and elsewhere, and was a dialogue coach on several films.

We get a sense of her approach through that phrase 'voice and text'. To call her – and others in her profession – a 'voice coach' is too limiting. As she says in the introduction to *The Actor and the Text* (1987):

> We must always be after the reaching out through words, and not a dulled, inward-looking speaking of dialogue. We have to honour a greater need, and that is to make what we say remarkable to the hearer.

In her opening chapter, we read:

> We have to work at language as well as voice; we have to practise it, in a sense, to get more adept at feeling its weight and movement. Just as, in everyday life, how a person uses language (or does not use language) is part of the essence of that person, so the actor has to be ready for the dialogue to take us into the world of the character.

In a 1996 workshop she summed up her essential insight:

> When we read a piece of text, our first impulse is to make sense of it. The danger is that, having come to a conclusion about the meaning, we often miss out on the surprises within the language.

She's chiefly thinking of the surprises that arise when we engage with articulation, rhythm, intonation, and the other effects that come from the full exploitation of the voice (SEE 16 APRIL). Anyone fortunate enough to work with her – as I did once – would certainly be surprised at the physicality of her techniques, engaging the whole body to develop an unselfconscious encounter with the text, as well as being startled by the personal linguistic earthiness (to put it mildly) which she incorporated into her vocal direction.

National Dictionary Day

This is a day celebrated in the USA, chosen because it was the birthday of Noah Webster, often called 'the father of the American dictionary'. The equivalent day in the UK, I suppose, would be Dr Johnson's birthday (SEE 18 SEPTEMBER), though there could be other contenders, such as Robert Cawdrey (SEE 27 JUNE). But the day has global implications, for wherever one lives in the English-speaking world, one experiences Webster's influence. Many of his spelling reforms (such as dropping the *k* in words like *musick*) have become standard English, and all global varieties have been influenced by American spelling.

Webster was born in 1758 in Connecticut, and died in 1843. He first became known as an educationalist, with textbooks on spelling and grammar, and in his *Dissertations on the English Language* (1789), published just six years after the end of the Revolutionary War, he states the need for an American frame of reference for the subject (SEE 4 JULY). This he supplied in *The American Dictionary of the English Language*, a twenty-five-year project published in 1828, and costing $20 – about $450 today. Its two quarto volumes ran to almost 2,000 pages and contained around 70,000 entries.

He writes in his Preface:

> A great number of words in our language require to be defined in a phraseology accommodated to the condition and institutions of the people in these states, and the people of England must look to an American Dictionary for a correct understanding of such terms.

The institutions were a particular focus of attention, and he lists several examples, such as *land-office*, *regent* of a university, *intendant* of a city, *senate*, *congress*, *court*, *assembly*, *plantation* and *marshal*, which 'are either words not belonging to the language of England, or they are applied to things in this country which do not exist in that'. Most of the words in the *Dictionary* weren't distinctively American, in fact, but there were enough, he felt, to warrant his title. It had great symbolic value, and is the source for his paternal lexicographical appellation.

Arthur Miller was born in 1915

He was born in New York City, and became one of America's leading playwrights, his best known play, *Death of a Salesman* (1949), winning the Pulitzer Prize for Drama. He was also a prolific essayist, often writing about drama, and it's in this connection that he frequently comments on the function of language, and especially about the intimate trading relationship between poetry and prose. He died in 2005.

A View From the Bridge (1955) was originally a verse drama, later revised into prose. He remarks, in a 2002 interview with his biographer Christopher Bigsby, that his verse dramas were important to him, not only in themselves but for what they taught him about writing: 'I made the discovery that in verse you are forced to be brief and to the point. Verse squeezes out fat and you're left with the real meaning of the language.'

The interaction between the genres is evident in the way he would try out some speeches in his notebooks in verse before writing his prose script. An example is Charley's speech at Willy Loman's funeral in *Death of a Salesman*. These lines appear in the notebook:

> He doesn't tell the law, or give you medicines
> So there's no rock bottom to your life.
> All you know [is] that on good days or bad,
> You gotta come in cheerful.
> No calamity must be permitted to break through
> Cause one thing, always you're a man who's gotta be liked.
> You're way out there riding on a smile and a shoeshine
> And when they start not smilin' back,
> It's the big catastrophe.

This is how they appear in the script:

> Willy was a salesman. And for a salesman, there is no rock bottom to the life. He don't put a bolt to a nut, he don't tell you the law or give you medicine. He's a man way out there in the blue, riding on a smile and a shoeshine. And when they start not smiling back – that's an earthquake.

As Bigsby puts it, 'It is spoken in prose but a prose charged with the poetic.'

Developmental Language Disorder Awareness Day

A surprising number of children have serious difficulty in understanding or producing spoken language, though all other aspects of their development seem to be normal. There's no evidence of hearing loss, brain injury, genetic conditions, or any of the other recognized mental or physical conditions known to affect language, such as autism spectrum disorder. And yet normal use and comprehension of speech are absent. Studies have shown that around 7 per cent of the child population have this condition to some degree – which means that in a class of, say, thirty children, two or three are likely to be having difficulties in understanding what the teacher is saying or making spoken contributions. They are often misdiagnosed as being just 'quiet' or 'shy'.

The condition has long been recognized in the world of speech and language therapy/pathology, but under a variety of different (and thus confusing) labels, such as 'specific language impairment', 'language disorder', 'language delay' and 'developmental language problem'. So in 2016 an international group got together to remove the confusion: the condition would henceforth be called Developmental Language Disorder, or DLD.

A new international volunteer-driven organization was formed: Raising Awareness of Developmental Language Disorder (RADLD), and this day is one of the initiatives. It's recognized globally, and by 2020 around forty countries were involved in arranging events to increase awareness of the condition among parents, relatives, carers, teachers, employers – all who interact with children, privately or professionally.

A terminological change may not seem much; but having a term about which there's a specialist consensus is of great value to those who need to estimate how many children need additional support, and to plan teaching services accordingly. It also helps to unify approaches from the various professions involved in helping these children – not only speech and language therapists and teachers, but clinical linguists, psychologists, paediatricians, nurses and others. It's a small but significant step forward.

Edna St Vincent Millay died in 1950

Born in 1892 in Maine, Millay became widely known as a poet, winning the Pulitzer Prize in 1923 for *The Harp-Weaver and Other Poems*, and providing a powerful voice for the growing feminism of her time. Her biographer, Nancy Milford, called her 'the herald of the New Woman'.

She was also a magazine celebrity in the 1920s, writing witty, satirical pieces as Nancy Boyd (the maiden name of her grandmother), especially for *Vanity Fair*, which brought her to the attention of the public. Her two 'voices' are amusingly related when she writes the preface to Boyd's collection of pieces, *Distressing Dialogues* (1924): 'Miss Boyd has asked me to write a preface to these dialogues, with which, having followed them eagerly as they appeared from time to time in the pages of Vanity Fair, I was already familiar.' The book includes 'Our All-American Almanac and Prophetic Messenger', with her target the moralizing temperament of the time, following the Volstead Act introducing alcohol prohibition. It was written as an eighteenth-century almanac, with astrological interpretations, and predicts forthcoming events in which the state takes over everything:

> NEW YEAR'S DAY, 1925. Cabarets closed, New York City; dancing abolished. Many private houses raided. Sale of crêpe paper and coloured balloons prohibited. Two men surprised in Central Park with pockets full of confetti; and given sixty days each. Slogan HAPPY NEW YEAR changed by Act of Congress to VIRTUOUS NEW YEAR. ...
>
> OLD CHRISTMAS DAY. Santa Claus excommunicated by Society for Suppression of Imagination in Children, 1932. Any allusion, either public or private, to this fictitious and misleading character prohibited under heavy penalty.
>
> All volumes of the untruthful adventures of (a) Alice in Wonderland, (b) Jack and the Beanstalk, (c) Little Red Riding-Hood, and (d) Cinderella, together with (e) the questionable episode of the Babes in the Wood; as well as the highly improbable tales of Hans Christian Andersen, and the senseless rhymes of Mary Vergoose: banned by S.S.I.C., removed from Public Libraries, and burned by Public Executioner in Central Park, 1933. ... Croquet, tiddledy-winks, and kindred games of chance abolished, 1934.

International Day of the Air Traffic Controller

The International Federation of Air Traffic Controllers' Associations was formed on this day in 1961, and since then it's been used as an opportunity for professionals to discuss air safety improvements and to raise public awareness about the nature of the job. One website sums it up:

> About 100,000 flights around the world take off and land each day. Their safety is dependent on air traffic controllers. They direct air traffic on the ground at runways and taxiways, monitor and direct the movement of planes through airspace, and issue landing and take-off orders to pilots.

The linguistic issue is obvious: how to do this clearly and succinctly.

The problem is identified in the opening statement of a manual issued by the International Civil Aviation Organization:

> Communications, or the lack thereof, has been shown by many accident investigations to play a significant role in those accidents. Of 28,000 Aviation Safety Reporting System reports, 70% cite problems related to information transfer.

The solution has been called *Aviation English*, widely known as *Airspeak* – English, because of its global reach, having been chosen as the lingua franca of air travel. It's what linguists call a 'restricted language', in which the terminology, syntax, pronunciation and discourse conventions are standardized. It covers all aspects of flight: aircraft identification, pre-flight status, line-up for departure, taxiing, take-off and initial climb, cruising, descent and landing, and approach to parking.

The phonetic alphabet (SEE 1 MARCH), is used for letters and numbers, and sequences are spelled out ('runway two seven' not 'twenty-seven'). Long sentences are reduced, often to single words ('acknowledge' = 'Let me know you have received and understood this message'). There is a standard vocabulary ('negative' = 'no') and fixed phrases ('I say again' for emphasis or clarity). And recommendations are made about speech style: for example, pausing before and after numbers, avoiding hesitation noises, and speaking slowly.

21 OCTOBER

Babbling Day

This is another day that has come out of the United States without any obvious origin or reason. Websites that recognize it talk vaguely about it offering an opportunity for people to speak at length and pointlessly to each other – though not just nonsense, as there's a *separate* day devoted to that (SEE 20 SEPTEMBER). One site tries to give the day a useful purpose by suggesting it's a chance to look critically at those who babble professionally, with politicians most often cited, for some reason. Another thinks that the day would be best celebrated by 'babbling like a baby'.

I suppose a linguist could find a point in today by using it to draw attention to research into that stage of child language acquisition. Babbling is the most familiar of all the types of sound a baby makes in its first year – the 'bababa, dadada' strings that typically emerge at around 6 months. This is called *reduplicative* babbling because of the repeated consonant sounds. And if these happen to be *m* or *d*, parents are delighted, as it sounds as if they're being named as *mama* and *dada*. Sadly, the strings are being used randomly, and have no meaning at this age. They'll be heard in children learning languages where the words for the parents are nothing like that.

After a couple of months, a much wider range of sounds comes to be heard – *variegated* babbling – some of which do show the influence of the language being learned. But most of the sounds only reflect the level of articulatory proficiency the child has reached: *d, b, m, g, w* are among the common sounds, but ones like *r, l, f, s, ʒ*, which require greater tongue positioning, are rare.

Babbling doesn't stop when first words begin, around the end of the first year (SEE ALSO 13 DECEMBER). Some children continue to babble long after they've begun to talk. One of my children could say about twenty words by the time he was 15 months, while still producing unintelligible conversation-like utterances with good English intonation and rhythm – what's sometimes described as 'jargon'. A role model for Babbling Day enthusiasts, perhaps.

Publication of the
OED Historical Thesaurus in 2009

A thesaurus enables people to find a word expressing a particular meaning out of all the possible words that a language has available in that semantic field (SEE 18 JANUARY). We choose a field, such as 'furniture' or 'happiness', and the work brings together the words (and sometimes phrases) that relate to it. An alternative approach, now common online, is to type a word into a search box + *thesaurus*, and up will come a listing of words of similar or related meaning – in the present-day language. For a long time, students of English have wished for a thesaurus that would do the same thing for older states of the language, and this is what the *Historical Thesaurus of the Oxford English Dictionary* (*HTOED*) provides.

It was a huge undertaking. A proposal for such a work was made by a British linguist, Michael Samuels, in 1965, at a meeting of the Philological Society. It would involve the charting of the semantic development of the entire language over a thousand years, using as source material the lexical data already included in the *OED*. It would be the first historical thesaurus for any language, and it took over forty years before the two-volume work appeared, with an online version viewable on the main *OED* website (ht.ac.uk). It was a breakthrough in the historical study of English, opening up new opportunities for historians, linguists, philologists, literary critics and language enthusiasts in general.

For students of literature, a historical thesaurus allows them to answer such questions as 'What words did Shakespeare have available to talk about...?' It brings together all the words for a topic from whatever period we wish to explore. And it's therefore a boon for writers of historical novels or screenplays who want to have their characters speak authentically. It would hardly be appropriate to have seventeenth-century characters use twentieth-century slang, for instance, and one of the commonest criticisms of historical writing comes from the failure of writers to carry out the required chronological checks. A historical thesaurus helps prevent lexical anachronism.

Harold Orton was born in 1898

Born in County Durham, after various university posts he became professor of English language and medieval literature at Leeds in 1946, remaining there until retirement in 1964. His special interest was dialectology, and his legacy was the Survey of English Dialects (1950–61) – an effort to capture as many regional words as possible before they died out. In collaboration with Eugene Dieth and others, the chief outcome was the magisterial *Linguistic Atlas of England* (1978). He died three years before its publication.

The Survey was based on responses to a questionnaire of over a thousand items, the informants (mainly working-class men over 60) coming from 313 parts of the country. Thirteen books of 'basic material' were published. The examples below come from Book 4, the responses from the Southern Counties. The range of variation is remarkable.

> What do you call these? (pointing to the handles of a scythe): *doles, grips, handles, hand-pins, hand-tings, straight-handles, nibs, nippets, noggets, nogs, snogs, tholes, toggers, tugs*
>
> Now tell me your words for the usual cries animals make? [These were the answers for horses in the fields]: *bray, hollo, neigh, nicker, nucker, nutter, snicker, snork, whicker, whinny, whistle, winker*

The task was considerable, not least because of the costs involved in training fieldworkers and sending them out for the hundreds of hours of transcription and recording required. Orton wrote in a 1952 paper:

> it takes something like a year of training to turn a phonetician and dialectologist into a satisfactory fieldworker. [Stanley Ellis was one – SEE 18 FEBRUARY] He must be fully aware of the aim and significance of every single question and fully understand the purpose and function of all the things and processes that he asks his informant to name. In addition to his academic qualities, certain personal qualities are essential: physical strength, energy, endurance, as well as integrity of mind, tact, powers of persuasion and unbounded enthusiasm for the work.

Quite a challenge! But he found them, and the result was a landmark in English dialectology.

Mrs Hale was born in 1788

Sarah Josepha Buell Hale was born in Philadelphia, and became nationally known through her writing and editing. Apart from her nursery-rhyme fame – 'Mary had a little lamb' appears in *Poems for Our Children* (1830) – she's remembered as the most influential arbiter of social behaviour in her day. She edited *Godey's Lady's Book* for forty years, and into her late eighties – she died in 1879.

She compiled what is surely one of the most remarkable books of the nineteenth century: *Mrs. Hale's Receipts for the Million* (1857). Its expansion: 'Containing Four Thousand Five Hundred and Forty Five Receipts, Facts, Directions, etc. in the Useful, Ornamental, and Domestic Arts, and in the Conduct of Life. Being a Complete Family Directory relative to…' and she lists thirty-seven categories: Accomplishments, Amusements, Beauty, Birds, Building, Children, Cookery…' Its coverage – some 245,000 words – was unprecedented.

There's no separate category on language, but many linguistic points are there within its sections, especially in 'Personal Matters'. They deal with such topics as the care of books, reading ('Never keep house without books'), games (anagrams, conundrums, riddles, but not puns – 'Gentlemen never pun'), the use of the voice, and, above all, conversational etiquette: 'Avoid talking about yourself… Like to listen rather than to talk… Look at the person to whom you speak… Never tell long stories…. Avoid swearing (An oath is but the wrath of a perturbed spirit)… Avoid provincialisms (Webster is the standard for pronouncing in the best society in the United States).'

While many of her observations reflect the social standards of her own time, several have permanent relevance:

> 4143. There is such a rush of all other kinds of words in our days, that it seems desirable to give kind words a chance among them.
> 4144. There are vain words, and idle words, and hasty words, and spiteful words, and silly words, and empty words, and profane words, and boisterous words, and warlike words.

Sounds like a description of some social media sites.

Chaucer died in 1400

The foremost poet of the English Middle Ages was born around 1343 in London, and became a civil servant, diplomat and courtier. The only evidence of his death is this date, engraved on his monument erected in Westminster Abbey 156 years later. His most famous work, *The Canterbury Tales*, is known from many manuscripts of the early fifteenth century, and its first printing by Caxton in 1476.

Many features of Chaucer's language and style show his influence on English, but the one I find most interesting occurs in 'The Reeve's Tale', as it's the first time regional dialect features are used for literary effect, and without any suggestion that they are inferior to the courtly speech of London. On the contrary. Northern dialect features are used by two young men who are well educated, students at Cambridge, and they succeed in getting revenge on the miller who has been defrauding their college of corn. It's the 'bad guy' who speaks in a southern way.

In pronunciation, the most noticeable feature is that several words which in the south would have been written with *o* or *oo* appear with *a* or *aa*. The word for 'no', for example, is spelled *na* when the students speak, and *no* when the others do. And there are several distinctively northern grammatical features. The reeve consistently uses a *-th* ending for the third-person singular present tense, whereas the students almost always use the northern *-s* ending (as in *has*, not *hath*). These lines illustrate their dialect.

> Quod John, 'and se howgates the corn gas in.
> Yet saugh I nevere, by my fader kyn,
> How that the hopur wagges til and fra.'

> *Said John, 'and see how the corn goes in.*
> *Yet saw I never, by my father's kin,*
> *How the hopper wags to and fro.'*

The miller would say 'goes' and 'fro' (SEE 8 JUNE). Chaucer's evident respect for the accent stands out at a time when other London writers were beginning to dismiss regional speech as inferior.

King Alfred died in 899

He was born in Berkshire in about 849, and became king in 871. His political and military achievements dominate accounts of his life, but his role in relation to the English language needs also to be recognized. The Viking invasions had destroyed education in England. During the early 890s he wrote a letter in which he identified the problem:

> It has very often come into my mind what learned men there once were throughout England ... and how people abroad looked to this country for learning and instruction; and how we should now have to get it from abroad, if we were to have it. So completely had it declined in England that there were very few people on this side of the Humber who could understand their service-books in English or translate even one written message from Latin into English, and I think there were not many beyond the Humber either. So few they were that I cannot think of even a single one south of the Thames when I came to the throne.

This is his solution:

> translate certain books, which it is most needful for all men to know, into the language that we can all understand, and make it happen – as we very easily can with God's help, if we have peace – that all young people who are now freemen in England, those that have the means, should devote themselves to study while they have nothing else to do, until the time that they know how to read written English well.

The results of his language planning were remarkable. Almost all surviving prose texts during the late ninth century and into the tenth were written in the dialect used by Alfred and his scribes. Today we call it West Saxon; for well over a century it became the most widely used form of English. If the Normans had lost at Hastings, it would probably have remained so. As it is, much of our knowledge of Old English comes from writings which we can trace back to Alfred's initiative.

Ntozake Shange died in 2018

Born in 1948 in New Jersey, Shange became a playwright, novelist and poet, best known for her first play, which won an Obie Award in 1977: *for colored girls who have considered suicide / when the rainbow is enuf.* She described it as a *choreopoem*: a series of poetic monologues accompanied by dance, music and song.

The opening of 'lady in brown' illustrates her creative use of spacing, punctuation, letter case and spelling. She describes falling in love with the Haitian revolutionary leader Toussaint Louverture in the library:

> de library waz right down from de trolly tracks
> cross from de laundry-mat
> thru de big shinin floors & granite pillars
> ol st. louis is famous for
> i found toussaint
> but not til after months uv
> cajun katie/ pippi longstockin
> christopher robin/ eddie heyward & a pooh bear
> in the children's room
> only pioneer girls & magic rabbits
> & big city white boys
> i knew i waznt sposedta
> but i ran inta the ADULT READING ROOM
>   & came across
>   TOUSSAINT
>   my first blk man

In 2010 she was diagnosed with a neurological disorder, forcing her to relearn basic skills and find new ways to write. In a 2017 interview she remarked with characteristic courage and humour:

> I have a new computer that does things without me asking it to do things. I don't have control over it, so the way I used to play with words on a page is very difficult for me now because I don't have control of where the words go. ... It also spell checks me, so I can't write Black English or Spanglish on a computer because it keeps underlining things. It is very disconcerting, but I persist.

Ted Hughes died in 1998

Born in 1930 in Yorkshire, Hughes began to write poetry as a child, later also writing children's stories and plays, translating and editing, notably and controversially the work of his first wife Sylvia Plath. He became the British Poet Laureate in 1983. His linguistic interest is evident in *Orghast* (1971), a play based on the Prometheus legend, and written in an invented dramatic language, 'purged of the haphazard associations of English', in which sound alone is used to express emotions. 'Theatre', he said, 'adapts language to a system of action; it is applied language.'

In a 1995 interview he spoke about the technological transition between old and new methods of writing. He would use a pen, and when he began to write with a typewriter he made 'an interesting discovery':

> I realized instantly that when I composed directly onto the typewriter my sentences became three times as long, much longer. My subordinate clauses flowered and multiplied and ramified away down the length of the page, all much more eloquently than anything I would have written by hand.

Word processors, he thought, extended this process, whereas...

> When you sit with your pen, every year of your life is right there, wired into the communication between your brain and your writing hand. There is a natural characteristic resistance that produces a certain kind of result analogous to your actual handwriting. As you force your expression against that built-in resistance, things become automatically more compressed, more summary and, perhaps, psychologically denser.

But times change...

> For those who start early on a typewriter or, these days, on a computer screen, things must be different. The wiring must be different. In handwriting the brain is mediated by the drawing hand, in typewriting by the fingers hitting the keyboard, in dictation by the idea of a vocal style, in word processing by touching the keyboard and by the screen's feedback. The fact seems to be that each of these methods produces a different syntactic result from the same brain. Maybe the crucial element in handwriting is that the hand is simultaneously drawing.

Walter Raleigh died in 1618

He was born in Devon in about 1552 and became a soldier, statesman, writer and explorer, playing a major role in the first expeditions to Virginia. He himself travelled twice to Guiana, but during his second visit some of his men attacked a Spanish outpost, thereby violating the British peace treaty with Spain. He was held responsible and executed.

His writing included several poems and works of prose, including an account of his Guiana travels, an unfinished *History of the World*, essays, and letters, including *Instructions to his Sonne, and to posterity*, in which he advises his son Carew about life. It includes this advice about how to speak well:

> Speaking much also, is a sign of vanity; for he that is lavish in words, is a niggard in deeds; ... be advised what thou dost discourse of, what thou maintainest; whether touching Religion, State, or Vanity; for if thou err in the first, thou shalt be accounted profane; if in the second, dangerous; if in the third, indiscreet and foolish: He that cannot refrain from much speaking, is like a City without Walls, and less pains in the world a man cannot take, than to hold his tongue; therefore if thou observest this Rule in all Assemblies, thou shalt seldom err; restrain thy choler, hearken much, and speak little; for the tongue is the instrument of the greatest good, and greatest evil that is done in the world.

Another piece of advice would prove prophetic:

> in all that ever I observed in the course of worldly things, I ever found that Mens fortunes are oftner made by their tongues than by their virtues, and more mens fortunes overthrown thereby also, than by their vices. And to conclude, all quarrels, mischief, hatred, and destruction, ariseth from unadvised Speech, and in much speech there are many errors, out of which thy enemies shall ever take the most dangerous advantage.

Danger indeed. It was the plotting of enemies that led in 1603 to an accusation of treason, conviction, imprisonment in the Tower, and his eventual execution.

Washoe died in 2007

She was a female chimpanzee, born in West Africa in 1965, who was the first non-human that learned to communicate using American Sign Language. She was named after Washoe County, Nevada, where the first research team worked (at the University of Nevada in Reno). Allen and Beatrix Gardener adopted the 10-month old chimp in 1966 from scientists who had thought to use her as part of a project into space exploration.

Previous attempts to teach chimps to speak had failed, because of physical differences between the animal and human vocal tracts. The Gardeners thought a more fruitful approach would be to tap into the potential of gesture and finger movements, as chimps had been observed to use a range of gestures in the wild; so they began to teach her American Sign Language. They simulated the environment of a human child as closely as possible, furnishing her living quarters, sharing their mealtimes, taking her on trips, and so on, and used only ASL when in her company.

She learned about 350 signs in all, for food, drink, objects in her everyday life, the names of the people working with her, actions such as 'go' and 'tickle', and basic requests such as 'more' and 'hurry'. An attempt was also made to see if she could combine these into simple sentences, as a human child would – an important step, as it would bear directly on the question of whether language is an innate, uniquely human ability, as many have argued. Some strings did emerge – signing 'water' + 'bird' upon seeing a swan, for example – but whether these showed genuine creative syntactic understanding or were simply a learned response to stimuli continues to be hotly debated.

Washoe moved to another centre when she was 5, and in 1980 to the Chimpanzee and Human Communication Institute at Central Washington University, where she died. Other projects have since worked with chimps, using plastic tokens for words or teaching them to press symbols on a keyboard. But Washoe has pride of place in stimulating fresh interest in the study of animal communication.

Louise DeSalvo died in 2018

Born in 1942 in New Jersey, DeSalvo became known as a writer on Italian-American culture, a scholar who wrote books on Virginia Woolf's life and works, and an editor and essayist on a range of literary topics. These include two on the practice of writing which incorporate features of a memoir into a pedagogical framework.

In *Writing as a Way of Healing: How Telling Our Stories Transforms Our Lives* (1999) she presents her view that writing about personal traumas will speed up the healing process. And in *The Art of Slow Writing* (2014) she addresses all the issues that face writers, from the preparations needed, through techniques that aid the process, to the final tasks of presentation and revision, and coping with the criticisms, rejection letters and self-doubt that all writers feel from time to time. She provides reassurance by illustrating from the 'slow writing' used by well-known authors such as Virginia Woolf, D.H. Lawrence and Stephen King. 'If we understand the writing process, learn how real writers work, and use that information to develop our unique identity as writers, we'll transform our writing lives.'

In her introduction, she draws a contrast with the fast world of today:

> We live in a world that values speed. Messages that used to take days or weeks to reach their recipients arrive in our e-mail in-boxes instantly, By comparison, James Clavell's *Shōgun* (1975) describes how, in the sixteenth century, a person would receive a reply to a letter sent to Europe four years later – if none of the ships carrying either missive sank. The people we communicate with expect our responses immediately. And all this back and forth e-mailing or texting, innocuous as it seems, shifts our attitude to time so we might begin to value only that which happens quickly. It can also rob us of our precious writing time – a writer friend having difficulty completing a book discovered she'd written more than three thousand words in e-mails in one day.

I lost track of the number of times I identified with the situations described in this insightful book.

Autistics Speaking Day

The day was founded by the Autistic Self Advocacy Network in 2010 as a way of raising understanding about the nature of the autistic condition – or, to be more accurate, conditions, for it isn't a single thing, but a spectrum of abilities, as this paragraph on its website illustrates:

> There is no one way to be autistic. Some autistic people can speak, and some autistic people need to communicate in other ways. Some autistic people also have intellectual disabilities, and some autistic people don't. Some autistic people need a lot of help in their day-to-day lives, and some autistic people only need a little help. All of these people are autistic, because there is no right or wrong way to be autistic. All of us experience autism differently, but we all contribute to the world in meaningful ways. We all deserve understanding and acceptance.

Autism is a developmental condition that affects how people experience the world around them. They think differently, process sensory input differently, move differently, socialize differently, and – especially relevant for this book – communicate differently. As the website puts it:

> We might talk using echolalia (repeating things we have heard before), or by scripting out what we want to say. Some autistic people use Augmentative and Alternative Communication (AAC) to communicate. For example, we may communicate by typing on a computer, spelling on a letter board, or pointing to pictures on an iPad. Some people may also communicate with behavior or the way we act. Not every autistic person can talk, but we all have important things to say.

And this is the day when autistic people have a special chance to say them – to advocate, share experiences, tell their stories, and communicate openly about autism using whatever means works best for them. And for everyone else, it's an opportunity to listen to these stories and deepen understanding of a condition that has so often been misunderstood.

Plan Your Epitaph Day

The day was created by American epitaph artist Lance Hardie in 1995. This is the 'Day of the Dead' in many countries, and 'All Souls Day' in Christian tradition. An alternative date, 6 April, was chosen to represent the Chinese Qingming Festival, often described as Tomb-Sweeping Day or Ancestors' Day.

Epitaphs are optional inscriptions on headstones, though also used on other memorials and in obituaries. They're normally chosen by a dead person's surviving relatives, and are commonly standard expressions, often suggested by the funeral company. A short text from the Bible or other sacred text is commonly used. Writers sometimes have a quotation from their work. The aspiration is to find something that would fit the personality or philosophy of life of the deceased, and something that will have some meaning to those who never knew the person, bearing in mind that the inscription could last for centuries.

Hardie felt that the responsibility should be in the hands of the living individual, who's in the best position to know what linguistic legacy they wish to have. As he says: 'It's your life – it's your death – it's your stone. You say something!' And many people have done just that. One of my favourites is Benjamin Franklin:

> The Body of B. Franklin, Printer; like the Cover of an old Book, Its Contents torn out, And stript of its Lettering and Gilding, Lies here, Food for Worms. But the Work shall not be wholly lost; For it will, as he believ'd, appear once more, In a new & more perfect Edition, Corrected and amended By the Author.

Linguistic decisions have to be made. Whose voice will be used – that of the deceased or of someone else? And in the first or third person? Abbreviations are risky, as are contemporary phrases and cultural references, which will lose meaning over time. It's quite a challenge, to summarize a life in a few words, and this day offers the chance to reflect upon it – or, of course, to decide not to have an epitaph at all.

Cliché Day

The origins and purpose of this day are totally unclear. Websites talk contradictorily about using it to either avoid or use clichés. The term came into English from French *clicher* during the 1800s. It was originally used in printing for the process of striking hot metal to make the cast for a piece of type. It then developed the meaning of an expression regarded as unoriginal or trite due to overuse, and by the end of the century it was being used in this way in English.

From the beginning clichés were viewed as a bad thing. It was a damning criticism for writers to be accused of cliché, and a similar condemnation was directed at speakers perceived to be speaking in a clichéd way. The problem, of course, was in the definition: how much use does there have to be for an expression to count as a cliché? And how many such expressions need to accumulate before speech or writing is considered clichéd. Parodies abounded. I created a two-minute sequence myself for a programme in my BBC radio series *English Now* in the 1980s. It began...

> If I may venture an opinion, when all is said and done, it would ill become me to suggest that I should come down like a ton of bricks, as large as life and twice as natural, and make a mountain out of a molehill on this issue. From time immemorial, in point of fact, the object of the exercise, as sure as eggs are eggs, has been, first and foremost, to take the bull by the horns and spell it out loud and clear...

Books such as Walter Redfern's *Clichés and Coinages* (1989) have to some extent rehabilitated the cliché, pointing out that there are occasions when they have an important role to play, such as offering an alternative to an embarrassing silence. It's when we sense that someone, especially a person in authority, is avoiding an issue or hiding a reality that clichés continue to attract justifiable critical attention.

Naomi Long Madgett died in 2020

Born in Virginia in 1923, Madgett became a poet, mentored by Langston Hughes (SEE 1 FEBRUARY), her works focusing on African-American spirituality and civil rights. She was named Detroit Poet Laureate in 2001. Frustrated by the lack of opportunity for black poets to get work published, in 1972 she founded Lotus Press, and it is her publishing achievement there which led to her sobriquet: 'the godmother of African-American poetry'.

She had firm views about the plight of poetry publishing. Asked in a 2017 interview by Morgan McComb why poetry doesn't sell, she replied:

> No one understands it – people expect poetry to be prose. They give up on it because they expect to read it as if it were a newspaper column and understand right away. That's not what poetry is all about. ... you don't need to understand everything about a poem. The average person who says they don't like poetry, they say, 'Well I don't know what they're talking about, why don't they come to the point?' That's not what poetry does ... Sometimes I don't even understand my own poems.

That last remark was accompanied by a laugh. And later in the interview I sense a smile in her admitting to be a workaholic. 'If I don't have work to do I have to invent something', and she wrote under her poem 'Nearing Jordan', 'I don't know what retiring means. If I didn't have work to do I would have to invent it':

> When you know that the shores of Jordan are not miles but steps away,
> And the chariot swings lower in the waning light of day
> You may hear an angel beckon come and rest eternally
> Then a gate will slowly open, but beyond it, you will see
> One large desk piled high with papers and a chair that bears your name
> You'll be happy to discover earth and heaven are the same
> You'll have manuscripts to edit, other writing jobs to do
> And your joy will last forever at your desk beyond the blue.

I know at least one academic who empathizes with that.

Ernest J. Gaines died in 2019

Born in 1933 in Louisiana, Gaines became a novelist and short-story writer, his early life on a plantation the setting for many of his works. J = James. He was a writer-in-residence at the University of Louisiana, Lafayette, from 1981 until retirement in 2004. In many interviews, and especially in his essay 'Mozart and Leadbelly' (1998), he talks about what influenced him as a writer, with this intriguing title later used for a collection of his stories and essays:

> The young writer finds his education both in the library and in the people around him. I've talked about this in 'Mozart and Leadbelly': Mozart is a symbol for form, which you pick up in books of all kinds, in the library; and Leadbelly is a symbol of the source for my work. That is, I learned both from the books I studied at San Francisco State, at Stanford, as well as from the people here, on this plantation, during my days growing up, the first fifteen years of my life.

And in an interview included in the collection he gives a memorable example:

> I remember I used to do a lot of walking in San Francisco in the morning, and there was this old man who used to sweep the streets before we got the motorized street sweepers ... and whenever I'd come back from my walk in the park, I'd see him pushing his broom. And, you know, I'd talk about baseball or football or whatever. But he would never leave a piece of paper or a piece of anything without brushing it up and moving it along to pick it up. And I thought, it's a wonderful thing that this man, this street sweeper, that he's so particular about everything that he does. That little piece of trash – to be sure that it's done. I feel the same way with my writing. The little things – you be sure that they're corrected...

And he concludes: 'writing, for me, is not just learning from novelists or short-story writers, but from all the things around us'. Mozart and Leadbelly again.

Richard Carew died in 1620

He was born in 1555 in Cornwall, and became a writer, translator and antiquarian, best known for the historical account of his county, *A Survey of Cornwall* (1602). However, those interested in the history of English will be more attracted to an essay that appeared soon after, and originally printed as a kind of appendix to the *Survey*. It was titled 'An Epistle concerning the Excellencies of the English Tongue', and seems to have been written in response to writers who considered English to be a poor language, especially when compared with Latin. Carew strongly argues the opposite, illustrating the way he thinks English is better than other languages in expressiveness, easiness, range (what he calls *copiousness*) and sweetness of sound. He draws attention to contemporary authors to make his points – including one of the earliest references to 'Shakespheare'.

His illustration of copiousness is especially interesting for its inclusion of a fine array of everyday idioms. This extract is from the 1614 printing, keeping the original punctuation:

> Moreover, the copiousnesse of our Language appeareth in the diversitie
> of our Dialects; for wee have Court and wee have Countrey English, we
> have Northerne, and Southerne, grosse and ordinarie, which differ each
> from other, not onely in the terminations, but also in many words, termes,
> and phrases, and expresse the same things in divers sorts, yet all right
> English alike, neither can any tongue (as I am perswaded) deliver a matter
> with more varietie then [than] ours, both plainely, and by proverbs and
> Metaphors: for example, when wee would bee rid of one, wee use to say,
> *bee going, trudge, packe, bee faring hence, away, shift,* and by circumlocution;
> *Rather your roome then your company, lets see your backe, come againe when I
> bid you, when you are called, sent for, intreated, willed, desired, invited, spare
> us your place, another in your stead, a ship of Salt for you, save your credite,
> you are next the doore, the doore is open for you, there is no body holdeth you,
> no body teares your sleeve,* &c.

The Royal National Institute for the Blind began talking books in 1935

They're usually called audio books today, but the 'talking book' was the popular description when the genre began. The initiative arose from the challenging situation facing the thousands of soldiers who had lost their sight during the First World War. Only some had been able to learn braille (SEE 4 JANUARY), often because their hands were badly injured. Captain Ian Fraser was one. The RNIB website takes up the story:

> He worked hard to learn braille at St. Dunstan's, a hostel built to help blinded veterans like him. One day, frustrated at how slowly he could read, he cried out, 'If books could only talk!' It was while listening to a gramophone at St. Dunstan's that he was inspired to record an entire 'Talking Book'.

The first studio was set up in London in 1934. The first two titles recorded were Agatha Christie's *The Murder of Roger Ackroyd* and Joseph Conrad's *Typhoon*, and these went out to listeners on this day in 1935. It would take around ten discs to record an entire novel. Special turntables had to be designed that would play at appropriate speeds.

A move from gramophone records to tape recordings came in 1960; and tape in turn was replaced by digital techniques in the 1990s. There's now a DAISY (Digital Accessible Information System) Consortium that defines technical standards for digital audiobooks. The first books on CD went out in 2002, with most fitting onto a single disc. Books on memory sticks became available in 2014, and a digital download service allowed access to a smartphone or tablet.

The tricky linguistic issues in recording an audiobook shouldn't be underestimated. Readers have to find a way of 'translating' such typographic conventions as subheadings, footnotes, indented quotations, cross-references, italics, and the like. But thousands of highly successful recordings have now been made, and the genre is today one of the fastest growing areas in the publishing industry.

Abet and Aid Punsters Day

There has already been one day in this book based on a pun (SEE 4 MAY), but today takes this category of wordplay to a whole new level. Its origin isn't recorded in any source I've been able to find, though some pundits say it's been around for decades. The aim, evidently, is to spend as much of the day as possible devising puns, and reacting to any that others make with an appreciative laugh rather than a punishing groan.

Puns aren't all the same. Taking the word *pun* as an example, some are purely auditory (*sponge*), some purely visual (*puny*), and some are both (*pungent*). Then there are puns on single words that sound the same (*bear* and *bare*) or that look the same (*bear* the animal / *bear* the action), and puns that rely on word sequence (*the door is ajar*). There are subgenres of puns. One of my favourites is the Tom Swifty, alluding to the name of one of the boy heroes whose exploits were melodramatically recounted in many books published in the 1910s: 'We're out of whiskey', Tom said dispiritedly', 'My electrocardiogram's fine', Tom said wholeheartedly.

Puns attract extreme views. In one opinion, associated with John Dryden and others, they are 'the lowest and most grovelling form of wit'. For the opposite view I choose Alfred Hitchcock: 'Puns are the highest form of literature.' Shakespeare I think would agree with Hitchcock, as entire books have been devoted to his wordplay, and pun duels (such as between pairs of lovers) are a notable feature of his plays. But whatever the great names say, a good pun is widely enjoyed, and it's a common experience to encounter what's been called 'ping-pong punning', when people try to outpun each other in a conversation. Without puns, advertisers and newspaper headline writers would be at a loss, the genre of 'joke books for kids' would dry up, stand-up comedians would lose many of their punchlines, and the makers of Christmas crackers would have to rely on homespun sayings.

Oh, alright. One more. 'Wouldn't you prefer a poodle?' asked Tom's father doggedly.

Janet Paisley died in 2018

Born to Scottish parents in 1948 in Ilford, Essex, Paisley grew up in
Scotland, and became a novelist, poet and playwright known for her
writing in English and in Scots, and for her eloquent advocacy in support
of Scots. At the 2013 Solas Festival, held in midsummer in Perthshire,
she made a powerful statement: 'In Defence of the Scots Language'.
A lack of public awareness was one of her themes:

> The Scots language is our national secret. We tell foreigners we speak
> English. They notice that we don't. In homes and classrooms, small
> children routinely translate into and out of Scots, but no one notices.
> In public, twa guid Scots speakers might converse entirely in Scottish
> English without ever discovering they share their native tongue.

Her talk reviewed the significant steps already taken by the Scottish
government and other bodies in education and the arts, concluding:

> Progress is slow. The day when all of our children have, as standard, a
> bilingual education in English *and* in Scots or Gaelic, is not close but it
> grows nearer. Gradually, on radio and television, we begin to hear voices
> that sound like people from Scotland, like us.

Towards the end of her speech, she gave an example:

> What do we lose without our language?

This:	Becomes this:
Think oan	Think on
doon burn, strath, brae an sea	down stream, plain, slope and sea
as watter tummles tae braid firth,	as water rushes to estuary,
we are aw ettled tae stravaig	we are all meant to roam

> It is no longer about Scotland or her people. If our lochs become lakes,
> and our bens turn into mounts, we lose our way, our unique way of
> thinking, and expressing ourselves, where we come from, and who we
> are. Who would we be without janitors and advocates, pinkies or oxters?
> Only we have care and custody of the Scots language. No one else will
> tend it.

Her words are a clarion call to action for all minority languages.

World Science Day for Peace and Development

The day was inaugurated by UNESCO, and first celebrated in 2002. The purpose is to highlight the role science plays in society and its relevance to everyday life, and to foster public debate about scientific issues. The UNESCO website breaks this down into four aims:

— Strengthen public awareness of the role of science for peaceful and sustainable societies;
— Promote national and international solidarity for shared science between countries;
— Renew national and international commitment for the use of science for the benefit of societies;
— Draw attention to the challenges faced by science in raising support for the scientific endeavour.

It might be thought that language isn't a relevant topic on this day, but not when we see linguistics under its alternative names. I once worked in the Department of Linguistic Science at Reading University. And there are several books on the subject where the title is 'speech sciences', in which the anatomy, physiology and neurology of speech provide a focus, as well as the physics of sound, which forms an important element in phonetics – or 'phonetic science', as it's also called.

The scientific element in language study has significantly increased in recent years in such areas as computer-assisted language learning, voice interaction with machines, and technical equipment that facilitates communication in those unable to use their bodies for normal listening, speaking, reading or writing.

The study of language in the service of peace already has a global presence through the growing field of peacelinguistics. It can also be seen in Linguapax, which evolved out of a UNESCO conference in 1987 on 'Teaching foreign languages for peace and understanding'. It was formalized as an Association at the UNESCO Centre of Catalonia in 2001, and dedicated to the promotion, preservation and activation of linguistic diversity. So linguists can legitimately celebrate this day too.

A.P. Herbert died in 1971

Alan Patrick Herbert, who used his two initials as an author, was born in Surrey in 1890. He began as a writer after service in the First World War, publishing his first novel, *The Secret Battle*, in 1919. He wrote in a wide range of genres, including many satirical articles for *Punch* magazine, especially on aspects of English law (having himself trained as a lawyer, though he never practised). He had a parallel political career as an independent Member of Parliament (1935–50).

He was especially known for his humorous writing, and this imbues his main language contributions. He wrote several articles for *Punch* on what he considered to be bad English usage – his 'Word War' – and reworked these for a collection of essays, *What a Word!* (1935). The tone of his approach is signalled on the half-title page:

> Being an Account of the Principles and Progress
> of 'The Word War' conducted in 'Punch', to
> the great Improvement and Delight of
> the People, and the lasting Benefit
> of the King's English, with
> many Ingenious Exercises
> and Horrible
> Examples

It included a chapter on 'Plain English', one of the earliest pieces advocating reform of unnecessarily complex writing. It came to fruition in Britain in the Plain English Campaign, founded in 1979.

Herbert concludes his book with an Appendix in which he sets up an 'Entrance Examination for Words, Phrases, and Usages Seeking Admission to the English Language'. He asks them: 'Are you intelligible? Are you pleasing? Are you legitimate? Are you needed?' Up to ten marks are awarded for each question; twenty are needed for election.

Most candidates fail. Of the twenty-six he reports, only five – *television, ticketeers, to sample, to diary* and *knock out* – pass. All the others fail, usually very badly, such as *recondition, motorcade, to diarize* and *to hospitalize. Unilateralism* is the worst failure, getting no marks at all.

Elizabeth Gaskell died in 1865

Often, in the manner of the time, referred to as Mrs Gaskell, she was born in London in 1810, and became known chiefly for her novels and short stories, many of which were published in Charles Dickens's *Household Words*. Although her writing was neglected for many years after her death, it became lauded in the later twentieth century, and *Cranford* (1853), *North and South* (1855) and *Wives and Daughters* (1865) were all adapted for BBC television. A Gaskell Society was formed in 1975, after events celebrating the 175th anniversary of her birth.

Family circumstances caused her to move to Knutsford, and later Manchester, where the industrial surroundings, workers' poverty and social conflict provided the context for the social realism in her writing, and also for her dialect realism, which makes her an essential figure in any account of the language of nineteenth-century literature. It's there from the very beginning, in her first novel, *Mary Barton* (1848), and she was scrupulous in her quest for accuracy in representing Lancashire speech. She complained to her publisher of errors in the first edition, made corrections and gave glosses to dialect words and phrases, aided by her husband. The 5th edition (1854) added two lectures on Lancashire dialect by William Gaskell – really detailed accounts of its history and use, and full of literary precedents going back to Anglo-Saxon times.

Here's a short selection of examples from *Mary Barton* (the glosses are from the original). We see local vocabulary and idiom: 'she was a farrantly lass' (comely), 'I was very frabbit with him' (peevish), 'don't mither your mammy for bread' (bother), 'you're right welcome'. Dialect grammar is there too, with singular nouns after numerals ('two shilling', 'two year') and old past forms of verbs ('I'm much afeard', 'well nigh five minutes agone', 'they've gotten it fixed again the gin-shop wall'). A dialect form of the comparative construction is seen in 'it seemed more like a wedding nor a funeral' (than). And grammar and vocabulary come together in many sentences, such as 'We han done our best to gi' the childer food' (children).

Dell Hymes died in 2009

Born in 1927 in Portland, Oregon, Hymes became one of the leading
sociolinguists of the twentieth century, known especially for the way
he developed the ethnographic study of language in use. Far more is
involved than the description of sounds, grammar and vocabulary, which
was always the focus of traditional descriptions – and, indeed, of much
contemporary linguistics. He described the complexity of the issues by
identifying sixteen components involved in communication:

1. the form of the message
2. its semantic content
3. its setting (time, place, circumstances)
4. its scene (the wider cultural context)
5. the speaker (the one originating a message)
6. the addressor (the person delivering it)
7. the hearer or audience
8. the addressee (the intended recipient)
9. the purpose (intended by the sender)
10. the purpose (seen by the community)
11. the key (its tone, manner or spirit)
12. the channel (speech, writing, semaphore...)
13. the style (formal, religious, legal...)
14. the social norms to be respected
15. the interpretation of those norms
16. the genre (poem, myth, proverb, curse...)

He was well aware that such a long list would be difficult to remember,
so he grouped them into eight types and coined a mnemonic:

SPEAKING
S   for setting and scene
P   for participants – speaker and audience
E   for ends – purposes and goals
A   for act sequence – the form and order of the event
K   for key (as above)
I   for instrumentalities – the styles used
N   for norms – the social rules governing interaction
G   for genres (as above)

First BBC broadcast in 1922

In May 1922 thirty-nine representatives of wireless manufacturing companies came together at the General Post Office's headquarters in London to discuss the future of broadcasting. They were anxious to avoid what was being described as 'chaos' in the USA, where there was competition between radio stations, wavelength interference, political influence and commercial advertising. The outcome of the meeting was a proposal for a single public-service organization, separate from government, and funded by a licence fee. As one of the speakers at the meeting said: radio stations should be

> run under one management so that they may be properly coordinated, so that there may not be more stations than are necessary, and so that they may be most economically and efficiently worked. I think that the most satisfactory way of doing that would be to create a separate entity in which all who have licences shall be interested, that should run the stations, and that should appoint the management of those stations.

The notion of a British Broadcasting Company emerged (the change to Corporation came in 1927, when it received its charter). Its first operating licence restricted broadcasting to news and information from just four news agencies. Daily broadcasts began in Marconi's London studio, 2LO (the call sign for London), in the Strand. A news bulletin went out at 5.33 p.m. along with a weather report, spoken by the director of programmes, Arthur Burrows, in an authoritative RP accent. On Christmas Eve he played Father Christmas in a play, *The Truth About Father Christmas*, thought to be the first broadcast drama. And for *Children's Hour* he was the first radio uncle: 'Uncle Arthur'.

It took some time for the linguistic variety we now associate with broadcasting to emerge. Sports commentary, for example, didn't arrive on the BBC until 1927 (SEE 22 JANUARY). The first edition of *Radio Times* was published in September 1923, but the listings were so sparse that its pages were filled with articles about the medium, advice for radio enthusiasts, and radio industry advertisements.

Marianne Moore was born in 1887

Born in Missouri, Moore became an influential modernist poet and critic, and editor of *The Dial* literary magazine (1925–29) in its final years. Her *Collected Poems* won the poetry Pulitzer Prize in 1951. T.S. Eliot, introducing a collection of her new and old works in *Selected Poems* (1935), gives her fulsome praise, describing her as 'one of those few who have done the language some service in my lifetime'. She died in 1972.

She seems to have thought of herself as a linguist manqué, judging by this remark in a 1961 interview for the *Paris Review*:

> The accuracy of the vernacular! That's the kind of thing I am interested in, am always taking down little local expressions and accents. I think I should be in some philological operation or enterprise.

However, her fascination with structure is evident, notwithstanding her distrust of the artifice of poetic form. The opening two (of five) stanzas of one of her most famous poems, 'Poetry' (which she later radically revised), illustrate both the suspicion and the structure. There is a strict discipline, with the corresponding lines of each stanza of equal syllabic length, patterned indention and occasional rhyming:

> I too, dislike it: there are things that are important beyond all this fiddle.
> Reading it, however, with a perfect contempt for it, one discovers that
> there is in it after all, a place for the genuine.
> Hands that can grasp, eyes
> that can dilate, hair that can rise
> if it must, these things are important not because a
>
> high sounding interpretation can be put upon them but because they are
> useful; when they become so derivative as to become unintelligible, the
> same thing may be said for all of us – that we
> do not admire what
> we cannot understand. The bat,
> holding on upside down or in quest of something to
>
> eat...

She influenced many later generations of American poets.

Chinua Achebe was born in 1930

He was born in Nigeria, and became one of the best-known African writers of the twentieth century, beginning with his novel *Things Fall Apart* (1958). He died in 2013. He was a prolific essayist and critic. In an interview in 1990, he reflected on the role of Nigeria's indigenous languages and the way they influence English.

> We come with this particular preparation which, as it happens, actually enriches the metropolitan languages. But that's not why we do it; we're not doing it in order to enrich the metropolitan language. We're doing it because this is the only way we can convey the story of ourselves, the way we can celebrate ourselves in our new history and the new experience of colonialism, and all the other things. We have had to fashion a language that can carry the story we are about to tell. ...
>
> It's not the only way we can tell our story, of course. I can tell our story in the Igbo language. It would be different in many ways. It would also not be available to as many people, even within the Nigerian environment. So this is the reality: This English, then, which I am using, has witnessed peculiar events in my land that it has never experienced anywhere else. The English language has never been close to Igbo, Hausa, or Yoruba anywhere else in the world. So it has to be different, because these languages and their environment are not inert. They are active, and they are acting on this language which has invaded their territory. And the result of this complex series of actions and reactions is the language we use. The language I write in. And, therefore, it comes empowered by its experience of the encounter with me.

English vocabulary and idiom are often described as having an increased 'richness' through an encounter with other languages, as its history from Anglo-Saxon times illustrates. Achebe uses the enrichment metaphor, and adds to it a notion of empowerment. It could be used with equal force by any second-language writer anywhere in the world.

National Unfriend Day

The day was created in 2010 by American television host Jimmy
Kimmel, who introduced it on his late-night talk for ABC, in an effort to
remind everyone of the true meaning of friendship. Several websites took
up the idea. One sums it up in this way:

> Ever scrolled through your Facebook and realised you don't recognise
> half the names popping up in your News Feed? Friend list at 1000 people
> and counting? Is your wall cluttered with posts you don't care about from
> people you don't remember?

This is the day, he suggested, when social media users make an honest
inventory of their list of friends:

> Please join us on this day of self-care to celebrate by simplifying our
> connections online and unfriending any and everyone who does not add
> joy to your online, social networking experience.

The modern use began in Usenet newsgroups, with an earliest
recorded usage in 2003. Facebook took it up in 2004. It then became so
widely used that the *Oxford English Dictionary* made it 'word of the year'
in 2009. The definition was 'to remove someone from a list of friends or
contacts on a social networking website'. It competed with *defriend* for a
while, but *unfriend* eventually gained the popular vote.

Unfriend actually has a long linguistic history before it came to be
adopted by social media. Its original use was as a noun. An *unfriend*
was, in effect, an enemy, and its use is recorded from the thirteenth
century, especially in Scotland. The use as a verb, or an adjective derived
from a verb, is much later, around the beginning of the seventeenth
century, with the meaning of 'friendless', 'deprived of a friend' (SEE ALSO
7 OCTOBER). Shakespeare uses it three times. Emilia in *The Two Noble
Kinsmen* worries about how she will 'comfort this unfriended, / This
miserable prince'. In *Twelfth Night* Antonio warns Sebastian about going
about the unfamiliar city 'unguided and unfriended'. And, perhaps most
famously, at the beginning of *King Lear* the king describes his daughter
Cordelia as 'unfriended, new-adopted to our hate'.

Margaret Atwood introduces
LongPen™ technology in 2006

It was the gruelling schedule of travelling for book tours, with all the stress involved, that led Canadian author Margaret Atwood – also known as an environmental activist – to invent a tele-remote device that would allow authors to do book signings without being physically present. Born in 1939 in Ottawa, she became internationally known for her novels, short stories, poems and essays, and is in great demand as a speaker. The idea hit her in spring 2004, she said in an interview, during a tour for her novel *Oryx and Crake*. It was in Denver at four o'clock in the morning 'after I'd flown from Japan, already did two events, one on the west coast and one in Denver, and had to get up very early to take a plane to Salt Lake City, and the same day take a plane to Boston'.

There has to be an easier way, and the LongPen™ was the solution. It consists of two twin units, each with a screen, webcam, speakers and microphone. The sender has a tablet that records pen strokes, and these are sent to a pen attached to a robotic arm at the receiving end, which reproduces the movements and inscribes a message and signature. There can be an audio and video conversation between the author and the fan.

The technology has limitations, such as the amount of writing it can cope with, and the dimensions a message can cover, and the legal status of signatures has yet to be tested, but it has been praised for being an ecologically efficient way of allowing authors to make promotional appearances without the expense and environmental damage of air travel. Carbon-free book tours. It also allows smaller bookshops or remote festivals to host events with an author that would otherwise not be cost-effective. Atwood also described it as a 'democratizing tool', allowing authors to interact with readers in places that would never normally see them. 'Suppose your book club exists in a community that has no bookstore: you could rent one of these from a nearby outlet – think rent-a-car.'

Ruth Stone died in 2011

Born in 1915 in Virginia, Stone began writing poetry as a child, and
would often tell this story when asked about her poetic inspiration:

> It's a funny thing. Even as a child, I would hear a poem coming toward
> me from way off in the universe. I wouldn't hear it. I would feel it, and
> it would come right toward me. If I didn't catch it, if I didn't run in the
> house and write it down, it would go right through me and back into the
> universe. So I'd never see it again. I'd never hear it again. I've lost about
> ninety-nine percent of my poems this way. Sometimes I would catch the
> last line and write it through the bottom up. I have to say, I never thought
> they were mine. They weren't mine. They belonged somewhere else.

She received some recognition for her early poems in the 1950s, and
during many years while teaching creative writing in several universities.
Her appointments were always short-term, and she didn't get a tenured
position until 77 – well past retirement age for most academics!
Widespread recognition came in her late eighties: her collection *Ordinary
Words* won the National Book Critics Circle Award in 1999; she was
named Poet Laureate of Vermont in 2007.

Words are the focus of her poem 'The Wound'. Here's its opening
sequence of two-line stanzas:

> The shock comes slowly / as an afterthought.
> First you hear the words / and they are like all other words,
> ordinary, breathing out of lips, / moving toward you in a straight line.
> Later they shatter / and rearrange themselves. They spell
> something else hidden in the muscles / of the face, something the throat
>   wanted to say.
> Decoded, the message etches itself in acid / so every syllable becomes a
>   sore. ...

And I love the image in Part 5 of 'The Poetry Factory', which
manufactures poems for all occasions:

> Barrels of thin words line the walls.
> Fat words like links of sausages
> hang on belts.

Nadine Gordimer was born in 1923

Born in Transvaal (now Gauteng), South Africa, Gordimer became a writer and political activist during and after the apartheid era in the country. She began to write as a teenager, wrote over two hundred short stories, and published her first novel, *The Lying Days*, in 1953. Several of her works were banned by the apartheid government. *The Conservationist* won the Booker Prize in 1974, and she received the Nobel Prize for Literature in 1991. She died in 2014.

Among her many awards, she was made an honorary fellow of the Modern Languages Association in 1984, and in a 2005 interview she affirmed her interest in languages. Her comments arose in a response to a question about how her style had developed. She was in no doubt that it came 'from reading since I was six years old, truly', and she went on:

> I suppose the love of words comes into it but then where do the words come from if you haven't had a long academic education, which I certainly didn't have. I don't know. Would I have been a different kind of writer, I sometimes ask myself, and, on the other hand, I often see in academics' fiction the stiffness and the set of academic language coming in. So maybe I was lucky. The only thing I really regret is that I would like to have studied languages, more languages. ... obviously English is my own but just to have studied foreign languages and not to have learnt an African language. So like most other South Africans, there I am sitting with my black friends and we're all talking in English and then I may go out of the room perhaps to get a bucket of ice or something and come back, we're having drinks together, and they have broken into their own language. They're talking Setswana, they're talking Zulu, whatever, and I am then a stranger in my own country and among my own people. So that's a great regret in my life.

World Hello Day

The day was created by two American graduates, brothers Brian and Michael McCormack, as a direct response to the conflict between Israel and Egypt, the Yom Kippur War, which took place during October 1973. Their proposal was a simple one. As they say on their website:

> Anyone can participate in World Hello Day simply by greeting ten people. This demonstrates the importance of personal communication for preserving peace.

'Hello' in any language, of course. But its history in English is interesting.

A word beginning with *h-* has been heard in Britain, as a way of attracting attention, since Anglo-Saxon times. *Hey* and *ho* are recorded in the thirteenth century, and *hi* in the fifteenth. Hunting shouts are known from that time, such as *hollo, hillo, holla, halloo*. When greeting each other, the Anglo-Saxons would say *hal* (pronounced 'hahl') in such expressions as 'be healthy'. It developed into *hail* in the Middle Ages.

The modern word makes its appearance in the early 1800s, used very informally. When it was written down, it appears with every vowel: *hallo, hello, hillo, hollo, hullo*. Today, *hello* is the usual spelling, about four times more common than *hallo*. It became more formal when the telephone was invented (SEE 7 MARCH), and people needed a standard way of starting a conversation or letting the other person know they were there. It continues to develop new uses, alongside the traditional one. At least since the 1980s it has acquired a negative tone, especially a disbelieving or sarcastic attention-getting use, implying that someone has failed to understand, said something foolish or missed the point in some way: 'I mean, hello! are you serious?'

I suppose this day could be celebrated just as well by using other greeting words. Its use as an informal greeting has come to be seriously challenged by *hi*, which became very common in the USA in the nineteenth century, and is now frequent in e-mails and other social media, two letters being a lot quicker to type than five. World Hi Day doesn't sound quite so impressive, though.

George Eliot was born in 1819

Born in Warwickshire as Mary Ann Evans, she became a poet, editor and translator, best known for her novels written under the pen name George Eliot. Her portrayals of the local speech of English rural society have been acclaimed for their realism, and she adds comments about how people talk – using vivid similes and even technical terms. Bartle Massey in *Adam Bede* is contemptuous about Mr Casson's way of talking: 'You're about as near the right language as a pig's squeaking is like a tune played on a key-bugle.' And Fred picks on one of Mary's words in *Middlemarch*: 'Not of the least use in the world for him to say he *could* be better. Might, could, would – they are contemptible auxiliaries.'

She also has a lyrical vein. In chapter 50 of *Adam Bede* she reflects on the scene between Adam and Dinah, addressing the reader:

> you will no more think the slight words, the timid looks, the tremulous touches, by which two human souls approach each other gradually, like two little quivering rain-streams, before they mingle into one – you will no more think these things trivial than you will think the first-detected signs of coming spring trivial, though they be but a faint indescribable something in the air and in the song of the birds, and the tiniest perceptible budding on the hedge-row branches. Those slight words and looks and touches are part of the soul's language; and the finest language, I believe, is chiefly made up of unimposing words, such as 'light', 'sound', 'stars', 'music' – words really not worth looking at, or hearing, in themselves, any more than 'chips' or 'sawdust'. It is only that they happen to be the signs of something unspeakably great and beautiful. I am of opinion that love is a great and beautiful thing too, and if you agree with me, the smallest signs of it will not be chips and sawdust to you: they will rather be like those little words, 'light' and 'music', stirring the long-winding fibres of your memory and enriching your present with your most precious past.

John Wallis was born in 1616

Born in Kent, Wallis became a clergyman and scholar, developing an interest in a wide range of subjects, notably mathematics, but including cryptography, logic, theology, music – and language. He was one of those who helped to found the Royal Society in 1660. He died in 1703.

He's remembered in language study as the first to call for a new, non-Latin approach to English grammar. His *Grammatica Linguae Anglicanae* (1653, 'Grammar of the English language') was written in Latin – the most widely used academic medium of his time – but he makes it very clear that his intention is to break away from the old grammatical tradition. He writes that his procedure is 'a completely new method, which has its basis not, as is customary, in the structure of the Latin language but in the characteristic structure of our own'. He keeps Latin terminology in his description, he says, chiefly because the terms are so well known, but his approach is unequivocal:

> Do not expect that everything in our language will be exactly equivalent to something in Latin. English, in common with nearly all modern languages, differs enormously in syntax from Greek and Latin (the main reason being that in English we do not distinguish different cases).

He was thinking of grammarians who would treat a noun in this way:

Cases	English	Latin
nominative	friend	amicus
vocative	O friend	amice
accusative	friend	amicum
genitive	of a friend	amici
dative	to or for a friend	amico
ablative	by, with or from a friend	amico

As the examples show, English expresses these notions through prepositions, not case endings.

Wallis's observations could have been written by any modern linguist. But for 300 years his insight was ignored, and I remember a grammar of the old kind still being used in my school in the 1950s.

Oulipo was founded in 1960

The name is an acronym in French, standing for *Ouvroir de littérature potentielle* – 'Workshop of Potential Literature' – a group of mainly French writers who created experimental works using techniques of constrained writing. The notion of writing to an imposed discipline is nothing new in poetry, as illustrated by acrostics, sonnets, haikus, limericks (SEE 12 MAY) and other poetic forms; but Oulipo extended the concept to all genres, motivating writers to explore the virtually limitless possibilities.

The constraints can be external, as when a work is created using only words extracted from a previously existing text (as with 'found poems') or limited by a technological length constraint (such as a Twitter character restriction – Twiction, or Twitterature). The length constraint can be internal, as when a text is restricted to monosyllables, or word length is made to vary according to strict patterns. Several texts use avoidance – writing a work that omits a particular letter (lipograms), punctuation mark or part of speech. The opposite is to insist on something always being present: each word in a text *must* contain a particular letter (reverse lipograms) or the same vowel (univocalics), or begin with the same letter (alliteratives). Linguistically sophisticated approaches are also found, such as creating a text that uses only words with a particular etymology, such as Anglo-Saxon, Romance or Latin.

There have been some famous creations, such as the 50,000-word novel *Gadsby* by Ernest Wright (1959), which uses no letter *e*, or the French equivalent by Georges Perec (one of the first members of Oulipo), *La Disparition*. Constrained writing is sometimes thought to be inevitably artificial. Not so, as these lines from *Gadsby* illustrate:

> Occasionally a sight bobs up without warning in a city, which starts a train of thought, sad or gay, according to how you look at it. And so, Lucy, Priscilla, and Virginia Adams, walking along Broadway, saw a crowd around a lamp post, upon which was a patrol-box; and, though our girls don't customarily follow up such sights, Lucy saw a man's form sprawling flat up against that post, as limp as a rag...

Anthony Burgess died in 1993

Born in Manchester in 1917, Burgess became a composer and writer, best known for his novel *A Clockwork Orange* (1952, later filmed by Stanley Kubrick), but the author also of librettos, screenplays, translations, literary criticism and essays. He was also a linguist in every sense of the word, learning several languages as he travelled the world (including Russian, Malay and Persian), teaching phonetics at a college of speech and drama, and writing two introductions: *Language Made Plain* (1964) and *A Mouthful of Air* (1992). He invented a prehistoric language for the film *Quest for Fire* (1981) and an Anglo-Russian youth slang for characters in *A Clockwork Orange. Joysprick* (1973) was an innovative stylistic study of the language of James Joyce (SEE 16 JUNE). Theatre interests led to writing on Shakespeare, and he was one of the first to explore the possibilities of reconstructing original pronunciation. His books, scripts, scores and artefacts are housed at the International Anthony Burgess Foundation in Manchester, UK.

He is typically inventive in the Introduction to *A Mouthful of Air*, where he searches for a word to describe the subject to his intended readership. Noting the existence of *illiteracy* and *innumeracy*, he first thinks of a way to capture the notion of an 'inability to read music', ponders *inmusicality* and thinks *musical illiteracy* might do. Then he turns to his book: 'I need, rather more desperately … a means of designating those to whom language as sound has little meaning.' He ponders *aphonic, aphonetic* and *phonetic illiteracy*, but finds them all too narrow. *Linguistic illiteracy* would probably have suited him better, though the only alternative he mentions is *linguistic ignorance*, by which he means 'lack of scientific, or quasi-scientific, knowledge of how language behaves'.

At the end of his Introduction he describes his book, self-deprecatingly, as 'a gentle rap on the door of linguistic knowledge. The door opens on a mansion with too many storeys, too many rooms. But we can learn enough for our purposes on the ground floor.' He makes a good tourist guide.

Birth of Ferdinand de Saussure in 1857

Born in Geneva, Saussure became the chief personality in the founding of twentieth-century linguistics, to the extent that he's seen as a turning point, with linguists often talking about language study before him as 'pre-Saussurean'. He published very little during his lifetime, and most of his ideas have come down to us thanks to his students collating their copious lecture notes after his death in 1913. The famous *Cours de linguistique générale* (Course in General Linguistics) appeared in 1916. It's there that we see such fundamental distinctions explained as the contrast between *diachronic* (historical) and *synchronic* (non-historical) dimensions of language study, the opposition between the abstract language system (*langue*) and the concrete act of speaking (*parole*), and the notion of language as a network of structures and systems – all very familiar to linguists today, but a powerful stimulus to the way scholars continued to study language in the first half of the century.

He was very much aware of the way times were changing, as philology morphed into linguistics, and was determined to make the new approach appealing. At the very beginning of his book he asks and answers a question that echoes down the years:

> What use is linguistics? Very few people have clear ideas on this point... But it is evident, for instance, that linguistic questions interest all who work with texts – historians, philologists, etc. Still more obvious is the importance of linguistics to general culture: in the lives of individuals and societies, speech is more important than anything else. That linguistics should continue to be the prerogative of a few specialists would be unthinkable – everyone is concerned with it in one way or another. But – and this is a paradoxical consequence of the interest that is fixed on linguistics – there is no other field in which so many absurd notions, prejudices, mirages, and fictions have sprung up. From the psychological viewpoint these errors are of interest, but the task of the linguist is, above all else, to condemn them and to dispel them as best he can.

Bebe Moore Campbell died in 2006

Born in Philadelphia in 1950, Campbell became a writer, journalist, essayist, broadcaster and teacher, known especially for her first novels, *Your Blues Ain't Like Mine* (1992) and *Brothers and Sisters* (1994), dealing with the harmful effects of racial violence. She was also a powerful advocate for mental needs within disadvantaged communities. In a 1996 interview, she was asked about the bidialectal use of language, such as used by Esther in *Brothers and Sisters*. She affirmed the importance for schools to teach standard English, to help people get on in the world, in its present state, but without projecting a negative attitude towards the use of Black Vernacular English.

> You may speak that at home. But you don't say 'He be coming in here' in my class. That's the way it works. ... The language is a metaphor for a certain kind of life. I mean white people can't come out of Yokumville and expect to get anywhere either. You've got to drop that, sometimes even an accent. I bet you if I turn on the news right now the people coming from Dahlus Texas delivering the news 'dohn't sohnd lahk thaht,' they sound like they just drove out of New Hampshire. There's that northeastern accent, and that's it. The first thing they said about Carter and Clinton [US presidents] was that they were hillbillies. So that's important. But Black English is a way to be connected with the black community. There's the power of Black English. ... But it's very important if you're going to navigate corporate America that you understand the invitation to be there is not an invitation to bring your cultural self in. That's for everybody across the board.

The interviewer asks if she can be intimate with someone who can't speak Black English.

> No. I can't. And the way I know is that with the very few white people whom I have really good feelings for I don't turn the censor on. When I let my hair down that much, then I trust you and I accept you. I know you know I know what's grammatical.

Nancy Mitford was born in 1904

Born in London, Nancy Mitford became a writer and journalist, known especially for her novels, such as *Love in a Cold Climate* (1948), and historical biographies. She died in 1973. For this book she's remembered for the way she popularized a stylistic distinction: the contrast between U (upper-class) English usage and its opposite, non-U.

The terms had been introduced in 1954 by linguistics professor Alan Ross in a study of the speech patterns of English social classes. An article was published in a Finnish academic journal, and was thus virtually unknown outside of a small circle of scholars. To illustrate his points, he used Mitford's novel *The Pursuit of Love* (1945). She then included his terms and some examples in an article on the English aristocracy that she was writing for *Encounter* magazine. She intended it to be no more than a humorous aside, but it was treated as deadly serious by her readers, many of whom began to worry about whether their usage was U or not – should they say *vegetables* (U) or *greens* (non-U), *bike* (U) or *cycle* (non-U), *pudding* (U) or *sweet* (non-U). The terms caught on, and were further popularized when her article and that of Ross were included in a book she edited in 1956 titled *Noblesse Oblige*, illustrated by cartoonist Osbert Lancaster (SEE ALSO 19 MAY).

It was surprising that people failed to appreciate the joke, which should have been evident from her over-the-top style; but it shows how sensitive people can be about linguistic 'correctness'. She takes Ross to task at one point:

> He speaks of the U-habit of silence, and perhaps does not make as much of it as he might. Silence is the only possible U-response to many embarrassing modern situations: the ejaculation of 'cheers' before drinking, for example, or 'it was nice seeing you', after saying goodbye. In silence, too, one must endure the use of the Christian name by comparative strangers and the horror of being introduced by Christian and surname without any prefix. This unspeakable usage sometimes occurs in letters – Dear XX – which, in silence, are quickly torn up, by me.

Charles Carpenter Fries was born in 1887

He was born in Pennsylvania, and became one of the leading American linguists of the first half of the twentieth century, directing the English Language Institute at the University of Michigan from its foundation in 1941 until 1956. He also had a historical interest, initiating the *Early Modern English Dictionary* and continuing as editor-in-chief for thirty years. He died in 1967.

He wrote widely on the application of linguistics to language teaching and learning in both mother-tongue and second-language contexts, but his most influential work in English language studies was *The Structure of English* (1952), which opened up a new dimension for the study of language. Buried in a footnote in his opening chapter is a statement that summarizes the biggest linguistic confrontation that would colour the remaining decades of the century:

> With the recent development of mechanical devices for the easy recording of the speech of persons in all types of situations there seems to be little excuse for the use of linguistic material not taken from actual communicative practice when one attempts to deal with a living language. Even though the investigator is himself a native speaker of the language and a sophisticated and trained observer he cannot depend completely on himself as an informant and use introspection as his sole source of material. He has a much more satisfactory base from which to proceed with linguistic analysis if he has a large body of mechanically recorded language which he can hear repeated over and over, and which he can approach with more objectivity than he can that which he furnishes from himself as informant.

Four years later, Noam Chomsky (SEE 7 DECEMBER) would reject this completely, and assert that a native speaker has an intuitive 'competence' that is far more powerful than any corpus of data could ever provide. Six years later, Randolph Quirk (SEE 12 JULY) would begin his Survey of English Usage, which hugely increased the database of recordings, and ushered in an era of corpus linguistics. The merits of both approaches continue to be debated.

Oscar Wilde died in 1900

Born in Dublin in 1854, Wilde became a poet, novelist and playwright, known especially for his series of social comedies written in the 1890s, such as *The Importance of Being Earnest*, and for his reputation in fashionable London society as a conversationalist and wit. Many of his aphorisms and epigrams were published in a collection in 1911 under the pen name of Sebastian Melmoth. Here's a baker's dozen that have language as their theme.

1. Conversation should touch on everything, but should concentrate itself on nothing.
2. Learnèd conversation is either the affection of the ignorant or the profession of the mentally unemployed.
3. Questions are never indiscreet. Answers sometimes are.
4. In England people actually try to be brilliant at breakfast. That is so dreadful of them! Only dull people are brilliant at breakfast.
5. Good intentions are invariably ungrammatical.
6. It is very vulgar to talk about one's business. Only people like stock-brokers do that, and then merely at dinner-parties.
7. Nowadays to be intelligible is to be found out.
8. Thought and language are to the artist instruments of an art.
9. There is only one thing in the world worse than being talked about, and that is not being talked about.
10. Words! Mere words! How terrible they were! How clear, and vivid, and cruel! One could not escape from them. And yet what a subtle magic there was in them! They seemed to be able to give a plastic form to formless things, and to have a music of their own as sweet as that of viol or of lute. Mere words! Was there anything so real as words?
11. I never talk during music — at least during good music. If one hears bad music it is one's duty to drown it in conversation.
12. If one doesn't talk about a thing it has never happened. It is simply expression … that gives reality to things.
13. It is perfectly monstrous … the way people go about nowadays saying things against one behind one's back that are absolutely and entirely true.

James Baldwin died in 1987

Born in New York City in 1924, Baldwin became a writer in several genres, beginning with the acclaimed novel *Go Tell It on The Mountain* (1953). He emigrated to France in 1948, returning to the USA in 1957 and becoming a leading literary voice during the civil rights movement. He returned to France in 1970. Many essays focus on African-American identity and racial issues, especially in his powerful 1979 essay 'If Black English Isn't a Language, Then Tell Me, What Is?' This beautifully crafted sentence expands his title:

> Now, if this passion, this skill, this (to quote Toni Morrison) 'sheer intelligence,' this incredible music, the mighty achievement of having brought a people utterly unknown to, or despised by 'history' – to have brought this people to their present, troubled, troubling, and unassailable and unanswerable place – if this absolutely unprecedented journey does not indicate that black English is a language, I am curious to know what definition of language is to be trusted.

In another paragraph he recollects its origins, thereby providing the social context that underpins any answer to his question:

> Black English is the creation of the black diaspora. Blacks came to the United States chained to each other, but from different tribes: Neither could speak the other's language. If two black people, at that bitter hour of the world's history, had been able to speak to each other, the institution of chattel slavery could never have lasted as long as it did. Subsequently, the slave was given, under the eye, and the gun, of his master, Congo Square, and the Bible – or in other words, and under these conditions, the slave began the formation of the black church, and it is within this unprecedented tabernacle that black English began to be formed. This was not, merely, as in the European example, the adoption of a foreign tongue, but an alchemy that transformed ancient elements into a new language: *A language comes into existence by means of brutal necessity, and the rules of the language are dictated by what the language must convey.*

The italics are his.

Date of the opening scene
of *Casablanca* in 1941

Casablanca is set at the beginning of the Second World War. About nine minutes into the opening scene we see Rick (Humphry Bogart), the owner of the Café Américain, sign a cheque for 1,000 francs, and the date is clearly 2 December 1941. He's taken aback when his love from the year before, Ilsa Lund (Ingrid Bergman), suddenly arrives: 'Of all the gin joints in all the towns in all the world, she walks into mine!' She approaches the café pianist, Sam, and asks him to play a tune. She assumes he knows which one she has in mind, so she says simply, 'Play it once, Sam.' He affects not to know what she means, so she repeats: 'Play it, Sam.' And then, 'Play "As Time Goes By".'

The point is: she doesn't say 'Play it again, Sam', which is how the remark has been transmitted down through the ages, even becoming a film title (by Woody Allen). It's a misquotation. And it's one of many. Sherlock Holmes never said 'Elementary, my dear Watson.' The nearest is when he says just 'Elementary', in 'The Adventure of the Crooked Man'. And the Internet is today a huge source of misquotation: looking up any one instance is likely to generate several versions, each slightly different from the other.

Elizabeth Knowles gives many examples of apocryphal quotations in her book *And I Quote: A History of Using Other People's Words* (2018). She also neatly summarizes the reason for using quotations:

> Quotations are part of the fabric of the language. We are often highly conscious of them: coverage of significant events and people is frequently marked by a clustering of related quotations, often from diverse sources. The most 'successful' quotations, which have a demonstrable longevity and are still with us today, are those that were originally unique to a particular time, place, or person (real or fictional), but that have a quality of universality that means that they can offer the perfect expression in response to another place, person, or circumstance.

3 DECEMBER

First text message sent in 1992

British programmer Neil Papworth had been working as a developer to create a Short Message Service for Vodafone using a mobile phone. His first test message was successfully sent to Richard Jarvis at Vodafone's headquarters in Newbury, Berkshire: it said simply 'Merry Christmas'. He had to send it on a personal computer, as mobile phones didn't have keyboards at that time. Jarvis read it on an Orbitel 901 – a large phone weighting over 4 pounds. He couldn't send a reply, as that option wasn't available either. By the end of the decade, mobiles had a QWERTY keyboard and a two-way text-messaging service, and the popularity of texting soared.

The limit of 160 characters seems to have resulted from a combination of technical constraints and a pragmatic judgement by the creators about the size of a 'typical' short message. The linguistic constraints were immediately appreciated, with users incorporating abbreviations into their messages, to the extent that the style was considered by some to be a new language, 'textese', and attracted criticism from pundits who felt that linguistic standards were deteriorating. In fact, the abbreviations were never a dominant feature of texts, usually amounting to only around 10 per cent of a typical message. 160 characters also allowed quite complex sentences to be sent. More important was the development of texting strategy, especially in marketing, to avoid wasteful use of character space. Adding a full link, for example, would use up many characters, whereas short links (such as Bit.ly) conserve them.

Texting style has evolved over time, partly reflecting linguistic developments, such as the emergence of emoticons and emojis, and partly a consequence of altered perceptions about the status of textisms among young people, where the proportion of abbreviations used has shown a steep decline since the early 2000s. As one 17-year-old said to me, during a school visit: 'I stopped using these abbreviations when I discovered my dad had started using them!' Evidently, they were then no longer cool.

Death of Daniel Jones in 1967

He was born in London in 1881, and after a period studying abroad he entered academic life, becoming head of the phonetics department at University College London in 1912, and setting up the country's first laboratory in experimental phonetics the following year. In 1921 he was appointed professor, the first in phonetics at a British university (SEE 3 JULY). He was undoubtedly the leading phonetician of the century, writing a series of influential textbooks, notably *An Outline of English Phonetics* (1919), and compiling the *English Pronouncing Dictionary* (1917), which he edited through a dozen editions in his lifetime.

DJ (as everyone called him) was continually being asked for advice about phonetic issues. He was a member of the Advisory Committee on Spoken English in the early years of the BBC, and George Bernard Shaw consulted him and his laboratory as he was writing *Pygmalion* – a relationship which motivated Beverley Collins and Inger Mees to call their biography of Jones *The Real Professor Higgins* (1999). Jones himself was unhappy with the way phonetics was presented in the play, as a means of social improvement through elocution, though he had a more relaxed view in later life, when the subject had become established and better known.

I was taught phonetics by phoneticians who were DJ's colleagues, and it's his emphasis on ear training and performance that characterizes his approach. In the opening chapter of the *Outline*, he writes: 'How to surmount the difficulties of pronunciation'. The first is:

a matter of 'ear-training' or more accurately 'cultivation of the auditory memory'. No one can hope to be a successful linguist unless he has a *good ear*. If his ear is unsensitive by nature, it may be made more sensitive by training; and if his ear is good by nature, it can be made still better by training.

The second is 'a matter of the *gymnastics of the vocal organs*', so that learners can produce the sounds they've heard. Both, he adds, require 'systematic practice' – in my case an hour a week over most of two academic years.

Nelson Mandela died in 2013

Born in the Eastern Cape region of South Africa in 1918, Mandela became world famous as the first black head of state in post-apartheid South Africa (1994–99), after a long period of imprisonment during the apartheid years (1967–90). He received the Nobel Peace Prize in 1993.

His Xhosa first name was Rolihlahla, and he explains the name by which he's now globally known in his autobiography, *Long Walk to Freedom*:

> On the first day of school my teacher Miss Mdingane, gave each of us an English name and said that thenceforth that was the name we would answer to in school. This was the custom among Africans in those days and was undoubtedly due to the British bias of our education. … Africans of my generation – and even today – generally have both a Western and an African name. Whites were either unable or unwilling to pronounce an African name, and considered it uncivilised to have one. That day, Miss Mdingane told me that my new name was Nelson. Why she bestowed this particular name upon me I have no idea. Perhaps it had something to do with the great British sea captain Lord Nelson, but that would be only a guess.

Locally he was known by his clan name, as he further explains:

> I am a member of the Madiba clan, named after a Thembu chief who ruled in the Transkei in the eighteenth century. I am often addressed as Madiba, my clan name, as a sign of respect.

In such a multilingual country as South Africa, it's perhaps not surprising that he makes memorable observations about language, as in this often-quoted remark, made during the closing address at the 13th International AIDS Conference in July 2000:

> It is never my custom to use words lightly. If twenty-seven years in prison have done anything to us, it was to use the silence of solitude to make us understand how precious words are and how real speech is in its impact upon the way people live or die.

Max Müller was born in 1823

He was born in Dessau, Germany, and became a philologist, specializing in the languages and religions of classical India, and making many translations of ancient texts. In 1846 he visited England for the first time, and became a member of the academic world in Oxford, where much to his surprise – as he claims in *My Autobiography: A Fragment* – he became professor of modern European languages in 1854; and in 1868 Oxford's first chair of comparative philology was created for him. He became a British citizen in 1855. He died in 1890, and the autobiography was published in 1891. It was called a fragment because it was only partly completed when he died, and his son edited and arranged its publication.

The autobiography is an informative and entertaining read, not only for its detailed picture of academic and intellectual life in nineteenth-century Oxford, but for its self-deprecating tone, and a style in which matters of high intellect are punctuated by humorous stories. His first encounters with the English language provide the focus of several anecdotes, such as how to choose the right form of address in a letter, and the dangers surrounding English accents. After arriving in London he goes in search of lodgings:

> The room which I took was almost entirely filled by an immense four-post bed. I had never seen such a structure before, and during the first night that I slept in it, I was in constant fear that the top of the bed would fall and smother me as in the German *Märchen* [fairy tales]. When the landlady came in to see me in the morning, after asking how I had slept, the first thing she said was, 'But, sir, don't you want another "pillar"?' I looked bewildered, and said: 'Why, what shall I do with another pillar? and where will you put it?' She then touched the pillows under my head and said, 'Well, sir, you shall have another "pillar" to-morrow.' 'How shall I ever learn English,' I said to myself, 'if a "pillar" means really a soft pillow?'

Noam Chomsky was born in 1928

Born in Philadelphia, Chomsky became the most influential figure in linguistics in the second half of the twentieth century, known for his radical repositioning of the subject (initially in the form of generative grammar, as presented in his 1957 book *Syntactic Structures*) and in his later years for his political activism. His approach includes such central notions as the role of native-speaker intuition as the source of linguistic data, and the view that children are born with a biologically innate language faculty (or universal grammar).

In the opening chapter of his 1975 book *Reflections on Language* he provides a succinct summary of his views after asking the question: 'Why study language?' (I've added a paragraph break):

> There are many possible answers, and by focusing on some I do not, of course, mean to disparage others or question their legitimacy. One may, for example, simply be fascinated by the elements of language in themselves and want to discover their order and arrangement, their origin in history or in the individual, or the way in which they are used in thought, in science or in art, or in normal social interchange. One reason for studying language – and for me personally the most compelling reason – is that it is tempting to regard language, in the traditional phrase, as 'a mirror of mind.'
>
> I do not mean by this simply that the concepts expressed and distinctions developed in normal language use give us insight into the patterns of thought and the world of 'common sense' constructed by the human mind. More intriguing, to me at least, is the possibility that by studying language we may discover abstract principles that govern its structure and use, principles that are universal by biological necessity and not mere historical accident, that derive from mental characteristics of the species.

It was this focus on the relationship between 'language and mind' (the title of another of his books) that changed the direction of linguisics so radically in the 1960s.

Thomas De Quincey died in 1859

He was born in Manchester in 1785, and became known as a writer, especially for *Confessions of an English Opium-Eater* (1821), and for a large number of essays and magazine contributions. Several of these explored linguistic topics: he wrote on style, rhetoric, the pronunciation of place names, and the 'destiny' of English (thinking especially of the consequences for the language of immigration into the USA).

He was an early advocate of the role of usage, as in his essay on 'Pronunciation', published posthumously. He's well aware of how people complain, and he addresses the reader:

> if I must teach him how to pronounce, and upon what learned grounds to pronounce, 40,000 words, and if polemically I must teach him how to dispose of 40,000 objections that have been raised (or that *may* be raised) against these pronunciations, then I should require at the least 40,000 lives (which is quite out of the question, for a cat has but nine) – seeing and allowing for all this, I may yet offer him some guidance as to his guide. One sole rule, if he will attend to it, governs in a paramount sense the total possibilities and compass of pronunciation. A very famous line of Horace states it. What line? What is the supreme law in every language for correct pronunciation no less than for idiomatic propriety? *'Usus, quem penes arbitrium est et jus et norma loquendi:'* usage, the established practice, subject to which is all law and normal standard of correct speaking.
>
> Now, in what way does such a rule interfere with the ordinary prejudice on this subject? The popular error is that, in pronunciation, as in other things, there is an abstract right and a wrong. The difficulty, it is supposed, lies in ascertaining this right and wrong ... in that preconception lies the capital blunder incident to the question. There *is* no right, there *is* no wrong, except what the prevailing usage creates. The usage, the existing custom, *that* is the law: and from that law there is no appeal whatever, nor demur that is sustainable for a moment.

John Milton was born in 1608

He was born in London, and became universally known for his poetry, with *Paradise Lost* considered to be one of the greatest poems in English literature. He also wrote many essays and pamphlets on religious, social and political topics, engaging with the great changes of his day – the English Civil War and the Restoration. He died in 1674.

His literary creativity had a linguistic parallel: first uses of over 500 words or senses, such as *awestruck, complacency, debauchery, ecstatic, exhilarating, extravagance, fragrance, irresponsible, pandemonium, stunning, terrific*. He also had much to say about language learning, in terms easily recognizable today. His letter-essay 'Of Education' criticizes current practice, which he asserts spends too much time on drilling structures and memorizing, and not enough on philosophical content ('solid things'):

> though a linguist should pride himself to have all the tongues that Babel cleft the world into, yet if he have not studied the solid things in them as well as the words and lexicons, he were nothing so much to be esteemed a learned man, as any yeoman or tradesman competently wise in his mother dialect only. Hence appear the many mistakes which have made learning generally so unpleasing and so unsuccessful.

The first part of his solution anticipates the elocutionist movement of the next century:

> I will point you out the right path of a virtuous and noble education ... first, they [learners] should begin with the chief and necessary rules of some good grammar, either that now used, or any better; and while this is doing, their speech is to be fashioned to a distinct and clear pronunciation, as near as may be to the Italian, especially in the vowels. For we Englishmen being far northerly, do not open our mouths in the cold air wide enough to grace a southern tongue; but are observed by all the nations to speak exceeding close and inward; so that to smatter Latin with an English mouth, is as ill a hearing as law French.

His reasoning has no standing in modern phonetics but was widely accepted at the time.

Emily Dickinson was born in 1830

Born in Massachusetts, Dickinson became recognized after her death as a major figure in American poetry. She spent a great deal of her life in home solitude, writing prolifically, in an unconventional style, with no titles, short lines, sporadic rhymes and half-rhymes, elliptical syntax, irregular capitalization, and a use of dashes (of varying length) that early editors replaced and some recent editions try to reproduce. She died in 1886.

A sprinkling of poems have aspects of language as their theme, sometimes with a spiritual underpinning. Here are three (SEE ALSO 28 APRIL).

The words the happy say
Are paltry melody
But those the silent feel
Are beautiful –

Silence is all we dread.
There's Ransom in a Voice –
But Silence is Infinity.
Himself have not a face. –

A Word made Flesh is seldom
And tremblingly partook
Nor then perhaps reported
But have I not mistook
Each one of us has tasted
With ecstasies of stealth
The very food debated
To our specific strength –

A Word that breathes distinctly
Has not the power to die
Cohesive as the Spirit
It may expire if He –
'Made Flesh and dwelt among us'
Could condescension be
Like this consent of Language
This loved Philology.

International UNICEF Day

The United Nation's International Children's Emergency Fund (UNICEF) was one of the brightest initiatives following the end of World War II, founded on this day in 1946. It became a permanent agency of the UN in 1953. The words International and Emergency were dropped, but United Nations Children's Fund provided no pronounceable acronym, so the earlier usage continued. It was awarded the Nobel Peace Prize in 1965.

Its website summarizes aims and achievements, with a powerful second sentence:

> UNICEF works in over 190 countries and territories to save children's lives, to defend their rights, and to help them fulfil their potential, from early childhood through adolescence. And we never give up.

The programme focuses on providing supplies, assistance and ways of improving the health, nutrition, education and general welfare of children, wherever they live and without making distinctions on political, religious, ethnic, gender or other grounds. A separate event, World Children's Day, is celebrated on 20 November. Each year has a theme: in 2021 its focus was to help children recover from interruptions and lost learning because of the pandemic.

Language isn't given a separate mention, but of course it's the facilitating force behind every UNICEF initiative, as it is with the UN International Day of Education (SEE 24 JANUARY) and related projects. The focus on children, however, motivates a different emphasis from any adult-orientated initiatives, and ties in with other programmes where children are an important factor, such as UNESCO's International Literacy Day (SEE 8 SEPTEMBER). There have also been several initiatives specifically related to language. Two examples. In 2021 UNICEF India prepared textbooks in tribal languages for children in a particular region who were unable to communicate in the official language, Hindi. And in 2017 UNICEF UK planned resource packs for refugee children faced with having to learn a new language. The covers showed a famous refugee: Paddington Bear.

E.R. Braithwaite died in 2016

Born in 1912 in Georgetown, Guyana, Braithwaite became a writer, known by his initials (Edward Ricardo), especially for his autobiographical novel *To Sir with Love* (1959). He studied in New York and then went to London, where he joined the RAF. After World War II he taught at a London East End school (the context for his novel), and when Guyana became independent changed career, was appointed the country's representative to the UN (1966–68) and then ambassador to Venezuela (1968–70). He later changed again, becoming writer-in-residence at several American universities.

In various interviews he affirmed his fascination with language: 'I write because I enjoy putting words together, and composing them in such a way that readers feel the excitement I feel.' And as he gained opportunities to engage in debate, he recalled his childhood:

> All the reading I had done, all the things my mother and father discussed with me at the dinner table … the language began to make sense. A point of view was discussed and you could make an interjection and make it imaginatively. When words can come together and paint pictures at your discretion, not somebody else's, you are doing it. You suddenly feel a relationship with words.

'There is something about all of us that relishes talk', he adds – even though it sometimes got him into trouble.

> I was playing in the backyard with some of my neighbour's children … We were playing marbles. And I became accustomed to hearing them using these richly descriptive words. I remember sitting at the dinner table with my mother and it popped out. I forgot to control my language – this word popped out. My mother took me by the hand into the bathroom, reached into the cabinet, took out a bottle which contained a black mixture called cascara… It is the essence of bitterness. If you take a little cascara in the mouth and you think you'll use some water to lessen the effect, it makes it worse. And my mother said, 'Any time I hear you using words like that, this bottle will be waiting for you!'

Elizabeth Bates died in 2003

Born in Kansas in 1947, Bates became professor of cognitive science at the University of California (San Diego), and was especially known for her research into the acquisition of language by children, and into the psychological and neurological processes in the brain that govern language use.

Her work on the early years of child development emphasized the cognitive and social factors that she believed were fundamental to language acquisition. She was especially interested in exploring the way children use other communicative strategies (such as pointing) to express their intentions before they are able to talk. Of especial interest, to my mind, was her analysis of utterances at around twelve months of age. In my *Listen to Your Child* I describe them in this way:

> Short utterances, just one or two syllables long, with a clear melody and rhythm, come to be made in a regular and predictable way. [daa] said Jamie, with a rising melody, one day; and the next day he said it several dozen times; and the next day, several hundred. No one was quite sure what it meant to begin with. It sounded as if he was trying to say *that*, but this interpretation didn't always fit the situation. It made sense when he said it while pointing at a passing cat. His mother immediately said 'What's that? It's a pussy-cat'. But it didn't seem to make sense when he said it in an off-the-cuff way over his mother's shoulder as he was being whisked off to bed. And everyone ignored it. Was it a word, or wasn't it?

These utterances weren't like babbling (SEE 21 OCTOBER), and they lacked the definite shape and meaning of 'first words'. Bates called them *proto-words*, thereby identifying an important and previously little recognized step in the early stages of a child learning to talk. In the transition from pre-language to language, children produce many of these proto-words, where the sounds are clear, but the meaning isn't. Only when the sound of an utterance and its meaning *both* become clear can we really begin to talk about 'first words'.

Aphra Behn was born in 1640

She was born in Kent. Little is known of her family or early life, but she became recognized as a playwright, writing over twenty plays for the reopened theatres after the Restoration. Her poems, translations and prose writings were also acclaimed. Among the last is her most famous work, written a year before her death, *Oroonoko* (1688), one of the earliest novels in English. The story, later adapted into a play, is about what happens to an African prince who is sold into slavery in Surinam, where he meets the narrator. An interesting linguistic detail occurs after his purchase by a Mr Trefry, who gives him special treatment as Oroonoko can speak both French and English.

> I ought to tell you, that the Christians never buy any Slaves but they give 'em some Name of their own, their native ones being likely very barbarous, and hard to pronounce; so that Mr. *Trefry* gave *Oroonoko* that of *Cæsar*; which name will live in that Country as long as that (scarce more) glorious one of the great *Roman*: for 'tis most evident he wanted no Part of the personal Courage of that *Cæsar*, and acted Things as memorable, had they been done in some Part of the World replenished with People and Historians, that might have given him his Due. But his Misfortune was, to fall in an obscure World, that afforded only a Female Pen to celebrate his Fame; tho' I doubt not but it had lived from others Endeavours, if the *Dutch*, who immediately after his Time took that Country, had not killed, banished and dispersed all those that were capable of giving the World this great Man's Life, much better than I have done.

There's been much debate about the narrator's identity – whether Behn herself or a fictitious character; but, either way, the comment that the story would have benefited if written by a man accurately captures the difficulties faced by women writers at the time.

International Tea Day

Many tea-producing countries celebrate their product on this day. It was created at the World Social Forum in 2004, and the following year the first such day was recognized in New Delhi. In 2015 the Indian government proposed a global event to the UN Food and Agriculture Organization, and the first UN Tea Day was celebrated in 2020 on 21 May – a day chosen because May is the season when harvesting begins in most tea-producing countries. But the December date is still used, and has some historical significance, as the famous Boston Tea Party of 1773 – a major dispute over tea taxation – took place the next day.

Tea-drinking has been known in China since at least the third millennium BCE, which makes its practice in Britain a baby by comparison. The first recorded usage in English is 1655. On 25 September 1660 Samuel Pepys wrote in his Diary: 'I did send for a cup of tee (a China drink) of which I never had drunk before.' The following year it was introduced into the Restoration court by Queen Catherine, and soon after it became a fashion to 'take tea', accompanied by an elegant apparatus of silver spoons, pots, stands, tongs and caddies.

The vocabulary of tea blossomed. Over the next fifty years we find a family of words introduced to describe all the bits and pieces needed in order to drink tea efficiently, such as *tea-pot*, *tea-spoon* and *tea-cup*. A century later society recognized the crucial notion of *tea-time*, which led to *tea-trays* and *tea-sets*. *Tea-bags* arrived in the nineteenth century; and in the twentieth we find an extension into the world of business, with *tea trolleys* and *tea breaks*.

No other drink has generated so many idioms, especially in the twentieth century. *Not for all the tea in China* seems to have started in Australia. *Tea and sympathy* became popular following its use as a title in a stage play and film from the 1950s. The most productive one of all is *cup of tea*, which emerged in the early 1900s, as in… *Linguistics is my cup of tea.*

Jane Austen was born in 1775

Born in Hampshire, Austen became a writer now recognized as one of the greatest female novelists, with her books, such as *Pride and Prejudice* and *Sense and Sensibility*, still widely read and often filmed. Acclaimed for their portrayal of contemporary English society, they contain innumerable insights into the language of the various social classes as reflected in her characters.

Less known, but just as important, are the comments about language and style that she makes in her letters. Of particular interest is the way she adopts the role of a literary critic in writing to her niece Anna, who had begun to write a novel of her own.

In a letter of 28 September 1814 she shows a particular dislike of what she calls 'novel slang' – the clichés of the typical Romantic novelist:

> Devereux Forster's being ruined by his Vanity is extremely good; but I wish you would not let him plunge into a 'vortex of Dissipation'. I do not object to the Thing. but I cannot bear the expression; – it is such thorough novel slang – and so old, I dare say Adam met with it in the first novel he opened.

Her comments are laced with a gentle humour, and she shows an appealing deference, as in this comment in July 1814:

> A few verbal corrections were all that I felt tempted to make – the principal of them is a speech of St Julians to Lady Helena – which you will see I have presumed to alter. – As Lady H. is Cecilia's superior, it wd not be correct to talk of *her* being introduced; Cecilia must be the person introduced – And I do not like a Lover's speaking in the 3d person; – it is too much like the formal part of Lord Orville, & I think is not natural. If *you* think differently however, you need not mind me.

Orville is a character in Fanny Burney's *Evelina* (SEE 13 JUNE).

Sadly, Anna lost interest in writing after her aunt's death in 1817, and according to her daughter she burned the manuscript some years later.

Dorothy L. Sayers died in 1957

Born in Oxford in 1893, Sayers became known as a crime novelist, featuring the amateur detective Lord Peter Wimsey. The *L* in her pen name stood for Leigh. She also wrote short stories, plays and essays, and (after studying modern languages at Oxford) made translations, notably of Dante's *Divine Comedy*. As an advertising agency copywriter, she's credited with the slogan 'It pays to advertise.' Several essays are about language; although she has her own pet likes and dislikes, she was vituperative about pedantry, as seen in 'The English Language' (1936), included in *Unpopular Opinions*:

> There are pedants, God mend their ears, who, having read some cheap-jack, rule-of-thumb, cramp-wit folly in a sixpenny text-book, would like to break our free idiom to the bit of an alien fashion. These are not the Latinists (who know better), but the Latinisers; they remember the Latin bones of language, and will have them dry bones. These are the pinching misers, who will hoard their gold, but will not put it out to gain. Of such are the dreary little men who write to the papers protesting – in the teeth of Chaucer, Bacon, Spenser, Shakespeare, Jonson, the English Bible, Milton, Burton, Congreve, Swift, Burke, Peacock, Ruskin, Arnold and the whole tradition of English letters – that a sentence must not end with a preposition. This is no matter of syntax; it is a matter of idiom; and the freedom to handle our prepositions is among the most glorious in our charter of liberties.

The essay contains several other punches:

> It is as dangerous for people unaccustomed to handling words and unacquainted with their technique to tinker about with these heavily-charged nuclei of emotional power as it would be for me to burst into a laboratory and play about with a powerful electro-magnet or other machine highly charged with electrical force. By my clumsy and ignorant handling, I should probably, at the very least, contrive to damage either the machine or myself; at the worst I might blow up the whole place. Similarly the irresponsible use of highly-electric words is very strongly to be deprecated.

Arabic Language Day

The day was established by the United Nations in 2012 as part of the policy to 'celebrate multilingualism and cultural diversity as well as to promote equal use of all six of its official working languages throughout the organization'. The date chosen remembers the day in 1973 when the General Assembly adopted Arabic as its sixth official language. Today, estimates suggest there are over 420 million speakers of Arabic in the world. It has official status in many countries, especially in North Africa and the Middle East, and is the liturgical language of Islam.

It has long been cited in linguistics as a classic example of *diglossia*, where two varieties of a language coexist in different cultural circumstances. At one level there is Modern Standard Arabic, derived from Classical Arabic (the language of the Quran); at another level there is Colloquial Arabic, spoken in different varieties within Arab countries.

Thanks to its political and cultural standing in past centuries, Arabic has been an important source of loanwords into English and other European languages. From the end of the twelfth century we see *saffron* and *admiral*; *mattress* in the thirteenth; and numerous examples in the fourteenth, especially in the fields of science and mathematics, such as *alchemy, alkali, azimuth* and *cipher*. Many are objects to do with trade, such as *cotton, lute* and *syrup*. Words relating to Arabic society and culture are increasingly noticeable during and after the fifteenth century, as travel between England and North Africa increased: *alcohol, jar, magazine, minaret, mosque, sheikh, sherbet, sofa, sultan, zero*. Most words arrived in English through an indirect route. *Tarragon*, for example, came into English via Spanish in the sixteenth century; *carafe* via French in the eighteenth. And the process continued into the twentieth century, though more slowly, with such cuisine terms as *falafel, hummus, kebab* and *tahini*. Often the route taken by a word isn't clear, with Persian, Turkish and other directions involved. But, one way or another, the *Oxford English Dictionary* lists over 1,400 words that have come into English that show the influence of Arabic, either directly or indirectly.

Emily Brontë died in 1848

Born in Yorkshire in 1818, Brontë became a poet and novelist, best
known for her only novel, *Wuthering Heights*, published in 1847 under
her pen name Ellis Bell. It's a classic of English literature now, and of
considerable linguistic interest for the way she incorporates Yorkshire
dialect into the speech of some of her characters, notably the old servant
Joseph. Over forty dialect words are used, such as *chimbley* (chimney),
flaysome (fearful), *laiking* (playful) and *thrang* (busy), and she takes pains
to represent the Yorkshire accent. But there was a problem.

After her death, her sister Charlotte – who had spent some time in
London – edited the text for the 2nd edition of 1850. In a letter to the
publisher, she said:

> It seems to me advisable to modify the orthography of the old servant
> Joseph's speeches; for though, as it stands, it exactly renders the
> Yorkshire dialect to a Yorkshire ear, yet I am sure Southerns must find
> it unintelligible; and thus one of the most graphic characters in the
> book is lost on them.

Her emendations were almost always to do with pronunciation:

> 1847: If Aw wur yah, maister, Aw'd iust slam t'boards i' their faces all
> on 'em, gentle and simple! Never a day ut yah're off, but yon cat uh
> Linton comes sneaking hithet

> 1850: If I war yah, maister, I'd just slam t'boards i' their faces all on
> 'em, gentle and simple! Never a day ut yah're off, but yon cat o' Linton
> comes sneaking hither

She didn't do it consistently, but the fact that she did it at all is an
interesting observation about contemporary dialect attitudes. It evidently
wasn't something that bothered Emily – or perhaps she wasn't aware of a
possible problem, not knowing the London scene as well as her sister.

The problem wasn't limited to the 1800s. Several twentieth-century
television series, such as *Birds of a Feather* and *Peaky Blinders*, had the
broad regional accents of the characters 'toned down'.

Dot Your i's Day

The origin of the day is unknown, but its intention is clear: to devote a day to carrying out tasks with minute care and without missing out any detail. The full form of the expression is 'dot your i's and cross your t's', which seems to date from the early decades of the nineteenth century, used by schoolteachers when urging their pupils to be careful in their handwriting. The earliest recorded usage is in 1820, when a writer to the Washington newspaper the *Daily National Intelligencer* commented:

> Pray, sir, what is the object of referring a bill to a committee – merely to dot the i's and cross the t's?

The first issue of the American *Scribner's Magazine* in 1887 contained a collection of unpublished letters of William Makepeace Thackeray (SEE 24 DECEMBER), who died in 1863. In one of these, written in 1849 to his friend Jane Octavia Brookfield, he remarks:

> See how beautifully I have put stops to the last sentence, and crossed the t's and dotted the i's!

It seems to have been a favourite expression of his, as he uses it again in another letter, in July 1850: 'I have been laboriously crossing all my t's'. It isn't clear just how widespread that 'reverse' usage was. Certainly in the twentieth century the dominant usage is for the i's to precede the t's.

Like the related expression, 'mind your p's and q's', the idiom illustrates an interesting exception to the rules governing the use of the apostrophe in English. People who are annoyed by such spellings as *potato's* and *agenda's* are prone to say that the apostrophe should never be used in a plural form. These idioms show that it sometimes can be, and the reason is clear. To write *ts, is, ps, qs* would interfere with easy reading, especially in the case of *is*, which is also a word. Some have tried to avoid the apostrophe issue in print by using fonts, making the *i* and *t* italic, and the *s* roman: *i*s, *t*s; but this has attracted criticism on aesthetic grounds, and isn't really an option in handwriting.

Crossword Puzzle Day

The first published crossword puzzle appeared in the edition of the *New York World* newspaper on this day in 1913. It was created by a journalist from Liverpool who emigrated to Pennsylvania in 1891: Arthur Wynne (1871–1945). He had an insider's awareness of newspapers, as his father edited the *Liverpool Mercury*, so it perhaps wasn't surprising that he found a job with the *Pittsburgh Press* and later the *New York World*, editing the 'fun' puzzle page. It was while he was working for the *World* that he devised what he called a 'word-cross' puzzle. The name would have stayed but for a typesetting error a month later, resulting in *cross-word*, and the hyphen was dropped soon after.

There had already been puzzles inserting words into various kinds of grids, but his innovation was to make the words across different from the words down, slotting them into a diamond array. All sorts of geometric shapes were used, in the early days, but the grid eventually became standard as a square. The puzzle was an instant success, but curiously the *World* was the only newspaper to publish crosswords until 1924, when the first collection of puzzles in a book appeared. Crosswords became a national craze in the USA, and then an international one. By the end of 1924 it had reached Britain, with Queen Mary among the early enthusiasts. US humorist Gelett Burgess (SEE 15 MAY) submitted a puzzle to the *World* later that year, and wrote a verse about it:

> The fans they chew their pencils,
> The fans they beat their wives.
> They look up words for extinct birds –
> They lead such puzzling lives!

It wasn't long until a cadre of professional compilers emerged (SEE 12 OCTOBER), and puzzles grew in size and complexity. There's a long literary history to be told, and fortunately it has been, by Adrienne Raphel in her book *Thinking Inside the Box* (2020), with the intriguing subtitle: *Adventures with Crosswords and the Puzzling People Who Can't Live without Them.*

Be a Lover of Silence Day

Another day whose origins are unknown, but whose purpose is clear: to look for opportunities to avoid the noise of everyday life. The day originally related to the absence of speaking; but it has also been used to obtain relief from the pressures of online communication.

You might think that silence is the enemy of language, but in fact it has an important linguistic role. It can provide a meaningful setting for speech, as when we 'break the silence'. We can introduce a silence to show puzzlement or indecision – 'I don't know what to say' – or an emotion, such as disapproval. And silence in the form of pausing is crucial to maintain speech intelligibility. In linguistic descriptions it's included as a prosodic feature, along with such other features as intonation. In my own research, I recognized three degrees of length: a pause equal to a beat of the speaker's rhythm, a shorter pause, and a longer one.

The dramatic potential of pause and silence has been exploited by several dramatists, such as Samuel Beckett and, above all, Harold Pinter, to the extent that the expression 'Pinter pauses' became widely used. Pinter himself had mixed feelings about it. On the one hand, he could see the dramatic power lying behind silence, as he said in a 1962 speech:

> There are two silences. One when no word is spoken. The other when perhaps a torrent of language is being employed. The speech we hear is an indication of that which we don't hear. It is a necessary avoidance, a violent, sly, anguished or mocking smokescreen. When true silence falls, we are still left with echo but are nearer nakedness. One way of looking at speech is to say that it is a constant stratagem to cover nakedness.

On the other hand, he thought people overrated them:

> These damn silences and pauses are all to do with what's going on... and if they don't make any sense, then I always say cut them. ... When I myself act in my own plays, which I have occasionally, I've cut half of them, actually.

Charles-Michel de l'Épée died in 1789

Born in Versailles in 1712, l'Épée became a Catholic priest and educator who founded the first school for the deaf in about 1760. He developed a pedagogical system which was influential in forming a climate for the development of sign languages in several countries. One of his pupils, Laurent Clerc, took his method to the USA (SEE 16 FEBRUARY). His major work was *Institution des sourds et muets par la voie des signes méthodiques* ('Institution of the Deaf and Dumb by Means of Systematic Signs', 1776).

In the opening chapter he mentions an apparent increase in the number of deaf people in Paris, and gives an explanation (translation by Francis Green, 1803):

> it is because that, until our days, those children who were born destitute of the faculties of hearing and speaking were kept secluded from society; the instruction of them having always been looked upon as being extremely difficult, if not impossible.

He goes on to report his school's successes, in words that have warmed the heart of teachers of the deaf ever since:

> At this day, *the case is altered*. Many of the Deaf and Dumb have been seen to exhibit themselves in the face of the whole world. The exercises they were to perform have been announced by the programmes or bills posted up to give notice of their intended performances in the school, which have excited the attention of the public. Persons of all ranks and conditions have attended there in crowds. The performers have been embraced, applauded, loaded with commendations, and crowned with laurels: those very children, that until then, had been considered as the outcasts of nature, have appeared with more distinction, and done more honor to their fathers and mothers, than their other children, who were not capable of doing the same things, and who have even blushed at it. Tears of joy and tenderness have accordingly succeeded to sighs and lamentations. These new kind of actors were shown with as great a degree of confidence and pleasure, as, until then, had been taken of precaution to keep them out of sight.

William Makepeace Thackeray died in 1863

He was born in 1811 in India (his father worked for the East India Company) and became an author and illustrator, best known for his novel *Vanity Fair* (1848), and for his satirical essays. From his prolific output, this time of the year suggests an extract from *The Christmas Books of Mr M.A. Titmarsh* (one of his pen names). It contains four stories, including *The Kickleburys on the Rhine* (1950). Lady Kicklebury is an aristocratic widow ('the Kickleburys date from Henry III') who appears in his comedy *The Wolves and the Lamb* (1854), and who is on a grand tour with her family. Mr Titmarsh, the narrator, is making the same tour.

The book was savagely attached by a reviewer for *The Times*, accusing Thackeray of writing a Christmas book for money:

> It has been customary, of late years, for the purveyors of amusing literature – the popular authors of the day – to put forth certain opuscules, denominated 'Christmas Books,' with the ostensible intention of swelling the tide of exhilaration, or other expansive emotions, incident upon the exodus of the old and the inauguration of the new year. We have said that their ostensible intention was such, because there is another motive for these productions, locked up (as the popular author deems) in his own breast, but which betrays itself, in the quality of the work, as his principal incentive. Oh! that any muse should be set upon a high stool to cast up accounts and balance a ledger!

Thackeray made an equally savage rejoinder, printed in a preface to the 2nd edition, which includes a devastating critique of the reviewer's style:

> And what a style it is, that great man's! What hoighth of foine language entoirely! How he can discoorse you in English for all the world as if it was Latin! … That is something like a sentence; not a word scarcely but's in Latin, and the longest and handsomest out of the whole dictionary.

If you read the whole riposte, I think you'd concur that Thackeray wins the battle. And Christmas books survive.

A'phabet Day

The joke may or may not be obvious. You're supposed to say: 'there's no *L* in the word Alphabet'. Then the penny may drop: No *L* ... Noël ... Christmas. You may well encounter it again if you pull a Christmas cracker. All I can say is that this was not my idea. I don't know who started it, or when, and nobody else seems to know either. Presumably the originator is in hiding somewhere.

Is there anything that can be salvaged from the day that would make it appeal to anyone other than inveterate punsters, who are complaining that they haven't had a day of their own since, oh, 8 November? It could be a source of Christmas Day games. Speak or write for a minute without using any word with *L* in it. Quite a difficut task. Or charades in which the only acceptable answers have to begin with *L*. Or, for those with a more academic temperament, find a word book and explore the etymology of names. Beginning with *Noël*, of course.

It comes from French, and ultimately Latin, where the verb *nasci* means 'to be born'. When it arrived in English, in the Middle Ages, it went in different directions. It could refer to the feast of Christmas itself or be an acclamation that Christmas has arrived. Chaucer's Franklin has it in his Canterbury Tale: '"Nowel" crieth every lusty man', and this use (since the 1800s usually spelled with a double *l*) became famous in a carol: 'The First Nowell'. It was also used as a first name, originally for children born or baptized today, and additionally as a surname. In the eighteenth century, carols came to be called 'Noels'.

Still, if all this is too much, we could call today 'Silent Night Day', as this was the day that carol was first performed in 1818. The lyrics to 'Stille Nacht' were written by a priest, Joseph Mohr, and performed in St Nikolaus's church in Oberndorf bei Salzburg in Austria. UNESCO declared it an intangible cultural heritage in 2011 in recognition of its role in fostering cultural diversity. No other carol has achieved such status.

Thomas Gray was born in 1716

He was born in London, and became known as a poet, chiefly for his 'Elegy Written in a Country Churchyard' (1751), which became one of the most quoted poems in English literature. Some of its expressions entered the language as a whole, such as 'kindred spirit'; and some inspired other writers, such as 'far from the madding crowd', which Thomas Hardy used as a novel title. Gray died in 1771.

He was also a prolific letter writer. In one, written to his friend Richard West in 1742, he made a remark that ensured him a place in the history of English poetic style:

> As to matter of stile, I have this to say: The language of the age is never the language of poetry.

The view is the opposite of that espoused by Wordsworth (SEE 15 SEPTEMBER). Gray goes on:

> Our poetry ... has a language peculiar to itself; to which almost every one, that has written, has added something by enriching it with foreign idioms and derivatives: Nay sometimes words of their own composition or invention. Shakespear and Milton have been great creators this way; and no one more licentious than Pope or Dryden, who perpetually borrow expressions from the former. ... And our language not being a settled thing (like the French) has an undoubted right to words of an hundred years old, provided antiquity have not rendered them unintelligible. In truth, Shakespear's language is one of his principal beauties; and he has no less advantage over your Addisons and Rowes in this, than in those other great excellencies you mention. Every word in him is a picture.

He quotes some lines from Shakespeare, and adds, somewhat ruefully:

> To me they appear untranslatable; and if this be the case, our language is greatly degenerated. However, the affectation of imitating Shakespear may doubtless be carried too far; and is no sort of excuse for sentiments ill-suited, or speeches ill-timed, which I believe is a little the case with me... Such is the misfortune of imitating the inimitable.

Charles Lamb died in 1834

He was born in London in 1775, and became known as a poet and essayist, as well as for his children's *Tales from Shakespeare*, written with his sister, Mary. He contributed to the *London Magazine* under the pen name of Elia, and later published two collections: *Essays of Elia* (1823) and *The Last Essays of Elia* (1833).

His *Last Essays* contains a series of sixteen 'Popular Fallacies', including 'That the worst puns are the best':

> If by worst be only meant the most far-fetched and startling, we agree to it. A pun is not bound by the laws which limit nicer wit. It is a pistol let off at the ear; not a feather to tickle the intellect. It is an antic which does not stand upon manners, but comes bounding into the presence, and does not show the less comic for being dragged in sometimes by the head and shoulders. What though it limp a little, or prove defective in one leg – all the better. A pun may easily be too curious and artificial.
>
> Who has not at one time or other been at a party of professors (himself perhaps an old offender in that line), where, after ringing a round of the most ingenious conceits, every man contributing his shot, and some there the most expert shooters of the day; after making a poor *word* run the gauntlet till it is ready to drop; after hunting and winding it through all the possible ambages [pathways] of similar sounds; after squeezing, and hauling, and tugging at it, till the very milk of it will not yield a drop further, – suddenly some obscure, unthought-of fellow in a corner ... has all at once come out with something so whimsical, yet so pertinent; so brazen in its pretensions, yet so impossible to be denied; so exquisitely good, and so deplorably bad, at the same time, – that it has proved a Robin Hood's shot; any thing ulterior to that is despaired of; and the party breaks up, unanimously voting it to be the very worst (that is, best) pun of the evening.

Susan Sontag died in 2004

She was born in New York City in 1933, and became a leading intellectual personality of her time, known especially for her writing, artistic criticism and political activism. She wrote in many genres, fiction and nonfiction, and several of her essays have language as their focus. Her essay 'On Style', published in her collection *Against Interpretation* (1966), was about the arts in general, but much of what she said can be applied to language in particular.

Style, she said, 'is the principle of decision in a work of art, the signature of the artist's will'. It is a mnemonic device, 'to preserve the works of the mind against oblivion':

> This function is easily demonstrated in the rhythmical, sometimes rhyming, character of all primitive, oral literatures. Rhythm and rhyme, and the more complex formal resources of poetry such as meter, symmetry of figures, antitheses, are the means that words afford for creating a memory of themselves before material signs (writing) are invented; hence everything that an archaic culture wishes to commit to memory is put in poetic form.

She also affirms the central role of metaphor – a major theme in linguistics in recent years: 'To speak of style is one way of speaking about the totality of a work of art. Like all discourse about totalities, talk of style must rely on metaphors. And metaphors mislead.' She amplified this in an interview for *Rolling Stone* in 1979:

> Metaphors are central to thinking, but it's like a kind of agnosticism: as you use them, you shouldn't believe them; you should know that they're a necessary fiction... You can say something is like something else, okay, then that's clean, because it's very clear what the differences are. But when you say, for example, that illness is a curse, it's a way of stopping your thinking and freezing you into certain attitudes. The intellectual project is inevitably involved with constructing new metaphors, because you have to use them to think, but at least you should be critical and skeptical of the ones you've inherited: unclogging your thought, letting in air, opening things out.

Don Marquis died in 1937

Born in Illinois in 1878, Marquis, a journalist and writer, is known especially for the characters of archy, a cockroach who had been a free-verse poet in a previous life, and mehitabel, an alley cat who was once Queen Cleopatra. The appeal of the archy books was due to the mix of philosophical and social comment produced by the insect and his unique typography. In the introduction to *archy and mehitabel* (1931), he explains:

> We came into our room earlier than usual in the morning, and discovered a gigantic cockroach jumping about upon the keys.
>
> He did not see us, and we watched him. He would climb painfully upon the framework of the machine and cast himself with all his force upon a key, head downward, and his weight and the impact of the blow were just sufficient to operate the machine, one slow letter after another.

archy writes long poems for Marquis on all kinds of subjects. There are no capital letters, as he can't work the shift key, and punctuation marks are absent. The opening of 'pete the parrot and shakespeare' illustrates:

> i got acquainted with
> a parrot named pete recently
> who is an interesting bird
> pete says he used
> to belong to the fellow
> that ran the mermaid tavern
> in london then I said
> you must have known
> shakespeare know him said pete
> poor mutt i knew him well
> he called me pete and i called him
> bill but why do you say poor mutt
> well said pete bill was a
> disappointed man and was always
> boring his friends about what
> he might have been and done...

Poor Bill: all he wanted, according to archy, was to write good poetry, and not melodrama. But he has a family to support...

Rudyard Kipling was born in 1865

He was born in Bombay (modern Mumbai), but lived for many years in the USA and then England, where he died in 1936. He wrote in many genres, and became famous for his children's books such as *The Jungle Book* (1894), *Kim* (1901) and *Just So Stories for Little Children* (1902). His poetry was also widely appreciated: in a BBC poll of 'The Nation's Favourite Poems' in 1996, his 'If...' came top. In 1907 he was awarded the Nobel Prize for Literature, the first writer in English to receive it.

He was also much in demand as a speaker, and – partly because of his multicultural background – language was often a topic. He published a collection of his speeches in *A Book of Words* (1928). It included this strong defence of learning Latin, in a speech to students at Wellington College in 1912.

> Here is my defence of this alleged wicked waste of time. The reason why one has to parse and construe and grind at the dead tongues in which certain ideas are expressed, is not for the sake of what is called intellectual training – that may be given in other ways – but because only in that tongue is that idea expressed with absolute perfection. If it were not so the Odes of Horace would not have survived. (People aren't in a conspiracy to keep things alive.) I grant you that the kind of translations one serves up at school are as bad and as bald as they can be. They are bound to be so, because one cannot re-express an idea that has been perfectly set forth. (Men tried to do this, by the way, in the revised version of the Bible. They failed.) Yet, by a painful and laborious acquaintance with the mechanism of that particular tongue; by being made to take it to pieces and put it together again, and by that means only; we can arrive at a state of mind in which, though we cannot re-express the idea in any adequate words, we can realise and feel and absorb the idea.

A linguistic New Year's Eve

Although the focus of these days has been on the English language, several others have been mentioned throughout the book. It seems appropriate to conclude my theme of linguistic diversity by wishing readers a Happy New Year in fifty of them from Europe and nearby.

In some countries there's more than one way of saying it, but I've space for only one choice here. I've also transliterated other writing systems into the Roman alphabet for ease of reading.

Albanian *Vitin e ri*
Arabic *Hilul as-sanah al-jadidah*
Basque *Urte berri on*
Belarussian *Z novym hodam I kaladami*
Bosnian *Sretan nova godina*
Breton *Bloavezh mat*
Bulgarian *Štastliva nova dogina*
Catalan *Feliç any nou*
Cornish *Bledhen nowydh da*
Croatian *Sretna nova godina*
Czech *Stàstný nový rok*
Danish *Godt nytår*
Dutch *Gelukkig nieuwjaar*
Esperanto *Feliĉan novan jaron*
Estonian *Head uut aastat*
Finnish *Hyvää uutta vuotta*
Flemish *Gelukkig nieujaar*
French *Bonne année*
Gaelic *Bliadhna mhath ur*
Galician *Próspero aninovo*
German *Frohes neues Jahr*
Greek *Eftyhisméno to néo étos*
Greenlandic *Ukiortaami pilluarit*
Hungarian *Boldog új évet*

Icelandic *Gleðilegt nýtt ár*
Italian *Felice anno nuovo*
Latvian *Laimīgu jauno gadu*
Lithuanian *Lasimingų naujųjų metų*
Luxembourgish *E glécklecht neit joer*
Macedonian *Srekna nova godina*
Maltese *I-sena t-tajba*
Manx *Blein vie noa*
Norwegian *Godt nytt år*
Polish *Szczesliwego nowego roku*
Portuguese *Feliz ano novo*
Romani *Baxtalo nevo berš*
Romanian *Un an nou fericit*
Romansch *In bien niev onn*
Russian *S novym godom*
Serbian *Srećna nova godina*
Slovak *Šťastný nový rok*
Slovenian *Srečno novo leto*
Spanish *Feliz año nuevo*
Swedish *Gott nytt år*
Turkish *Mutlu yıllar*
Ukrainian *Z novym rokom*
Welsh *Blwyddyn newydd dda*

And not forgetting:

Latin *Annum faustum*; Old English *Glæd niwe gear* (the second *g* pronounced as in *year*); Scots *Haud Hogmanay*.

Appendix

8 MARCH

Two deliberate typos: a double colon in the last line of the second paragraph; an extra *r* in errors in the fourth paragraph.

22 MARCH

The Third Man quotation. It's said towards the beginning of the film, when the porter at Harry Lime's apartment tells Holly Martins that a 'third man' helped carry Lime's body, after his car accident. Martins asks him what this man looked like. The porter replies that he didn't see his face, and adds these words, looking out into the street: 'It might have been… just anybody'.

The Prisoner quotation. 'Be seeing you' is the farewell spoken by the brainwashed inhabitants of 'the village', from which the prisoner (played by Patrick McGoohan) is trying to escape.

12 OCTOBER

Crossword clue solutions: *advertisement, Berlin, Edam, pet.*

Literary references
& further reading

JANUARY

1 Maria Edgeworth, *Castle Rackrent* (Oxford University Press, 2008). Marilyn Butler, *Maria Edgeworth: A Literary Biography* (Oxford University Press, 1990).

2 Malcolm Coulthard, Alison Johnson and David Wright, *An Introduction to Forensic Linguistics* (Routledge, 2016).

3 J.R.R. Tolkien, *The Fellowship of the Ring* (Allen & Unwin, 1954), ch. 8. Jan Wayne Hammond and Christina Scull, *The Lord of the Rings: A Reader's Companion* (HarperCollins, 2014).

4 Margaret Davidson, *Louis Braille: The Boy Who Invented Books for the Blind* (Scholastic, 1991).

5 Leung Ping-kwan, in *Modern Chinese Literature and Culture* 17 (1), 2005, pp. 18–19, 32. Foreign Language Publications, Ohio State University. Esther M.K. Cheung (ed.), *City at the End of Time: Poems by Leung Ping-kwan* (Hong Kong University Press, 2012).

6 David Crystal and Rosemary Varley, *Introduction to Language Pathology*, 4th edn (Wiley, 2005).

7 Allan Ramsay, *The Ever Green* (1724), Preface; *The Gentle Shepherd* (1725), 1–4. *The Poems of Allan Ramsay* (1724; Nabu Press, 2012).

8 Marcia Biederman, *Scan Artist: How Evelyn Wood Convinced the World that Speed-Reading Worked* (Chicago Review Press, 2019).

9 Dr Seuss, *If I Ran the Zoo* (HarperCollins, 2000).

10 Susan Pedersen, *The Guardians: The League of Nations and the Crisis of Empire* (Oxford University Press, 2015).

11 Adam Grant and Francesca Gino, 'A Little Thanks Goes a Long Way: Explaining Why Gratitude Expressions Motivate Prosocial Behavior', *Journal of Personality and Social Psychology* 98 (6), 2010, pp. 946–55.

12 Paul Taylor, *Text-to-Speech Synthesis* (Cambridge University Press, 2009).

13 Michael Rosen, *What is Poetry? The Essential Guide to Reading and Writing Poems* (Walker Books, 2016).

14 Stephen Crain, *The Emergence of Meaning* (Cambridge University Press, 2012).

15 Stella Brook, *The Language of the Book of Common Prayer* (Andre Deutsch, 1965).

16 Keith Houston, *The Book* (Norton, 2016).

17 David Crystal, *Spell It Out: The Singular Story of English Spelling* (Profile, 2012).

18 Nick Rennison, *Peter Mark Roget: A Biography* (Pocket Essentials, 2007).

19 Victoria A. Fromkin (ed.), *Errors in Linguistic Performance: Slips of the Tongue, Ear, Pen and Hand* (Academic Press, 1981).

20 Gordon Campbell, *Bible: The Story of the King James Version 1611–2011* (Oxford University Press, 2010).

21 George Orwell, 'Politics and the English Language', in *Essays* (Penguin, 2014), p. 356. *The Road to Wigan Pier* (Penguin, 2014), p. 52.

22 David Hendy, *The BBC: A People's History* (Profile Books, 2022).

23 Andrew Robinson, *The Story of Writing* (Thames & Hudson, 1999).

24 International Linguistics Olympiad, ioling.org.

25 'To a Haggis', in *Poetical Works of Robert Burns* (Chambers, 1990). Ian McIntyre, *Robert Burns: A Life* (Constable, 2009).

26 Toad Hollow, nationaltoday.com/toad-hollow-day-of-encouragement.

27 G.J. Leigh (ed.), *Principles of Chemical Nomenclature* (Blackwell, 1998).

28 Paul Ticher, *Data Protection and the Cloud* (ITGP, 2018).

29 'Words', in *A Few More Verses* (1889; Palala Press, 2015). *The Collected Works of Susan Coolidge* (Musaicum Books, 2017).

30 *O These Men, These Men* (1935; Moyer Bell, 1995), ch. 3. Anne Hall, *Angela Thirkell: A Writer's Life* (Unicorn, 2021).

31 Backward Day, nationaltoday.com/national-backward-day.

FEBRUARY

1 Langston Hughes, *The Weary Blues* (1926; Open Road Media, 2022). Arnold Rampersad (ed.), *The Collected Poems of Langston Hughes* (Vintage, 1995).

2 'Slavery' (Cadell, 1788), in *The Complete Works of Hannah More* (Hardpress, 2019). Patricia Demers, *The World of Hannah More* (University Press of Kentucky, 1996).

3 Saint Blaise:The Iconography, www.christianiconography.info/blaise.html.

4 Frederick James Furnivall, *Dictionary of National Biography*, 1912 Supplement, vol. 2, p. 61.

5 David Crystal, *Words on Words* (Oxford University Press, 2006).

6 John Macalister, *A Dictionary of Maori Words in New Zealand English* (Oxford University Press, 2005).

7 'Seven Dials', in *Sketches by Boz* (Macrone, 1836; Penguin Classics, 1995). G.L. Brook, *The Language of Dickens* (Deutsch, 1970).

8 Ingrid Tieken-Boon van Ostade, *The Bishop's Grammar* (Oxford University Press, 2011).

9 Alexander Tulloch, *It's All Greek: Borrowed Words and their Histories* (Bodleian Publishing, 2018).

10 'Interviewing Fleur Adcock', 28 March 2018, www.jogosflorais.com/interview/2018/7/interviewing-fleur-adcock. 'Dragon Talk', in *Dragon Talk* (Bloodaxe Books, 2010). Janet Wilson, *Fleur Adcock* (Northcote House, 2008).

11 Daniel Paul O'Donnell and Dawn Collins, *Cædmon's Hymn: A Multimedia Study, Archive and Edition* (Brewer, 2005).

12 *Autobiographies: Charles Darwin* (Penguin, 2002).

13 Gordon Bathgate, *Radio Broadcasting: A History of the Airwaves* (Pen & Sword, 2020).

14 'On the Writing of Lyrics', *Vanity Fair*, June 1917. Robert McCrum, *Wodehouse: A Life* (Viking, 2004).

15 Peter Gilliver, *The Making of the Oxford English Dictionary* (Oxford University Press, 2016).

16 David F. Armstrong, *The History of Gallaudet University* (Gallaudet University Press, 2014).
17 Christina Rutherford Macpherson (1895), *Waltzing Matilda manuscript notated by Christina Macpherson (the Bartlam–Roulston manuscript)*, nla.gov.au/nla.obj-23495736. Richard Magoffin, *Waltzing Matilda 1895–1995* (Robert Brown, 1995).
18 Clive Upton, David Parry & John Widdowson, *Survey of English Dialects* (Routledge, 2014).
19 George Birkbeck Hill, *Johnsonian Miscellanies* (Clarendon Press, 1897), vol. 2, p. 11. *Boswell's Life of Johnson*, 19 September 1777. Gwen Hampshire (ed.), *Elizabeth Carter 1717–1806: An Edition of some Unpublished Letters* (University of Delaware Press, 2005).
20 Shelagh Rixon and Richard Smith, *A History of IATEFL: The First 50 Years of the International Association of Teachers of English as a Foreign Language* (IATEFL, 2017).
21 David Crystal, *Language Death* (Cambridge University Press, 2000).
22 Pamphlet first published in London by Benj. Tooke, 1712. Jack Lynch (ed.), *Jonathan Swift's 'A Proposal for Correcting, Improving and Ascertaining the English Tongue'*, jacklynch.net/Texts/proposal.html.
23 John Man, *The Gutenberg Revolution* (Bantam, 2009).
24 'Behind the Name', www.behindthename.com/namedays.
25 Issues published in London by T. Gardner, 1745. Kathryn R. King, *A Political Biography of Eliza Haywood* (Routledge, 2012).
26 *The True Story of the Three Little Pigs*, by A. Wolf, as told to Jon Scieszka (Viking, 1989). David Crystal, *Language Play* (Penguin, 1998; updated 2013 at www.davidcrystal.com).
27 David Crystal, *The Disappearing Dictionary* (Macmillan, 2015).
28 Tony Crowley, *The Liverpool English Dictionary: A Record of the Language of Liverpool 1950–2015 on Historical Principles* (Liverpool University Press, 2017).
29 'How first woman stole language from tuli-tuli the beast', first published at www.Janetkagan.com, February 2005. *The Collected Kagan* (Baen Books, 2016), www.baen.com.

MARCH

1 Civil Aviation Authority, *Radiotelephony Manual*, 22nd edn, 2016, www.caa.co.uk.
2 Elias Nason, *A Memoir of Mrs Susanna Rowson* (Munsell, 1870), archive.org/details/amemoirmrsusano1nasogoog.
3 Third Person, sites.google.com/site/talkinthirdperson.
4 David Crystal, *Making Sense: The Glamorous Story of English Grammar* (Profile, 2017).
5 'Language and Literature from a Pueblo Indian Perspective', in L.A.Fiedler and A. Baker (eds), *English Literature: Opening Up the Canon* (Johns Hopkins University Press, 1979).'Language and Literature from a Pueblo Indian Perspective', www.leeann hunter.com/gender/wp-content/uploads/2012/11/SilkoLanguageLiterature.pdf.
6 *Artemus Ward in London* (Ward, Lock, 1867), p. 72. Charles Farrar Browne, *The Complete Works of Artemus Ward*, www.gutenberg.org/files/6946/6946-h/6946-h.htm.
7 Charlotte Gray, *Reluctant Genius: Alexander Graham Bell and the Passion for Invention* (Arcade, 2006).
8 Chartered Institute of Editing and Proofreading, www.ciep.uk.

9 *Memoirs of Wm. Cobbett, Esq. M.P.* (A. Mann, 1835), p. 19. William Cobbett, *A Grammar of the English Language in a Series of Letters* (William Benbow, 1818).

10 Faustin S Delany, 'A Sketch of the Life of Miss Hallie Quinn Brown', in *Bits and Odds: A Choice Selection of Recitations for School, Lyceum, and Parlor Entertainments* (Chew, 1884), p. 7. Annjennette Sophie McFarlin, Hallie Quinn Brown, *Black Woman Elocutionist*, 1845(?)–1949 (Washington State University, 1975).

11 Keith Williams, *The English Newspaper: An Illustrated History to 1900* (Springwood Books, 1977).

12 Tim Berners-Lee, *Weaving the Web: The Past, Present and Future of the World Wide Web by Its Inventor* (Orion, 1999).

13 A.A.M. Duncan (ed.), John Barbour, *The Bruce* (Canongate, 2007). Charles Jones, *The English Language in Scotland: An Introduction to Scots* (Tuckwell Press, 2001).

14 Gemma Elwin Harris, *Big Questions from Little People – Answered by Some Very Big People* (Faber & Faber, 2012). *Does My Goldfish Know Who I Am?* (Faber & Faber, 2013). David Crystal, *Listen to Your Child* (Penguin, 2nd edn, 2017).

15 Verisign, www.verissign.com.

16 John Millar (Jonas Stepšis), 'My Father Was a Smuggler', www.draugas.org/news/my-father-was-a-smuggler.

17 'The History of TESOL International Association', www.tesol.org.

18 David and Hilary Crystal, *Wordsmiths and Warriors* (Oxford University Press, 2013), ch. 41.

19 Dave Keeling, *The Little Book of Laughter* (Independent Thinking Press, 2013).

20 Jonathan Gottschall, *The Storytelling Animal: How Stories Make Us Human* (Mariner Books, 2013).

21 The Poetry Society, poetrysociety.org.uk.

22 The LaMarche and Pollak conversation, www.youtube.com/watch?v=Kyo3Qe-5S-k.

23 Allan Metcalf, *OK: The Improbable Story of America's Greatest Word* (Oxford University Press, 2010).

24 Ralph Iron (Olive Schreiner), *Story of an African Farm* (1883; Penguin, 1979), ch. 1. Ruth First and Ann Scott, *Olive Schreiner: A Biography* (Schocken, 1980).

25 *Letters of Anna Seward, Written between the Years 1784 and 1807, in Six Volumes* (Ramsay, 1811), vol. 1, letter 10, p. 79; letter 17, p. 72. Teresa Barnard, *Anna Seward: A Constructed Life* (Routledge, 2009).

26 N.F. Blake, *Caxton's Own Prose* (Deutsch, 1973), pp. 55, 57. N.F. Blake, *Caxton and His World* (Deutsch, 1969).

27 Peter Brook, *The Empty Space: A Book about the Theatre: Deadly, Holy, Rough, Immediate* (Simon & Schuster, 1968; Penguin Classics, 2008).

28 'The only surviving recording of Virginia Woolf', www.bbc.com/culture/article/20160324-the-only-surviving-recording-of-virginia-woolf. Quentin Bell, *Virginia Woolf: A Biography* (Pimlico, 1996).

29 John J. Gumperz, *Discourse Strategies* (Cambridge University Press, 1982).

30 Henry Petroski, *The Pencil: A History of Design and Circumstance* (Knopf, 1990).

31 James M. Powell, *Medieval Studies: An Introduction* (Syracuse University Press, 1992).

APRIL

1 The Unbelievable Hamlet Discovery, www.davidcrystal.com. Martin Wainwright, *The Guardian Book of April Fool's Day* (Aurum, 2007).

2 International Board on Books for Young People, www.ibby.org.

3 Bernard Weinraub, 'The Artistry of Ruth Prawer Jhabvala', *New York Times Magazine*, 11 September 1983, www.nytimes.com/1983/09/11/magazine/the-artistry-of-ruth-prawer-jhabvala.html. James Ivory, *Solid Ivory: A Memoir* (Corsair, 2021).

4 S.A. Barney, W.J. Lewis, J.A. Beach and O. Berghof (eds), *The Etymologies of Isidore of Seville* (Cambridge University Press, 2006; online 2009), www.cambridge.org/core/books/etymologies-of-isidore-of-seville.

5 Algernon Charles Swinburne, *A Century of Roundels* (Chatto & Windus, 1883), number 63. Francis O'Gorman, *Algernon Charles Swinburne: Selected Writings* (Oxford University Press, 2020).

6 AZQuotes: Isaac Asimov, www.azquotes.com/author/605-Isaac_Asimov. Isaac Asimov, *I, Asimov: A Memoir* (Doubleday, 1994).

7 Yvonne Vera, *Under the Tongue* (Baobab Books, 1996; Farrar, Straus & Giroux, 2002), ch. 11. Robert Muponde and Mandivavarira Maodzwa-Taruvinga (eds), *Sign and Taboo: Perspectives on the Poetic Fiction of Yvonne Vera* (Weaver Press, 2002).

8 Peter Bakker et al., *What is the Romani Language?* (University of Hertfordshire Press, 2000).

9 The recording can be heard here, along with some technical detail, en.wikipedia.org/wiki/Phonautograph.

10 Doris Pilkington/Nugi Garimara, *Follow the Rabbit-Proof Fence* (University of Queensland Press, 1996), ch. 7. Doris Pilkington/Nugi Garimara, *Home to Mother*, children's edition of *Follow the Rabbit-Proof Fence* (University of Queensland Press, 2006).

11 Geoffrey Hughes, *Swearing: A Social History of Foul Language, Oaths and Profanity in English* (Blackwell, 1991).

12 Beverly Cleary, *Ramona Quimby, Age 8* (Dell, 1981). Stephen Krashen, *Free Voluntary Reading* (Libraries Unlimited, 2011).

13 'Word Up: The Secret Story of Scrabble', BBC Culture, www.bbc.com/culture/article/20150911-word-up-the-secret-story-of-scrabble.

14 Helen Keller, *The Story of My Life* (1903; Penguin, 2010), ch. 4. www.gutenberg.org/ebooks/2397. Kim E. Nielsen, *Beyond the Miracle Worker: The Remarkable Life of Anne Sullivan Macy and her Extraordinary Friendship with Helen Keller* (Beacon Press, 2010).

15 House of Vigdis, english.hi.is/university/verold_vigdis_house.

16 Jane Setter, *Your Voice Speaks Volumes* (Oxford University Press, 2019).

17 R.H. Blyth, *A History of Haiku* (Greenpoint, 2022).

18 Robert A. Hall Jr, *A Life for Language: A Biographical Memoir of Leonard Bloomfield* (John Benjamins, 1990).

19 *Detached Thoughts* (1821), petercochran.files.wordpress.com/2009/03/detached_thoughts.pdf. J. Drummond Bone (ed.), *The Cambridge Companion to Byron* (Cambridge University Press, 2005).

20 Raymond Chang and Margaret Scrogin Chang, *Speaking of Chinese* (Andre Deutsch, 1980).

21 Joan Swann, Rob Page and Ronald Carter (eds), *Creativity in Language and Literature: The State of the Art* (Red Globe Press, 2011).

22 'On a Book Entitled *Lolita*', *Anchor Review* 2, 1957, pp. 1–13. *New York Times* interview, 19 April 1969, www.kulichki.com/moshkow/nabokow/Inter11.txt. Andrew Field, *Vn: The Life and Art of Vladimir Nabokov* (Crown, 1986).

23 World Book Day, www.unesco.org/en/days/world-book-and-copyright-day.

24 Anthony Trollope, *An Autobiography* (CSP Classic Texts, 2008), ch. 10. N. John Hall, *Anthony Trollope: A Biography* (Clarendon Press, 1991).

25 License Plates, en.wikipedia.org/wiki/Vehicle_registration_plate.

26 Daniel Oberhaus, *Extraterrestrial Languages* (MIT Press, 2022).

27 Kenneth Silverman, *Lightning Man* (Da Capo Press, 2003).

28 Thomas H. Johnson (ed.), *Emily Dickinson: The Complete Poems* (Faber & Faber, 1970), items 883, 1212. Edward Hirsch, *The Heart of American Poetry* (Library of America, 2022).

29 Alfred Hitchcock, in *Encyclopædia Britannica*, 14th edn (1965), 'Motion Pictures: Film Production'. Interview for *Cinema* 5 (1) (1963), p. 34; reprinted in Sidney Gottlieb (ed.), *Hitchcock on Hitchcock*, vol. 1 (1995). Patrick McGilligan, *Alfred Hitchcock: A Life in Darkness and Light* (Wiley, 2004).

30 Otto Jespersen, *Mankind, Nation and Individual* (Allen & Unwin, 1946), ch. 5, p. 74. A. Juul, H.F. Nielsen and J.E. Nielsen (eds), *A Linguist's Life* (Odense University Press, 1995), ch. 16, p. 247. Otto Jespersen, *Language: Its Nature, Development and Origin* (Allen & Unwin, 1922; Legare Street Press, 2021).

MAY

1 Jeffrey A Auerbach, *The Great Exhibition of 1851* (Yale, 1999).

2 Gordon Campbell, *Bible: The Story of the King James Version 1611–2011* (Oxford University Press, 2010), p. 87. David Crystal, *Begat: The King James Bible and the English Language* (Oxford University Press, 2011).

3 David Crystal and Hilary Crystal, *Wordsmiths and Warriors: The English Language Tourist's Guide to Britain* (Oxford University Press, 2013).

4 Michael Kaminski, *The Secret History of Star Wars* (Legacy Books, 2008).

5 Milton M. Azevedo, *Portuguese: A Linguistic Introduction* (Cambridge University Press, 2005).

6 Henry David Thoreau, *Walden: or Life in the Woods* (1854), ch. 6, 'Visitors'. Bradford Torrey, *The Writings of Henry David Thoreau: Journal*, Volume 1: *1837–1846* (Houghton Mifflin, 1906), entries at 14 July 1845, 27 July 1840. Laura Dassow Walls, *Henry David Thoreau: A Life* (University of Chicago Press, 2017).

7 Elizabeth Isele, 'Casey Miller and Kate Swift: Women Who Dared to Disturb the Lexicon', Virginia Polytechnic, 1994, scholar.lib.vt.edu/ejournals/old-WILLA/fall94/h2–isele.html. Casey Miller and Kate Swift, *The Handbook of Nonsexist Writing: For Writers, Editors, and Speakers* (Lippincott Williams & Wilkins, 1980).

8 Allen Mawer, *Place-Names and History* (University of Liverpool Press, 1922). Caroline Taggart, *The Book of English Place Names* (Ebury Press, 2011).

9 Betty Patchin Greene, 'A Talk with Freya Stark', *Aramco World*, September/October 1977, archive.aramcoworld.com/issue/197705/a.talk.with.freya.stark.htm. Freya Stark, *A Winter in Arabia* (John Murray, 1940), 6 January, p. 93. Jane Fletcher Geniesse, *Passionate Nomad: The Life of Freya Stark* (Modern Library, 2001).

10 Thomas Young's review of *Adelung* in *The Quarterly Review* 10 (10), October 1813, Article 12. Andrew Robinson, *The Last Man who Knew Everything* (Oneworld, 2006).

11 Douglas Adams, *The Hitchhiker's Guide to the Galaxy* (Pan, 1979), ch. 5. Douglas Adams and John Lloyd, *The Meaning of Liff* (Pan, 1983), Preface. Douglas Adams, *The Ultimate Hitchhiker's Guide* (Portland House, 1997).

12 Edward Lear, *A Book of Nonsense* (Frederick Warne, 1846). G. Legman (ed.), *The Limerick* (Bell, 1964).

13 Grace Warrack (ed.), *Revelations of Divine Love* (Chump Change, 1901; Oxford University Press, 2015). Jamina Ramirez, *Julian of Norwich: A Very Brief History* (SPCK, 2017).

14 Paul Ferris (ed.), *Dylan Thomas: The Collected Letters* (Macmillan, 1985), 21 December 1933, p. 73; 21 May 1934, p. 137. Andrew Lycett, *Dylan Thomas: A New Life* (Weidenfeld & Nicolson, 2003).

15 Gelett Burgess, *Burgess Unabridged: A New Dictionary of Words You Have Always Needed* (Frederick A. Stokes, 1914; Facsimile Publisher, 2015). Gelett Burgess, *Are You a Bromide?* (Huebsch, 1906).

16 Year 1763 in James Boswell, *Life of Samuel Johnson* (Charles Dilly, 1791; Pomona Press, 2006). Marlies K. Danziger and Frank Brady, *Boswell: The Great Biographer, 1789–1795* (McGraw Hill, 1989).

17 Anna Brownell Jameson, *A Commonplace Book of Thoughts, Memories and Fancies* (Appleton, 1855; Kessinger, 2007), p. 60. Clara Thomas, *Love and Work Enough: The Life of Anna Jameson* (University of Toronto Press, 1967).

18 Ottar Grepstad, 'Language Museums of the World', Centre for Norwegian Language and Literature, 2018, www.nynorsk.no/wp-content/uploads/2020/02/814-20180314-Language-museums-OG.pdf.

19 *John Betjeman's Collected Poems* (John Murray, 3rd edn, 1973), pp. 157, 254, 293. Bevis Hillier, *John Betjeman: The Biography* (John Murray, 2007).

20 Randolph Quirk, Sidney Greenbaum, Geoffrey Leech and Jan Svartvik, *A Comprehensive Grammar of the English Language* (Longman, 1985).

21 UN World Day, www.un.org/en/observances/cultural-diversity-day.

22 Arthur Conan Doyle, *Through the Magic Door*, serialized in *Cassell's Magazine*, December 1906–November 1907, ch. 1, www.arthur-conan-doyle.com/index.php/Through_the_Magic_Door. Andrew Lycett, *Conan Doyle: The Man Who Created Sherlock Holmes* (Weidenfeld & Nicolson, 2008).

23 Eric Partridge, *A Dictionary of Slang and Unconventional English* (Routledge, 1937), Preface. David Crystal (ed.), *Eric Partridge: In His Own Words* (Andre Deutsch, 1980).

24 Stuart A.P. Murray, *The Library: An Illustrated History* (ALA Editions, 2009).

25 Bede, *The Ecclesiastical History of the English People* (Oxford University Press, 2008), ch. 1. David Crystal, *The Stories of English* (Penguin, 2004).

26 Kate Loveman (ed.), *The Diary of Samel Pepys* (Everyman, 2018), entries for 6 August 1665, 9 August 1667. Claire Tomalin, *Samuel Pepys: The Unequalled Self* (Knopf, 2002).

27 *The Statutes at Large of England and of Great Britain* (Eyre & Strahan, 1811), vol. 4, p. 678. James Shapiro, *1606: Shakespeare and the Year of Lear* (Faber & Faber, 2016).

28 Edwidge Danticat, interview with Maya Angelou, 'A Phenomenal Woman', *Playboy*, 1999. *I Know Why The Caged Bird Sings* (Random House, 1969), ch. 29. *The Collected Autobiographies of Maya Angelou* (Random House, 2004).

29 Clayton Lindsay Smith, *The History of Trade Marks* (Literary Licensing, 2012).

30 Rob Pope, *Creativity: Theory, History, Practice* (Routledge, 2005).

31 Walt Whitman, 'Slang in America', *The North American Review* 141, November 1885. John Hollander (ed.), *Leaves of Grass: The Complete 1855 and 1891–92 Editions* (Library of America, 2011).

JUNE

1 Mitchell Carnell, *Say Something Nice: Be a Lifter @ Work* (Charleston Publishing, 2012). Patricia Wallace, *The Psychology of the Internet* (Cambridge University Press, 2001).

2 A. Hayford, 'Kobina (A Little African Boy)', in Adelaide M. Cromwell, *An African Victorian Feminist: The Life and Times of Adelaide Smith Casely Hayford 1868–1960* (Routledge, 2004). *Sierra Leone Weekly News*, 5 March 1949, p. 3.

3 Eirini Kartsaki (ed.), *On Repetition: Writing, Performance and Art* (Intellect Books, 2016).

4 Sally McClain, *Navajo Weapon* (Books Beyond Borders, 1994).

5 Margaret Drabble, *A Writer's Britain: Landscape in Literature* (Thames & Hudson, 1979), Foreword. Glenda Leeming, *Margaret Drabble* (Northcote House, 2004).

6 Philip Durkin, *Borrowed Words: A History of Loanwords in English* (Oxford University Press, 2015).

7 *Memoirs of the Life and Writings of Lindley Murray* (Palala Press, 2016).

8 Grace Tierney, *Words the Vikings Gave Us* (Wordfoolery Press, 2021).

9 International Council on Archives. www.ica.org/en.

10 Douglas Adams, *The Hitchhiker's Guide to the Galaxy* (Pan, 1979), ch. 21. György Moldova, *Ballpoint: A Tale of Genius and Grit, Perilous Times, and the Invention that Changed the Way We Write* (New Europe Books, 2012).

11 Discoveries, www.gutenberg.org/files/5134/5134-h/5134-h.htm. Ian Donaldson, *Ben Jonson: A Life* (Oxford University Press, 2011).

12 David Crystal, *Pronouncing Shakespeare: The Globe Experiment* (Cambridge University Press, 2005; 2016).

13 'An Italian Singer's Views of England', Frances Burney, *Journals and Letters* (Penguin Classics, 2001). www.gutenberg.org/files/5826/5826-h/5826-h. htm#link2H_4_0103. Claire Harman, *Fanny Burney: A Biography* (HarperCollins, 2001).

14 Alexander John Ellis, *On Early English Pronunciation* (Philological Society, 1875; Forgotten Books, 2018), vol. 4, ch. 21. Entry in *Oxford Dictionary of National Biography* (Oxford University Press, 2004).

15 David Carpenter, *Magna Carta* (Penguin Classics, 2015).

16 Anthony Burgess, *Joysprick: An Introduction to the Language of James Joyce* (André Deutsch, 1973), p. 17. Edna O'Brien, *James Joyce: Author of Ulysses* (Weidenfeld & Nicolson, 2020).

17 J.R. Firth, *The Tongues of Men* (Watts, 1937; Oxford University Press, 1964), ch. 10. F.R. Palmer (ed.), *Selected Papers of J.R. Firth* (Longman, 1968).

18 'Thought and Word', in Henry Festing Jones (ed.), *The Note-Books of Samuel Butler* (Fifield, 1912). Peter Raby, *Samuel Butler: A Biography* (Vintage, 1991).

19 Laurie Bauer, *English Word-formation* (Cambridge University Press, 1983).

20 *The Diary of John Evelyn* (Everyman, 2006), www.gutenberg.org/files/41218/41218-h/41218-h.htm.

21 David Crystal, *Sounds Appealing: The Passionate Story of English Pronunciation* (Profile Books, 2018), ch. 6.

22 Simon Winchester, *The Surgeon of Crowthorne* (Viking, 1998).

23 Janine Vangool, *The Typewriter: A Graphic History of the Beloved Machine* (UPPERCASE Publishing, 2015).

24 Ambrose Bierce, *The Devil's Dictionary* (1906; Bloomsbury, 2008). Carey McWilliams, *Ambrose Bierce: A Biography* (Literary Licensing, 2011).

25 Judith Wright, *Phantom Dwelling* (Angus & Robertson, 1985). Veronica Brady, *South of My Days: Judith Wright Biography* (Angus & Robertson, 1998).

26 Paul Baker, *American and British English* (Cambridge University Press, 2017).

27 Robert Cawdrey, *A Table Alphabeticall of Hard Usual English Words* (Edmund Weaver, 1604), reprinted as *The First English Dictionary* (Bodleian, 2007). Entry in *Oxford Dictionary of National Biography* (Oxford University Press, 2004).

28 Jan Francis Schiller, *Paul Broca* (Oxford University Press, 1992).

29 James Maguire, *American Bee: The National Spelling Bee and the Culture of Word Nerds* (Rodale Books, 2006).

30 P. Seargeant and C. Tagg (eds), *The Language of Social Media: Identity and Community on the Internet* (Palgrave Macmillan, 2014).

JULY

1 Harriet Beecher Stowe, *Oldtown Folks* (Fields, Osgood, 1869; West Margin, 2022). Katie Griffiths, *Harriet Beecher Stowe: Author and Abolitionist* (Cavendish Square, 2016).

2 David Crystal, *The Gift of the Gab: How Eloquence Works* (Yale, 2016).

3 David Crystal, *The Oxford Dictionary of Original Shakespearean Pronunciation* (Oxford University Press, 2016).

4 Noah Webster, *Dissertations on the English Language* (Isaiah Thomas, 1789), www.gutenberg.org/files/45738/45738-h/45738-h.htm. Stuart Berg Flexner, *I Hear America Talking* (Touchstone, 1976).

5 Christine Watson, 'Autobiographical Writing as a Healing Process: Interview with Alice Masak French', *Canadian Literature* 167, 2000, pp. 32–42. Alice Masak French, *My Name is Masak* (Peguis, 1977).

6 Jean Stein interview with William Faulkner, *Paris Review* 4, 1956, pp. 28–52; reprinted in Malcolm Cowley (ed.), *Writers at Work* (Viking, 1958), pp. 119–41. Carl Rollyson, *The Life of William Faulkner: The Past Is Never Dead, 1897–1934* (University of Virginia Press, 2020).

7 Richard Brinsley Sheridan, *The Critic*, 1779, act 1, scene 2. Linda Kelly, *Richard Brinsley Sheridan: A Life* (Faber & Faber, 2009).

8 Raja Rao, *Kanthapura* (Orient, 1938), Foreword. J.P. Tripathi, *Raja Rao: the Fictionist* (B.R. Publishing Corporation, 2003).

9 Franz Boas, *Introduction to the Handbook of American Indian Languages* (1911, reprinted by Georgetown University Press), pp. 28–9, 31. Rosemary Lévy Zumwalt, *Franz Boas: The Emergence of the Anthropologist* (UNP Nebraska, 2019).

10 Edmund Clerihew Bentley, *Biography for Beginners* (Werner Laurie, 1905), *Baseless Biography* (Constable, 1939). E. Clerihew Bentley, *The First Clerihews* (Oxford University Press, 1982).

11 Thomas Bowdler, *The Family Shakespeare* (Longman, 1807), Preface. Noel Perrin, *Dr Bowdler's Legacy* (Godine, 1992).

12 David Crystal, *Let's Talk: How English Conversation Works* (Oxford University Press, 2020).

13 Sara Yasin, interview extracts at Index on Censorship, 30 October 2012, www.indexoncensorship.org/2012/10/nigeria-wole-soyinka-poet-writer. Wole Soyinka, *Aké: The Years of Childhood* (Collings, 1981).

14 Desiderius Erasmus and Richard Taverner, *Proverbs or Adages* (Scholars' Facsimiles and Reprints, 1977). Christopher Hollis, *Erasmus* (Cluny Media, 2022).

15 David Crystal, *Internet Linguistics* (Routledge, 2011).

16 Interview by Kristin L. Matthews, 'Renaissance Woman', in *Callaloo* 39 (3) 2016. 'How We Speak' in *Clarity as Concept: A Poet's Perspective* (Third World Press, 2006). Mari Evans, *I Am a Black Woman* (Morrow, 1970).

17 Marcel Danesi, *The Semiotics of Emoji: The Rise of Visual Language in the Age of the Internet* (Bloomsbury, 2016).

18 John Hart, *An Orthographie* (W. Seres, 1569; Scolar Press, 1969), Preface. Valerie Yule and Ishi Yasuko, 'Spelling Reform', in *The Routledge Handbook of the English Writing System* (Routledge, 2016).

19 'An Appeal for Cultural Equity', *World of Music* 14 (2), 1972. www.culturalequity.org/alan-lomax/appeal. 'Song Structure and Social Structure', *Ethnology* 1 (4), 1962, pp. 425–51. John Szwed, *The Man Who Recorded the World: A Biography of Alan Lomax* (Arrow, 2011).

20 Deborah Schiffrin, *Discourse Markers* (Cambridge University Press, 1987), Preface. Michael Stubbs, *Discourse Analysis* (Blackwell, 1983).

21 Jonathan Miller, *The Body in Question* (Jonathan Cape, 1978), p. 95. Kate Bassett, *In Two Minds: A Biography of Jonathan Miller* (Bloomsbury, 2012).

22 William Hayter, *Spooner: A Biography* (Virgin, 1977).

23 Jerry Seinfeld, *Seinlanguage* (Bantam, 1993).

24 Robert Graves, *On English Poetry* (Knopf, 1922), ch. 33. Bruce King, *Robert Graves: A Bibliography* (iC-Haus, 2008).

25 *Specimens of the Table Talk of S.T. Coleridge* (John Murray, 1837), 3 July 1833, 27 May 1830. *Biographia Literaria*, ed. Adam Roberts (Edinburgh University Press, 2014).

26 Aleksander Korzhenkov, *Zamenhof: The Life, Works and Ideas of the Author of Esperanto* (Mondial, 2010).

27 Hilaire Belloc, 'A Guide to Boring', in *A Conversation with a Cat and Others* (Cassell, 1931). Hilaire Belloc, *Essays* (Ghose, 2014).

28 Letter to Richard Watson Dixon, 6 October 1878, in *Gerard Manley Hopkins: Selected Letters*, ed. Catherine Phillips (Oxford University Press, 1991). Norman White, *Hopkins: A Literary Biography* (Oxford University Press, 1995).

29 Braj Kachru, 'Standards, Codification and Sociolinguistic Realism: The English Language in the Outer Circle', in R. Quirk and H.G. Widdowson (eds), *English in the World* (Cambridge University Press, 1985), p. 12. Braj Kachru, *The Alchemy of English* (Pergamon, 1986).

30 LeRoy Robinson interview in *Naosite* 67 (4), 1988 (Nagasaki University); 'The Ruined Gopuram' on e.g. sites.google.com/site/jeanarasanayagam. Jean Arasanayagam, *The Life of the Poet* (Sarasavi, 2017).

31 *Diderot's Early Philosophical Works*, trans. Margaret Jourdain (Open Court Publishing, 1916), p. 173. tems.umn.edu/pdf/Diderot-Letters-on-the-Blind-and-the-Deaf.pdf. P.N. Furbank, *Diderot: A Critical Biography* (Knopf, 1992).

AUGUST

1 Arnold Kellett, *Ee By Gum, Lord! The Gospels in Broad Yorkshire* (Smith Settle, 1996), p. 1. Yorkshire Dialect Society. www.yorkshiredialectsociety.org.uk.

2 'Note on Vaudeville Voices', in Leroi Jones (ed.), *The Moderns: An Anthology of New Writing in America* (Corinth Books, 1963), p. 345. William Burroughs, 'Note on Vaudeville Voices', www.writing.upenn.edu/~afilreis/88v/burroughs-cutup.html.

3 Jennifer Reese, *The Salon Interview*, 26 February 1998, www.salon.com/1998/02/26/cov_si_26int. P.D. James, *Time to Be in Earnest: A Fragment of Autobiography* (Faber & Faber, 2000).

4 'Byron and Shelley on the Character of Hamlet', *New Monthly Magazine* 29, October 1830, p. 330, supposedly recorded by an eyewitness, and attributed to Mary Shelley. *A Defence of Poetry*, www.gutenberg.org/files/5428/5428-h/5428-h.htm. John Worthen, *The Life of Percy Bysshe Shelley: A Critical Biography* (Wiley-Blackwell, 2019).

5 Toni Morrison, Nobel Lecture, 7 December 1993, www.nobelprize.org/prizes/literature/1993/morrison/lecture. Barbara Kramer, *Toni Morrison: A Biography of a Nobel Prize-Winning Writer* (Enslow, 2013).

6 Robin Dunbar, *Grooming, Gossip and the Evolution of Language* (Faber & Faber, 1997; 2004).

7 Global Speakers Federation, www.globalspeakersfederation.net.

8 Terry Nation, *Doctor Who Magazine* interview, 30 September 2009, drwhointerviews.wordpress.com/category/terry-nation. Alwyn W. Turner, *Terry Nation: The Man Who Invented the Daleks* (Aurum, 2013).

9 Los Pinos Declaration, en.unesco.org/sites/default/files/los_pinos_declaration_170720_en.pdf.

10 Julia Mood Peterkin, 'The Wind', *Poetry*, November 1923, p. 60. Frank Durham (ed.), *The Collected Short Stories of Julia Peterkin* (University of South Carolina Press, 1970).

11 Chris Weigant interview in *Huffington Post*, 25 May 2011, huffpost.netblogpro.com/entry/exclusive-interview-with_b_206057. Geoffrey Nunberg, *The Years of Talking Dangerously* (PublicAffairs US, 2009).

12 Joyce Pettis interview, *Melus* 17 (4), Winter 1991–2, pp. 117–29. 'From the Poets in the Kitchen', *New York Times*, 9 January 1983. Paule Marshall, *Triangular Road: A Memoir* (Basic Civitas Books, 2009).

13 Joyce Carol Thomas, *The Blacker the Berry* (Amistad Books for Young Readers, 2022). Interview reported in *Washington Post*, 23 August 2016. Joyce Carol Thomas, *Marked by Fire* (Jump at the Sun, 2007).

14 *Scots Magazine*, July 1761, p. 389, digital.nls.uk/learning/scottish-enlightenment/source/description-of-a-lecture-series-given-in-edinburgh-by-thomas-sheridan-1761. Thomas Sheridan, *A Course of Lectures on Elocution* (1761; Gale ECCO, 2010).

15 E. Nesbit, *Wings and the Child* (Hodder & Stoughton, 1913), ch. 9, p. 90. Elisabeth Galvin, *The Extraordinary Life of E. Nesbit* (Pen & Sword, 2018).

16 Marcus Tullius Cicero, trans. Michael Fontaine, *How to Tell a Joke: An Ancient Guide to the Art of Humor* (Princeton University Press, 2021).

17 William J. Clinton Statements, Office of the Independent Counsel, 9 September 1998, vol. 3, Document Supplement, Part A, p. 510. David Crystal, *The Story of Be* (Oxford University Press, 2017).

18 John White, 'Narrative of His Voyage', in *The Roanoke Voyages 1584–1590* (Hakluyt Society, 1955), vol. 2, pp. 598–622. James Horn (ed.), *Captain John Smith: Writings, with Other Narratives of Roanoke, Jamestown, and the First English Settlement of America* (Library of America, 2007).

19 'Oafishness Sells Good, Like an Advertisement Should', in *You Can't Get There From Here* (Dent, 1957). *The Old Dog Barks Backwards* (Little Brown, 1972). Linell Smith and Isabel Eberstadt (eds), *Candy is Dandy: The Best of Ogden Nash* (Mandarin, 1983).

20 Aug Jim Bell, *The Interstellar Age: Inside the Forty-Year Voyager Mission* (Dutton, 2016).

21 Lady Mary Wortley Montagu, *The Turkish Embassy Letters* (Virago, 1994), 16 March 1718. Jo Willett, *The Pioneering Life of Mary Wortley Montagu: Scientist and Feminist* (Pen & Sword History, 2021).

22 Quotations from various websites, such as azquotes.com. Barry Day, *Dorothy Parker: In Her Own Words* (Taylor, 2004).

23 Tom McArthur, *Longman Lexicon of Contemporary English* (Longman, 1981), p. vi. Tom McArthur, *Worlds of Reference* (Cambridge University Press, 1986).

24 'The Library of Babel', in James Irby (ed.), *Labyrinths: Selected Stories & Other Writings* (New Directions, 2007). Edwin Williamson, *Borges: A Life* (Viking, 2004).

25 Thomas Dekker, *The Bel-man of London* (Nathaniell Butter, 1608), quod.lib.umich.edu/e/eebo/A20042.0001.001/1:4?rgn=div1;view=fulltext. Thomas Dekker, *The Shoemaker's Holiday* (Bloomsbury, 2017).

26 William and Elizebeth Friedman, *The Shakespearean Ciphers Examined: An Analysis of Cryptographic Systems Used as Evidence that Some Author Other Than William Shakespeare Wrote the Plays Commonly Attributed to Him* (Cambridge University Press, 1957), ch. 1. G. Stuart Smith, *A Life in Code: Pioneer Cryptanalyst Elizebeth Smith Friedman* (McFarland, 2017).

27 Neville Alexander, *Language Policy and National Unity in South Africa/Azania* (Buchu Books, 1989), p. 61. Allan Zinn, *Non-Racialism in South Africa: The Life and Times of Neville Alexander* (Sun Press, 2016).

28 S. Chapman, *Paul Grice: Philosopher and Linguist* (Palgrave Macmillan, 2005).

29 Sybil Marshall, 'Natural Development', in *An Experiment in Education* (Cambridge University Press, 1963), ch. 3.

30 *Beyond Babel: English on the World Stage*, Infonation (Foreign and Commonwealth Office, 2002), Programme 2, ch. 4. John Kani, *Nothing But the Truth: A Play* (Wits University Press, 2003).

31 'Autobiography vs. Biography vs. Memoir', www.blurb.com/blog/memoirs-biographies-autobiographies.

SEPTEMBER

1 Simon Garfield, *To the Letter: A Journey Through a Vanishing World* (Avery, 2013).

2 Laura Riding, *Collected Poems* (Cassell, 1938; repr. Trent Editions, 2011). 'The Promise of Words', *London Review of Books* 17 (7), 7 September 1995, pp. 23–4. Elizabeth Friedmann, *A Mannered Grace: The Life of Laura (Riding) Jackson* (Norton, 2005).

3 George Firmage (ed.), *E.E. Cummings, A Miscellany Revised* (October House, 1965), pp. 314–15. (Pantheon, 2014). Susan Cheever, *e.e. cummings: A Life* (Pantheon, 2014).

4 Andrew Blum, *The Weather Machine: A Journey Inside the Forecast* (HarperCollins, 2019).

5 'How I Write', *Wordsetc: South African Literary Journal*, First Quarter, 2011, p. 32. Lindy Stiebel and Michael Chapman (eds), *Writing Home: Lewis Nkosi on South African Writing* (UKZN Press, 2016).

6 William Bradford, *Of Plimoth Plantation* (1620; Wright & Potter, 1898), Second Book, p. 114, www.gutenberg.org/files/24950/24950-h/24950-h.htm#a1620. Nathaniel Philbrick, *Mayflower: A Story of Courage, Community, and War* (Viking, 2006).

7 C.K. Ogden and I.A. Richards, *The Meaning of Meaning* (Kegan Paul, 1923).

8 Geoff Barton, *Don't Call it Literacy! What Every Teacher Needs to Know about Speaking, Listening, Reading and Writing* (Routledge, 2012).

9 Kurt W. Beyer, *Grace Hopper and the Invention of the Information Age* (MIT Press, 2009).

10 Mary Wollstonecraft, *Thoughts on the Education of Daughters* (J. Johnson, 1787), chapters on 'Moral Discipline', 'Reading'). Lyndall Gordon, *Vindication: A Life of Mary Wollstonecraft* (Virago, 2006).

11 'Romeo and Juliet', first piece in *Code Poems* (Open Book Publications, 1968). Charles Bernstein interview in *LINEbreak*, 1995, writing.upenn.edu/epc/authors/weiner/Weiner-Hannah_LINEbreak_1995_full-transcript.pdf. Geoff Ward, *Language Poetry and the American Avant-Garde* (Ryburn, 1993), p. 3.

12 H.L. Mencken, *Prejudices, Third Series* (Cosimo, 1922), ch. 7, p. 146. 'Gamalielese', *Baltimore Sun*, 7 March 1921. Terry Teachout, *The Skeptic: A Life of H.L. Mencken* (HarperCollins, 2004).

13 Dedicatory letter in *The Book of the Courtier* (Penguin, 1976). John Strype, *The Life of the Learned Sir John Cheke* (John Wyat, 1705; Franklin Classics, 2018).

14 Cynthia Haven interview in *The Cortland Review*, 14 November 2000, web.stanford.edu/~clh/articles/stevenson.html. Anne Stevenson, *About Poems and How Poems Are Not About* (Bloodaxe, 2017).

15 Preface, *Lyrical Ballads*, 2nd edn (Longman, 1801). A.S. Byatt, *Unruly Times: Wordsworth and Coleridge in Their Time* (Nelson, 1970; Vintage, 1997).

16 Geoff P. Smith, *Growing Up with Tok Pisin* (Battlebridge, 2002).

17 David Crystal, 'Going Especially Careful in *The Third Man*', www.davidcrystal.com. Letter to Eva Kearney, 28 April 1978, in Richard Greene (ed.), *Graham Greene: A Life in Letters* (Abacus, 2008), p. 350. Dermot Gilvary and Darren J.N. Middleton (eds), *Dangerous Edges of Graham Greene: Journeys with Saints and Sinners* (Continuum, 2011).

18 David Crystal (ed.), *Dr Johnson's Dictionary: An Anthology* (Penguin, 2005).

19 Robert Louis Stevenson, *Treasure Island* (Cassell, 1883), ch. 28. International Talk Like a Pirate Day, nationaltoday.com/talk-like-pirate-day.

20 David Crystal, *The Story of English in 100 Words* (Profile, 2011), number 82, Doobry.

21 Walter Scott, *Chronicles of the Canongate* (Cadell, 1827), ch. 6. Graham Tulloch, *The Language of Walter Scott* (Routledge, 1999).

22 David Crystal, *Evolving English: One Language, Many Voices* (British Library, 2010), pp. 87, 141. Tirthankar Roy, *The East India Company: The World's Most Powerful Corporation* (Penguin, 2016).

23 Anne E. Baker et al. (eds), *The Linguistics of Sign Languages* (Benjamins, 2016).

24 David Crystal, *Making a Point: The Pernickety Story of English Punctuation* (Profile Books, 2015).

25 Joshua Steele, *The Melody and Measure of Speech* (J. Almon, 1775; Scolar Press, 1969), pt 1, p. 4. David Crystal, *Prosodic Systems and Intonation in English* (Cambridge University Press, 1969).

26 European Day of Languages, edl.ecml.at.

27 *William Safire on Language* (Times Books, 1980), blurb and introduction. William Safire, *Take My Word for It* (Henry Holt, 1987).

28 Roger Beard and Andrew Burnell, *Language Play and Children's Literacy* (UCL Institute of Education Press, 2021).

29 *The Rudiments of Grammar for the English-Saxon Tongue* (Bowyer, 1715), Preface, p. ix,

www.gutenberg.org/files/15329/15329-h/15329-h.htm. Elizabeth Elstob, in the *Oxford Dictionary of National Biography*, doi.org/10.1093/ref:odnb/8761.

30 David Bellos, *Is That a Fish in Your Ear? Translation and the Meaning of Everything* (Penguin, 2012).

OCTOBER

1 Martin Willoughby, *A History of Postcards* (Studio, 1992).

2 Dave Moss, *Number Plates: A History of Vehicle Registration in Britain* (Shire Publications, 2006).

3 Richard K. Bass, *GMDSS: A Guide for Global Maritime Distress Safety System*, 2nd edn (Tele-Technology, 2007).

4 Ten codes, en.wikipedia.org/wiki/Ten-code.

5 Teachers' day, www.unesco.org/en/days/teachers-day.

6 Interview with Alexandra Johnson, *Christian Science Monitor*, 23 March 1978, pp. 20–21. 'Invitation to Miss Marianne Moore', in *Poems: The Centenary Edition* (Chatto & Windus, 2011). George Monteiro (ed.), *Conversations with Elizabeth Bishop* (University Press of Mississippi, 1996).

7 'False Friends-like', in *Poems of Rural Life in the Dorset Dialect* (Kegan Paul, 1879), Second Collection, p. 290. Alan Chedzoy, *William Barnes: A Life of the Dorset Poet* (Dovecote Press, 1985).

8 'Essay on Conversation', 1741–2, fullreads.com/essay/an-essay-on-conversation. Martin C. Battestin and Ruthe R. Battestin, *Henry Fielding: A Life* (Taylor & Francis, 2019).

9 W.B. Jones, *The Story of the Post Office, Containing a History of the World's Postal Service* (Forgotten Books, 2012).

10 'Street Names' in *Next Sunday* (Pearl, 1956); repr. in R.K. Narayan, *A Writer's Nightmare: Selected Essays 1958–1988* (Penguin, 1988), p. 94.

11 *The Second Person Singular and Other Essays* (Oxford University Press, 1922; Kessinger, 2010). 'Composure' and 'The Little Language', in *In a Book Room*, repr. in *Essays*, Centenary Edition (Newman, 1947), pp. 50, 55. June Badeni, *The Slender Tree: A Life of Alice Meynell* (Tabb House, 1981).

12 Francois Greeff, *The Hidden Code of Cryptic Crosswords* (Foulsham, 2003), pp. 103ff. Roger Millington, *The Strange World of the Crossword* (Hobbs, 1974).

13 The English Project: www.englishproject.org.

14 'Letter case', at en.wikipedia.org/wiki/Letter_case.

15 Cicely Berry, *Voice and the Actor* (Macmillan, 1974). Cicely Berry, *The Actor and the Text* (Virgin, 1987), Introduction.

16 Noah Webster, *The American Dictionary of the English Language* (S. Converse, 1828), Preface. A.P. Cowie (ed.), *The Oxford History of English Lexicography* (Clarendon Press, 2009), vol. 1.

17 In Christopher Bigsby, *Arthur Miller* (Weidenfeld & Nicolson, 2008), p. 154. Notebook text in Bigsby, 'Arthur Miller: Poet', *Michigan Quarterly Review* 37 (4), 1998.

18 Developmental language disorders, radld.org.

19 'Our All-American Almanac' in Nancy Boyd, *Distressing Dialogues* (Harper, 1924). Nancy Milford, *Savage Beauty: The Life of Edna St. Vincent Millay* (Random House, 2002).

20 David J. Smith, *Air Traffic Control Handbook*, 11th edn (Crecy, 2021).

21 Marilyn May Vihman, *Phonological Development* (Blackwell, 1996).

22 David Crystal, *Words in Time and Place* (Oxford University Press, 2014).

23 Harold Orton, 'A New Survey of Dialectal English', *Journal of the Lancashire Dialect Society* 2, p. 6. Harold Orton and Martyn F. Wakelin (eds), *The Southern Counties*, vol. 4 of *Survey of English Dialects: Basic Material* (Arnold, 1967), pp. 247, 343. Clive Upton et al., *Survey of English Dialects: The Dictionary and Grammar* (Routledge, 1994; 2014).

24 Sarah Josepha Hale, *Mrs. Hale's Receipts for the Million* (Peterson, 1857), www. gutenberg.org/files/46254/46254-h/46254-h.htm. Melanie Kirkpatrick, *Lady Editor: Sarah Josepha Hale and the Making of the Modern American Woman* (Encounter, 2021).

25 Simon Horobin, *Chaucer's Language* (Red Globe Press, 2012).

26 Simon Keynes and Michael Lapidge (eds), *Alfred the Great* (Penguin, 1983), p. 123. Justin Pollard, *Alfred the Great* (John Murray, 2005).

27 Ntozake Shange, 'lady in brown', in *For Colored Girls...* (Collier Books, 1989). Interview by Jamara Wakefield for *Shondaland*, 4 December 2017, www.shondaland. com/live/a13999488/ntozake-shange-interview. Ntozake Shange, *Wild Beauty: New and Selected Poems* (2017; Simon & Schuster, 2022).

28 Interview with Drue Heinz, 'The Art of Poetry' 71, *The Paris Review* 134, Spring 1995. Jonathan Bate, *Ted Hughes: The Unauhorised Life* (Collins, 2016).

29 *Sir Walter Raleighs instructions to his sonne and to posterity* (Benjamin Fisher, 1632; EEBO Editions, 2010), pp. 49, 51, 53. Penny Williams, *Sir Walter Raleigh: In Life and Legend* (Bloomsbury, 2011).

30 R. Allen Gardner (ed.), *Teaching Sign Language to Chimpanzees* (SUNY Press, 1989).

31 Louise DeSalvo, *The Art of Slow Writing* (Macmillan, 2014), Introduction. Louise DeSalvo, *Writing As a Way of Healing: How Telling Our Stories Transforms Our Lives* (Harper San Francisco, 1999).

NOVEMBER

1 Autistic Self Advocacy Network, autisticadvocacy.org. Temple Grandin, *The Autistic Brain: Thinking across the Spectrum* (Rider, 2014).

2 Samuel Fanous (ed.), *Epitaphs: A Dying Art* (Bodleian Publishing, 2016).

3 Walter Redfern, *Cliches and Coinages* (Wiley-Blackwell, 1989).

4 Interview with Morgan McComb, in '"Everything is Here and Now":The Polyvocal Poetry of Naomi Long Madgett' (MA thesis, University of Kansas, 2019), p. 89; includes the extract from 'Nearing Jordan', p. 90. Naomi Long Madgett, *Pilgrim Journey* (Lotus, 2006).

5 Title essay and interview in *Mozart and Leadbelly: Stories and Essays* (Knopf, 2005). Ernest J. Gaines, *Lesson Before Dying* (Knopf, 1997).

6 Richard Carew, 'An Epistle concerning the Excellencies of the English Tongue' (Jaggard, 1603), www.gutenberg.org/cache/epub/9878/pg9878.html. S. Mendyk, 'Richard Carew (1555–1620)', in *Oxford Dictionary of National Biography* (Oxford University Press, 2004).

7 'Celebrating the History of Talking Books', www.rnib.org.uk/reading-services/ celebrating-history-talking-books.

8 John Pollack, *The Pun Also Rises* (Gotham Books, 2011).

9 National Collective transcript, www.nationalcollective.com/2013/07/03/

janet-paisley-in-defence-of-the-scots-language. Billy Kay, *Scots: The Mither Tongue* (Mainstream, 2006).

10 World Science Day, www.un.org/en/observances/world-science-day.

11 A.P. Herbert, *What a Word!* (Methuen, 1935), title page, p. 240. A.P. Herbert, *A.P.H.: His Life and Times* (Heinemann, 1970).

12 Jenny Uglow, *Elizabeth Gaskell: A Habit of Stories* (Farrar Straus & Giroux, 1993).

13 Dell Hymes, *Foundations in Sociolinguistics: An Ethnographic Approach* (Tavistock, 1974), p. 62. Dell Hymes, *Now I Know Only So Far: Essays in Ethnopoetics* (University of Nebraska Press, 2003).

14 David Hendy, *The BBC: A People's History* (Profile Books, 2022).

15 Interview by Donald Hall, 'The Art of Poetry' 4, *The Paris Review* 26, Summer–Fall 1961. 'Poetry', in Alfred Kreynborg (ed.), *Others for 1919: An Anthology of the New Verse* (Nicholas L. Brown, 1920). Linda Leavell, *Holding On Upside Down: The Life and Work of Marianne Moore* (Farrar Straus & Giroux, 2013).

16 Interview by Charles H. Rowell, *Calaloo* 13 (1), 1990, pp. 86–101. Ezenwa-Ohaeto, *Chinua Achebe: A Biography* (Indiana University Press, 1997).

17 National Unfriend Day, nationaltoday.com/national-unfriend-day.

18 Interview by Oliver Burkeman, 'Atwood Sign of the Times Draws Blank', *Guardian*, 6 March 2006. LongPen technology: syngrafii.com/solutions/longpen.

19 Chard deNiord, 'Ruth Stone: An Interview', *American Poetry Review*, July–August 2010, pp. 49–54. 'The Wound' and 'The Poetry Factory', in *Ordinary Words* (Paris Press, 2000). Bianca Stone (ed.), *Essential Ruth Stone* (Copper Canyon, 2020).

20 Simon Stanford interview (transcript with audio), 26 April 2005, www.nobelprize.org/prizes/literature/1991/gordimer/interview. Ronald Suresh Roberts, *No Cold Kitchen: A Biography of Nadine Gordimer* (Real African Publishers, 2001).

21 World Hello Day, www.worldhelloday.org.

22 George Eliot, *Adam Bede* (John Blackwood, 1859), ch. 50. Nancy Henry, *The Life of George Eliot: A Critical Biography* (Wiley-Blackwell, 2012).

23 J.A. Kemp (ed.), *John Wallis's Grammar of the English Language* (Longman, 1972), p. 277. Frank Palmer, *Grammar*, 2nd edn (Penguin, 1984).

24 Ernest Vincent Wright, *Gadsby* (Fourth Ramble House Editions, 2004), p. 79. Philip Terry, *The Penguin Book of Oulipo* (Penguin, 2019).

25 Anthony Burgess, *A Mouthful of Air* (William Morrow, 1992), Introduction. Andrew Biswell, *The Real Life of Anthony Burgess* (Picador, 2006).

26 Ferdinand de Saussure, *Course in General Linguistics* (Philosophical Library, 1959), p. 7. John E. Joseph, *Saussure* (Oxford University Press, 2012).

27 Martha Satz, interview *in Southwest Review* 81 (2), 22 March 1996. Bebe Moore Campbell, *Brothers and Sisters* (Putnam, 1994).

28 Nancy Mitford, *Nobless Oblige: An Enquiry into the Identifiable Characteristics of the English Aristocracy* (Hamish Hamilton, 1956), p. 43. Selina Hastings, *Nancy Mitford* (Hamish Hamilton, 1985).

29 C.C. Fries, *The Structure of English* (Harcourt Brace World, 1952), pp. 3–4. Charles Carpenter Fries, *American English Grammar* (Appleton-Century-Crofts, 1940).

30 (1) *The Critic as Artist*, pt 2; (2) ibid., pt 1; (3) *An Ideal Husband*, act 1; (4) ibid.; (5) *Miscellaneous Aphorisms* (Sebastian Melmoth); (6) *The Importance of Being Ernest*, act 1; (7) *Lady Windermere's Fan*, act 1; (8) *The Picture of Dorian Gray*, Preface; (9) ibid., ch. 1; (10) ibid., ch. 2; (11) ibid., ch. 4; (12) ibid., ch. 9; (13) ibid., ch. 15. Matthew Sturgis, *Oscar: A Life* (Apollo, 2018).

DECEMBER

1 James Baldwin, 'If Black English Isn't a Language, Then Tell Me, What Is?', *New York Times*, 29 July 1979, sect. E, p. 19. David Leeming, *James Baldwin: A Biography* (Arcade, 2015).

2 Elizabeth Knowles, *And I Quote...: A History of Using Other People's Words* (Oxford University Press, 2018), p. 2. Ruth H. Finnegan, *Why Do We Quote? The Culture and History of Quotations* (Open Book Publishers, 2011).

3 David Crystal, *Txtng: the gr8 db8* (Oxford University Press, 2008).

4 Daniel Jones, *An Outline of English Phonetics* (Heffer, 1918; 1957), p. 3. Beverley Collins and Inger M. Mees, *The Real Professor Higgins: The Life and Career of Daniel Jones* (Mouton de Gruyter, 1999).

5 Nelson Mandela, *Long Walk to Freedom* (Little, Brown, 1994), p. 13. Speech, 14 July 2000. South African Government Information Website, ID NMS083. Nelson Mandela, *Conversations with Myself* (Pan, 2011).

6 Max Müller, *My Autobiography: A Fragment* (Scribner, 1901), ch. 6. Max Müller, *Lectures on the Science of Language* (Scribner, 1862; Cambridge University Press, 2013).

7 Noam Chomsky, *Reflections on Language* (Temple Smith, 1976), p. 3. Neil Smith, *Chomsky: Ideas and Ideals* (Cambridge University Press, 2016).

8 Thomas De Quincey, 'Pronunciation', in Alexander H. Japp (ed.), *The Posthumous Works of Thomas de Quincey* (Heinemann, 1893), vol. 2, p. 219. Frances Wilson, *Guilty Thing: A Life of Thomas De Quincey* (Bloomsbury, 2016).

9 John Milton, 'Of Education, to Master Samuel Hartlib', 1644, milton.host. dartmouth.edu/reading_room/of_education/text.shtml. Thomas N. Corns, *Milton's Language* (Blackwell, 1990).

10 Thomas H. Johnson, *Emily Dickinson: The Complete Poems* (Faber & Faber, 1970), items 1750, 1251, 1651. Richard Benson Sewell, *The Life of Emily Dickinson* (Harvard University Press, 1998).

11 UNICEF history, www.unicef.org/history.

12 Interview in 2009 recalled in Indranie Deolall, 'An Author and a Gentleman', *Starbroek News*, 29 December 2016. E.R. Braithwaite, *To Sir with Love* (Bodley Head, 1959).

13 David Crystal, *Listen to Your Child* (Penguin, 2017), p. 40. Elizabeth Bates, *Language and Context* (Academic Press, 1976).

14 Montague Summers (ed.), *The Works of Aphra Behn*, vol. 5 (Heinemann, 1915); *Oroonoko, or The Royal Slave* (1688; Penguin, 2003), p. 169. Janet Todd, *Aphra Behn: A Secret Life* (Fentum Press, 2017).

15 Victor H. Mair, *The True History of Tea* (Thames & Hudson, 2009).

16 Deirdre Le Faye (ed.), *Jane Austen's Letters* (Oxford University Press, 1997), pp. 277, 267. K.C. Phillips, *Jane Austen's English* (Andre Deutsch, 1970).

17 'The English Language' in *Unpopular Opinions* (Gollancz, 1946), p. 95. 'Creative Mind', p. 57. Barbara Reynolds, *Dorothy L. Sayers: Her Life and Soul* (St Martins Press, 1993).

18 Mary S Serjeantson, *A History of Foreign Words in English* (Routledge & Kegan Paul, 1935), pp. 213ff.

19 Margaret Smith (ed.), *The Letters of Charlotte Bronte* (Clarendon Press, 2000), vol. 2, 1848–1851, p. 479. Claire O'Callaghan, *Emily Brontë Reappraised: A View from the Twenty-First Century* (Saraband, 2018).

20 *Scribner's Magazine* 1, 1887, p. 557. *A Collection of Letters of Thackeray, 1847–1855* (Scribner, 1888), p. 124. David Crystal, *Making a Point: The Pernickety Story of English Punctuation* (Profile, 2015), chs 28 and 29.

21 Adrienne Raphel, *Thinking Inside the Box* (Penguin, 2020).

22 Speech at National Student Drama Festival, 1962, extracts in 'The Echoing Silence', *Guardian*, 31 December 2008. Mark Taylor-Batty, *The Theatre of Harold Pinter* (Bloomsbury, 2014), p. 206. Michael Billington, *Harold Pinter* (Faber & Faber, 2007).

23 Francis Green, 'Extracts from the "Institution des Sourds et Muets" of the Abbé de L'Epée', *American Annals of the Deaf and Dumb* 13 (1), 1861, pp. 8–29. Harlan Lane, *When the Mind Hears: A History of the Deaf* (Random House, 1984).

24 Preface to M.A. Titmarsh, *The Kickleburys on the Rhine*, 2nd edn. public-library.uk/ ebooks/53/54.pdf. *The Christmas Books of Mr M.A.Titmarsh* (Estes and Lauriat, 1883; A Word to the Wise, 2013).

25 Andrew Gant, *Christmas Carols: From Village Green to Church Choir* (Profile Books, 2016).

26 Letter to Richard West, 8 April 1742, www.thomasgray.org/cgi-bin/display. cgi?text=tgal0119. Robert Mack, *Thomas Gray: A Life* (Yale, 2000).

27 Charles Lamb, 'Popular Fallacies IX', in *Last Essays of Elia* (Everyman, 1908), p. 306. Charles Lamb, *The Essays of Elia* (1823, 1833; Franklin, 2018).

28 Susan Sontag, 'On Style', in *Against Interpretation and Other Essays* (Dell, 1966; Penguin, 2009). Interview for *Rolling Stone*, 4 October 1979, www.rollingstone.com/ culture/culture-news/susan-sontag-the-rolling-stone-interview-41717. Benjamin Moser, *Sontag: Her Life* (Penguin, 2020).

29 'the coming of archy', in *archy and mehitabel* (Ernest Benn, 1933), reprinted in *the archy and mehitabel omnibus* (Faber & Faber, 1998), p. 7. 'pete the parrot and shakespeare', p. 101. Edward Anthony, *O Rare Don Marquis: A Biography* (Doubleday, 1952).

30 'The Uses of Reading', 25 May 1912, in *A Book of Words* (Macmillan, 1928), ch. 11. www.kiplingsociety.co.uk/readers-guide/rg_words_intro.htm. Rudyard Kipling, *Something of Myself* (Macmillan, 1937).

31 Happy New Year in many languages, omniglot.com/language/phrases/newyear. htm.

Index

abbreviations 15 Jun
Abet and Aid Punsters Day 8 Nov
Aboriginal languages 10 Apr
academies 22 Feb, 20 Jun
accents 12 Feb, 19 Dec
Achebe, Chinua 16 Nov
Act to restrain abuses 27 May
Adams, Douglas 11 May
Adcock, Fleur 10 Feb
Aesop's Fables 26 Mar
African-American English 1 Dec
Airspeak 20 Oct
Alexander, Neville 27 Aug
Alexander Graham Bell Day 7 Mar
Alfred, King 26 Oct
Alien Day 26 Apr
All Fools' Day 1 Apr
alphabet for radiotelephony 1 Mar
American and British English 26 Jun, 4 Jul,
    6 Sep
Amerindian languages 9 Jul
ampersands 8 Sep
Angelou, Maya 28 May
Anglo-Saxon 25 May, 29 Sep, 7 Oct
animal communication 30 Oct
anthropology 9 Jul
A'phabet Day 25 Dec
aphasia 28 Jun
Arabic Language Day 18 Dec
Arasanayagam, Jean 30 Jul
archives 9 Jun
archy and mehitabel 29 Dec
Asimov, Isaac 6 Apr
Ask a Question Day 14 Mar
Atwood, Margaret 18 Nov
audiobooks 7 Nov
Austen, Jane 16 Dec
Australian English 17 Feb
Autistics Speaking Day 1 Nov
autobiography 31 Aug

Babbling Day 21 Oct
backward(s) language 31 Jan
Baldwin, James 1 Dec
ballpoint pens 10 Jun
Barbour, John 13 Mar
Barnes, William 7 Oct
Bates, Elizabeth 13 Dec
BBC 22 Jan, 14 Nov
Bede, St 25 May
bees, spelling 29 Jun
Behn, Aphra 14 Dec
Bell, Alexander Graham 7 Mar
Belloc, Hilaire 27 Jul
Bentley, Edmund Clerihew 10 Jul
Berners-Lee, Tim 12 Mar
Berry, Cicely 15 Oct
Betjeman, John 19 May
Bible translation 20 Jan, 23 Feb, 2 May
Bierce, Ambrose 24 Jun
Big Word Day 21 Apr
Biographer's Day 16 May
biros 10 Jun
Bishop, Elizabeth 6 Oct
Black English 1 Dec
Blah Blah Blah Day 17 Apr
Blaise, St 3 Feb
blends 19 Jun
blindness 4 Jan, 14 Apr, 7 Nov
bloody 11 Apr
Bloomfield, Leonard 18 Apr
Bloomsday 16 Jun
blurb 15 May
Boas, Franz 9 Jul
Book Day 2 Apr, 23 Apr
Book of Common Prayer 15 Jan
Book Publishers' Day 16 Jan
book smuggling 16 Mar
books for children 2 Apr, 28 Sep
Borges, Jorge Luis 24 Aug
boring speech 27 Jul

Boswell, James 25 Mar, 16 May
Bowdler, Thomas 11 Jul
Boyd, Nancy 19 Oct
Bradford, William 6 Sep
Braille, Louis 4 Jan
Braithwaite, E.R. 12 Dec
broadcasting 22 Jan, 14 Nov
Broca, Pierre Paul 28 Jun
Brönte, Emily 19 Dec
Brown, Hallie Quinn 10 Mar
Browne, Charles Farrar 6 Mar
Brus, The 13 Mar
bugs 9 Sep
Burgess, Anthony 16 Jun, 25 Nov
Burgess, Gelett 15 May
Burgher English 30 Jul
Burney, Fanny 13 Jun
Burns Night 25 Jan
Burroughs, William S 2 Aug
Butler, Samuel 18 Jun
Byron, Lord 19 Apr
Cædmon 11 Feb
Campbell, Bebe Moore 27 Nov
Cansfield, Joyce 12 Oct
cant 25 Aug
car names 2 Oct
Carew, Richard 6 Nov
Carter, Elizabeth 19 Feb
Casablanca 2 Dec
case in typesetting 14 Oct
catalogues 24 May
Cawdrey, Robert 27 Jun
Caxton, William 26 Mar
CB codes 4 Oct
Chaucer, Geoffrey 25 Oct
Cheke, John 13 Sep
chemistry terms 27 Jan
Children's Book Day 2 Apr
children's speech 21 Oct, 13 Dec
chimpanzee communication 30 Oct
Chinese Language Day 20 Apr
Chomsky, Noam 7 Dec
Cleary, Beverly 12 Apr
clerihews 10 Jul
Cliche Day 3 Nov
Clinton, Bill 17 Aug
Cobbett, William 9 Mar
code talkers 4 Jun
Coleridge, Samuel Taylor 25 Jul
College of Speech Therapists 6 Jan
Comprehensive Grammar of the English
    Language, A 20 May
computer bugs 9 Sep
context of situation 17 Jun
conversation 25 Feb, 12 Jul, 28 Aug, 8 Oct
Coolidge, Susan 29 Jan

Coverdale, Myles 20 Jan
creativity 21 Apr, 30 May
creole 2 Jun
crosswords 12 Oct, 21 Dec
cryptography 26 Aug
cultural diversity 21 May
Cummings, E.E. 3 Sep
cut-ups 2 Aug
Daily Courant, The 11 Mar
Daleks 8 Aug
Danish invasions 8 Jun
Dare, Virginia 18 Aug
Darwin, Charles 12 Feb
Data Protection/Privacy Day 28 Jan
deaf education 16 Feb, 31 Jul, 23 Dec
DEAR Day 12 Apr
Declaration of Independence (US) 4 Jul
Dekker, Thomas 25 Aug
De Quincey, Thomas 8 Dec
DeSalvo, Louise 31 Oct
Developmental Language Disorder Awareness
    Day 18 Oct
Devil's Dictionary, The 24 Jun
dialects 18 Feb, 27 Feb, 26 Jun, 1 Aug, 23 Oct, 19
    Dec
Dickens, Charles 7 Feb
Dickinson, Emily 28 Apr, 10 Dec
dictionaries 18 Mar, 15 Apr, 23 May, 27 Jun,
    16 Oct
Dictionary of Slang, A 23 May
Diderot, Denis 31 Jul
discourse markers 20 Jul
domain names 15 Mar
Dot Your i's Day 20 Dec
Doyle, Arthur Conan 22 May
Drabble, Margaret 5 Jun
Drop Everything and Read Day 12 Apr
Dylan Thomas Day 14 May
East India Company 22 Sep
Edgeworth, Maria 1 Jan
editing 8 Mar
education 24 Jan
Eliot, George 22 Nov
Ellis, Alexander 14 Jun
Ellis, Stanley 18 Feb
elocution 10 Mar, 14 Aug
eloquence 2 Jul, 7 Aug
Elstob, Elizabeth 29 Sep
Elvish 3 Jan
emojis 17 Jul
encouragement 26 Jan
encyclopedias 4 Apr
endangered languages 18 Feb, 21 Feb, 5 Jul, 9
    Aug
English Academy 22 Feb, 20 Jun
English Dialect Dictionary 27 Feb

English Language Day 23 Apr, 13 Oct
English Language Teaching 20 Feb, 17 Mar
English teaching in schools 29 Aug
epitaphs 2 Nov
escalator 29 May
Esperanto 10 Jan, 26 Jul
ethnomusicology 19 Jul
European Day of Languages 26 Sep
extraterrestrial languages 26 Apr, 8 Aug
extraterrestrial life 20 Aug
etymology 4 Apr
Evans, Mari 16 Jul
Evelyn, John 20 Jun
fairy tales 26 Feb
Faulkner, William 6 Jul
fear of speaking 2 Jul
Female Spectator 25 Feb
Fielding, Henry 8 Oct
film-making 3 Apr, 29 Apr
film quotations 22 Mar, 21 Jun, 2 Dec
Finnbogadóttir, Vigdis 15 Apr
Firth, J.R. 17 Jun
folksong 19 Jul
football commentary 22 Jan
forensic phonetics 2 Jan
Franklin, Benjamin 17 Jan
Freedom from Fear of Speaking Day 2 Jul
French, Alice Masak 5 Jul
Friedman, Elizebeth Smith 26 Aug
Fries, Charles Carpenter 29 Nov
Fromkin, Victoria 19 Jan
Furnivall, Frederick 4 Feb
Gaines, Ernest J. 5 Nov
Gallaudet University 16 Feb
Garimara, Nug 10 Apr
Gaskell, Elizabeth 12 Nov
geek 9 Jan
gender-neutral language 7 May
gestures 31 Jul
gibberish 20 Sep
global language 10 Jan, 29 Jul
Global Speakers Federation 7 Aug
Globe theatre 12 Jun
glossopoeia 3 Jan
Gordimer, Nadine 20 Nov
gossip 6 Aug
grammar 4 Mar, 1 Jul, 29 Aug
grammars 8 Feb, 9 Mar, 30 Apr, 20 May,
    7 Jun, 23 Nov
gratitude expressions 11 Jan
Graves, Robert 24 Jul
gravy 29 Mar
Gray, Thomas 26 Dec
Great Exhibition 1 May
Greek 9 Feb
Greene, Graham 17 Sep

Grice, Paul 28 Aug
Gullah 10 Aug
Gumperz, John 29 Mar
Gutenberg, Johannes 23 Feb
haiku 17 Apr
Hale, Mrs 24 Oct
HAL 9000 12 Jan
handwriting 23 Jan
Harry Potter books 26 Jun
Hart, John 18 Jul
Hayford, Adelaide Casely 2 Jun
Haywood, Eliza 25 Feb
hello 7 Mar, 21 Nov
Herbert, A.P. 11 Nov
historical thesaurus 22 Oct
Hitchcock, Alfred 29 Apr
Hitchhikers Guide to the Galaxy, The 11 May
Hong Kong English 5 Jan
Hopkins, Gerard Manley 28 Jul
Hug a Medievalist Day 31 Mar
Hughes, Langston 1 Feb
Hughes, Ted 28 Oct
Hymes, Dell 13 Nov
IATEFL 20 Feb
Indian English 8 Jul
indigenous languages 21 Feb, 9 Aug
innovation 21 Apr
interactional sociolinguistics 29 Mar
Internet 15 Mar
interpreters 30 Sep
Irish English 1 Jan
is in English 17 Aug
Isidore of Seville 4 Apr
Island Languages Day 18 Feb
James, P.D. 3 Aug
Jameson, Anna Brownell 17 May
Jaws 21 Jun
jazz poetry 1 Feb
Jerome, St 30 Sep
Jespersen, Otto 30 Apr
Jhabvala, Ruth Prawer 3 Apr
Johnson, Samuel 2 Feb, 19 Feb, 16 May, 18 Sep
jokes 16 Aug
Jones, Daniel 3 Jul, 4 Dec
Jonson, Ben 11 Jun
Joyce, James 16 Jun
Julian of Norwich 13 May
Juneteenth Day 19 Jun
Kachru, Braj 29 Jul
Kagan, Janet 29 Feb
Kani, John 30 Aug
Keller, Helen 14 Apr
King James Bible 2 May
Kipling, Rudyard 30 Dec
Knowles, Elizabeth 2 Dec
Krio 2 Jun

Lamb, Charles 27 Dec
landscape and literature 5 Jun
language disorders 18 Oct
language education 24 Jan
language greetings 31 Dec
language planning 27 Aug
language play 6 Mar, 24 Nov
language teaching 20 Feb, 17 Mar, 5 Oct
laughing 19 Mar
League of Nations 10 Jan
Lear, Edward 12 May
Lee, W.R. 20 Feb
Leiden University Library 24 May
L'Epée, Charles-Michel de 23 Dec
Let's Laugh Day 19 Mar
letter-writing 25 Mar
Letter-Writing Day 1 Sep
Leung Ping-kwan 5 Jan
lexicography 22 Jun, 23 Aug
library classification 24 May
Library of Babel, The 24 Aug
License Plates Day 25 Apr
limericks 12 May
Linguistics Olympiad 24 Jan
listening 16 Jul
literacy 8 Sep
Lithuanian 16 Mar
Liverpool English 28 Feb
logic 14 Jan
Lomax, Alan 19 Jul
Longman Lexicon 23 Aug
LongPen™ 18 Nov
Lord of the Rings, The 3 Jan
Lowth, Robert 8 Feb
Lyrical Ballads, The 15 Sep
Machiavelli 12 Oct
Madgett, Naomi Long 4 Nov
Magna Carta 15 Jun
makars 7 Jan
Mandela, Nelson 5 Dec
Māori 6 Feb
Marquis, Don 29 Dec
Marshall, Paule 12 Aug
Marshall, Sybil 29 Aug
Mawer, Allen 8 May
maxims of conversation 28 Aug
Mayflower, The 6 Sep
McArthur, Tom 23 Aug
Meaning of 'is' Day 17 Aug
Meaning of Meaning, The 7 Sep
medieval studies 31 Mar
Melody and Measure of Speech 25 Sep
memoir 31 Aug
Mencken, H.L. 12 Sep
Meynell, Alice 11 Oct
Millay, Edna St Vincent 19 Oct

Miller, Arthur 17 Oct
Miller, Casey 7 May
Miller, Jonathan 21 Jul
Milton, John 9 Dec
Minor, William Chester 22 Jun
Mitford, Nancy 28 Nov
Montagu, Lady Mary Wortley 21 Aug
Moore, Marianne 15 Nov
More, Hannah 2 Feb
Morrison, Toni 5 Aug
morse 3 Oct
Morse Code Day 27 Apr
Mother Language Day 21 Feb
mother languages 5 Mar, 10 Apr, 15 Apr, 5 Jul,
    9 Aug
Müller, Max 6 Dec
multilingualism 21 Feb, 26 Sep
Murray, James 15 Feb, 22 Jun
Murray, Lindley 7 Jun
museums 18 May
musical quotations 21 Jun
Nabokov, Vladimir 22 Apr
name days 24 Feb
name your car 2 Oct
Narayan, R.K. 10 Oct
Nash, Ogden 19 Aug
Nation, Terry 8 Aug
Native American literature 5 Mar
NATO Phonetic Alphabet 1 Mar
Navaho code talkers 4 Jun
nerd 9 Jan
New Conversations Day 12 Jul
newspapers 11 Mar
New Year's Eve 31 Dec
New Zealand English 6 Feb
Nez, Chester 4 Jun
Nkosi, Lewis 5 Sep
nonsense speech 20 Sep
novel-writing 6 Jul
Nunberg, Geoff 11 Aug
Ogden, C.K. 7 Sep
OK Day 23 Mar
Old Norse 8 Jun
original pronunciation 12 Jun, 3 Jul
origins of language 29 Feb
Orton, Harold 23 Oct
Orwell, George 21 Jan
Oulipo 24 Nov
Oxford English Dictionary 4 Feb, 15 Feb, 22 Jun,
    22 Oct
Paisley, Janet 9 Nov
Papua New Guinea 16 Sep
Parker, Dorothy 22 Aug
Partridge, Eric 23 May
PAT computer 12 Jan
Patterson, Banjo 17 Feb

pauses 22 Dec
peace linguistics 10 Nov
Pencil Day 30 Mar
Pepys, Samuel 26 May
Peterkin, Julia Mood 10 Aug
phonautograph 9 Apr
phonetics 2 Jan, 14 Jun
pidgins 16 Sep
Pilgrim Fathers 6 Sep
Pilkington, Doris 10 Apr
Pinter, Harold 22 Dec
pirate speech 19 Sep
place-names 8 May
plain English 13 Sep, 11 Nov
Plan Your Epitaph Day 2 Nov
poetry 13 Jan, 21 Mar, 28 Apr, 3 Sep, 17 Oct
Poetry Break Day 13 Jan
Poetry Reading Day 28 Apr
political speech 21 Jan
portmanteau words 19 Jun
Portuguese Language Day 5 May
postal services 9 Oct
Postcard Day 1 Oct
prescriptivism 8 Feb, 9 Mar
printing press 23 Feb, 26 Mar
Privacy Day 28 Jan
Professional Speakers Day 7 Aug
pronouns and gender 7 May
pronunciation 18 Mar, 14 Jun
proofreading 8 Mar
proverbs 14 Jul
pseudonyms 12 Oct
public speaking 2 Jul, 7 Aug
publishing 16 Jan
Pueblo 5 Mar
puffing 7 Jul
Punctuation Day 24 Sep
puns 8 Nov, 25 Dec, 27 Dec
Pygmalion 11 Apr
questions 14 Mar
Quirk, Randolph 20 May, 12 Jul
quotations 15 Jan, 22 Mar, 21 Jun, 2 Dec
radio CB codes 3 Oct
radio commentary 22 Jan
Radio Day 13 Feb
radiotelephony alphabet 1 Mar
Raleigh, Walter 29 Oct
Ramsay, Allan 7 Jan
Rao, Raja 8 Jul
Read a Child a Book You Like Day 28 Sep
Reader's Digest 5 Feb
reading 8 Jan, 2 Apr, 12 Apr, 28 Sep
recording of the voice, earliest 9 Apr
Repeat Day 3 Jun
rhyming 19 Aug
rhythm and metre 10 Feb

Richards, I.A. 7 Sep
Riding, Laura 2 Sep
Roanoke Island 18 Aug
Roget, Peter Mark 18 Jan
Romani 8 Apr
roundel 5 Apr
Rowling, J.K. 26 Jun
Rowson, Susanna 2 Mar
Russian Language Day 6 Jun
Safire, William 27 Sep
Saussure, Ferdinand de 26 Nov
Say Something Nice Day 1 Jun
Sayers, Dorothy L. 17 Dec
Schiffrin, Deborah 20 Jul
Schreiner, Olive 24 Mar
Science Day for Peace 10 Nov
science fiction 26 Apr, 8 Aug
science of language 10 Nov
scientific terms 27 Jan, 1 May
Scots 7 Jan, 25 Jan, 13 Mar, 9 Nov
Scott, Walter 21 Sep
Scouse 28 Feb
Scrabble Day 13 Apr
screenwriting 3 Apr
Seinfeld 23 Jul
Seward, Anna 25 Mar
sexism 7 May
Shakespeare, William 23 Apr, 27 May, 3 Jul, 11
    Jul, 4 Aug, 26 Aug, 30 Aug
Shakespeare's Globe 12 Jun
Shange, Ntozake 27 Oct
Shatner, William 22 Mar
Shaw, George Bernard 11 Apr
Shelley, Percy Bysshe 4 Aug
Sheridan, Richard Brinsley 7 Jul
Sheridan, Thomas 14 Aug
Sherlock Holmes Day 22 May
short-messaging service 15 Jul
Sierra Leone Creole 2 Jun
sign language 16 Feb, 23 Sep, 30 Oct
silence 22 Dec
Silent Night Day 25 Dec
Silko, Leslie Marmon 5 Mar
slang 23 May
slips of the tongue 19 Jan, 22 Jul
slow writing 31 Oct
social media 30 Jun, 15 Jul
sociolinguistics 29 Mar
Sontag, Susan 28 Dec
SOS 3 Oct
South Africa 27 Aug
South African English 24 Mar
Soyinka, Wole 13 Jul
speech and language therapy 6 Jan, 18 Oct
speed reading 8 Jan
spelling bee 29 Jun

spelling dictionary *2 Mar*
spelling humour *6 Mar*
spelling reform *17 Jan, 18 Jul*
Spooner's Day *22 Jul*
sports commentary *22 Jan*
sprung rhythm *28 Jul*
Stark, Freya *9 May*
Star Trek 22 Mar
Star Wars Day *4 May*
Statute of Pleading *13 Oct*
Steele, Joshua *25 Sep*
Stevenson, Anne *14 Sep*
Stone, Ruth *19 Nov*
storytelling *5 Mar*
Storytelling Day *20 Mar*
Stowe, Harriet Beecher *1 Jul*
style *28 Dec*
Sullivan, Anne *14 Apr*
Survey of English Dialects *18 Feb, 23 Oct*
Survey of English Usage *20 May*
Sutcliffe, Peter *2 Jan*
swearing *27 May*
Swift, Jonathan *22 Feb, 29 Sep*
Swift, Kate *7 May*
Swinburne, Algernon Charles *5 Apr*
Table Alphabeticall 27 Jun
Talk in Third Person Day *3 Mar*
Talk Like a Pirate Day *19 Sep*
Talk Like Shakespeare Day *23 Apr*
Talk Like William Shatner Day *22 Mar*
Talking Books *7 Nov*
Taverner, Richard *14 Jul*
taxonomy *24 May*
teachers *20 Feb, 17 Mar, 5 Oct*
Tea Day *15 Dec*
TESOL *17 Mar*
telephones *7 Mar*
Tell a Fairy Tale Day *26 Feb*
Ten-Four Day *4 Oct*
tennessine *27 Jan*
terminology *27 Jan, 1 May*
texting *3 Dec*
Thackeray, William *20 Dec, 24 Dec*
Thank-you Day *11 Jan*
theatre *27 Mar, 27 May*
thesaurus *23 Aug, 22 Oct*
Thesaurus Day *18 Jan*
Third Man, The 17 Sep
third-person pronouns *3 Mar*
Thirkell, Angela *30 Jan*
Thomas, Dylan *14 May*
Thomas, Joyce Carol *13 Aug*
Thoreau, Henry David *6 May*
tip of the tongue *19 Jan*
Toad Hollow *26 Jan*
Tok Pisin *16 Sep*

Tolkien Day *3 Jan*
toponymy *8 May*
trademarks *29 May*
translation *14 Jul*
Translation Day *30 Sep*
Trollope, Anthony *24 Apr*
Twitter *15 Jul*
2001: A Space Odyssey 12 Jan
typesetting *14 Oct*
Typewriter Day *23 Jun*
U and non-U *28 Nov*
Unfriend Day *17 Nov*
UNICEF Day *11 Dec*
United States Declaration of Independence
    4 Jul
usage *20 May, 11 Aug, 27 Sep*
vehicle registration plates *25 Apr*
Vera, Yvonne *7 Apr*
Vigdis House *15 Apr*
vocabulary size *5 Feb*
voice *3 Feb, 16 Apr, 15 Oct*
voice recording, earliest *9 Apr*
Voyager 2 *20 Aug*
Waitangi Day *6 Feb*
Walker, John *18 Mar*
Wallis, John *23 Nov*
Waltzing Matilda 17 Feb
Ward, Artemus *6 Mar*
Washoe *30 Oct*
weather forecasting *4 Sep*
Webster, Noah *4 Jul, 16 Oct*
We Love Memoirs Day *31 Aug*
Weiner, Hannah *11 Sep*
What Katy Did series 29 Jan
Whitman, Walt *31 May*
Wiggin, Kate *28 Sep*
Wilde, Oscar *30 Nov*
Wodehouse, P.G. *14 Feb*
Wollstonecraft, Mary *10 Sep*
women's rights *10 Sep*
Wood, Evelyn *8 Jan*
Woolf, Virginia *28 Mar*
Word Nerd Day *9 Jan*
Wordsmith Day *3 May*
Wordsworth, William *15 Sep*
World Wide Web *12 Mar*
Wright, Ernest *24 Nov*
Wright, Joseph *27 Feb*
Wright, Judith *25 Jun*
writing process *31 Oct*
Yada Yada Yada Day *23 Jul*
Yesi *5 Jan*
Yorkshire Day *1 Aug*
Yorkshire Ripper *2 Jan, 18 Feb*
Young, Thomas *10 May*
Zamenhof, Ludwik Lajzer *26 Jul*